Duty, Honor, Victory

Duty, Honor, Victory

America's Athletes in World War II

Gary L. Bloomfield

The Lyons Press
Guilford, Connecticut
An imprint of The Globe Pequot Press

To my father, Army Command Sergeant Major Robert D. Bloomfield, whose competitive spirit instilled in me a love for sports and all the great heroes he idolized, whose love of country was rock solid, unwavering. Of all the great heroes I've written about here, none has inspired me more than Dad.

First Lyons Press paperback edition, 2004

The Lyons Press is an imprint of The Globe Pequot Press.

Designed by M.A. Dubé

ISBN 1-59228-548-1 (paperback)

The Library of Congress has previously cataloged an earlier (hardcover) edition as follows:

Bloomfield, Gary L.
  Duty, honor, victory : America's athletes in World War II / Gary L. Bloomfield.
    p. cm.
  ISBN 1-59228-067-6 (alk. paper)
  1. Athletes--United States--Biography. 2. World War, 1939-1945--Biography. 3. United States--Armed Forces--Sports. I. Title.
  D810.A79B56 2003
  940.53'73'088796--dc22   2003015616

10 9 8 7 6 5 4 3 2 1

Printed in the United States of America

Contents

1. Prelude to War in Europe and the Pacific

"WAR! THAT MAD GAME THE WORLD SO LOVES TO PLAY."

— *Jonathan Swift*

"IT'S NOT SO IMPORTANT WHO STARTS THE GAME, BUT WHO FINISHES IT."

— *John Wooden, UCLA basketball coach*

AS YOUNGSTERS GROWING UP IN THE 1920s, TED AND JOEY D. dreamed of playing big-league baseball someday.

By 1941, not only had their dreams come true, but both were superstars, long before the term was ever dreamed up, setting records for hitting that have remained unreachable for more than sixty years.

Ted Williams had a sizzling .406 batting average with the Boston Red Sox that year, and Joe DiMaggio posted a remarkable 56-game hitting streak with the rival New York Yankees. (Ironically, five years earlier the Yankees had scouted Ted Williams and tried to sign him, but his mom had demanded one thousand dollars up front. The Yankees backed off, and the Red Sox snatched him up.) Baseball was the big drawing card in sports in 1941.

But while most of the country was following these baseball exploits, elected officials in Washington, D.C., were more concerned about the United States being drawn into the conflicts raging in Europe and the Far East. The Selective Service Training Act was signed on September 16, 1940, calling for all men between twenty-one and thirty-six to register for the draft. On October 29 draft numbers were assigned. In July of 1941, a second lottery was held in New York to draft young men into the armed forces. Each eligible male would be assigned a separate number. Quite simply, first names chosen were the first to be called up.

Joe DiMaggio Gets His Draft Notice

On that July 17—the day after twenty-six-year-old Joe DiMaggio's hitting streak ended—another young man, an unknown named Joe DiMaggio, who was five years younger than the Yankees' Joltin' Joe, made the news when he became the second eligible male chosen in the draft.

Newspaper editors couldn't resist the coincidence and declared "DiMaggio Joins the Army," setting off a wave of panic among Yankees fans, while BoSox fans projected a run for the pennant.

OPPOSITE: After coming to power in 1933, Adolf Hitler (center with gloves) set out to expand German territory, threatening all of Europe. He would use the 1936 Olympics in Berlin to showcase Aryan superiority.
National Archives photo

ABOVE: On July 17, 1941, a lottery was implemented for all eligible males to be drafted. Yankee fans had a scare when it was announced that Joltin' Joe DiMaggio was selected as the second one chosen for induction. But it was another Joe, five years the junior to his more famous namesake, who got his notice from Uncle Sam.

But after Pearl Harbor, every eligible male expected to be called, and the Yankee Clipper was no exception. He would eventually be stationed in Hawaii with the 7th Air Force.
U.S. Marine Corps photo

Gearing Up for the Impending Conflict

In the following months thousands of young men would be mustered into the armed services. America was not yet officially at war, but the country was being pulled into the European conflict and would not be able to remain on the sidelines much longer.

"What I knew of the world's turmoil came mostly from 'War Cards' which, like baseball cards, came packed with penny bubble gum," recalled Russell Baker in his autobiography, *Growing Up.* "These [cards] depicted Japanese atrocities in China, Italian atrocities in Ethiopia, and slaughters of women and children in the Spanish Civil War. From these I knew that Japan was bad and China good, that Italy was bad and Ethiopia good. The lesson on Spain was confusing. One side murdered nuns and the other bombed helpless villages, but I was uncertain which side was which."

As exciting as that summer of 1941 was for sports fans—when Ted Williams and Joe DiMaggio set milestones that thousands of baseball players have since tried to break, with only a few coming close—many immigrants were worried about family and friends caught up in the turmoil back in Europe. DiMaggio's own parents had come to the United States from the island of Sicily.

The Far East was also boiling over, as Japan threatened the entire region, but among American immigrants it didn't merit the same concern as Europe.

A Raving Lunatic Gains Support

Germany was in the midst of catastrophic depression and wide-scale unemployment following World War I, when the terms of the Versailles Treaty left the country powerless. An ex-corporal who had been gassed in World War I had tried making a living as an artist and often stood on street corners attracting passersby as he ranted and raved, criticizing the current government.

He took potshots at Germany's leaders and declared that, if he were in power, he would restore the country to its rightful place as a world leader. He would give the German people back their pride and acquire more living space by expanding homeland territory into disputed areas of border countries, such as the Alsace region of France.

Though he was labeled a lunatic and a crackpot, what this comic-looking

ABOVE: *In 1937, Japanese forces swept across China, advancing on Shanghai. They hoped to extend their sphere of influence across Asia and down through Indonesia.* U.S. Information Agency photo

BELOW: *The elite Polish cavalry was no match for Nazi tanks, planes, and infantry that stormed across the border on September 1, 1939. Nazi blitzkrieg tactics would terrorize all of Europe and north Africa in coming years.* Polish Archives photo

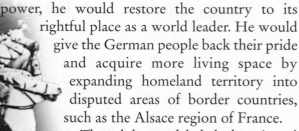

upstart was saying was exactly what the German masses had felt since the end of the Great War. His popularity grew, and with a small group of followers—mostly street thugs and drunks—Adolf Hitler led the National Socialist German Workers' Party, called simply the Nazis, to unprecedented strength.

By coalition government, Hitler rose to power and took over in 1933. He then combined that post with the presidency when the much-revered war hero Paul von Hindenburg died of natural causes in mid-1934.

Almost immediately, Hitler set his far-fetched plans in motion, and the Nazis imposed his will on every facet of German life. By abolishing all political affiliations, Hitler eliminated any organized opposition that might protest his radical views.

Tightening the Stranglehold

After denouncing the Treaty of Versailles—which Germany had been forced to sign after World War I, agreeing to pay for damages incurred by all nations involved in the fighting, and limiting its armed forces to 100,000 men, Hitler defiantly ordered the formation of a military force rivaling any to date.

The former corporal was envisioning a military juggernaut that could overwhelm any foe. Hitler planned to unleash a lightning bolt, which he would call his Blitzkrieg, that could strike down any army foolish enough to stand in its way.

Forcing Out the Jews

Hitler also felt that the Aryan race—blue-eyed, blond-haired, strong, and intelligent—was destined to rule the world. All other ethnic people, such as

BELOW: *The battleship* Arizona's *1935 football team included All-Americans Buzz Borries (middle of back row with Navy sweatshirt) and Slade Cutter (back row, third from left). Many members of the squad were still with the* Arizona *when it perished at Pearl Harbor six years later.*
Photo courtesy of USS *Arizona* Memorial

blacks, Slavs, and Jews, he deemed inferior. Hitler would order a rewriting of racial doctrine to reflect this distorted Nazi viewpoint.

Jewish schoolteachers and doctors were forced to quit, so as not to come in contact with German students or patients. Jewish merchants were boycotted, and their shops were looted and burned. Excessive taxes were imposed on Jews. The pressure continued, forcing many Jewish families to move to other countries. Those Jews who remained felt that the difficult times would eventually pass, as they always had before.

Their decision to tough it out, to endure whatever new law the Nazis decreed against them, would be a fatal mistake, for Hitler fully intended to cleanse Germany, leaving only the Aryan race to eventually rule the world. It would be essential to his Thousand-Year Reich.

Center Stage to the World

In 1931 the International Olympic Committee had chosen Berlin to host the 1936 Summer Olympic Games. Hitler planned to use the international sporting event to showcase his army of Aryan super-athletes. To defuse world criticism about his treatment of Jews, Hitler conveniently allowed one Jewish athlete—fencer Helene Meyer—to represent Germany at the Olympic Games. Germany also hosted the 1936 Winter Games at Garmisch-Partenkirchen, and Hitler again reluctantly added one Jewish athlete—hockey star Rudi Ball—to the national team. These Jewish athletes were unwitting pawns in Hitler's elaborate ruse. He felt only athletes of true German stock had any chance of claiming Olympic gold.

But someone forgot to tell the Black Auxiliaries—the ten black athletes of the U.S. track and field team—that they were supposed to let their Aryan hosts win every event at the Berlin Olympics!

BELOW: *The American contingent marches into Berlin's Olympic Stadium on the first day of the track and field events. No one, except maybe the U.S. athletes, expected them to dominate the medal sweep, at the same time embarrassing Adolf Hitler's Aryan supermen.* National Archives photo

During the months leading up to the Summer Games, Hitler extolled Aryan superiority while criticizing the United States as it selected its best athletes for the national team: "The Americans ought to be ashamed of themselves for letting their medals be won by Negroes." Though he felt confident European athletes would win every event, Hitler vowed, "I myself would never shake hands with one of them [Negroes]."

The Americans Disprove Hitler's Beliefs

During the first and second day of competition in Berlin, European competitors did win, and Hitler attended the medal ceremonies. But on the third day, America's Black Auxiliaries began to dominate the field. And Adolf Hitler disappeared from the viewing stand at the Reichsportfeld.

Jesse Owens led the American team and swept the 100- and 200-meter dash. But he struggled in the broad jump. "The broad jump was an event that I was supposed to win with some ease," Owens wrote. "But on this day something was going wrong."

With a mark of only 23 feet 6 inches, Owens was in danger of being eliminated from an event he usually dominated. "But there happened to be a young German broad jumper, Luz Long, the greatest of them all in his own country, who was watching as I took my qualifying jumps."

After Owens fouled twice, Long walked over, in front of the thousands of German spectators, and checked Owens's takeoff mark. He also checked his steps and suggested a different starting spot on the runway. At this point Owens had little to lose. "Thanks to his suggestions and confidence in me, I was able to produce a leap which qualified and opened up the pathway to ultimate victory.

"Luz Long jumped 25 feet 9 inches for a new Olympic record. I managed 26 feet 5 inches and so won. Luz was second; but in my book of sportsmanship he ranks first."

ABOVE: *At the Berlin Olympics, American Jesse Owens personally shattered the myth that Aryan supermen— blonde hair, blue eyes, physical dynamos— were a far superior breed of athlete, destined to conquer the world. The Nazis failed to tell Owens or any of the other Black Auxiliaries of the American contingent of this supposed superiority.* Library of Congress photo

After Owens won the broad jump, Long encouraged him to circle the Olympic track. And Long encouraged the German crowd to cheer Jesse Owens as a deserving Olympic hero.

Owens later wrote, "You can melt down all the medals and cups I have, and they wouldn't be a plating on the 24-carat friendship I felt for Luz Long at that moment."

Jesse Owens was not the only American who reaped gold, silver, and bronze in track and field events at the Berlin Olympics. John Woodruff captured gold in the 800 meters, Archie Williams took the 400 meters, and Cornelius Johnson walked away with the high jump, while David Albritton took the silver medal in that event.

Owens went for his fourth medal when he teamed up with Ralph Metcalfe, Frank Wykoff, and Foy Draper to set a world record in the 400-meter relay. Originally Sam Stoller and Marty Glickman had trained with Wyckoff and Draper for the relay, "but the morning of the day we were to run . . . Sam and I, the only Jews on the [American] track team, were being replaced by Owens and Metcalfe," recalled Glickman.

Jesse Owens protested the change but was told to follow orders, and so he reluctantly agreed to run the relay.

"I believe we were dropped," recalled Glickman, "to save Hitler further embarrassment by having two Jews stand on the winning podium before 120,000 Germans and the world's news media. The only way we could have lost that race is if we had dropped the baton."

Seven years later Foy Draper would be killed during the fighting in North Africa, while Marty Glickman would serve with the Marines in the Pacific Campaign.

All told, the Black Auxiliaries—those same American athletes Hitler had deemed "inferior"—would win eight gold medals, three silvers, and two bronzes at the 1936 Berlin Summer Games.

Other Notable Olympians

In the Olympic marathon, Sohn Kee Chung of Korea easily outdistanced the field. But in the 1936 Summer Games, Sohn was not running for his own country. Instead, he represented Japan, which had occupied the Korean peninsula since the war with Russia in 1904–05.

As they would also do in occupied China, the Japanese imposed their language, rules, and culture on the Korean people. Though Sohn had shattered the world record in the marathon, the Japanese would not allow him to represent his own country, which had become a puppet state. Nor would they allow him to use his Korean name while representing Japan. Instead, he was entered as Kitei Son of Japan.

He won the marathon easily, with another Korean runner, Nam Sung Yong, coming in third. During what should have been his proudest moment, while on the medal stand, Korean Sohn Kee Chung could not watch as the Japanese flag was raised while the Japanese national anthem played.

"It was humiliating torture. I hadn't run for Japan. I ran for myself and for my oppressed Korean people," Sohn would say later.

Numerous other Olympians would be caught up a few years later in World War II, serving stateside, in Europe, or in the Pacific. Among the Americans were the following.

Glenn Morris, who took the gold medal at Berlin in the decathlon and broke a world record set two years earlier by German champion Hans Sievert, would go on to play pro football with the Lions in 1940 before joining the Navy as an assault boat commander, where he survived numerous deadly beach landings.

Katherine Rawls had won the silver medal in springboard diving at both the 1932 and '36 Olympics and won the bronze as a member of the 4x100-meter freestyle relay team. When male pilots were needed overseas for the bombing campaigns, she joined the Women's Airforce Service Pilots—the WASPs—to fly planes from manufacturing plants to military air bases.

Adolph "Sonny" Kiefer was considered America's best backstroker in the 1930s, winning the 100-meter event in Berlin. A year earlier he had shattered eleven American and world records, and he went on to break another seventeen over the next decade. During World War II Kiefer served in the Navy, overseeing the swimming program for new recruits.

John Macionis swam on the American 4x200-meter relay team that captured the silver medal at the 1936 Olympics. He would later serve in the Coast Guard, which had the vital mission of patrolling and protecting America's shorelines from Nazi and Japanese submarines.

Marshall Wayne won a gold medal at Berlin in the high dive and a silver in springboard diving. While assigned to the Eighth Air

Force in Europe, he flew perilous bombing missions. After his plane was hit, and shot down, local Italians helped him to a British aid station nearby. Tendons and ligaments in his left leg were torn and would require numerous operations and months of rehabilitation, but he would never return to competitive diving.

Nazi Hypocrisy

When they had free time during their stay in Berlin, some American Olympians saw a disconcerting side of German society.

Helen Stephens, who won gold medals in 1936 in the 100-meter dash and the 4x100-meter relay, recalled, "Those German girls who were attached to us as English-speaking guides said they were going to beat the hell out of us come the next war, and in that very stadium there were tunnels underneath for air raid shelters. And all those training fields adjacent to the stadium were filled with thousands of German schoolchildren marching around with broomsticks and swords—the Hitler Youth, the Boy Scouts." Stephens would later run exhibition races against Jesse Owens during the war years to raise money for a variety of charities.

Francis Johnson, a member of the 1936 gold medal basketball team, which had to play the championship game outdoors and on a muddy field, also remembered seeing the Hitler Youth. "They said it was the same as our

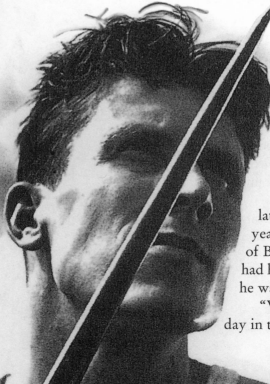

BELOW: *Glenn Morris, the gold medal winner in the decathlon in Berlin, would later be wounded in WWII.*
Library of Congress photo

Boy Scouts, but they had all of these youths out training, just going out and marching and popping their heels. It was actually a young military group."

Johnson also noticed Nazi efforts to control the masses: "In downtown Berlin . . . on every street corner there was a loudspeaker, and there was always music playing on those loudspeakers. But the German officials could cut in and broadcast throughout the whole city of Berlin anytime they wanted. In a matter of seconds they could shut down everything in the city through this speaker system." Johnson would later join the Navy and serve on an aircraft carrier during the Pacific Campaign.

Eight-hundred-meter gold medalist John Woodruff, who later joined the Army in 1941 and served as an officer for five years, added: "We did see soldiers marching to and fro in the city of Berlin, but we didn't pay any attention to them. Of course, we had heard quite a bit about Hitler. There was a lot of talk about how he was persecuting the Jews.

"We did talk to a young German athlete who visited with us one day in the Olympic Village. We asked him what the Germans thought of Hitler. He told us that they thought he was a great man. He had opened up all of those factories to make war armaments so everybody had a job. They thought that was wonderful.

"As a result of the aftermath of World War I, when the Germans had to pay all of those reparations and were brought to their knees, they were looking for a savior, so to speak, and there he was. I guess they didn't anticipate what he really had in mind; they didn't know."

Another American athlete got a frightening glimpse of what was being created in those war armaments factories, in clear violation of the Versailles Treaty. Gold medal 400-meter sprinter Archie Williams recalled: "There was an airport right near the Olympic Village, so one day Gene Venzke [who ran the mile and was interested in planes] said, 'Let's go over and take a peek at those planes,' We crawled under this fence, and someone yells, 'Halt!' We got the hell out of there. Then we saw this plane go by—whoosh. I'd never seen a plane that fast before. And they were only supposed to be flying gliders. That was the fastest glider in the world."

Williams would soon learn that the "glider" he had seen was a German ME-109. Five years later Williams would join the Army Air Corps and serve as a flight instructor for the Tuskegee Airmen, a group of black pilots who would confront hundreds of ME-109s in the skies over Europe.

A Hollow Peace Proclamation

During the closing ceremonies of the Berlin Summer Olympics, Dr. Joseph Goebbels, Nazi propaganda minister, stated, "The Eleventh Olympic Games take their place in world history as an event full of happiness and peace.

"It may be said of them that they have ushered in a new epoch of true peace in all those fields of activity which join nations together."

The so-called "new epoch of true peace" only masked Nazi Germany's true intention of expanding its empire throughout all of Europe and northern Africa. Those who had seen or experienced the Nazi stranglehold on German society, and the Jewish community especially, knew that happiness and peace were not looming on the horizon for Europe.

The Games in Garmisch

Though overshadowed by the Summer Olympics, the Winter Games at Garmisch in southern Germany were also deemed a success, showcasing Nazi pomposity. Many Americans, by now aware of the Jewish Question in Europe, chose not to compete. One of those was sprint skater Jack Shea, who had won gold four years earlier at Lake Placid and had many Jewish friends. "I received a lot of adverse comments about that from other athletes, but I've always been proud of that position." More than a thousand contestants from around the world did compete in skiing, speed skating, hockey, bobsledding, and figure skating events. Among them were Alec Bright, who had been a hockey letterman at Harvard and then received a pro offer from Montreal. As an Olympian, Bright competed in downhill skiing against competitors much younger than himself. (He was thirty-nine at Berlin.) In World War II's European Campaign he would fly with the highly decorated Eighth Air Force. Roy Mikkelsen was a great ski jumper who served with the prestigious Tenth Mountain Division and the Ninety-ninth Norwegian American Battalion. These units would endure some of the toughest battles in Europe.

The 1940 Olympic Games were slated for Finland but were cancelled after the Soviet invasion in 1939. Those Games were moved to Japan, which would soon be at war with China. Thus, after the 1936 Olympics, there would be a twelve-year lull, until the Games returned to war-torn London in 1948.

Hitler's Quest for Living Space Begins

Immediately after the Nazi Games, Hitler resumed his racial cleansing of the German homeland, moving "inferior races" to ghettos and concentration camps, laying the groundwork for massive death camps in Eastern Europe with the sole purpose of eliminating the unwanted masses, especially the Jews.

He also continued his threats to dominate Europe, though neighboring

BELOW: *America's gold medal winning 4x100-meter relay team at the Berlin Olympiad was composed of Jesse Owens, Ralph Metcalfe, Foy Draper, and Frank Wykoff.* National Archives photo

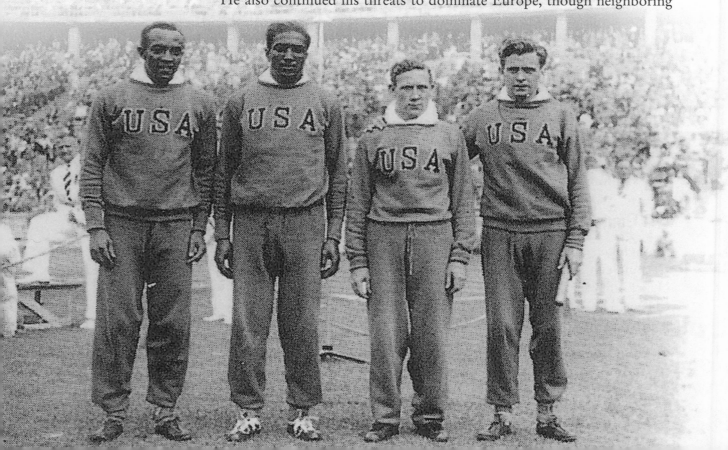

countries underestimated Nazi Germany's military strength, feeling Hitler's bark was worse than his bite.

After occupying the Sudetenland and Austria within eighteen months of the Summer Games, then invading Czechoslovakia and Poland in 1939, Nazi forces charged north into Denmark and Norway, west into the Netherlands, Luxembourg, and France, east into Yugoslavia and Russia, and south to North Africa. Hitler was no longer interested in simply claiming disputed regions of surrounding countries. He set out to conquer the world.

After talks between Hitler and Benito Mussolini, Germany and Italy formed the Axis powers in 1939. Now virtually all of Europe was threatened by this Pact of Steel between the ex-corporal and Il Duce. Japan would later join the Axis powers, bringing the Far East into its sphere.

Foreseeing America's Participation

In response to Germany's invasion of Poland on September 1, 1939, American sportswriter Red Barber wrote: "Day by day it grows more difficult to support the pretty fiction that the future of civilization lies somewhere between Tony Galento's fist and Lou Nova's profile, or that the sun will be blotted out if Penn's football team fails to whip Yale. Somehow these matters don't seem nearly so important as they did a year or even a month ago. It cannot be so very long before it will become advisable and perhaps necessary to pay strict attention to the net yards gained from scrimmage by Villanova or the batting average of Joe DiMaggio.

"So we'll go on whipping up our daily portion of froth and bubbles, remembering that as long as the battles we witness are fought with bats instead of bayonets, with headgears instead of gas masks, and with gloves instead of guns, some measure of sanity will be preserved in the land."

Brutus Hamilton, who had been the U.S. decathlon coach at the Berlin Olympics, lamented the cancellation of the Helsinki Games and what was unfolding in Europe: "The 1940 Olympic Games, which would have been history's greatest are out of the question. Finland would have been a perfect host, but bombs are falling in Helsinki!

"Your track coach doesn't know what it is all about. He knows from the Games at Antwerp, Paris, Amsterdam, Los Angeles and Berlin that the young men are splendid sportsmen who ask nothing more of life than to lead normal lives, work for their food and shelter, to be reasonably secure and to be able to rise as high as their ability may carry them.

"Now instead of meeting on the field of play they face each other on the fields of battle. Grand men, every one of them. How they would have enjoyed competing at Helsinki! How they would love to get together as they did in Berlin and sing till nearly dawn! But that's over now. A bomb, a piece of steel, a machine gun bullet, and their strong, well-conditioned bodies sink to earth . . . Oh, Heaven, may it stop!"

Japan Threatens Entire Pacific

Japan's military planners set out to control every region in the Pacific, first invading Manchuria in mid-September 1931.

By July of 1937, Japan and China were at war, though with its mighty war machine, Japan clearly had the upper hand.

Similar to the Nazis and their concept of racial superiority, Japanese zealots felt that theirs was the true master race, destined to rule all of Asia and eventually the world. Their glorious 2,600-year history, untainted by Western influence, was evidence of their self-serving beliefs.

Going after Vital Resources

Britain, France, and Holland had territories in Southeast Asia containing vital oil, rubber, coal, and tin reserves, which they tried to protect with garrisoned troops and WWI–era battleships. Japan had limited natural resources of its own and thus set out to conquer and control those regions of the Pacific Rim.

BELOW: *Japanese military leaders knew they could not control the Pacific as long as the U.S. fleet remained at Pearl Harbor. Relying on its pilots taking off from aircraft carriers, Japan attacked Hawaii at dawn on December 7, 1941.* Japanese War Museum photo

The Japanese constructed a massive arsenal of planes, aircraft carriers, warships, tanks, and cannons in virtual secrecy in the late 1930s to carry out its conquests.

When it suddenly unleashed its fury, Japan stunned the world with its awesome firepower. Only Nazi Germany, on the other side of the world, had a military as formidable as Japan's.

America Supports Allies along the Rim

The United States had sent fighter aircraft and pilots, food, munitions, and supplies to help the Chinese in their fight with Japan. America also sent antiquated and rusting warships and untested seamen, aircraft, and pilots to Australia and New Zealand to protect those territories and the surrounding waters.

Just as in Europe, the United States was trying to stay out of a war far removed from its own shores. Instead, it sent weapons, ammunition, and supplies, plus small contingents of personnel who acted as advisers or trainers, to those countries that were being threatened.

Keeping America Out of the Fight

Japanese leaders knew that eventually America would stand beside its friends in the Far East and join the fight. They also realized they couldn't win a war against the Americans, unless they could somehow hit first and hit hard, with a crippling blow.

Many of Japan's military leaders had visited or received military training in the United States and were very familiar with U.S. strategy and deployment of its existing forces. Japanese commanders determined that the most effective way to nullify America's military might in the region would be to destroy the Pacific fleet based at Pearl Harbor in the Hawaiian Islands.

But their own warships could not get close to within firing range without being detected somewhere along the way. Only large numbers of planes launched from aircraft carriers, flying at night and attacking at dawn, on a weekend when American soldiers and sailors would still be sleeping, would catch them unprepared and most vulnerable.

The Japanese formulated a plan many considered impossible. Then they set out to destroy the dragon while it slept in its island paradise.

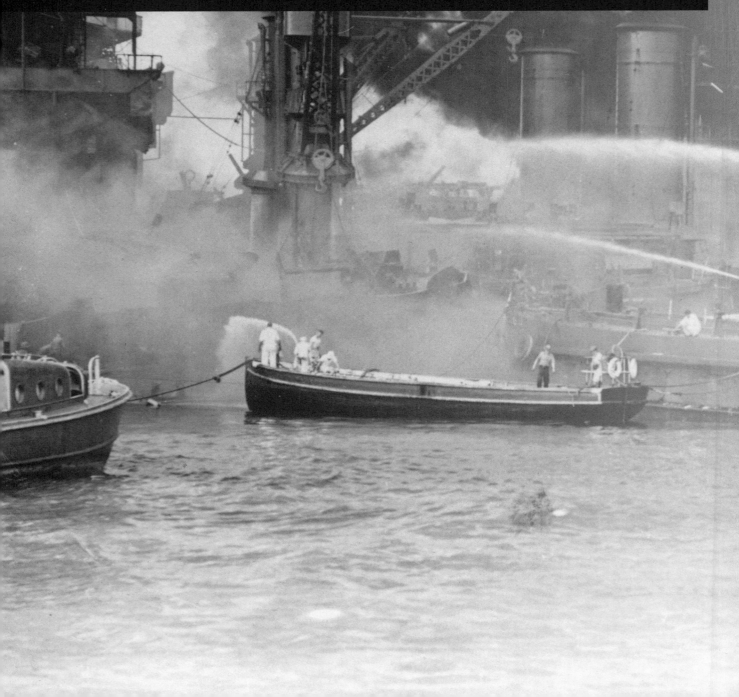

"IF YOU GET KNOCKED OUT ON YOUR FEET, YOU CARRY ON, AND YOU DON'T REALIZE WHAT'S HAPPENING— YOU JUST KEEP FIGHTING."

—*Navy Seaman Joseph George, all-Navy boxer, at Pearl Harbor*

"THERE IS NO SUCH THING AS DEFEAT EXCEPT WHEN IT COMES FROM WITHIN. AS LONG AS A PERSON DOESN'T ADMIT HE IS DEFEATED, HE IS NOT DEFEATED—HE'S JUST A LITTLE BEHIND AND ISN'T THROUGH FIGHTING."

—*Darrell Royal, University of Texas football coach*

"THE NEXT WAR MAY WELL START IN THE AIR, BUT IN ALL PROBABILITY IT WILL WIND UP, AS DID THE LAST WAR, IN THE MUD."

—*Anonymous, 1925*

OPPOSITE: *Pearl Harbor survivors and civilian volunteers manned fire and rescue boats, searching for others still alive within the wreckage. Some of those volunteers included members of the San Jose State football team, visiting Hawaii to play a round-robin football tournament.* U.S. Navy photo

BY 1900 THE JAPANESE HAD ADOPTED BASEBALL AS their national sport, introduced there by American missionaries in the past decade. The Japanese not only played the game very well but also idolized American ballplayers.

In 1927 Negro Leagues ballplayers toured Japan and impressed their hosts with their style of play. Though mostly unknown overseas, these "kokujin," which included Raleigh "Biz" Mackey and Herbert "Rap" Dixon, were immensely popular in Japan. They played against Japanese collegians, introduced their shadowball routine of engaging in lively infield practice without any ball, and dazzled the spectators with their base running and long-distance throwing skills.

In 1934 a team of major league all-stars stocked with numerous future Hall of Famers were amazed that everywhere they went, the Japanese fans and players were so knowledgeable about them.

"You'd think being so many miles away and being such a different culture, the whole thing would have been strange to them. But apparently they had been following big-league baseball for years and they knew all of us," remembered Detroit Tiger Charlie Gehringer, among the top five in 1933 in batting average, total bases, and hits.

The American contingent to Japan included some of the greatest players in baseball history: Lou "The Iron Horse" Gehrig, Jimmie Foxx, and the most popular player of that era, Babe Ruth.

ABOVE: *President Franklin D. Roosevelt addresses Congress on December 8, 1941, denouncing the attack on Pearl Harbor as "the day that will live in infamy," declaring war on Japan.* National Archives photo

The previous year Foxx led the American League in batting average (.356), total bases, slugging, runs batted in, and home runs. Gehrig was right behind him in each of those categories, and he led the league in runs scored, with 138. Ruth busted down the fences from 1920 to 1932 before that visit to Japan, clubbing at least 40 home runs each year (except 1922, when he hit 35, and 1925, when he hit 25 round-trippers).

"Those Japanese fans had never seen anything like those big guys—Ruth, Foxx and Gehrig," Charlie Gehringer continued. "They just couldn't believe anybody could hit a ball so far."

One of the Japanese pitchers who struck out Gehringer, Ruth, Gehrig, and Foxx in order was fastballer Eiji Sawamura. Pulling off this feat rocketed him to instant immortality. Tragically, he would become an enemy casualty a decade later during World War II's brutal Pacific Campaign.

Moe Berg was another of the all-stars on that 1934 tour of Japan. During some free time in Tokyo, he shot photos around the city. But these were not just tourist shots. They were shots of key military and industrial installations. A master of foreign languages, Berg enjoyed his "hobby" as a spy. He wasn't sure if the photos would be of any use but thought it certainly wouldn't hurt to take them since he was in Tokyo anyway. His sightseeing completed, Berg rejoined his all-star teammates, who dazzled the Japanese fans with massive home runs like they'd never seen before. (Berg certainly wasn't swatting any home runs of his own: from 1923 to 1933 he had hit a grand total of three four-baggers.)

After playing eighteen games in Japan, the American all-stars boarded a ship bound for the Philippines with a refueling stop in Shanghai, where they

RIGHT: The USS Arizona's 1937 baseball team included pitcher Marion "Pat" Tobin (front row, second from right), who played minor league ball in San Diego after he left the Navy later that year. In 1941 he made it to the major leagues, playing for the Athletics. Tragically though, many of his former Arizona teammates were killed when the battleship was sunk by Japanese planes at Pearl Harbor.
U.S. Navy photo

were coaxed to disembark and play a pickup game against U.S. Marines and missionaries there. This was one overseas skirmish the Marines didn't mind losing, 22–1.

Sports Activity at Pearl Harbor

In 1935 the battleship USS *Arizona* had one of the best football squads in the Navy, led by Annapolis all-American halfback Buzz Borries and tackle Slade Cutter, another all-American borrowed from the battleship *Idaho* for the football season.

Pitcher Marion "Pat" Tobin was a dominating pitcher for the *Arizona* team in the mid-1930s, which was good enough to hold its own during spring training games against major league clubs touring Hawaii. When his hitch in the Navy was over in 1937, Tobin played minor league ball for the San Diego Padres when they were part of the Pacific Coast League. In 1941 he had a brief stint with the Philadelphia Athletics, appearing in only one game.

But also during that 1941 baseball season, as if to send an ominous signal to the United States, Japan suddenly banned America's game from being played anywhere in the country. At the same time, Japanese military forces were preparing for a surprising and devastating attack that would, they were hoping, lead to the conquest of the entire Pacific.

The Japanese Throw a Sucker Punch

In the early days of December 1941, Hawaii was buzzing with sports events, both collegiate and among the numerous military units stationed there.

When the San Jose State Spartans football team arrived in Honolulu on December 3 to play a round-robin tournament with two other teams, none of the Spartans, nor any of the other athletes visiting the islands, suspected that their lives would be completely disrupted in a few days. Some had aspirations of playing football as professionals, and a good performance in the upcoming games might attract offers from some of the big-league teams. Other graduating players simply knew they would be playing their final collegiate game and wanted a good showing.

At the University of California, Los Angeles (UCLA), Jackie Robinson had lettered in track, football, baseball, and basketball. When he left the

LEFT ABOVE: *Moe Berg (center) was a full-time major league ballplayer and part-time spy, who travelled extensively overseas to snoop around and monitor the progress of Imperial Japan's military buildup and years later, Nazi Germany's atomic weapons development. In 1934 he toured Japan with other major league all-stars and took that opportunity to photograph key installations and factories in Tokyo. His photos were used eight years later by the Doolittle Raiders to select bombing targets.* Photo courtesy of the O.S.S.

LEFT BELOW: *Navy All-American gridiron star Slade Cutter would later be stationed at Pearl Harbor and served on the USS Arizona in 1935, playing for the battleship's football squad, which many considered one of the best anywhere. Later in the Pacific Campaign, Cutter would skipper a submarine, and harass and sink enemy transports and warships.* U.S. Naval Academy Archives photo

university after two years, Robinson found that none of the pro teams—in baseball, basketball, or football—would allow blacks to play, no matter how good they were. His only offer came from the Honolulu Bears, a minor league football team in Hawaii. Robinson worked in construction during the week and played ball on Sundays for two months in 1941, earning one hundred dollars a game. After the last game of the season, Robinson boarded a ship and returned home to California, on December 5, 1941, unaware that farther out in the Pacific, Japanese naval forces were converging on the Hawaiian Islands.

That Friday night, December 5, a boxing smoker was held at Pearl Harbor. One of the pugilists was Navy Boatswain's Mate Joe George, a Golden Gloves and three-time Navy heavyweight champ, assigned to the *Vestal*, a repair ship berthed alongside the battleship *Arizona* at Pearl Harbor.

The next day, at nearby Schofield Barracks, the Army post held its football championships, with the Twenty-first Infantry, which boasted numerous college players, beating the Thirty-fifth Infantry Regiment 13–6. One of the Thirty-fifth Infantry Regiment's top players was Army Sergeant Emil Matula, who, when not playing football, was section leader for an 81-mm mortar platoon.

That same day the islands' annual Shrine football game pitted the Willamette University Bearcats against the University of Hawaii Rainbows.

On Sunday, December 7, the Navy at Pearl Harbor planned to hold its baseball championships, involving teams from the battleship *Arizona* and the carrier *Enterprise*. But the flattop, along with nine destroyers and three cruisers escorting it, was still at sea two hundred miles away, delayed by rough weather. The ball game would have to be delayed until the Mighty E made it back to Pearl.

But that game was never played, for the peaceful dawn of December 7 was suddenly shattered by the roar of hundreds of Japanese planes descending on Battleship Row at Pearl Harbor.

The visiting collegiate football players were awakened by what sounded like thunder directly overhead. They were stunned, watching in horror from their hotels as swarms of Japanese planes dropped bombs and torpedoes on the berthed war ships at Pearl and parked aircraft at Hickam Field. It was almost too horrible to imagine, as the entire harbor was engulfed with fire and smoke.

Just two months after the New York Yankees had won the '41 World Series, 360 Japanese warplanes loaded with bombs and torpedoes were doing their damnedest to destroy the United States Pacific fleet.

One of those enemy pilots was Lieutenant Tasuo Ichihara, a bear of a sumo wrestler assigned to the carrier *Shokaku.* Another was Lieutenant Fusata Iida, assigned to the carrier *Soryu.* He was one of Japan's best young pilots and excelled in both tennis and baseball. In addressing his pilots before the Pearl Harbor mission, Iida stated that, in the event of engine problems, "I will fly straight to my objective and make a crash dive into an enemy target rather than an emergency landing." He fully expected his fellow pilots to follow suit.

ABOVE: *Throughout the Pacific Campaign, Hawaii was used as a staging area and training site for thousands of U.S. troops. Sports, such as football, promoted physical conditioning and teamwork—two assets that commanders felt would lead to victory on the beachheads and in the jungles of the South Pacific.*
U.S. Army photo

Athletes Caught in the Attack

Amidst the chaos and carnage of the surprise attack at Pearl Harbor were individual acts of heroism and moments of tragedy. Former Annapolis tackle William "Killer" Kane was already on duty that morning, as officer of the day—a day that would stretch into forty-eight grueling hours—scrambling to rescue the wounded, dispatching makeshift fire teams, and directing volunteers pouring into the area.

Joe George, the heavyweight boxer from the repair ship *Vestal,* was amazed that torpedoes from enemy planes passed right under his ship, because it rested so high in the water. "All those torpedoes were coming toward us, and nothing ever exploded because they were going under us and hitting the *Arizona,* which was berthed alongside." George and his fellow crewmen worked tirelessly to help sailors from the *Arizona* cross over by rope to the *Vestal* while still under attack.

Major Allan Shapley, the slugging first baseman and coach for the Arizona baseball team and former running back for the Naval Academy's national championship squad in 1926, tried to reach the anti-aircraft gun on the mainmast of the crippled battleship but was strafed by enemy warplanes and was forced to dive into the water littered with debris and bodies and burning fuel. One of his shipmates was Marine Corporal Earl Nightingale, attached to the *Arizona*, himself a top-notch swimmer who struggled along with Shapley to swim over to nearby Ford Island.

Claude Ricketts, another member of Navy's 1926 championship team, was on board the mighty battleship *West Virginia*. After suffering several torpedo hits, the *West Virginia* was doomed. As damage control officer, Ricketts knew she would roll over if he didn't scuttle her, flooding compartments so she would settle upright. Because of these actions, the *West Virginia* was repaired in quick order and later was dispatched to the fight for a little payback against the Japanese.

Former Naval Academy star halfback Gordon Chung-Hoon from the *Arizona* was on a weekend pass in Honolulu when he heard the battle unfolding. Like other servicemen in town, he attempted to get back to his duty station at Pearl Harbor but was stopped by traffic jams and road-blocks. By the time Chung-Hoon reached the *Arizona*, the mighty warship was little more than a smoldering wreck, with many of his shipmates trapped inside.

Navy lightweight boxing champ Joe Fisher watched the aerial assault from the nearby liberty landing of Aiea and helped the wounded swimming to safety. Another onlooker was Honolulu resident Toy Tamanaha, a top-ranked flyweight boxer. Tragically, Tamanaha was inside a store when it was hit by a shell. "I just sat there, looking at my legs. They were all mangled." Tamanaha would never fight again. Both of his legs had to be amputated.

Emil Matula, the football player for the Thirty-fifth Infantry Regiment, was alerted, along with the rest of his unit, to ward off an anticipated invasion of enemy troops. In the coming years the Thirty-fifth Regiment would deploy to unheard of Pacific islands for epic battles with the Japanese.

A Heavy Toll

Eight battleships, three destroyers, and three cruisers were crippled or sunk at Pearl, along with 188 planes destroyed and another 31 badly damaged. The death toll was staggering: 2,403 dead, with another 1,104 wounded in the attack. More than 1,100 of the dead were entombed forever in the battleship *Arizona*.

As bad as the carnage was, the Japanese had failed to trap the vital American aircraft carriers at Pearl. Fortunately, the *Lexington* and *Saratoga* were at sea, with their own support fleet of ships. The *Enterprise* pulled into smoldering Pearl at dusk on December 8. The Big E's crew stood on the deck, silently disbelieving what they were seeing. (All three flattops would play crucial roles in future battles with Japanese naval forces in the Pacific.)

On December 7, 1941, America was suddenly plunged into World War II. The scheduled football and baseball games in Hawaii were never played, and the college athletes were stranded in Hawaii for two weeks until a hospital ship, the *President Coolidge,* took them back to the West Coast, along with the Pearl Harbor wounded. Some of the players remained in Hawaii to provide help wherever needed, thus becoming the earliest wartime volunteer athletes. Many trooped down to the local recruiting offices and signed up to serve in one of the armed forces "for the duration."

The News Filters In

At Griffith Stadium in Washington, D.C., the Redskins and Philadelphia Eagles were grinding it out midafternoon on December 7. The devastating news from Hawaii was not known publicly yet, but everyone at the game

BELOW: *Billowing smoke hides much of the damage along Battleship Row at Pearl Harbor. U.S. losses included fourteen warships, 188 planes, and 2,403 killed, with thousands more wounded.*
U.S. Navy photo

was distracted by the hundreds of military and political leaders being directed over the loudspeaker to return to their offices.

"We didn't know what the hell was going on," remembered Redskins quarterback Slingin' Sammy Baugh. "I had never heard that many announcements one right after another. We felt something was up, but we just kept playing."

Reporters up in the press box had seen a flash report: "The Japanese have kicked off. War Now!"

The crowd that remained knew something big must be going on, but it wasn't until after the game, which the Redskins won 20–4, that the spectators and the rest of the nation learned about the attack on Pearl Harbor.

At that game was Navy Reserve Ensign John F. Kennedy, a natural athlete who played end for Harvard's junior varsity football team in 1936 and was a vital member of "the greatest Harvard freshmen swimming team ever assembled." (While physical problems would force him to curtail collegiate sports and bother him all his life, Kennedy's athleticism would be a lifesaver later when he commanded a PT boat in World War II's South Pacific Campaign.)

At New York's Polo Grounds that afternoon, the Giants and Dodgers were literally slugging it out: a full squad of potential recruits was helped off the gridiron and a few were taken to the hospital. The game was played in honor of Giants star running back Tuffy Leemans, but the Dodgers steamrolled them 21–7, while news of the attack spread through the crowd. Hundreds of fans left the football game to confirm what they couldn't believe. Very quickly Tuffy Leemans Day became Pearl Harbor Day.

The next day President Franklin D. Roosevelt declared war on Japan and the other Axis powers, Germany and Italy.

Overnight Japan was despised for its act of cowardice at Pearl Harbor. The *Sporting News* implied that if baseball was in fact Japan's national pastime, the country could never have committed such a despicable act: "Through our great game runs an inherent decency, fair dealing . . . and respect for one's opponents. That is the very soul of . . . our national game [which] never touched . . . [Japan] . . .

" . . . the Japanese could [not] have committed the vicious, infamous deed of . . . December 7 . . . if the spirit of the game ever had penetrated their yellow hides."

BELOW: *A newsboy in Redding, California, announces the shocking news that the Japanese have attacked Pearl Harbor. Soon every man, woman, and child in the United States was mobilizing for both the war in Europe and the war against Japan. Everyone was expected to do his part. No one wanted to be labeled a slacker.* Library of Congress photo

Dorrie Miller

AMONG THE MANY HEROES AT PEARL HARBOR WAS twenty-two-year-old Dorie Miller, serving on the *West Virginia* as a steward. In high school he was a battering-ram running back, and at Pearl he was heavyweight boxing champion.

When the Japanese planes swarmed overhead, Miller rushed to one of the ship's machine guns and started blasting the enemy planes. The *West Virginia* was hit by two bombs and at least six torpedoes, but Miller stayed at his gun; he was credited with shooting down at least two, possibly four, of the enemy invaders. (Varying accounts dispute the actual tally.)

For his actions Miller received the Navy Cross. And for black Americans demanding equality, including the right to serve their country in the armed forces, Dorie Miller became a true war hero.

Tragically, two years later he would be killed while serving on the *Liscome Bay* when a torpedo slammed into the ship.

RIGHT: *Seaman Dorrie Miller was heavyweight boxing champion in Hawaii while serving as a steward on the battleship* West Virginia. *When the Japanese attacked Pearl Harbor, Miller rushed to a machine gun on deck and blasted the enemy planes swarming overhead.* National Archives photo

BACKGROUND: *Japanese attack Pearl Harbor, December 7, 1941.* Corbis photo

Jackie Robinson Shatters the Barrier

GROWING UP IN PASADENA, CALIFORNIA, JACKIE ROBINSON idolized his older brother, Mack, who was a member of the 1936 Olympic team that shattered Adolf Hitler's myth about the superiority of the Aryan race. Jesse Owens attracted most of the attention at the Berlin Games, but there were many great athletes on that American team, including Mack Robinson, who had placed second to Owens in the 220-meter sprint and would later set an AAU record in the broad jump.

Jackie Robinson loved baseball but was also great in basketball, football, and track. After being selected as a junior college all-American in football while attending Pasadena Junior College, he transferred to the University of California at Los Angeles in 1939.

After years as an also-ran in football, UCLA's wins piled up once it began recruiting black athletes, including Kenny Washington and Woody Strode, who would both serve in the military during World War II and eventually play pro ball.

Jackie Robinson quickly became noted as a great open-field runner, a scat back, who could juke his way right into the end zone. UCLA would go undefeated that year, with six wins and four ties. And as soon as football season was over, Robinson hit the hard courts, leading the Pacific Coast Conference's Southern Division in scoring average.

Some opposing coaches felt Robinson could be one of the greatest players in the game, if he would concentrate on just basketball. But in the spring the baseball team started practicing, and he headed for the ball diamond. And after that it was track season, where Robinson would win the NCAAs in the broad jump.

But then in early 1941, Robinson dropped out of UCLA and accepted a temporary position as a coach with the National Youth Administration, which folded soon afterward.

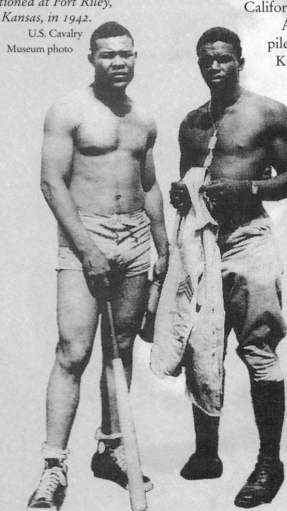

BELOW: *Army Lieutenant Jackie Robinson (right) and heavyweight boxing champ and Army Private Joe Louis, work out together while stationed at Fort Riley, Kansas, in 1942.*
U.S. Cavalry Museum photo

That summer the *Chicago Tribune* invited Robinson to play in an all-star game against the Chicago Bears, NFL champs that year. Though the Bears won, as everyone expected, by a score of 37–13, Robinson made an impression when he caught a pass and scored a touchdown. From that game he received an invitation to play for the Honolulu Bears, which promised him one hundred dollars per game and a construction job during the week.

After the final game of the season, Robinson boarded a steamship and left Hawaii, on December 5, 1941—just two days before Japan's attack on Pearl Harbor turned the world upside down. Robinson returned to Los Angeles and played semipro basketball with the Red Devils.

Months later he received his draft notice and went into the Army. During a brief hitch at Fort Riley in central Kansas, Robinson would experience the racism that every Negro athlete had felt.

During some free time, Army Lieutenant Robinson passed by a ball game and asked if he could play. But a white officer told him that he would have to play with the colored team instead. On that Fort Riley field was major leaguer Pete Reiser, who would later recall, "That was a joke. There was no colored team. The black lieutenant didn't speak. He stood there for a while, watched us work out, and then he turned and walked away. I can still remember him walking away by himself."

Robinson underwent training to be an armor officer, leading a platoon of tanks from the 761st Tank Battalion at Camp Hood in Texas. But because of a verbal altercation with a bus driver, Robinson was held on charges and faced a court-martial while his unit deployed overseas.

After writing letters and making phone calls, promising bad publicity for the Army just at a time when the walls of segregation were being torn down, Robinson eventually beat the charges against him and received an honorable discharge from the Army in November 1944.

That winter he accepted a coaching position with the basketball team at Sam Houston College in Texas. He also received an offer to play baseball for the Kansas City Monarchs, beginning with the 1945 season.

Three years earlier, while in California, he had played an exhibition game against Negro League players and never received the pay he was promised. When he received the Monarchs offer, Robinson remembered that incident, and nearly turned down the offer. But Kansas City was considered the classiest of all the Negro Leagues teams. The Monarchs were better paid and better treated than other players, and thus the team attracted the best players, which led to continued success on the field. Robinson joined the Monarchs, but only for a short stint. On August 28 of that year he signed on to join the Brooklyn Dodgers organization.

Among Negro Leagues players, Jackie Robinson was not most people's choice to break the major leagues color barrier. Any number of players, including Monte Irvin, Satchel Paige, or Cool Papa Bell, would have been just as good. In fact, many players felt these other men were more deserving because they had paid their dues, playing for years in the Negro Leagues.

But Jackie Robinson was the "sure bet" choice because he was a World War II veteran and a collegiate star who excelled at several sports, attracting a large following of both white and black fans.

Still, Robinson knew he would be facing not only hostile crowds wherever he played, but also racist opponents who would try to hurt him when he came up to bat ran the bases. Many simply refused to play in the same game with him.

At the conclusion of his first year as a Dodger, having played in 150 games, with a .297 average, 12 home runs, 175 hits, and 48 runs batted in, Robinson was selected as the *Sporting News* National League Rookie of the Year. The *Sporting News* wrote: "That Jack Roosevelt Robinson might have had more obstacles than his first-year competitors, and that he perhaps had a harder fight to gain even major league recognition, was no concern of this publication. This sociological experiment that Robinson represented, the trailblazing that he did, the barriers he broke down, did not enter into that decision. He was rated and examined solely as a freshman player in the big leagues—on the basis of his hitting, his running, his defensive play, his team value."

Whether they wanted him to fail or succeed, baseball fans everywhere followed the amazing exploits of Jackie Robinson, who proved Negro Leaguers belonged in the major leagues.

Jackie Robinson joined the Brooklyn Dodgers in April 1947. But Negro Leaguers actually played on the same teams as white ballplayers a full two years earlier, in April and May 1945, when U.S. forces stationed in Italy and North Africa formed their own all-star teams to compete for the Mediterranean Theater championships. At the same time, teams from England, France, Belgium, Holland, and Germany were playing for the European Theater championship.

Among the many players who competed in these two tournaments were Kansas City Monarchs catcher Joe Greene, Newark Eagles superstar pitcher Leon Day, and Monarchs slugger Willard "Home Run" Brown, just to name a few.

Some of the major league ballplayers who teamed up with the Negro Leaguers were pitcher Ewell "the

BELOW: *Jackie Robinson experienced Army warfare of the past when he rode a cavalry horse at Fort Riley in 1942, then prepared for modern warfare, as a tank commander at Camp Hood in Texas.* U.S. Cavalry Museum photo

Whip" Blackwell and Ben Zientara of the Cincinnati Reds, Harry "the Hat" Walker and Sam Nahem of the Cardinals, Johnny Wyrostek and Russ Bauers of the Pittsburgh Pirates, and Ken Heintzelman of the Philadelphia Phillies.

Harry "the Hat" Walker had faced Willard "Home Run" Brown of the Monarchs while competing for the European crown and recalled, "I pitched against him on the Riviera. He like to killed me with a line shot, hit my glove, thank God, not my face."

Brown, representing the European champions, then faced Ewell Blackwell, pitching for the Mediterranean team: "We were playing in Nice, France. Leon Day of the Newark Eagles played for us; that's the only reason we could beat them. I hit a home run off Blackwell. I remember it so well, because the next time up I got hit!"

Negro Leagues hurler Leon Day was the winning pitcher for the European team, beating the Med team by the score of 8–0, capped by two home runs from Willard Brown.

In that championship game, in the spring of 1945, the two Negro Leaguers had more than held their own against major league stars. Leon Day and Willard Brown proved they belonged on the same team with white ballplayers . . . two years before Jackie Robinson was recognized as the first black ballplayer to make it to the majors.

3. Thousands Volunteer for Some Big-Time Payback

> "WE ARE IN TROUBLE AND THERE'S ONLY ONE THING
> FOR ME TO DO . . . RETURN TO THE SERVICE."
>
> —*Hank Greenberg, Detroit Tigers*

BEGINNING IN THE MID-1930s, AS NAZI GERMANY AND Imperial Japan flexed their military might, America's leaders knew it was just a matter of time before this country entered the fray. In September 1940 President Roosevelt signed into law the country's first peacetime draft, which called for training 1.2 million men, with an additional 800,000 for the Reserves. The draft was implemented in October 1940 using a lottery system. Those eligible men with a low lottery number (determined by their birthday) would be called up immediately.

Minor league outfielder Billy Southworth, who played with Toronto, enlisted in the Army Air Corps months before Pearl Harbor. And Pennsylvania Senators outfielder Bill Embrick, another minor leaguer, was the first ballplayer to be called up in the newly implemented draft. Even before Pearl Harbor, two major league players—Phillies pitcher Hugh Mulcahy and Hammerin' Hank Greenberg of the Detroit Tigers—joined the service.

Mulcahy, the first major leaguer to be drafted, had the misfortune of pitching for the last place Philadelphia Phillies from 1937 to '40.

Greenberg, who was Jewish, had read the news reports and heard the radio broadcasts about Jews being harassed, herded up, and confined in overcrowded ghettos and concentration camps in Europe. In 1938 he slugged out fifty-eight homers and was harassed by spectators in every city he played in. Many Jewish leaders and publications felt this anti-Semitism took a toll on Greenberg's efforts to break Babe Ruth's record of 60 home runs in a single season. Despite the racial taunting, Greenberg would not retaliate: "Nobody else could have withstood the foul invectives that were directed toward Greenberg, and he had to eat them. Or else he would be thrown out of every game he played," recalled catcher Birdie Tebbetts.

During the 1940 season Greenberg led the Tigers to the American League championship. The team hoped for a repeat run at the crown in 1941, so losing the power of Greenberg was a devastating blow.

"I came to feel that if I, as a Jew, hit a home run I was hitting one against Hitler," he would write in *Story of My Life*. But Greenberg knew that

BELOW: *After surrendering, U.S. and Filipino soldiers were rounded up and force-marched from the Bataan peninsula for sixty miles north in early 1942. Hundreds died along that route, forever after known as the infamous Bataan Death March. Thousands survived, only to spend the remainder of the war in a POW camp.*

One of those prisoners was Mario "Motts" Tonelli, former Notre Dame All-American scat back, who would spend forty-six months in confinement. Mason Chronister, Penn Relay long distance runner, would die in camp after being severely beaten by Japanese guards.
National Archives photo

OPPOSITE: *Crewmen aboard the USS* Yorktown, *May 1943.*
Corbis photo

this Nazi menace couldn't be stopped by playing baseball, and so, after leading the league with 41 home runs and 150 RBIs in 1940, he joined the Army after playing in just nineteen games of the '41 season. In early December, having completed his hitch, he was discharged and headed home to rejoin the Tigers. But two days after hearing the news about the attack at Pearl Harbor, Greenberg volunteered as an officer with the Army Air Corps.

"I have not been called back. I am going back of my own accord." he explained. "Baseball is out the window as far as I'm concerned. I don't know if I'll ever return to baseball." In fact, four years later he would return to the Tigers in time to play in the 1945 World Series. The next year he again led the league in homers and RBIs.

But in early December 1941, after the attack on Pearl Harbor, swatting baseballs was the last thing Greenberg was thinking about. He knew there were more important things to do for his country.

Avenging a Despicable Act

Within days after the Japanese attack on Pearl Harbor, thousands of young men went down to their local recruiting offices and signed up for the military, hoping to fight and defeat "them God-damned Japanese." One of those young men was Cleveland Indians fireball pitcher Bob Feller, who was considered the best pitcher in baseball when he enlisted in the Navy.

Feller was one of the American League's most dominating pitchers, even throwing a no-hitter in 1940 when he was just twenty-one. He also led the league that year in strikeouts (261), innings pitched (320), complete games pitched (31), and wins (27).

Just months before Pearl Harbor, Feller again led the American League in wins (25), strikeouts, shutouts, innings pitched, and games pitched. He could have bided his time and waited to be drafted, possibly pitching all or at least part of the 1942 season. Yet after Pearl Harbor, Rapid Robert knew there were more important things to do than play baseball.

"I can throw a few strikes for Uncle Sam," he told reporters after arriving at Norfolk, Virginia, for training. "I always wanted to be on the winning side and this time I know I'm with a winner."

He would serve with a gun crew aboard the USS *Alabama* in both the North Atlantic and South Pacific until the end of the war in 1945.

Hundreds of thousands of men had volunteered to fight just days after Pearl Harbor, but many more would be needed. America would now have to wage two separate wars, in Europe/North Africa and the entire Pacific, from Alaska to India.

For the United States it truly was a world war. And if it dragged on for years, as many feared it would, every healthy young man could expect to eventually get a letter from Uncle Sam requesting that he join the conflicts overseas.

American families had been preparing for the Chanukah and Christmas holidays when the attack on Pearl Harbor occurred. Many quickly realized it might be their last time together as fathers, brothers, and sons prepared to go to war.

There would be little to celebrate that New Year's Eve.

An Unhappy New Year

The traditional Rose Bowl Game in Pasadena, California, slated for New Year's Day, 1942, was in jeopardy, because civil defense leaders were worried about large crowd gatherings along the West Coast. And there were rampant rumors that Japanese "sympathizers" living in the area might sabotage large gatherings. Naturally there was concern that after crippling America's Pacific fleet in Hawaii, the Japanese would soon attack the western United States. The Rose Bowl game, between Duke and Oregon State, was moved to the Duke campus at Durham, North Carolina.

Oregon State won that subdued game, 20–16. Many of the players on both teams would be wearing a different uniform in a few short months. Tragically, too many of them would not survive World War II. Four who joined the Marines and were killed in the Pacific were Oregon State running back Everett Smith, who drowned in an amphibious assault; Duke tackle Bob Nanni, who fell at Iwo Jima; his teammate Wally Griffith, who was killed eleven months after the game; and Fellow Blue Devil Al Hoover, caught up in the bloody battle of Peleliu, who pounced on an enemy grenade to save his buddies, costing him his life.

BELOW: *Japanese tanks rumble into Manila, passing by the Philippine legislature, just weeks after the attack on Pearl Harbor.*
Japanese War Ministry photo

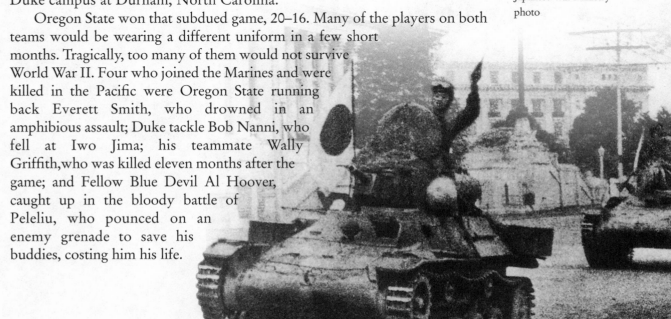

Japanese Juggernaut Advances

After the surprise attack on the American fleet at Pearl Harbor, the Japanese continued their assault on other regions of the Pacific.

Guam, largest of the Mariana Islands, was hit only hours later. Enemy planes chewed up the island's defenses, which were manned by only five hundred U.S. troops. Three days later, six thousand Japanese troops stormed ashore and overran the American garrison there, taking them prisoner.

Other U.S. servicemen on Wake Island, 2,300 miles west of Hawaii, intercepted radio reports about the attack at Pearl Harbor and prepared to come under fire. The next day, as President Roosevelt was officially declaring war on Japan, enemy ships and planes bombed and strafed Wake. Marine, Army, and Navy servicemen on the island were able to hold off the invading force temporarily, but by December 23 Wake had also fallen.

The Philippines were the next U.S. stronghold to come under attack and looked to be the next domino to fall in the Pacific. The American and

Filipino defenders had known weeks earlier that war was about to disrupt the islands. By November 27 they were put on alert. Just three days later many of the American officers gathered at the Army-Navy Club on Manila Bay to hear the broadcast of the football game between West Point and the midshipmen from Annapolis.

American pilots of the Far East Air Force were itching for a fight, braced to defend the islands from enemy planes based at Formosa and on carriers lurking in the Pacific. War was imminent, and those pilots in the Philippines wondered if maybe they were just a trip wire to pull the United States into war with Japan. On December 6 the Fifth Interception Command issued a brief statement to dispel some of the rumors: "Men, you are not a suicide squadron yet, but you are damned close to it. There will be war with Japan in a few days. It may come in a matter of hours."

Among the American pilots facing impossible odds were Don Pagel, Don "Shorty" Crosland, and Frankie Bryant of the Thirty-fourth Pursuit Squadron. Pagel had been a star halfback for his high school football team in Aurora, Illinois; Crosland played varsity basketball for his high school; and Bryant played football for North Texas State Teachers College before joining the Army Air Corps.

Some American pilots erroneously felt the Japanese pilots would not engage them in a dogfight, that they were all nearsighted, and their nervous system couldn't withstand all the aerial acrobatics! It wouldn't take long to learn just how mistaken they had been, when swarms of Japanese zeroes swooped down and destroyed those American planes that couldn't get aloft.

Many American pilots perished when Japanese planes strafed them, but Pagel, Crosland, and Bryant continued to fly sorties against Japanese ships as they landed troops in the Philippines.

The bulk of the American planes of the Far East Air Force had been destroyed while still on the ground, leaving the remainder of the pilots to launch futile strikes, knowing they would probably be shot out of the skies.

Thirty-three American pilots were killed in the initial Philippines Campaign, while more than eighty had become infantrymen until they were taken prisoner. Fewer than fifty were evacuated to Australia to continue the fight.

Anton Bilek, a pitcher for the base team at Clark Air Field in the Philippines prior to the Japanese attack, explained the fate of some of his teammates: "At shortstop we had Armando Viselli. He died in a reconnais-

ABOVE: *Mario "Motts" Tonelli had been an All-American ball carrier for the Fighting Irish but he saw little action during WWII, spending nearly four years "on the sidelines." Sergeant Tonelli had endured the Japanese bombardment of Bataan, the brutality of the notorious Death March, where hundreds of American and Filipino captives succumbed, and forty-six months of captivity in a POW camp.* AP Wide World photo

sance flight over Lamon Bay on the twenty-second of December 1941. We had two catchers. Beck was hit on the first day the Japanese bombed at Clark Field and his leg was badly mangled. The other catcher was Dumas. He was killed on the first day at Iba."

Two former West Point teammates who would end up at the Bataan Peninsula together were Maurice Daly and Tom Trapnell. Daly was with the Army Air Corps at Clark Air Field and watched as all of their aircraft were either blasted out of the skies or destroyed on the ground. The crewmen and support personnel of the decimated air squadrons who survived the initial enemy air attacks were absorbed into Army units scattered throughout the Philippines.

Even after surrendering, Daly continued to fight the Japanese, even as a POW, standing up for his fellow prisoners. But after two very long years of deprivation, he would succumb while lying next to longtime teammate Tom Trapnell aboard a POW ship bound for Japan.

Battling at Manila Bay

ABOVE: *The day after attacking Pearl Harbor, the Japanese hit Wake Island, one of the U.S.-held outposts in the Pacific soon overrun by enemy forces. It would take two years for the Allies to reclaim Wake, shown here when a Dauntless dive-bomber makes a pass on the island in December 1943.*
U.S. Navy photo

American and Filipino ground forces were already in place and prepared for the fight, assured that reinforcements were on the way from the United States if they could slowly give ground and hold off the Japanese until then.

The Twenty-sixth Cavalry Regiment was brash and gritty, boasting the finest polo team in the Army. Ed Ramsey, who had played polo while in law school at Oklahoma University, would lead a horse platoon into battle near the Philippine village of Morong. In desperation the valiant cavalrymen charged, knowing that for centuries the thundering hooves and heart-stopping sight of a cavalry charge had terrified enemy soldiers.

But on January 16, 1942, Lieutenant Ramsey would spearhead the final charge of mounted cavalry. He and a few survivors would join up with partisan forces and fight on in the hills and jungles of the Philippines.

None of the Americans or their Filipino allies expected what was about to take place near the capital of Manila, at a small peninsula known as Bataan, and on a nearby island the shape of a tadpole, called Corregidor.

As Japanese forces surrounded the Allies and pushed them back toward Bataan, some American and Filipino soldiers surrendered, while others swam for two miles to get to the fortified stronghold of Corregidor.

The Japanese pounded the defenders there with artillery shelling for twenty-seven straight days. Though they had little food or water, inadequate medicine to care for the wounded, and not enough ammunition to keep on fighting, the Americans and Filipinos refused to surrender, still hoping rein-forcements would arrive in time to save them. But on April 9 the battling bas-tards of Bataan surrendered. Then on May 5, Corregidor finally fell.

Minor league catcher Frank Mancuso had been in training as an army paratrooper in April 1942 when he tumbled out of a plane head first and got his legs tangled in the lines of his chute. He landed hard, breaking his leg and wrenching his back. He remained behind while his unit deployed to the Philippines and was decimated in the fighting on Bataan and the Japanese bombardment of Corregidor. (After rehabilitating his leg, Mancuso would be called up to the St. Louis Browns in 1944 and played that year in the team's only World Series appearance, batting .667 in two games. His back injury continued to bother him, though, preventing him from looking up to catch pop flies. He called it quits forty-three games into the 1947 season.)

Those Americans and Filipinos who survived the bombardment of Bataan and Corregidor were taken prisoner and had to endure what became known as the Bataan Death March to prison camps farther north. Sweltering heat, no food or water, and brutal Japanese guards decimated the weary pris-oners of war, who were force-marched sixty miles. While exact casualties will never be known, it is estimated that six hundred Americans and five thousand to ten thousand Filipinos died on the route.

Sergeant Mario "Motts" Tonelli, former Notre Dame all-American run-ning back, survived the Death March and spent forty-six harrowing months in a Japanese prison camp. He was released at the end of the war, in 1945.

Medical officer Alvin Poweleit was an imposing figure at the beginning of the siege at Bataan and Corregidor, but after weeks of starvation this

BELOW: *During the Japanese bombard-ment of Corregidor in March and April of 1942, American and Filipino defenders sought refuge in the Malinta Tunnel. Many couldn't stand the confinement and ventured outside, despite the continual pounding of enemy artillery shells.* U.S. Army photo

former pro boxer was, like most of the Death March survivors, little more than a walking skeleton.

Olympic sharpshooter Martin Gison was one of the thousands of Filipino scouts who would spend the duration of the war in a POW camp. He would survive and three years later represent his country at the 1948 Olympics.

Some Would Not Return

Official War Department statistics show that more than 5,200 Americans died either during the Bataan Death March or in the prison camps. One of those was Mason Chronister, a long-distance runner who participated in the 1940 Penn Relays. He had been captured on Bataan and endured the Death March but later died in a prison camp after being beaten by Japanese guards.

Charles Humber, team captain on West Point's 1930 football team, led the Thirty-first Infantry Battalion at Bataan and fought until there was nothing but rocks to throw at the Japanese forces. After surrendering, Humber endured the Death March but would perish on a POW ship just months before the war in the Pacific ended.

Another casualty was Paul Bunker, former West Point all-American tackle and halfback. He had been a classmate of General Douglas MacArthur several decades earlier. MacArthur had even written about Bunker, saying, "I could shut my eyes and see again that blond head racing, tearing, plunging—210 pounds of irresistible power."

During the early siege of Corregidor, MacArthur was reunited with his old classmate, who was commander of the Fifty-ninth Coast Artillery Regiment on The Rock. But President Roosevelt ordered MacArthur to leave the besieged island, and he reluctantly left behind his old friend, promising to send reinforcements that never came, leaving Bunker to defend an indefensible stronghold.

When U.S. and Filipino forces on Corregidor finally surrendered, after enduring weeks of enemy bombing, Bunker unceremoniously lowered the Stars and Stripes and raised the white flag.

Bunker was among those taken prisoner, as was Captain Austin Shofner of the Fourth Marines, former varsity lineman with Tennessee. Bunker died a year later in a POW camp on Formosa.

BELOW: *American and Filipino soldiers endure the sweltering heat and brutal treatment from their Japanese guards during the seemingly-endless Bataan Death March in April of 1942. Unknown thousands died along the route.* National Archives photo

"THEY STARTED IT, WE'LL FINISH IT."

—*popular rally cry in 1942*

THOSE FOOTBALL AND BASEBALL PLAYERS WHO DIDN'T march down to the induction center and enlist tried to squeeze out a few more months with their teams, continuing to play until they were drafted and it was time to join the military. To delay that induction notice from Uncle Sam, many athletes found war-essential jobs in factories in the same city they played for or within easy traveling distance, working during day shifts and practicing with the team after hours, playing games as usual at night and on the weekends but skipping day games.

Lefty "Goofy" Gomez, who had retired as a pitcher for the New York Yankees after compiling Hall of Fame statistics, worked at the Norden bomb sight plant and continued to pitch for a semipro team in New York on Sundays. The Norden sights allowed bomber crews to pinpoint their "sticks," or bombs, over enemy targets. Gomez had led the American League in wins in 1934, with 26, and again in 1937, with 21. He also led the league in strikeouts, with 163 in 1933; 158 the following year; and 194 in 1937. He was a perfect 6–0 in five World Series, in 1932 and from 1936 to 1939. He finally called it quits after pitching in just one game in 1943.

St. Louis Browns pitcher Denny Galehouse worked five or six days a week at the Goodyear Aircraft plant in Akron, Ohio, helping to churn out thousands of vital plane tires. He was also the selective service rep at the plant, recommending which of his coworkers should receive deferments from the draft. Galehouse then caught up with the Browns to throw on Sundays. In 1944 he also pitched in two World Series games for the Browns, winning one and losing one and posting a 1.50 earned run average.

Another Brownie, outfielder Chet Laabs, also had a full-time job in a war factory, which exempted him from the draft but limited the number of games he could play for the Browns. He was there at the end of the 1944 season, playing in five games when the Browns made it to the Series. The Browns lost in six games to their cross-town rivals, the Cardinals.

OPPOSITE: *Good-byes were tearful because everyone knew it was for the duration of the war, however long that might be.* U.S. Army Signal Corps photo

ABOVE: *Douglas Aircraft's Long Beach, California plant, October 1942.* Corbis photo

135155

One of the most powerful black basketball teams, the Washington Bears, scheduled its games on weekends because the players worked in New York and Washington, D.C., for Grumman Aircraft. In 1943 the Bears posted an amazing 66–0 record.

Collegiate alpine skier Dick Durrance, who had participated in the 1936 Olympic Games in Germany, worked at plane manufacturer Boeing Aircraft during the war.

By 1944 all-pro halfback Dutch Clark was coaching a semipro football team dubbed the Seattle Bombers, made up of shipyard workers.

Negro Leagues baseball player Buddy Burbage ended his fifteen-year pro career to work on the East Coast at the Philadelphia Naval Shipyard during the war years. And heavyweight boxer Jersey Joe Walcott worked in the Camden, New Jersey, shipyards, lacing on the gloves only once in three years.

Another Negro Leagues star, with the overpowering Homestead Grays, was Vic Harris. The Grays won nine consecutive Negro National League titles from 1937 to 1945, and Harris played for or managed all of them, though in 1943 and '44 he relinquished the managing duties to work in a defense plant, catching up and playing with the team whenever he could.

Val Picinich had an eighteen-year career in baseball, first as a catcher and then as a minor league manager in West Virginia and Pennsylvania. Soon after the attack on Pearl Harbor he took a job with the Bath Iron Works in Maine. He was trying to start up a company baseball team when he contracted influenza and passed away in 1942.

Minor league pitcher Sal Maglie struggled through five seasons trying to crack the big leagues. In 1943 and '44 he set aside his aspirations and went to work at a defense plant. Then in 1945 Maglie took the mound for Jersey City, posting a nondescript 5–4 record. (Maglie would work on developing a wicked curveball during a stint in the Mexican League and in 1950 joined the Giants as an over-the-hill, thirty-three-year-old rookie! As if to make up for lost time, Sal the Barber (also known as the Renaissance Assassin, Sinister Sal, and other, less-flattering monikers) posted records of eighteen wins and four losses, 23–6 and 18–8. And at thirty-nine years young, pitching for the Dodgers, Maglie notched a no-hitter. (Sal earned the nickname "the Barber" because of a nasty disposition and the tendency to "shave" opposing batters under the chin with a blazing fastball.)

Whether to avoid public criticism and the draft or to earn extra money and do their part for the war effort, many ballplayers worked full-time in factories during the off-season. And if those factories made war-related products—anything from tanks, planes, and jeeps to gloves, tents, and parachutes—the men who worked there didn't have to worry much about being drafted, at least not at first.

Enemy Presence Forces Scheduling Changes

In the weeks after the attack on Pearl Harbor, with the U.S. Pacific fleet in shambles, there was concern that the Japanese would invade the West Coast. Rumors of sabotage and clandestine invasions raised security issues. A ban on large gatherings was imposed. College football's Rose Bowl was moved from Pasadena, California, to North Carolina. Night games were also curtailed or moved to sites away from the coast and out of range of any enemy battleships that could lob shells at such an easy target as an illuminated stadium packed with thousands of people.

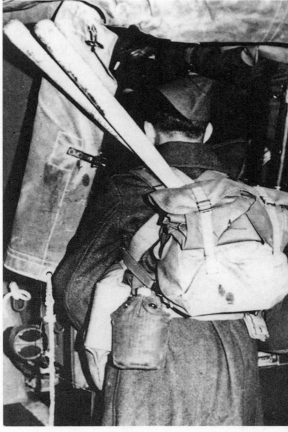

Baseball's Western International League started its games earlier in the day to avoid using stadium lights. Game broadcasters would issue this warning during pregame announcements: "Should an air raid siren sound while you're watching a game, don't leave the ball park. A sticker on the back of your seat will tell you what to do. If you are to move at all, red and green arrows will direct you beneath the stands. You'll probably be sitting in the best bomb shelter in the neighborhood."

In the Atlantic, German U-boats were sinking many Allied transport ships and tankers bound for Europe. Military leaders theorized that the illumination from coastal city lights was silhouetting the vulnerable transports. Blackouts were ordered, forcing all outdoor sporting events to suspend play at dusk. Even dog- and horseracing tracks stopped relying on photo finishes because spotlights and flash equipment violated dim-out rules.

ABOVE: *With only a backpack for personal items, most GIs carried photos of loved ones, maybe a Bible, or other small valuables. This serviceman took his prized possessions— two baseball bats, a ball, and glove— hoping to play a little ball when he wasn't dodging enemy bullets.* U.S. Office of War Information photo

Radio announcers were prohibited from mentioning weather conditions at sporting events, such as explaining a rain delay or describing football players slipping and sliding on an ice-glazed field, for fear the information might aid enemy eavesdroppers. During one exceedingly long rain delay, Cardinals pitcher turned pitchman Dizzy Dean expressed his exasperation when he huffed, "If you folks don't know what's holding up this game, just stick your head out the window!"

San Francisco's Cow Palace had been built in 1941 to host the Grand National Stock Show and Rodeo. But during the war years the stock show and rodeo was suspended, and the massive arena was used as a staging area for troops bound for the Pacific theater. It also served as a repair warehouse where women and children worked in shifts to support the war effort.

Women Join the Workforce

Thousands of factory workers who were exempt from serving because their jobs were critical did join the military, because at the time it was the patriotic thing to do.

They were replaced by single and married women who wanted to do more for the country than just bake cookies for the servicemen and write love letters.

The twenty-minute film *The Hidden Army* tugged at audiences' heart-strings when it showed wives and mothers crying after getting word that a loved one had been killed overseas. The film's narrator stressed that "there is no such thing as a slight falling off of production because there's no such thing as a slight death." This film was shown in movie theatres across the country and caused many women to rethink their role in the family and the community.

ABOVE: *Women Production Aides.* Corbis Photo

As millions of women went to work and proved they were able to do even the toughest and dirtiest of "men's jobs," those male coworkers who preferred to do their part close to home suddenly became eligible for military service.

Prior to World War II women were expected to stay home, raise the children, and do all the housework. But from 1942 until the end of the war in late 1945, women were needed in a variety of jobs traditionally done by men, who were overseas fighting the Germans and the Japanese.

The commitment of countless women was second to none, as revealed by the daily pledge of workers at the Union Wire Rope plant: "I pledge allegiance to our servicemen and to the nation for which they fight: united in production, for victory . . ."

Without these women, who built planes and ships and still managed to raise their children while their husbands, sweet-hearts, and brothers were overseas, America would not have won World War II until many years later.

Uncle Sam Wants YOU!

When the draft was first implemented in late 1940, all men between the ages of twenty-one and thirty were required to register. Soon after Pearl Harbor, the government expanded the age window to between eighteen and sixty-four, with men between twenty and forty-five susceptible to immediate call-up.

Initially all single men were considered "most eligible," and many thousands received their draft notices. All other men were slotted into categories, such as single with a war-related job, or married but with no children and no job that contributed to the war effort. The least likely to be drafted were married men who had children and worked in a job critical to the war, which included farming.

Washington Redskins quarterback Sammy Baugh returned to his ranch in Texas, fully expecting to be drafted. But the War Department felt he could support the war effort better by raising cattle, so he remained behind, traveling back and forth between his ranch and football games in the fall.

Cleveland Indians fireball pitcher Bob Feller could easily have received an exemption because his family owned a farm. Instead, he enlisted for naval combat duty the day after Pearl Harbor.

Many men who registered for the draft were later categorized as 4-F, or physically unfit. As many as a third of all inductees failed their physical exams and were sent home.

Minor leaguer Stan Partenheimer was drafted by the Army but was quickly mustered out after it was revealed he had a crippling leg injury, traced back to a pickup football game he played as a kid. In 1944 and '45 he had brief stints as a southpaw pitcher with the Red Sox and Cardinals, but again his leg hampered his efforts, and he soon retired.

By the 1944 and 1945 seasons, a majority of pro football and baseball players were either too young or too old to serve or were 4-Fs, unable to handle the physical rigors of the military though still capable of throwing a fastball or hitting a home run, withstanding a bone-jarring tackle, or streaking downfield to catch a touchdown pass.

Old-Timers Return

At the beginning of the '44 season, there were 157 big-league baseball players who were exempted from the military. Of that number, 113 were classified 4-F (38 of these were dubbed "over the hill," too old for the services but not quite ready for a rocking chair).

Among the old-timers called back to fill out the big-league rosters for another go-around was the great Jimmie Foxx, a superstar in the 1930s who had captured three MVP awards and pounded 534 home runs.

During the war Foxx worked at a Philadelphia oil plant and managed a minor league team in the Piedmont League. He returned with the Philadelphia Phillies for fifteen games in 1944, and eighty-nine in 1945.

In his final game, against the Reds, Foxxie took the mound and was posting a no-hitter through the sixth inning. Once the Reds got a hit off him, Foxx was lifted. "But we won that game, which made me the leading

ABOVE: *Slingin' Sammy Baugh was an All-American quarterback at Texas Christian and later led the Washington Redskins to the NFL crown in 1937 and '42. He watched as many of his teammates were drafted into one of the services, but Sammy was deemed too important . . . as a rancher back home in Texas, where he continued to raise cattle for the war effort, making it back to D.C. every weekend during the fall to continue playing for the 'Skins.* Photo courtesy of Texas Christian University

percentage pitcher in the National League for that year. I had one victory and no defeats. But it was the end of the road for me."

In the 1930s the Wild Horse of the Osage, Pepper Martin of the St. Louis Cardinals, had led the league in stolen bases, with twenty-six in 1933, twenty-three the next year, and twenty-three in 1936. Martin came back from the war in 1944 for another hitch with the Cards.

Eight years after calling it quits after just seventeen games in 1937, Babe Herman squeezed into a Brooklyn Dodgers uniform for one more season in '45, playing in thirty-seven games, mostly as a slow-footed pinch-hitter.

Supporting the War Effort

To generate public interest in both baseball and the war effort, major league teams played exhibition games against college and military teams, which were loaded with former pro players. Great Lakes Naval Station in Chicago, Fort Ben Harrison in Indianapolis, Lakehurst Naval Air Station and Camp Kilmer in New Jersey, West Point, and the Naval Academy were all competitive against the depleted big-league squads.

Benefit games were also held across the country to raise money for Army and Navy relief programs. Such funds were given to the families of servicemen killed or those wounded and unable to work. Other benefit games were held in support of the Red Cross, the USO, War Bonds, and hundreds of other charities.

In 1942 the Big Train and the King of Swat—Walter Johnson and Babe Ruth—came out of retirement for a charity game at New York's Yankee Stadium. Johnson had led the league in wins with thirty-six in 1913, twenty-eight in 1914, twenty-seven in 1915, twenty-five in 1916, twenty-three in 1918, and twenty-three in 1924. His earned run average was tops in 1912 and '13, 1918 and '19, and 1924. His dominance was most evident, though, as a strikeout pitcher. In 1912 he mowed down 303 batters in just fifty games. That year and through 1919 he was practically unhittable. He again led the league in strikeouts in 1921, 1923 and '24.

Babe Ruth's numbers, of course, are etched in stone. Though he started out as a pitcher, with a record of eighty-nine wins and forty-six losses from 1914 to 1919, he is best known for what he could do with a piece of timber at home plate. In eleven seasons from 1919 to 1931, the Sultan of Swat had led the American League in home runs, first with the Boston Red Sox and then, beginning in 1920, with the New York Yankees. He also led the league in runs batted in and total runs in 1919–21, 1926, and 1928. By the time he called it quits in 1935, the Babe had clobbered 714 home runs, a mark that seemed impossible to reach until Hammerin' Hank Aaron broke the record in 1974.

For one last time, in 1942, the Big Train stood on the pitcher's mound at Yankee Stadium and served up seventeen pitches to a giant of a man he'd faced many times before. To the delight of Yankee fans, Babe lofted two of Johnson's pitches into the stands, recalling his glory days. Eighty thousand dollars was raised for the war effort that day.

In late 1941, Ruth had made a personal effort to support the cause, when he stopped by the war bonds office in New York and wanted to purchase $100,000 worth. But when he was told the limit was fifty grand a year, he flipped out the appropriate amount and left the other $50,000 for another bond he'd pick up on January 2.

Johnny Beazley was a rookie pitcher for the Cardinals in 1942 and pitched in exhibition games to raise money for the Army Relief Fund.

BELOW: *Walter "Big Train" Johnson and Babe Ruth came out of retirement in August 1942 to face each other again, raising $80,000 for war relief charities. Catcher Benny Bengough and umpire Billy Evans were also on hand to witness this sentimental confrontation between two Hall of Fame stars.*

National Archives photo

He would then join the Army Air Corps for the duration, missing three seasons of what had been a promising career.

Boxing and wrestling exhibitions, golf tournaments, and football scrimmages were also held during the war years to raise funds.

Pointing Fingers at Athletes

Criticisms were understandably hurled at any athletes who seemed to be shirking their patriotic duty, even though they were legitimately exempted from the draft. One of those was Boston Red Sox slugger Ted Williams—the Splendid Splinter—who fell into the secondary exemption category of having a "collateral dependent," meaning he was supporting his mother. Even with the exemption Williams had to endure stinging criticism from both the public and the press. He decided to join the Navy, eventually becoming a Marine Corps fighter pilot and instructor.

Williams served from 1942 through 1946 before returning to the Red Sox to pick up where he left off in 1941: tormenting opposing pitchers with his batting prowess.

By early 1945, criticism about 4-F ballplayers—especially those with "trick" knees, perforated eardrums, and mysterious back ailments—had reached the director of war mobilization and reconstruction, James Byrnes, who ordered a reevaluation of all 4-F athletes, saying, "It is difficult for the public to understand, and certainly it is difficult for me to understand, how these men can be physically unfit for military service and yet be able to compete with the greatest athletes of the nation in games demanding physical fitness."

After this reevaluation, many men who were previously designated 4-F were deemed fit to fight and thus eligible to serve in the military. Some were drafted in 1945, but most lucked out when Germany surrendered in May of that year and Japan bowed out four months later.

Suspended for the Duration

Travel restrictions, the loss of players, and fewer fans forced several football teams to shut down. Teams accustomed to traveling in luxury railroad cars were forced to ride on troop trains with servicemen.

By 1943 the Cleveland Rams suspended play and the Philadelphia Eagles and Pittsburgh Steelers merged to form the Phil-Pitt Steagles. Philly later

BELOW: *Exempt from serving in the military because he supported his mother, Boston Red Sox slugger Ted Williams endured media criticism through the 1942 season then enlisted in the Navy. He would serve as a fighter pilot and instructor, missing three full seasons of baseball before returning in 1946.* Army Air Corps photo

broke away, so the Steelers merged with another war-depleted team, the Chicago Cardinals, to form the Card-Pitt.

Shortages Lead to Rationing

Every American was forced to make sacrifices during WWII so that more precious materials could be recycled and used to make war goods. Gasoline and many food items were rationed, limiting the amount each family could use each month, which affected every facet of American life. Tin cans, rubber, chewing gum wrappers, and cooking grease were just a few of the many household goods that were collected in every neighborhood.

Sports teams took advantage of fan support to assist in the war effort. The minor league Louisville Colonels hosted a "Waste Fat Night" and collected more than 2,500 pounds of fat and grease!

When the Japanese overran the islands and territories of the South Pacific and Indonesia, they also took control of the world's rubber resources. The U.S. needed rubber for tires and fan belts, gaskets and washers, and hundreds of other parts used in jeeps and tanks, ships and submarines, and airplanes, along with all the equipment to maintain and repair them.

But very quickly rubber was in short supply, and its use in nonessential items was curtailed. Americans were asked to turn in scrap rubber and to limit their driving, thus extending tire wear. Drivers who zipped around a little too fast often heard the Victory honk—three taps and a long blast, which was Morse Code for the letter V—urging them to remember the war effort and slow down to conserve gas and rubber.

The Professional Golfers Association appealed to its players to turn in cut and damaged golf balls so the rubber cores could be reprocessed. By 1943 rubber was so critical that golf ball production was halted. Numerous golf courses shut down, and in 1942 the government discussed converting clubhouses and locker rooms into hospitals and convalescent wards for the war wounded.

During the 1942 baseball season, fans were asked to throw back foul balls instead of keeping them. In Atlanta, the balls were prestamped with a value from twenty-five cents to fifty dollars. Fans lucky enough to catch one of those money balls and survive being mugged by other jealous spectators could redeem them for war bonds, cash, or stamps.

By 1943 there was a shortage of both horsehide and the cores used to make baseballs. Several alternatives were tried but failed. Finally, a substitute—the balata ball, which used a gum substitute in place of the normal rubber sheathing—was developed for the '43 season, and it proved to be as resilient as . . . a rock.

Baseball schedules were structured to limit cross-country trips, and many traditional rivalries were skipped until the end of the war, replaced by games with teams in closer proximity. Games were often played in half-empty stadiums, witnessed only by fans who lived within walking distance. Gasoline and oil were rationed. Often the allowed amount wasn't even enough to get to work and back. Leisure travel during the war years, including cross-town trips to a baseball or football game, was banned in January 1943, and many spectators were forced to stay home and listen to their favorite teams battle it out over the radio. Naturally, attendance suffered at all sporting events throughout the country.

The Indianapolis 500, along with all other car and motorcycle races, was suspended from 1942 to '45 due to the gas and rubber restrictions.

Hunters were asked to turn in their pelts, which would be used to line the gloves, boots, hats, and coats desperately needed by the troops overseas, especially in Europe and Alaska. With meat strictly rationed, outdoorsmen relied on wild game to supplement their food stocks. Excess meat was shared with others in the community on limited meat rations.

Throughout the early 1940s, the entire nation was asked to share what little they had with those who needed it most. But in part because of this communal bonding, the American war effort was eventually victorious on both fronts, Europe and the Pacific.

BELOW: *Numerous household goods were turned in at recycling points in every community. In Roanoke, Virginia, school children carry jars and cans of fat and grease to be turned in, which will be used in making explosives.* Library of Congress photo

Women at War

> "I WAS GOING TO GO INTO SERVICE. IF MY BROTHER
> DID, WHY COULDN'T I? I WASN'T GOING TO SIT HOME
> AND BE POLLY BY THE FIRE."
>
> —*Anonymous woman, voicing the feelings of hundreds*

FIGHTING A WAR IN BOTH EUROPE and the Pacific demanded that every able-bodied American citizen, both men and women, do their patriotic duty. Millions of men signed on for the duration, but back home the planes, ships, and tanks still needed to be built to replace those being destroyed in battle. American women stepped forward and almost overnight became known as "Rosie the Riveter."

During the war years, from 1941 through 1945, women factory workers were vital to winning both the European and Pacific Campaigns. From patrol boats and submarines to aircraft carriers and battleships, they built more than 76,000 naval vessels; rolled nearly 300,000 aircraft off the assembly lines; tooled more than 20 million pistols and rifles; and assembled a staggering 41 billion rounds of ammunition—from bullets and grenades to tank rounds, naval shells, and aircraft bombs—with delicate care.

Thousands of women also demanded a role in the military, and by early 1943 all of the armed forces—the Army and its aerial component, the Army Air Corps, the Navy, the Marines, and the Coast Guard had opened their ranks to women.

BELOW: *Rosie the Riverter poster by J. Howard Miller.* Corbis photo

OPPOSITE: *While serving at Fairfield-Suisun Army Air Base in California, women from the Air Transport Command formed a basketball team that competed successfully against other military and collegiate squads in the region.* Army Air Force photo

Also, as Allied forces in Europe prepared for the invasion of the mainland, more servicemen in the states were shifted into combat units and rushed overseas. Women filled their slots, mostly in administrative jobs.

"*Semper Paratus*—Always Ready" was the Coast Guard motto, and when the service's women reserve component was formed on November 23, 1942, it took the name SPAR for short. Though assigned shore duties along the East and West Coasts, many SPARs were also deployed to the territories of Alaska and Hawaii, primarily in clerical positions.

Betty Hicks was a SPAR apprentice seaman at Palm Beach, Florida. The drill field there just happened to be the same golf course where Hicks won the 1940 Palm Beach championship tourney.

During World War I about three hundred women had served in the Marine Corps, but they disbanded soon after the Armistice. On February 13, 1943, the Marines established the Women's Reserves, reaching a peak strength of more than 18,000 by the end of the war. By utilizing women Marines in admin slots, the corps was able to deploy more men to the front lines. A day after winning the Tam O'Shanter golf title in early 1943, Patty Berg joined the Marines Women's Reserves.

The Women's Army Auxiliary Corps was established on May 14, 1942. The next year the service became known as the Women's Army Corps, or WAC. The WAC was the largest of the distaff units, with a peak strength of more than 99,000 by April 1945. More than 17,000 WACs deployed overseas, in every theater, including China-Burma-India, Alaska, North Africa, the Southwest Pacific, Italy, France, and Southeast Asia.

More than 5,500 WACs endured the harsh conditions of the Pacific Campaign, from Australia to New Guinea, Hollandia, and up to the Philippines. Besides the withering humidity, monsoon rains, equatorial temperatures, and "man-eating" insects, the women endured air raids, artillery barrages, and sniper fire.

On transport and hospital ships, these women were just as susceptible to

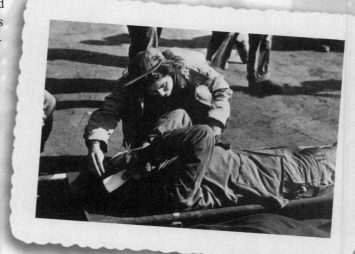

attack from enemy planes and submarines as any of their male counterparts.

Of the 201 Army nurses who died overseas, sixteen were killed as a result of such enemy action. Nurses captured during the siege of Corregidor in early 1942 became prisoners of war in the Philippines for thirty-seven months, until the end of the war. (Five Navy nurses captured on Guam were transported to a camp in Japan.) Besides struggling to survive in camp, all of the nurses did their best to care for other sick and wounded POWs.

LEFT: American women demanded a role in the military, forcing the creation of distaff units in the Army, Navy, and Coast Guard. Women would soon deploy to Europe and the Pacific, supporting every campaign, primarily in administrative and medical roles, including this nurse serving in England. U.S. Army photo

BELOW: As the war effort cranked up, most plants shifted from producing consumer goods to defense-related materiels. Westinghouse set aside toasters and washers to assemble millions of rounds of munitions. Records of the Women's Bureau photo

The men in uniform, especially those in combat, certainly appreciated the role Army nurses played in WWII. To show their gratitude, hundreds of servicemen published a letter in the *European Stars and Stripes* newspaper on Oct. 21, 1944:

"To all Army nurses overseas:
"We men were not given the choice of working in the battlefield or the home front. We cannot take any credit for being here. We are here because we have to be.
"You are here because you felt you were needed. So, when an injured man opens his eyes to see one of you, concerned with his welfare, he can't but be overcome by the very thought that you are doing it because you want to. You endure whatever hardships you must to be where you can do us the most good."

Army General Douglas MacArthur knew how important these nurses were and recognized the risks they willingly took:

"The Army nurse is the symbol to the soldier of help and relief in his hour of direst need. Through mud and mire, through the murk of campaign and battle, wherever the fight leads, she patiently, gallantly, seeks the wounded and distressed. Her comfort knows no parallel. In the hearts of all fighting men, she is enshrined forever."

Several prominent female athletes joined the WACs. Expert swimmer and horsewoman Mary Jane Ford was serving as an X-ray technician in Wisconsin when she saw a soldier drowning in a nearby lake. Ford dove in and swam to the GI, who drowned

before she could rescue him. For her efforts Ford was awarded the Soldier's Medal—making her the first woman to receive the award for heroism.

Another top female swimmer in the WACs was Helen Rains, national senior breaststroke champion.

Playing second base and lead-off hitter for the Fort Sheridan, Illinois, softball team was Lorraine Worth, who had honed her diamond skills while playing ball for Kalamazoo, Michigan.

Private Marie McMillin served as a parachute rigger at Fort Benning, Georgia. She watched as soldiers with very little jump experience joined the newly created airborne units. Few were aware that, prior to joining the WACs in mid-1943, McMillin had logged 690 jumps and held the women's record for a 24,800-foot jump eleven years earlier at the Cleveland Air Races.

The WAVES—Women Accepted for Volunteer Emergency Service—augmented the U.S. Navy, with a peak strength of 90,000 by mid-1945. Tennis champion Helen Jacobs joined the WAVES in late 1942.

Taking to the Skies

Though restricted from flying combat missions, members of the Women's Airforce Service Pilots (WASP) played key roles in WWII. A similar unit, the Women's Auxiliary Ferrying Squadron (WAFS), was formed in September 1942 and eventually merged with the WASP.

Well-known aviatrix Jacqueline Cochran stepped forward in 1939 with a plan to use women pilots wherever needed during the impending conflicts in Europe and the South Pacific, thus freeing up male pilots to deploy overseas.

In aviation circles Cochran was known as a highly competitive pilot. She entered her first air

race in 1935 and then won the prestigious Harmon Trophy three years in a row. Cochran was the only woman to compete in the 1938 Nationals. Flying a Seversky SEV-S2, she beat nine male pilots, coming in first, twenty-three minutes before the next finisher. In 1939 Cochran became director of the WASP.

Once women aviators learned of Jackie Cochran's idea to muster as many of her peers as possible, more than 25,000 applications poured in. Each of the 1,830 women accepted for the stringent training had logged a minimum of two hundred hours in the air. Those who made it to graduation were assigned as test pilots for fighter and bomber aircraft being rushed into production, and as instructors for male aviation cadets. Women also flew newly assembled aircraft from the factory to the coasts for shipment overseas.

Olympic diver and swimmer Katherine Rawls was one of the original WASPs who ferried planes cross-country. In 1932 she had won a silver medal in Olympic springboard diving; she pulled off the same feat in Berlin in 1936, where she also earned a bronze medal as part of the 4x100-meter relay team. In Amateur Athletic Union competition she won thirty-three medals in swimming and diving before retiring in 1938.

Unlike their male counterparts, most of whom had no choice but to join the military, all of the women who served in the armed forces were volunteers, the unsung heroines who played a vital yet little-publicized role in America's greatest victory.

The All-American Girls Baseball League

Mobilizing for war proved costly to professional baseball. Though President Roosevelt felt baseball should continue during WWII, he could not exempt any ballplayers from military service "for the good of the game." As a result, half of all the big-league players had gone to war by the end of the 1942 season.

And the minor leagues, loaded with younger players still in their teens, were decimated by the military draft, with three thousand players either in the armed forces or working in defense-related factories. Of the twenty-six minor leagues, only nine could field their full complement of teams for the 1943 season. The rest suspended operations or trimmed their number of teams during the war.

LEFT TOP: *Nancy Harkness Love, director of the U.S. Women's Auxiliary Ferry Squadron, prepares to fly a plane from the assembly plant to a base on the coast. Thousands of women served as stateside pilots, freeing up their male counterparts to fight in both the Europe and Pacific theaters.* National Archives photo

BELOW: *Pilot Nancy Harkness Love and Betty Gillies, her co-pilot, were the first women to fly the B-17 Flying Fortress heavy bomber.* U.S. Air Force photo

That fall the Office of War Information considered canceling the 1943 season, deeming the excessive travel demands of baseball a huge waste of fuel and an imposition on railroad cars better utilized to move men and materiel to the coasts for deployment overseas.

Chicago Cubs owner Philip Wrigley got together with Branch Rickey of the Brooklyn Dodgers and other major league club owners to consider a contingency plan in case major league baseball was ordered to suspend operations for the rest of the war. The group decided to create a new league that wouldn't be susceptible to the military draft: the All-American Girls Softball League.

Wrigley was aware that female athletes in other sports were popular, and in early 1943 he wrote, "In two or three years' time it's possible that girls' softball may be recognized by the press and radio as of major league possibilities. When that time arrives, girl [softball players] will have the same opportunity to gain nationwide recognition and acclaim as Helen Wills and Helen Jacobs in Tennis; Patty Berg and Helen Hicks in Golf; Gertrude Ederle, Gloria Callen, and Eleanor Holm in Swimming."

To avoid the cross-country travel restrictions that threatened the major leagues, only four women's teams were formed, all in the Chicago area: the Rockford Peaches in Illinois, the Racine Belles and Kenosha Comets in Wisconsin, and the South Bend Blue Sox in Indiana.

Each of these cities were factory towns. The novelty of watching women ballplayers would be a relaxing pastime for workers after a long shift at the plant, or so Wrigley reasoned.

In later years other teams would be added: the Milwaukee Chicks and Minneapolis Millerettes in 1944; the Fort Wayne Daisies in '45; the Muskegon Lassies and Peoria Redwings in '46; and the Chicago Colleens and Springfield Sallies in '48. The Belles would move from Racine to Battle Creek, then on to Muskegon, Michigan; the Chicks played only one year in Milwaukee and then uprooted to Grand Rapids; and the Lassies shifted to Kalamazoo after five seasons in Muskegon.

When the league held tryouts, players from throughout the country, Cuba, and Canada showed up to pursue a dream come true. Those deemed good enough to play were assigned according to their ability to ensure a competitive balance among the four teams.

BELOW: *The Rockford Peaches in Illinois were the dominant team in the All-American Girls Professional Baseball League, winning the championship in 1945, then three in a row from '48 to '50.* Photo courtesy of the Northern Indiana Historical Society

Many of the girls had to choose between jobs back home, which paid ten to twenty dollars a week, or baseball, which lasted for only four months but paid forty-five to eighty-five dollars a week. Most sent part of their earnings home to support their families. Some of the girls even considered joining one of the armed services. And nearly all saw a loved one—a boyfriend, husband, brother, or even father—join the military.

Dorothy Kamenshek of Cincinnati wanted to join the Army in 1942, at age seventeen. Her mom refused, but she did allow Dottie to try out for the girls league being formed in Chicago. Dottie made the cut and was assigned to the Rockford Peaches, where she became not just a regular on the all-star team but what many feel was the best player in the league.

Another player who considered joining was Connie Wisniewski. Connie had actually wanted to play in the All-American Girls League, but when her mother scoffed at that idea, saying "only bad girls leave home," Connie threatened to join the Army instead "and be gone for four years."

Reluctantly, her mom gave her blessing, and Connie joined the Milwaukee Chicks and tossed a 23–10 record in her first year. In 1945 "Iron Woman" pitched in forty-six games and recorded a phenomenal 32–11 mark. Her earned run average that season was an untouchable 0.81, meaning opponents averaged fewer than one run a game whenever she pitched!

During the off-season, Connie supported the war effort by assembling airplanes at the nearby General Motors plant.

Mary Rountree, a well-known softball catcher in Miami, had three brothers in the military. She would wait until they returned from the war before leaving home to play pro ball in 1946.

Athletic ability was the primary criteria for being selected to play. But for all of the girls,

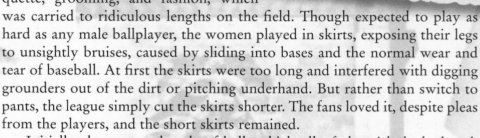

"femininity was to be stressed at all times," according to league bylaws, which further stated: "Every effort is made to select girls of ability, real or potential, and to develop that ability to its fullest power. But no less emphasis is placed on femininity, for the reason that it is more dramatic to see a feminine-type girl throw, run and bat than to see a man or boy or a masculine-type girl do the same things. The more feminine the appearance of the performer, the more dramatic her performance."

Classes were held in hair styling, etiquette, grooming, and fashion, which was carried to ridiculous lengths on the field. Though expected to play as hard as any male ballplayer, the women played in skirts, exposing their legs to unsightly bruises, caused by sliding into bases and the normal wear and tear of baseball. At first the skirts were too long and interfered with digging grounders out of the dirt or pitching underhand. But rather than switch to pants, the league simply cut the skirts shorter. The fans loved it, despite pleas from the players, and the short skirts remained.

Initially the teams played softball, which all of the girls had played, though on the sandlots back home when they played with their brothers and neighbor boys.

But many of their managers, including Hall of Fame stars such as Jimmie Foxx and Max Carey, pushed the league to change to baseball. Pitchers used to throwing underhand windmills for years suddenly had to rear back and throw overhand, with varying degrees of accuracy.

Softball pitcher Joanne Winter received a telegram offer from the Racine Belles manager, Johnny Gottselig, a big-league player in hockey for the Chicago Blackhawks. Joanne's brother John had already enlisted, so she joined the Belles, posting an 11–11 record her first year and torching the league in 1946 with a 33–10 record, which included 183 strike-outs and 63 consecutive scoreless innings.

The next year, sidearm pitching was allowed, followed by the switch to baseball and overhand pitching in 1948. Winter tallied a respectable 25–13 record in 1948.

Male ballplayers and their fans naturally felt the women's game was a step removed from the big leagues, until several of the established stars saw the women play. New York Yankee first baseman Wally Pipp proclaimed

that Dottie Kamenshek was the "fanciest-fielding first baseman I've ever seen, man or woman."

Besides femininity, patriotism was on full display at every game the women played. As part of pregame activities, both teams would line up at home plate to form a V, symbolizing the victory everyone in America was striving for. "The Star-Spangled Banner" was also played, a tradition started during the war years that continues today.

Many of the games sponsored war bond sales, recruiting drives, and blood donations. And despite playing ballgames every day during the four-month season, the women also put on exhibitions for military trainees and hospitalized veterans.

The players—with loved ones of their own fighting overseas—developed a special bond with disabled servicemen. And for Mickey Maguire, Milwaukee Chicks catcher, seeing hospitalized veterans was a reminder of her own loss. Prior to a game between the Chicks and the Kenosha Comets on June 9, 1944, Maguire was told that her husband, Corporal Thomas Maguire, was killed in Italy, a campaign of brutal combat where thousands of Americans died. Mickey Maguire could have skipped that game and everyone would have understood. But instead she strapped on her gear, asked that no one outside the team be told of her loss until after the game, and went out and played what reporters later called "the most dramatic exhibition of courage shown in the girls loop."

In her own poignant way, Mickey Maguire set an example for countless American families who put aside their grieving and continued to do their part to help America win the war against Germany and Japan

LEFT AND BACKGROUND: *Female soldiers of the Women's Army Corps participated in the Victory Parade after the liberation of Paris in 1944.* Women's Army Corps Museum photo

BELOW: *Just like their male counterparts, teams from the All-American Girls League conducted spring training in Florida, such as here at Opa-Locka, when troop trains weren't crammed with servicemen headed overseas.* Photo courtesy of the Florida State Archives

5. Lands Down Under Become Pacific Staging Areas

"A FRIGHTFUL JAPANESE BROADCAST HAS STEELED US FOR THE WORST. A JAPANESE PROFESSOR WAS DESCRIBING NEW ZEALAND AND HOW IT WOULD BE DEVELOPED BY THE JAPS. HE SAID THAT THE LUSH FIELDS, THE WEALTH, THE CITIES WERE IN THEIR GRASP AT LAST. THE DAY OF RECKONING WITH INSOLENT NEW ZEALANDERS WAS AT HAND. IMMORTAL JAPANESE TROOPS WOULD KNOW WHAT TO DO."

—*James Michener,* Tales of the South Pacific

OPPOSITE: *In April 1942, the impossible was accomplished when Army B-25 Mitchell bombers took off from the aircraft carrier USS Hornet and bombed Tokyo. The Japanese had thought their home islands were unreachable, and so they were stunned when sixteen bombers known as the Doolittle Raiders appeared overhead.* National Archives photo

WITH PEARL HARBOR CRIPPLED AND TRYING TO REPAIR the ships damaged in the December 7 attack, and with the Philippines now in enemy control, American troops began pouring into Australia and New Zealand, staging areas for future confrontations across the South Pacific. If the Japanese managed to overrun these two Allies, there would be no safe haven anywhere in the region for American ships to get fuel, supplies, and ammunition or to be repaired if damaged in a battle at sea.

Japanese naval aircraft did strike the Australian port at Darwin, sinking twelve Allied ships with torpedoes and bombs on February 19, 1942. But Australia did not come under further attack, though its air and naval forces fought the Japanese in other areas of Southeast Asia.

Enjoying the Lands Down Under

Americans stationed in Australia and New Zealand felt almost like they were in paradise. The locals spoke English and ate pretty much the same kind of food as in the States, and the young ladies there were fascinated with the dashing American servicemen. In fact, more than 12,000 GIs eventually married their Aussie and New Zealand sweethearts!

When they weren't getting ready for combat, the GIs kept in shape by playing sports with each other and against local athletes, who wanted nothing more than to beat these Yanks who were stealing their girls!

One of the mates who tried to inflict some pain was Australian heavyweight boxing champion Herb Narvo, who was serving with the Royal Australian Air Force. He climbed into the ring against an

ABOVE: *While preparing to confront the Japanese in the South Pacific, U.S. and New Zealand soldiers compare weapons and tactics.* Department of Defense photo

unknown American, U.S. Army Corporal Al Hoosman. After slugging it out for nine rounds, it was Hoosman who was declared the winner.

The Australians were shocked that this unknown Yank could beat their champion. But the Americans knew that Hoosman had been the Pacific Coast Golden Gloves champion, with a perfect record of 25–0 before he joined the Army and shipped out to the South Pacific.

New Zealand heavyweight Tom Heeney was serving with the Seabees (Navy construction battalion). In 1928 he had lost to World Heavyweight Champion Gene Tunney.

If there were any other Australian or New Zealand fighters wanting to take on a Yank, they might end up in the ring facing Private Albert Henley, another Golden Glove titlist from Philadelphia, or Private William Breed, a middleweight contender from Pittsburgh. Tommy Loughran, world light heavyweight champion, and American welterweight Barney Ross both deployed to the lands down under and later saw action with the Second Marine Division.

Another of the many American boxers who served in uniform down under was S. J. Fischel, who doubled as a trainer for other pugilists. While stationed in New Zealand, Fischel hosted a popular local radio program, "The American Hour," broadcast every Sunday night for U.S. troops.

BELOW: *During their off-duty time, American soldiers in Australia enjoyed the company of local Aussie women, hundreds of whom became war brides.* ANZUS Veterans photo

American Games Confuse the Aussies

The Australians tried to learn how to play baseball but had difficulty comprehending the rules. It wouldn't matter, because the Americans were unbeatable.

During one game the American pitcher was Cotton States minor leaguer Johnny Lund. He won the game 4–1, striking out nine batters, but the Aussies were more amazed that Lund could pitch with such a bad toothache! They didn't realize the bulge in his cheek was a massive wad of chewing tobacco.

The U.S. military had not yet sent sports equipment to its troops in Australia in 1942, so the Americans there had to play touch football rather than bone-jarring tackle. After watching a game of touch, the Australians couldn't understand why this game was so popular in the States. Their own version, known as rugby, was much more brutal, or so they claimed. Rugby players were often carried off the field with broken bones and teeth missing.

They also couldn't understand the constant huddles in football, the time-outs, and the measurements for first downs. The Aussies quickly decided that American football—touch football—was inferior to rugby. They felt touch was for girls. Real men played rugby or soccer.

George Barr, who had been selected to the U.S. all-star soccer squad while playing for the Brookhattans, played for several Aussie teams while stationed down under. He would also try to teach his GI buddies the intricacies and footwork of soccer, but most of them stuck with baseball and "sissy" football.

Softball and basketball were also girls-only sports in Australia and New Zealand. The balls for both were mushier and didn't last very long when the Americans abused them with their roughneck play.

Footballs made locally were also fatter, almost like rugby balls, and baseball bats broke often. It would be early 1943 before American sports equipment—including boxing gloves, tennis rackets, and golf clubs—began arriving for the U.S. servicemen in Australia. All that was needed for foot races was a smooth road or open, flat land. The Americans weren't lacking for competitive track stars. Their stable included Indiana miler Mel Trutt and Duke University's track captain, John B. Nania, just to name two.

Honing a Fighting Edge

The GIs knew they would soon be battling the Japanese, and so they were encouraged to maintain a fighting edge by competing in sports.

General Douglas MacArthur, commander of Allied forces in the Pacific, felt confident that the Japanese would eventually be defeated, because American servicemen had developed "gameness and fortitude" while competing in athletics, especially football and boxing.

MacArthur himself grew up playing sports, first at West Texas Military Academy and then at West Point. "I had always loved athletics and the spirit of competition moved me to participate in as many sports as possible. [At West Texas] I became the quarterback on the eleven, the shortstop on the nine, the tennis champion of the campus."

MacArthur had become commandant at West Point in 1919 and overhauled the academy's athletics program. "The problem of athletic training was one to my heart," he later would write in *Reminiscences*. "For many years, athletics at West Point had consisted of an excellent system of military gymnastics, but it was apparent from the experiences of the World War that course of training should be planned not only to fit future officers physically for the rigors of military service, but also to qualify them as physical directors and instructors for their future commands."

As commandant, Dauntless Doug determined that every cadet at West Point should become adept at a variety of sports—including football, basketball, and baseball, but also hockey, golf, soccer, lacrosse, tennis, and track—all of which quickly became part of the course load. Only the best in each sport participated at the varsity level, but intramural games and meets pitted teams from the cadet companies against each other.

BELOW: *Douglas MacArthur (far right), with the varsity baseball squad at West Point in 1901, believed athletics prepared young officers for the military, teaching leadership, communication, and above all else, teamwork, which would prove to be vital in combat.* U.S. Military Academy photo

"Nothing brings out the qualities of leadership, mental and muscular co-ordination, aggressiveness, and courage more quickly than this type of competition," stressed MacArthur. "Physical qualities may well determine the destiny of the intellect. To emphasize these truths I had carved on the stone portals of the gymnasium these words:

> Upon the fields of friendly strife
> Are sown the seeds
> That, upon other fields, on other days
> Will bear the fruits of victory.

During World War II, many key leaders came from West Point or one of the other military schools and academies such as Texas A&M and the Virginia Military Institute, and, of course, the Naval Academy—and the majority of these commanders developed the attributes of teamwork, communication, and leadership while participating in athletics. MacArthur would later stress, "Nothing is more synonymous of our national success than is our national success in athletics."

Aussies Learn a Lesson

On America's Independence Day in 1943, a team of Army football players beat a Navy team, 14–0. Both squads had the appropriate pads and helmets to bang away on each other.

Among the spectators were partisan American soldiers and sailors, their Aussie girlfriends, and disgruntled Australian servicemen, still denigrating this version of football as a sissy's game. During halftime, trotting horses came out pulling chariots, vying for the tounge-in-cheek Mustache Cup!

After several arguments and challenges broke out, the inexperienced Australians agreed to get on the field and try tackle football against those "sissy" GIs. Naturally, they assumed all that padding would protect them, until they got plastered by two-hundred-pound solid-body American players with a little something to prove.

After a few of their mates got carried off the field with assorted fractures and missing teeth, the Aussies quickly learned that American football wasn't such a sissy game, after all!

In sports, the Aussies enjoyed the competition, but in the battles to come, they were glad they would be fighting side by side with the Yanks.

BELOW: *American and Australian soldiers pitted their best against each other in a variety of sports, including horse racing at Queensland in 1942.* Australian Archives photo

GIs Desperate for Sports News

It was bad enough the Americans had to wait for months before they got equipment to play football. They also couldn't get any news about their favorite collegiate teams. The American Red Cross found a solution. With the help of an announcer in San Francisco, the Red Cross recorded an abbreviated version of the games, then rebroadcast fifteen-minute game summaries during the college football season. The GIs in Australia looked forward to Sundays when these recaps were piped over radios and loudspeakers.

New Zealand Also Hosts Yanks

New Zealanders opened their sports facilities to the American units training at nearby bases. At Papakura, "we played a couple of football games and soccer. We also had impromptu contests of our trucks in hill climbing bouts," recalled one soldier serving with Battery B of the 135th Artillery Battalion. "The commanding officer of the 1st Field Regiment presented our commander with a brass shell case from an 8-inch cannon, captured from a German ammo dump in 1916."

At Auckland, marines of the 169th and 172nd Regimental Combat teams played football games and donated the $5,036 in gate receipts to local charities. Wellington opened its civic skating rink and the Glide skating rink to marines and sailors, who played hockey and basketball. Baseball teams from the Second and Eighth Marines used nearby Athletic Park.

On January 31, 1943, a game between American League and National League baseball players in the military was held at Athletic Park in Wellington. Baseball and football games were played regularly here, and even though local New Zealanders attended these sporting events, few understood the baffling rules for either.

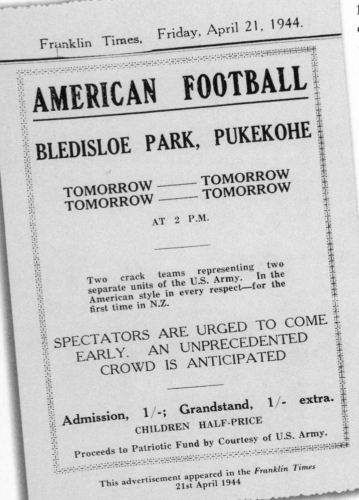

Franklin Times, Friday, April 21, 1944.

AMERICAN FOOTBALL

BLEDISLOE PARK, PUKEKOHE

TOMORROW —— TOMORROW
TOMORROW —— TOMORROW

AT 2 P.M.

Two crack teams representing two separate units of the U.S. Army. In the American style in every respect—for the first time in N.Z.

SPECTATORS ARE URGED TO COME EARLY. AN UNPRECEDENTED CROWD IS ANTICIPATED

Admission, 1/-; Grandstand, 1/- extra.
CHILDREN HALF-PRICE
Proceeds to Patriotic Fund by Courtesy of U.S. Army.

This advertisement appeared in the *Franklin Times* 21st April 1944

Target: Tokyo

Despite all the fun and games in Australia and New Zealand, battles were being fought without much success in other parts of the Pacific. Nothing could stop the Japanese. In fact, some Americans feared that if the enemy couldn't be stopped, they would be invading the West Coast very soon.

U.S. military strategists knew they had to strike back at Japan, and soon. After deciding that a few well-placed bombs in the Japanese emperor's back yard might do the trick, they dug out those "tourist" photos Moe Berg had shot in 1934 and studied them to see which facilities and industries in and around Tokyo were worth hitting.

Moe Berg had already retired from baseball in 1939 and resumed his clandestine activities for the Office of Strategic Services. (He would later be instrumental in confirming that Germany's nuclear weapons plans were far behind the Allied efforts. For his work Berg was awarded the Medal of Freedom. But when he was ordered not to say what he had done during World War II to deserve such a prestigious award, Berg declined the medal, which is now in the Baseball Hall of Fame.)

Berg's photos revealed a city with numerous military targets. And wouldn't a little payback for Pearl Harbor be a great morale booster for every American? But with no forward-based airfields close enough to Japan, and no long-range carrier bombers capable of making the round trip, it seemed like an impossible mission, one that only a widowmaker might dream up.

Ever since the thirteenth century, the Japanese had believed that a "divine wind" protected their country from evil invaders. American military strategists decided that maybe a little "ill wind" was needed to destroy that age-old myth.

In April 1942 the Japanese were quite surprised when sixteen B-25 Mitchell bombers lumbered overhead and dropped a few dozen explosives on Tokyo and other industrial cities in Japan. Thanks to those photos that Moe Berg had shot eight years earlier, Jimmy Doolittle's pilots knew exactly where to drop their bombs. American bombers hit a steel factory, oil refineries, boat docks, ammunition and supply warehouses, and an aircraft factory during the daylight raid.

To avoid anti-aircraft fire, the pilots flew at rooftop level, startling the Japanese citizens, who wondered where these noisy bombers with the strange markings on the wings had come from. One American pilot, as he flew over a baseball game in Tokyo, even leaned out and mockingly shouted,

ABOVE: *Jimmy Doolittle was a well-known aviator prior to WWII, but after he led sixteen Mitchell Bombers to Tokyo in April of 1942, he became a bona fide war hero.* National Archives photo

"What's the score?!" The U.S. pilots also flew over Tokyo's Meiji Stadium, where only a few years earlier Moe Berg and the other American all-stars had played baseball.

A few days later, when asked where the American bombers had come from, FDR stated simply: "Shangri-la!" But, in fact, they had been launched off the deck of the aircraft carrier *Hornet*—an impossible mission that only a lunatic would think of and that only a band of fools would attempt . . . and somehow they pulled it off.

The sparkplug for the raid on Tokyo was Doolittle, famous in the 1920s and '30s as a daredevil and cross-country pilot. When he was just fifteen, Doolittle had been the West Coast's amateur bantamweight champ. But his love of flying was stronger, though the tenacity he used in the boxing ring would remain with him as he pushed the limits of flying further than anyone had ever dared. He shattered both speed and distance flying records.

Among the many pilots and crewmen assembled for this impossible mission to launch bombers from the perilously short platform of an aircraft carrier and bomb Tokyo was Lieutenant George Barr (no relation to Sergeant George Barr, the American soccer star stationed in Australia). In his younger days, Lieutenant Barr played varsity basketball for Northland College in Ashland, Wisconsin. Though tall and lanky, he was pure speed and grace on the hardcourt. As one of the Army pilots who'd volunteered for the Tokyo mission, Barr was hailed as a hero.

But for forty months he would languish in a Japanese prison in Peking. All of the bomber pilots had planned to deliver their "presents" to the emperor in Tokyo and then fly to airfields in China. But they ran out of fuel (one did land safely in Russia) and the crews either parachuted or crash-landed in China, where Japanese patrols hunted them down.

Robert Bourgeois, who had played ball for the base team at Barksdale Field in Louisiana, was a bombardier on the mission. A day at sea on the *Hornet* the air crews were told for the first time that their destination was Tokyo. "It was like a football game when the score is three to three and there are only a couple of seconds left, and some guy kicks a field goal, and then everything is bedlam. That was the way we and the Navy boys [on the *Hornet*] were. They were cheering us on."

After dropping its payload over Japan, his plane headed for the China coast but ran out of fuel. The crew bailed out and were rescued by local partisans. After making it back to friendly lines, Bourgeois remained in the Far East, serving in the China-Burma-India Campaign.

Jimmy Doolittle was disconsolate after ditching his plane over China, knowing he had probably lost all of his planes and most of his men. "They'll court-martial me for this," he would tell his engineer, Sergeant Paul Leonard.

ABOVE: *New B-25 bombers lined up for final inspection and tests at the flying field of a Western Aircraft plant. General Doolittle, who flew in a B-25 in the raid on Tokyo, has called this ship the best military plane in existence. It performs brilliantly at its 25,000-foot ceiling.* Library of Congress photo

"No, Colonel, they're going to give you the big medal," Leonard assured him, "and another plane. And when they do, I'd like to fly with you."

Partisans rescued Doolittle and some of the crewmen, but eight were captured. Three of those were executed; one died while in captivity. Barr and three others were eventually liberated.

It was considered a "daring and spectacular mission," and newspaper headlines around the free world flashed the long-awaited news: "Tokyo Bombed! Doolittle Do'od it!"

After more than four months of Japanese domination, the raid on Tokyo boosted the morale of every American, especially those service members in the Pacific. More importantly, it forced Japan to divert men and warships to defend the homeland. Maybe the United States could somehow defeat the Japanese after all.

Baseball Gets "Green Light"

"THE IDEA OF BASEBALL IS A TEAM, AN OUTFIT, A SECTION, A GANG, A UNION, A CELL, A COMMANDO—IN SHORT, A TWENTIETH-CENTURY SETUP OF OPPOSITE NUMBERS. BASEBALL TAKES ITS MYSTIC NINE AND SCATTERS THEM WIDE. A KIND OF INDIVIDUALISM THEREBY RETURNS, BUT IT IS LIMITED—ETERNAL VIGILANCE IS THE PRICE OF VICTORY."

—*Jacques Barzun,* God's Country and Mine

"THE PHILOSOPHY ON THE FIELD WAS TOTALLY DIFFERENT THAN IT IS TODAY. BASEBALL WAS A FORM OF WARFARE PLAYED UNDER A SET OF RULES THAT WERE NOT NECESSARILY DRAWN UP BY THE LEAGUE OFFICIALS."

—*Leo Durocher*

THE SERIOUSNESS OF WORLD WAR II OVERSHADOWED PROfessional and collegiate sports, and just days after Pearl Harbor the *Sporting News* echoed baseball's stance concerning America's entry into the war: "Uncle Sam, we are at your command. The game stands at attention, ready for whatever role it may be called upon to play."

Mel Ott had just taken over as manager of the New York Giants and responded abruptly when he heard about the attack on Pearl: "Young fellows eligible for military service, whether they are clerks or ballplayers, are going to rush to the colors . . . the first thought by everybody is the defense of our country."

Hammerin' Hank Greenberg of the Detroit Tigers had just been discharged from the Army in early December 1941. But after the Japanese attacked Hawaii, Greenberg didn't hesitate: "We are in trouble and there is only one thing to do—return to service. I have not been called back. I am going of my own accord. Baseball is out the window as far as I'm concerned. I don't know

RIGHT: *By early 1944 hundreds of major leaguers were serving overseas, in every theater and every campaign. These lucky sailors played mostly exhibition games in Hawaii to entertain the troops and raise money for the war effort.* U.S. Navy photo

if I'll ever return to baseball." He would serve with the Twentieth Bomber Command in the China-Burma-India Campaign.

(Greenberg did in fact return to the Tigers midway through the 1945 season. In his first game back on July 1, facing the Philadelphia Athletics, he hit a home run, dispelling any doubts about whether his skills had diminished after missing more than three full seasons.)

Just before spring training in 1942, baseball Commissioner Kenesaw Mountain Landis considered canceling the season, feeling it wouldn't be appropriate to be playing baseball or other sports while young Americans were fighting and dying overseas. Athletes could better serve their country by joining the military or working full-time in factories. All sports activities could be postponed until after the war.

American correspondent Quentin Reynolds chimed in from Berlin with his feelings about the issue, reporting for *Collier*'s magazine: "Hitler has killed a great many things in the past few years . . . do not let him kill baseball."

Newspapers all over the country debated the issue, but the Feather River *Bulletin* in California's Plumas County may have said it best: "Baseball is more than a National Game. It is America's anchor. It keeps the ship of state fast to its moorings in a balanced life. American boys play ball. 'PLAY BALL!' is their battle cry, not 'HEIL HITLER.'

"While little fascists are learning to throw hand grenades, little Americans are learning to groove one over the plate. But woe betide the enemy when an American boy finds it needful to throw hand grenades!"

But President Franklin D. Roosevelt, in his "green light" letter to Landis, stated, "I honestly feel that it would be best for the country to keep baseball going. There will be fewer people unemployed and everybody will work longer hours and harder than ever before. And that means that they ought to have a chance for recreation and for taking their minds off their work even more than before.

"Even if the actual quality to the teams is lowered by the greater use of older players, this will not dampen the popularity of the sport. Here is another way of looking at it—these players are a recreational asset to at least 20 million of their fellow citizens—and that in my judgment is thoroughly worthwhile." But even with FDR's approval, the game would endure sacrifices and restrictions, personnel turmoil, and tragedy from 1942 through 1946.

ABOVE: *In civilian life back in New York, Harry Danning of the Giants and Red Ruffing of the Yankees played against each other in the 1936 and '37 World Series. While in the Army they were teammates, playing for the sixth Ferrying team at Long Beach, California.* U.S. Army photo

Spring Training Restrictions

For major league baseball, spring training in warm weather regions was affected by the war's travel restrictions. During the spring of 1942, just a few months after Pearl Harbor and FDR's declaration of war, the sixteen major league teams were still training in Florida and California.

The next year, though, all available trains were needed to transport war goods and service personnel, not out-of-shape baseball players headed south for a little fun in the sun. All teams were asked to utilize training facilities closer to home. For some, home in February and March meant subfreezing temperatures and several inches of snow. Batting and fielding practices were hampered by long underwear, winter coats, and gloves!

The Brooklyn Dodgers trained at the U.S. Military Academy, but only when Army cadets weren't using the gymnasium and athletic fields.

RIGHT: George Munger, St. Louis Cardinals pitcher was fairly accurate on the mound, posting an 11–3 record in 1944. After joining the Army he tested his accuracy with an M1 rifle while training at Fort Benning, Georgia.
U.S. Army photo

The St. Louis Cardinals set up camp at Cotter Field, which was little more than a dump until local towns-folk cleaned up and resodded the diamond. In early

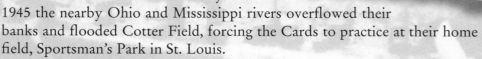

1945 the nearby Ohio and Mississippi rivers overflowed their banks and flooded Cotter Field, forcing the Cards to practice at their home field, Sportsman's Park in St. Louis.

The Chicago Cubs trained in French Lick, Indiana, and marked off a ball diamond on the local golf course, the only field level enough to play on.

Several other Midwest teams also relocated to Indiana. Among them were the Cincinnati Reds at Indiana University, the Indians at Purdue, and the Tigers at Evansville.

When harsh weather prevented outdoor practice, the teams were forced to find alternate sites: the Yankees used a deserted aircraft hangar, and the White Sox prepared for the upcoming season in a horse stable.

Finding competition, though, was a hit-or-miss situation. Many major league teams set up exhibition games on military bases in the area, not only to keep interest up and raise funds for the war effort, but also to get in some practice against an assemblage of pro and college athletes in uniform. And every month, more and more ballplayers were getting called up to serve, often decimating a team pushing for a World Series berth.

Former St. Louis Cardinals pitcher Dizzy Dean spoke for the ballplayers when he said, "If the government thinks our efforts should be turned toward winning the war, let's quit baseball without a squawk and get in there and fight. But I also say this—if they tell us to play, then the game owes too much to the public not to go ahead. The people need baseball and they want it. There'll be enough fellas for the teams. The game just won't be as fast, that's all."

Newspaper columnist Red Smith added, "As long as the battles we witness are fought with bats instead of bayonets, with headgears instead of gas masks, and with gloves instead of guns, some measure of sanity will be preserved in the land."

And Admiral Ernest King spoke for the military leaders when he added, "Baseball has a rightful place in America at war. All work and no play seven days a week would soon take its toll on national morale."

In 1943 Wisconsin Representative La Vern Dilweg spoke before the House of Representatives about whether or not baseball should continue: "What does baseball do for America? It provides an opportunity for hundreds of thousands of war workers to relax in the fresh air and sunshine—and to

LEFT: *Many military bases were loaded with ballplayers. These eight, including five major leaguers, were stationed at the Army Air Forces' Waco Flying School in Texas. They are (top row), Tigers outfield prospect Walter Evers, Detroit catcher George Tebbetts, Senators outfielder Bruce Campbell, and Cleveland outfielder Buster Mills. The bottom row is East Texas League pitcher Mickey Mandjack; Tiger catcher Mike Popovich and his brother, who was a minor league pitcher with the White Sox; and Senators pitcher Sid Hudson.* U.S. Army photo

ABOVE: *Big-league ballplayers who played in Hawaii in 1944, were (standing) Sergeant Walter Judnich of the Browns, Corporal Mike McCormick from the Cincinnati Reds, Yankee slugger and Army sergeant Joe DiMaggio, (kneeling) Sergeant Dario Lodigiani of the White Sox and the Senators' Gerald Priddy.* Seventh Air Force photo

continue to enjoy something that has been a significant part of American life for almost 100 years. Baseball news is a refreshing balance against the worrisome news that we are fighting a war. War news is 'must' reading—it is work. Sports news is refreshment—it is fun.

"These, I believe, are sound, logical arguments for the maintenance of spectator sports on the American scene, but the strongest argument of all, perhaps, is that men in our fighting forces—men in the fox holes, men who have achieved glorious victory in Africa, men who are battling the Japs to a standstill in the Pacific, awaiting only the day when they will launch the victory offensive, and men who are poised for the victorious invasion of Europe—want spectator sports to continue on the home front and hungrily await news of sports results.

"Where can you get a better example of a community rallying around a spectator sport than in Brooklyn, where the exploits of the 'Beloved Bums' on the baseball diamond are the personal concerns of every fan in the most rabid baseball community in America?"

To keep up the morale of area factory workers, Braves owner Bill Veeck scheduled ball games after shift changes for his Milwaukee players. Other owners followed suit.

"We played games at nine and ten o'clock in the morning so the factory workers on the night shift could see ball games," recalled Don Johnson, a replacement player for the Chicago Cubs. "And even at that hour we loaded the park. He served them Wheaties and cream."

(Bill Veeck would himself see action in the South Pacific during World War II. A heavy artillery gun crushed his right leg, which would have to be amputated. He hobbled home on crutches and relinquished ownership of the Braves, despite three league pennants during his reign. He would later purchase the Cleveland Indians, sign the first Negro Leagues ballplayer in the American League, fellow veteran Larry Doby, and oversee their march to a World Series title in '48.)

A call to suspend play would circulate again within days after the invasion of Fortress Europe, on June 6, 1944, at Normandy, France.

But Arthur Daley would write in his "Sports of the Times" column: "Once the stunning impact of the invasion news has worn off there will not be the same irresistible urge to glue ear to radio for last-minute bulletins and human nature again will demand entertainment as a distraction from the war—movies, the theater and all other diversions, including sports. After all, it still is part of our American way of life and that is one of the things we are fighting for."

As dismal as the replacement players were, America's game would not be suspended.

Quality of Play Diminishes

Baseball would continue throughout the war, though the caliber of play would deteriorate, as most rosters lost their first-line players. White Sox skipper Jimmy Dykes responded smugly when asked which teams might have a good shot at winning the pennant: "Any team that can keep nine men on the field will be dangerous." While more than 3,400 ball players served in the military, the teams were filled out by the aged, the underaged, the lame, the short, and the tall—basically anyone who was exempt from the military.

Sports columnist Red Smith pointed out that a player with a bum knee should not be on the front lines because that man's leg could "fold in a situation where one man's failure might cost a dozen lives."

And when the criticism continued that athletes might be shirking their patriotic duty, Smith fired off another salvo: "It ought to be clear to everybody that the big lug is playing ball because the draft board hasn't seen fit to call him and because [the military] can't find any other earthly use for him. Same like you. Same like me."

BELOW: *Not all service teams were loaded with big-league players and prospects, but there were plenty of wannabes, such as students at the Bryan Air Forces Instructors School in Texas.* Army Air Forces photo

The St. Louis Browns gave Pete Gray—a one-armed outfielder—a try. Gray had lost his right arm when he was a boy, but that didn't stop him from pursuing his dream to one day play baseball. In 1943 and '44, Gray played for the Memphis Chicks, batting .333 his second year, and stealing 68 bases. He was selected the Southern Association's MVP, and sportswriters in Philadelphia called him "the most courageous athlete of 1944." In 1945 Gray played in seventy-seven games for the Browns, serving as an inspiration to injured war veterans.

The Cincinnati Reds called up fifteen-year-old pitcher Joe Nuxhall. "Probably two weeks prior to that, I was pitching against 7th, 8th and 9th-graders," Nuxhall recalled. "All of a sudden, I look up and

there's Stan Musial [of the St. Louis Cardinals]. It was a scary situation."

While Nuxhall was the youngest ballplayer in the majors, there were hundreds of other teenagers given a shot. In fact, there was such a drain on the minor leagues—both from the military and the big-league clubs—that many teams suspended play during the war.

In 1940 there were 314 minor league teams, spread over forty-three leagues. By 1943—when manpower demands were building up for the invasion of mainland Europe—there were only sixty-two teams and nine leagues remaining.

ABOVE: *Joe DiMaggio (left) with the seventh Army Air Force in Honolulu in 1944 endured miniscule soldierly tasks but mostly played exhibition baseball during WWII.*
National Archives photo

The St. Louis Cardinals, for example, lost 265 minor leaguers during the war years, and consequently, its farm system dwindled from twenty-two teams down to just six.

"Manpower was so sparse that the desperate Dodger scouts were snatching beardless shortstops from the cradle and dropping their butterfly nets over Spanish War veterans who had played the outfield alongside Willie Keeler," mocked John Lardner in *Sport*. He was referring to the Dodgers bringing back Babe Herman for a few weeks in 1945. Herman hadn't played ball in thirteen years and was considered baseball's worst outfielder, "a constant danger to his own life."

After witnessing four years of diminishing talent, Chicago sports columnist Warren Brown was asked about the 1945 World Series, which pitted the Detroit Tigers against the Chicago Cubs. With complete candor, Brown stated, "I don't see how either team can possibly win."

Even the quality of sports writing suffered, mandated by the Associated Press in May of 1942 when it sent out this memo to all of its writers and editors: "There should be a ban on flowery, over-enthusiastic lyrical sports writing for the duration. Remembering the exploits of military heroes, it does not seem appropriate to overdo the use of such words as 'courageous,' 'gallant,' 'fighting.' It doesn't take much 'courage' to overcome a two-run lead in the ninth."

Major Leaguers Answer the Call

Some opponents of sports still felt athletes were shirking their responsibility to the war effort by "playing games when other young men are fighting and dying overseas." But when they received their induction notices, hundreds of major leaguers and thousands of minor league ballplayers signed up for the armed forces, for the duration of the war, however long that would be.

Joe DiMaggio and Enos Slaughter were stationed in the Pacific. The Yankee Clipper was in a noncombat job, playing centerfield in exhibition ball games to entertain the troops for the Seventh Air Force at Hawaii's Hickam Field. Some of DiMaggio's teammates in Hawaii included fellow Yankee second baseman Joe Gordon, Washington Senator Gerry Priddy, Walt Judnich and Johnny Beazley of the Browns, Cleveland outfielder Hank Edwards; Mike McCormick from the Cincinnati Reds, Dario Lodigiani from the White Sox, and future major leaguers Charlie Silvera of the San Francisco Seals and Ferris Fain from the Kansas City Blues.

Hawaii was overflowing with Army and Navy senior officers who scoured the ranks of the troops arriving from the mainland, looking for prized athletes, such as DiMaggio.

The Navy at Pearl Harbor had numerous teams littered with pro players, such as New York Giants first baseman Johnny "Big Cat" Mize, the Dodgers' Pee Wee Reese, Phil Rizzuto of the Yankees, Johnny Lucadello of the Browns, George "Skeets" Dickey from the White Sox, St. Louis Cardinal Stan Musial (who was discharged in 1946 and rushed back to rejoin his team in that year's World Series), Detroit Tigers outfielder Barney McCosky, and Cubs pitcher Vern Olsen and his battery mate Marv Felderman.

With such potent talent it was only natural that the Army generals and Navy admirals at Hawaii bragged about which service had the better team. In 1944 the Navy all-stars took the field against their Army counterparts for Hawaii's own "World Series."

Detroit pitcher Virgil Trucks noticed just how important this series was to the military brass when he said, "The Army had DiMaggio and all those ballplayers and the Navy didn't have as much.

"The Navy was looked down on and Admiral Nimitz didn't go for that. He brought out all of those major league ballplayers who were in the Navy back in the States and challenged the Army to that World Series."

All told there were thirty-six major league players in Hawaii for the epic eleven game series, which the Navy would dominate eight games with one tie.

"We, the Navy, cleaned their clock," Rizzuto remembered. "Here was this game played at the height of the war, in a war zone, and we were told more money was bet on this game than any game in history to that point."

BELOW:
In the big leagues they were rivals, in the armed forces they were bigger rivals, but in the South Pacific Phillies pitcher and Army PFC "Big Jim" Bivin, Lieutenant "Long Tom" Winsett of the Red Sox, and Marine Corporal Cal "Preacher" Dorsett of the Indians, were teammates, taking on all challengers.
U.S. Marine Corps photo

Countless more big leaguers weren't as lucky as their counterparts in Hawaii. They were thrown into the fight, enduring some of the most horrific battles in the European and Pacific Campaigns. Country Boy Slaughter of the Cardinals was with the Fifty-eighth Bomb Wing in the Mariana Islands, where the battles of Guam, Saipan, and Tinian took place.

Knowing how important baseball was to American servicemen, Japanese signal units would jam broadcasts of stateside games, which only encouraged GIs in the Pacific to fight harder!

Edwin Snider was a sailor on the submarine tender USS *Sperry,* who had a special interest in those radio broadcasts. As Duke Snider he would clobber four home runs in both the 1952 and 1955 World Series for the Dodgers, on his way to Cooperstown and the Baseball Hall of Fame.

One of Snider's Dodger teammates was Carl Furillo, the Reading Rifle, who served with the Seventy-seventh Division in the South Pacific Campaign.

Halfway around the world, the Germans produced a radio program filled with sports scores—and Nazi propaganda.

To prevent German soldiers dressed in American uniforms from penetrating the lines, sentries would ask baseball-related questions, and might be shot on sight if the didn't know the right answers.

Boston Braves pitcher Warren Spahn even quipped: "I used to pity any guy in our outfit who wasn't a baseball fan because he would be in deep trouble."

Near the end of the European Campaign, Boston Braves pitcher Warren Spahn was with the 276th Combat Engineers and was nearly killed when the Remagen Bridge in Germany collapsed without warning, just minutes before he would have been walking across it. Several other GIs on the bridge weren't so lucky, perishing in the crash or drowning in the water below.

Spahn would return to the Braves and continue to post Hall of Fame stats. But even when he had a bad game it was better than what he had experienced during World War II: "When I came back I thought, 'Wow, what a great way to make a living. If I goof up, there's going to be a relief pitcher coming in. Nobody's going to shoot me.'"

BELOW: *The Army and Navy in Hawaii had their own battles going on, stocking their already over-stocked service teams with major league ballplayers, such as Sergeant Joe DiMaggio (left) and Navy Chief Specialist Pee Wee Reese (third from left), posing with Vice Admiral Robert Ghormley and Brigadier General William Flood.*
U.S. Navy photo

Another ballplayer who ended up at Remagen was Kansas all-stater Ralph Houk, who served with the Eighty-ninth Cavalry Recon Squadron of the Ninth Armor Division. By September of 1944 the division was thrown into the Battle of the Bulge. During one skirmish in Luxembourg, cut off from other units of the division, Houck sneaked through enemy lines, climbed inside a tank destroyer, and engaged and destroyed the enemy armored column blocking his men. In another engagement, an enemy sniper spotted Houck in his sites and pulled the trigger. The bullet penetrated his helmet, but miraculously Houck wasn't hurt. He would earn the Silver Star, Bronze Star, and Purple Heart, and returned to baseball after the war. (He would become manager of the New York Yankees in late 1960, winning three American League pennants and two World Series.)

Rocco Francis Marchegiano also had big-league dreams, but he was drafted in 1943 and assigned to the 150th Combat Engineers, which would see action at Normandy and across northern France and into Germany. Marchegiano had done some amateur boxing in the Army but his first love was still baseball. After his discharge in 1947, he tried out as a catcher with the Chicago Cubs but didn't get an offer. He stepped back into the boxing ring as Rocky Marciano and won the heavyweight crown in 1952.

Lawrence "Yogi" Berra was playing minor league ball in Norfolk when he joined the Navy and committed the unforgivable sin of volunteering . . . for rocket boats, seeing action in the Normandy and Southern France invasions in 1944. Years later war veterans would tease Berra with "Didn't anybody ever tell you, never volunteer?"

(After the war Yogi joined the powerful New York Yankees, which won ten World Series crowns and fourteen American League pennants during his sixteen years as a catcher. Yogi would be chosen Most Valuable Player in 1951, '54, and '55, capping his career with induction into the Hall of Fame in 1972.)

Mickey Cochrane was a five-sport athlete at Boston University before he joined the Philadelphia Athletics as a catcher. He earned Most Valuable Player honors in 1928 and led the A's to three American League crowns. He joined the Detroit Tigers and promptly repeated as MVP, backstopping them to two league championships and the 1935 World Series title.

Cochrane was already four years removed from baseball when Pearl Harbor was attacked. He would join the Navy and serve as physical fitness training officer and baseball coach at the sprawling Great Lakes Training Center in Illinois. Under his leadership, the Great Lakes team would compile a record of 48–2 in 1944. Among the teams it defeated were eleven of twelve big-league squads.

The Great Lakes base commander, Captain Robert Emmet, was an avid sports fan who took great pride in being the "general manager" of one of World War II's best baseball franchises. Emmett saw the role the game played for both the athletes and the spectators, stating, "Baseball is a genuine incentive to wholesome thinking. When a man's mind is alive with interest and enthusiasm, then there is no room for homesickness or depressive thoughts."

Though located two oceans away from harm, Mickey Cochrane would be emotionally wounded by World War II when he received tragic news that his only son, Gordon, was killed in action.

Brooklyn Dodgers left-handed pitcher Larry French posted a 15–4 record in 1942, his final hurrah in the big leagues. His overall record was 197 wins, 171 losses. He was often asked why he didn't stick around long enough to make it to that magical 200. But the following January French was in the Navy.

"When I went into the Navy on January 8, 1943, they ordered me to the Brooklyn Ship Yard, of all places. So, since there was a curtailment on travel, the Dodgers trained in a fieldhouse at West Point, just up the river. Each weekend I'd go up there and work out with them, and when the season opened I was ready to pitch.

"I petitioned the Secretary of the Navy to let me pitch eight ball games, all to be done on my own time and on weekends in Brooklyn, and I would give the Navy Relief Society $8,000 for the eight games. I was confident I could get my three wins in eight tries. But I was turned down."

French would soon be on his way to Fortress Europe and participated in the Normandy invasion. A year later his world tour would include a stop at one of the most brutal battles of the Pacific Campaign: Okinawa.

After the war, French never went back to baseball to try for those elusive three wins.

Another Brooklyn Dodger, outfielder Pete Reiser, proved to be his own worst enemy, crashing into outfield walls with reckless abandon and using his head instead of his bat to connect with pitched balls. In his first big-league season, he was beaned twice and smacked into a wall, yet still managed to hit .343 and win the National League batting title in 1941.

"After the '42 season I decided to join the Navy. So I went and took a physical, but because of all the injuries I'd had playing ball, I turned up 4-F. They told me no induction center in the country would take me. Then I get a call from the Army. January 13, 1943, I'm inducted.

"I go to Fort Riley, Kansas. I stayed there for a couple of years, playing center field. We ended up with a hell of a ball club. We had Joe Garagiola, Lonny Frey, Creepy Crespi, Harry Walker, Al Brazle, Murry Dickson, Rex Barney, Ken Heintzelman. We whomped everybody we played."

W. C. Heinz would later write about Reiser: "In two and a half years in the minors, three seasons of Army ball, and ten years in the majors, Pete Reiser was carried off the field 11 times.

"Nine times he regained consciousness either in the clubhouse or in hospitals. He broke a bone in his right elbow, throwing. He broke both ankles, tore a cartilage in his left knee, ripped the muscles in his left leg, sliding. Seven times he crashed into outfield walls, dislocating his left shoulder, breaking his right collarbone and, five times, ending up in an unconscious heap on the ground. Twice he was beaned, and the few who remember still wonder how great he might have been."

In 1946 Reiser was back with the Dodgers, scampering for thirty-four stolen bases, including eight dashes for home plate.

Another future Dodger was Carl Erskine, who was drafted into the Navy and served his hitch in Boston, where he spent his off-duty hours throwing batting practice for the Boston Braves. (He would later sign with the Dodgers and compiled a 122–78 record over twelve seasons, including two no-hitters.)

Ted Williams, the superstar Boston Red Sox slugger, was granted a deferment but came under criticism in the press, though fans continued to cheer him. He did enlist in the Navy Air Corps on June 2, 1942, and began studying for flight school until the end of baseball season. It turned out to be a triple crown effort: 36 home runs, 137 RBIs, and a .356 batting average—highest in all three stats.

Williams quickly proved to be an excellent pilot during naval aviation school, which included fellow big-leaguers Johnny Sain, Buddy Gremp, Joe Coleman, and Johnny Pesky. After transferring to Jacksonville, Florida, for operations training, Williams knew a combat assignment was inevitable.

Charlie Gehringer also ended up at Jacksonville. "Ted Williams was stationed there at the time," he recalled. "They had a league of service teams down there. Upon arriving I went to see the commanding officer. He was a great sports fan, and he told me how happy he was to see me."

Gehringer planned on coaching baseball, not playing, until he was informed by his CO,

BACKGROUND AND BELOW: *Major Greg "Pappy" Boyington was the brash leader and fighter ace of the Marine Corps' "Black Sheep Squadron." By the fall of 1943 their ball caps were worn out or lost so they sent word back to major league baseball that they would blast one Jap plane for each new cap sent to them. The St. Louis Cardinals sent over twenty caps and the Black Sheep kept their promise. In fact they downed forty-eight enemy planes, with Boyington credited with fourteen of those.* U.S. Marine Corps photo

"If you don't play I'll send you so far they won't know where to find you!" Gehringer decided to play ball.

"Later I was talking to Williams. Ted was so hepped up about flying those night fighters he couldn't think about anything else. I asked him if he was going to come out for the team."

Williams didn't think he'd have time, but of course the commander managed to persuade him to play. "Those commanding officers took the whole baseball thing pretty seriously," Gehringer recalled.

Williams managed to hone his flying skills and braced himself for a combat assignment, but on his way to the Far East the Japanese surrendered. He had served thirty-eight months in the Navy.

Back with Boston in 1946, and teamed with fellow ex-GIs Pesky, Bobby Doerr, Dom DiMaggio, Mickey Harris, Joe Dobson, and Tex Hughson, Williams led the BoSox to the pennant. (Williams later served in the Marines and was re-called during the Korean War.)

Elden Auker was a workhorse pitcher for Detroit, Boston, and St. Louis, compiling a 130–101 record. But when war was declared he knew what he had to do: "Everybody was into the war effort. If you weren't contributing, something was wrong with you."

According to the National Baseball Hall of Fame, thirty future inductees from the major leagues and Negro Leagues fought in World War II. They included University of California and Philadelphia Athletics outfielder Sam Chapman (who had also been selected to play football in Detroit), who spent four years as a pilot and Dodgers slugger Gil Hodges, who served with the Sixteenth Anti-Aircraft Battalion and saw combat at Tinian and Okinawa. The granite-muscled marine was discharged in February of 1945 and would become a superstar with the Dodgers, playing in seven Fall Classics and six All-Star Games. Tragically, many more budding stars never had the opportunity to rack up Hall of Fame statistics. They were killed or severely hurt in battle.

BELOW: *Former St. Louis Cardinals pitcher Dizzy Dean hung up his glove and turned to the broadcast booth (center). When baseball was decimated by the manpower demands of WWII, the Dizzy spoke out: "If the government thinks our efforts should be turned toward winning the war, let's quit baseball without a squawk and get in there and fight."* AP Wide World photo

War Takes Its Toll

Major league baseball lost more than fifty players wounded in combat. Many never regained their playing skills.

Gordon Houston, minor league outfielder with Texarkana, was the first pro ballplayer killed in World War II, on February 12, 1942. Eight months later, on October 31, another minor leaguer, Billy Hebert from the Oakland Oaks, was killed at Guadalcanal.

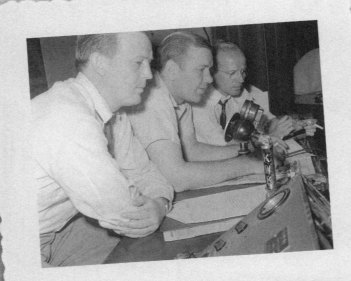

Frostbitten feet during the Battle of the Bulge hurt Cecil Travis, a batting wiz for the Washington Senators whose average fell after the war. In 1941 he was the major league's top shortstop and pounded out a .359 batting average, with fifty-five extra base hits. While serving with the Seventy-sixth Division in Europe, Travis recalled, "You were moving fast in that action. Heck, you was in that snow, and you was out in that weather, and you was lucky you got to stay in an old barn at night. The thing about it, you'd sit there in those boots, and you might not get 'em off for days at a time. And COLD! You'd just shake at night. Your feet would start to swelling, and that's how you'd find out there was something really wrong. You'd pull your boots off and your feet is swelling."

Minor-league pitcher John Grodzicki, an Army paratrooper, was hit in the upper thigh on March 30, 1945, when a German shell exploded close by, killing three others during action near Wesel, along the Rhine. He had had a brief five-game stint with the Cards in 1941, but never made it back to the big leagues after the war.

Phil Marchildon had won seventeen games for the A's in 1942 before joining the Royal Canadian Air Force. As a tail-gunner in a heavy bomber, Marchildon saw plenty of action on bombing runs over Fortress Europe. During a mission over Kieler Bucht, Denmark, in mid-1944, his plane was hit by enemy flak and the crew bailed out. Marchildon and a fellow crewman were captured and sent to a Nazi prison camp in Poland.

He would languish there, emaciated, until Allied forces advanced and threatened to overrun the camp. The POWs were then force-marched by their Nazi captors to another camp farther west. In May 1945 British forces liberated Marchildon and his fellow POWs.

The former A's pitcher had lost weight and returned home in mid-1945 too weak to play baseball. "I'd kind of drift away from concentration," recalled Marchildon. "I'd think about how lucky I was to get out of it all. I was more fidgety than before . . . war nerves, that's what they called it."

(But by the 1946 season Marchildon had built up his strength to resume his big-league career. He returned to the A's for four seasons and then called it quits in 1950 after one game with the Boston Red Sox.)

Elmer Gedeon, who played five games with the Washington Senators in 1939, was killed while fighting at St. Pol, France, in April 1944. Harry O'Neill, who played in just one game for the Philadelphia Athletics in 1939, was killed on Iwo Jima on March 6, 1945.

Lou Brissie was hurt in Italy when shell fragments ripped into his legs, hands, and shoulder. He recuperated and went on to pitch for the A's.

ABOVE: *Major league rosters were decimated by the war, and youngsters, old-timers, and even one-armed minor league outfielder Pete Gray were given a shot. While playing for the Memphis Chicks, Gray was selected league MVP, then was called up by the St. Louis Browns in '45. Though obviously he couldn't serve in the military, Gray was a morale booster to the thousands of disabled servicemen returning home.* AP Wide World photo by Harry Harris

Bert Shepard was flying a P-38 over Germany when he got strafed and lost a leg. He would be captured and spend time in a German POW camp, all the while recuperating his leg and getting used to pitching with a prosthetic leg so he could one day pitch in the major leagues. He finally got his shot with the Senators soon after the war.

Negro Leaguers Finally Break the Barrier

An important aspect of baseball tied directly to WWII was integration. It was well known throughout the country for years that some of the best players and most exciting games were in the Negro Leagues. But breaking the color barrier didn't occur until U.S. Senator Happy Chandler, who took over as baseball commissioner when Landis died, declared that "If they (black ballplayers) can fight and die in Okinawa, Guadalcanal, in the South Pacific, they can play baseball in America. And when I give my word, you can count on it."

By the end of the 1945 season, Branch Rickey of the Dodgers had signed Army veteran, UCLA college star and Kansas City Monarchs rookie Jackie Robinson to a contract with the Montreal Royals. But Rickey fully intended to promote him to Brooklyn as soon as the coaches felt he was ready.

Major league owners responded by voting whether or not to add African-Americans to their rosters. That vote was a lopsided 15–1 against,

with the lone dissenting vote cast by Branch Rickey. But he knew it wouldn't stand up to any legal challenges and so, in 1947, Jackie Robinson would become the first black player in the major leagues. This opened the door for other black players such as Willie "Say Hey" Mays, Ernie Banks, Larry Doby, Monte Irvin, and the granddaddy of them all—Satchel Paige—to play in "the bigs."

Ironically, during the war years, baseball at all levels struggled to field competitive teams, and yet, because of World War II, Negro Leagues players were finally given the opportunity to prove they could play and succeed in the major leagues. It was long overdue.

Divine Intervention

While serving overseas, Brooklyn Dodgers boss Larry MacPhail visited the Vatican in Rome and was introduced to the Pope in 1944.

"I suppose you would like me to bless the Dodgers for you?" the Pope inquired. MacPhail, knowing his team, like every other team, had lost its best players to the armed forces, replied, "Your Holiness, I'm afraid it's too late for that. The last time I looked at the standings, they were in last place."

Three seasons later though, the Dodgers were back in first place, as National League champions. And playing first base for "dem Bums" was Jackie Robinson, National League Rookie of the Year.

> "EVERY MEMBER OF OUR BASEBALL TEAM AT WEST
> POINT BECAME A GENERAL: THIS PROVES THE VALUE OF
> TEAM SPORTS FOR THE MILITARY."
>
> —*General Omar Bradley*

NATURALLY, THE MILITARY WANTED THE HEALTHIEST MEN, from every state and every profession, and by 1943 every sport had been devastated by the call-up. According to *Yank* magazine, "Maybe Brigadier General Hershey ought to know that he's got a million-dollar baseball club, enough golfers to fill five or six Ryder cups, more boxing champions and near-champions . . . and enough football players to round out an average-sized Notre Dame football squad."

It seemed that more pro and college athletes were being asked to join than any other group of men. Actually, because they were well known, whenever sports stars traded in their team uniforms for Army green or Navy white and denim, the newspapers wrote about them, and so they were simply in the news more than men from other professions.

While everyone was glad to see that these players were doing their part for the war effort, many fans were also sad because it meant they wouldn't be able to cheer for them again until after the war . . . if they made it back in one piece.

Uncle Sam Calls

For any young man who received a letter from the government saying he was drafted, he could end up wherever he was needed, in any branch of the military—the Army, Army Air Corps, Marine Corps, Navy, or the Coast Guard. If a young man enlisted, he could choose which armed service he went into, as long as he passed a physical. For example, if he wanted to be a pilot in the Army Air Corps, he couldn't be color-blind or have poor eyesight.

College football lineman Art Donovan recalled, "I went over and joined the Marines. I went home that night, and my father said, 'So Arthur, you're going into the Army, huh?' And when I told him no, I had joined the Marines, Jesus Christ, he began hollering at my mother, 'Kiss him goodbye, Mary, he's going to get killed! He's going to get that fat ass shot right out from under him!'

"I tried to explain to him that I had to join something and that the Marines seemed to promise the most action. But he wouldn't hear any of it.

OPPOSITE: *A shortage of weapons forced trainees to use wooden machine guns and rifles, and throw baseballs instead of hand grenades at Army posts and Marine boot camps throughout the country.* National Archives photo

ABOVE: *Numerous athletes received their training at the massive Norfolk Naval Station in Virginia. Among the major league ballplayers spending time at Norfolk were Pee Wee Reese of the New York Giants, Phil Rizzuto from the cross-town rival Yankees, and Hugh Casey, a teammate of Pee Wee's with the Giants.* U.S. Navy photo

Through all his years in the service, the Marines were always the ones my father had seen die first."

Donovan would see the action he signed up for, ending up in the thick of the Pacific Campaign. Others waited for Uncle Sam to ask for them.

Many who were drafted couldn't pass the induction physical. National Physical Fitness Director John Kelly had established an eight-point criteria that every recruit should be able to accomplish: run a mile in seven minutes; throw a baseball 150 feet; high jump a minimum of three feet six inches; sprint 100 yards in 14.5 seconds; walk a mile in ten minutes; broad jump 13 feet; throw a twelve-pound shot 32 feet; and jump over five low hurdles in 19 seconds. Any new recruit over age thirty-five should accomplish at least six of the eight tasks, and anyone under thirty-five should be able to beat all of them.

But concerned about each serviceman's combat readiness, Kelly warned, "It is estimated that fifty percent of our armed forces, when inducted, cannot swim well enough to save their lives, and lack the strength, agility and endurance to jump ditches, scale walls, throw missiles and stand up under forced marches." Put simply, "a majority of those accepted did not possess skills necessary for self-protection." Because so many recruits lacked the physical stamina to make it through basic, America's athletes quickly took on leadership roles.

Using Athletic Prowess in the Military

BELOW: *Unsure of what American troops would face in combat, Army instructors developed "dirty fighting" techniques, which included Judo and other martial arts.* National Archives photo

After joining one of the armed services, the young men had to go to basic training, or boot camp. Those enlisting in the Navy were sent to bases in Norfolk, Virginia, and San Diego, California; the Great Lakes Naval Base in Illinois; or the Brooklyn Navy Yard in New York. Army recruits were sent to Fort Riley, Kansas; Fort Sill, Oklahoma; or one of many other training sites. And the Air Corps, Marines, and Coast Guard had their own training sites.

Boot camp taught recruits how to fire and clean a rifle; shine their boots, which got dusty or muddy from marching all day; peel onions and cry at the same time; toss a grenade far enough not to get caught up in the blast; and salute sharply and stand at attention like a statue.

With such an array of skills to learn in a limited amount of time, athletes already adept at hand and eye coordination and

in good physical condition seemed to excel at basic training. Hunters naturally had an edge with marksmanship and were pegged to become snipers in the Army and Marine Corps.

Baseball slugger Ted Williams of the Red Sox was known to have excellent eyesight and discipline at home plate, waiting for pitches he could pounce on. After joining the Marines, he had his eyes tested at 20/10, then blasted the air gunnery range, setting a new Marine Corps record for accuracy. He would become an instructor for future pilots.

American horseman Bill Steinkraus was at Yale when he joined the Army and would serve with the last cavalry regiment still using horses, in Southeast Asia during World War II. (He would later participate in six Olympics, winning the gold medal in 1968 for individual jumping.)

Athletes were more adept on the physically demanding obstacle courses than regular recruits, who hadn't endured the regimen of training and exercise. In fact, many of the best athletes became physical fitness instructors. One was Oklahoma high school football player Darrell Royal, stationed at Will Rogers Field until 1946. (Royal would play collegiately at Oklahoma during the glory years of 1946 to 1949, earning all-America honors. He would later make his mark in football as head coach at the University of Texas, posting a record of 167–47–5.)

Heavyweight wrestler Lou Thesz served in the Army, teaching hand-to-hand combat to new recruits. From 1937 and through the '40s he would win and lose the heavyweight title several times before becoming undisputed World Heavyweight Champion in 1950.

Another wrestler, Illinois amateur champion Chris Gestrich, was in great shape but couldn't stand up straight during his induction physical at Fort Warren. Doctors thought maybe he had a curved spine, but Gestrich explained, "I've stood in a crouch so much while wrestling I just can't stand up straight anymore."

LEFT: *Military trainees quickly learn that the enemy can strike at any time, including a gas attack during a baseball game. At Camp Stoneman in California trainees attempt to play ball with gas masks on.* U.S. Army photo

BELOW: *While preparing for deployment to the South Pacific, members of the 81st Infantry Division enjoy a ball game at San Luis Obispo, California. Soon the Wildcats would endure heavy fighting at Guadalcanal, Peleliu, and the Philippines.* U.S. Army photo

Baseball players showed great accuracy at throwing hand grenades, which were about the same size as a baseball, though slightly heavier. New York Giants all-pro tackle (1942–44) and national shot put record-holder Al Blozis had heaved a grenade sixty-five yards and was proclaimed the Army champion until Corporal Michael Rizzo, a former end with the Long Island College football team, bested the mark by twenty yards.

Negro Leagues all-star catcher Frank Duncan, who played primarily with the Kansas City Monarchs, was known for gunning down runners who tried to steal second base. On the marksmanship range while undergoing Army training, he again displayed his accuracy, hitting thirty-one out of thirty-two bull's-eyes from 200 yards.

The Navy's training program for PT boat skippers and crewmen at Melville, Rhode Island, also valued athletes, not only for their conditioning but for their ability to function with others. In the highly volatile arena of the South Pacific, teamwork could very well save the lives of these devil boatmen.

Navy Lieutenant Bill Specht was in charge of this training and equated the functioning of a PT boat crew to that of a well-drilled football squad. But he also stressed that "there is one important difference with that eleven-man football team. When the whistle blows and the game starts, there are no substitutes. If a PT [crewman] goes out, a teammate must take over the missing man's job as well as his own. Another thing, this game is being played against professionals [the Japanese]—and they're plenty tough. They make up their own rules, and they change rules without warning. One slip on your part and they'll kick hell out of you."

To teach the art of street brawling to PT boat cadets, Specht called on martial arts expert and pro wrestler Butch Smith, who warned: "The Nips are first-rate fighters in hand-to-hand combat. And there ain't any referees where you're going. Never give the other bastard an even break; he won't give you one. Kick him in the balls, gouge his eyes out, break his goddamned arm."

Olympic gold medal 100-meter backstroke swimmer Adolph "Sonny" Kiefer—considered one

BELOW: *Whether to settle a grudge or to instill a warrior's attitude, boxing was a popular diversion at military training sites. During a post tournament at Gowen Field in Idaho in 1944, PFC Ed Keefer (right) grits his teeth and knocks out his opponent.* Army Air Force photo

of the greatest swimmers in the 1930s and who set seventeen world records from 1935 to '44—was in charge of the Navy's swimming program during the war years.

Of course, some of the simplest things required of every serviceman, like marching in formation, were virtually impossible for some athletes. "In our barracks we had Bobby Riggs, the tennis player," recalled former Tigers outfielder Barney McCosky. "He couldn't [march] in a straight line. In tennis you've got to move sideways, so he duck-walked. I had to put him at the back of the line. Same with Willie Pep, the boxer. He couldn't walk a straight line and couldn't march."

Besides marching, recruits in every service did jogging every day, along with lots of exercises, especially push-ups and sit-ups. They also learned how to cuss and smoke a lot. And many learned how lonely it could be being away from home for the first time in their life. That was basic training, where all recruits learned the fundamentals of life in the military.

Some Athletes Joined Service and Became . . . Athletes!

Of course, many athletes weren't expected to learn the basics at basic.

"When I think back about my time in boot camp in Norfolk, Virginia, the word 'coddled' came to mind," remembered New York Yankee ballplayer Phil Rizzuto, who joined the Navy.

LEFT: *After completing his military training, daddy came home on holiday leave. But after the New Year it was time to say good-bye again.* National Archives photo

BELOW: *During a lull before being thrown into battle, Wildcats of the 81st Infantry Division do early morning calisthenics. They would later see heavy fighting at Guadalcanal, Palau, New Caledonia, and the Philippines, eventually serving on occupation duty at Honshu, Japan after the war.* 81st Infantry Division photo

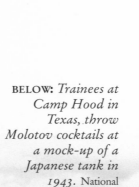

"I spent the required number of weeks in boot camp [but] because I had the good fortune to play for the Yankees, in what was at the time last year's World Series, I did not learn anything. When they had knot tying 101, the chief would say, 'Rizzuto, come up here.' He would sit me down on a chair or a bench and the sailors would all practice tying knots on me.

"I missed some underwater drills and even bedmaking. I was coddled, recoddled, and while I left camp certified as someone who could be in charge of a gun crew, the fact is I was not even in charge of my right arm."

After basic training, most recruits from each of the services (except maybe for the coddled!) then went on to specialized training, sometimes at the same location but often in another part of the country. This is where they learned to do the specific job they would be doing while in the military. For example, cooks learned how to make scrambled eggs for two hundred hungry soldiers, tankers learned how to drive a noisy tank with their feet, and Navy pilots learned how to land safely on an aircraft carrier.

Former West Point football player and hard-nosed coach Ralph Sasse, who served with the 301st Tank Battalion in World War I, was a proponent of armor tactics. Along with George "Blood and Guts" Patton, he foresaw the dominant role tanks would play in future battles.

Though he longed to get in the fight, Sasse remained stateside to train new armor commanders and crews. He would have to read about their successes on faraway battlefields in Europe and the Pacific.

LEFT: *The jungles of the South Pacific were unfamiliar territory for American soldiers and Marines being trained in the States and rushed to the frontlines. The Unit Jungle Training Center in Hawaii was opened in September of 1943 to rectify that issue.* U.S. Army photo

Tragic Consequences

When mistakes were made during training, the consequences could be severe.

While learning to fly fighter planes, both Henry Mazur, former football captain at West Point, and Joe Bartlett, Georgia Tech shot put champ and half-back, had to bail out when they lost control of their planes. As they ejected, both were hit by the planes' tail sections. Mazur was not hurt, but Bartlett was killed.

Bobby Pair of Georgia Tech's 1940 football team was killed in a plane crash near Oklahoma City in 1943. He was the third member of Georgia Tech's Orange Bowl squad to die in World War II. The others were center Slim Sutton and halfback Bobby Beers.

Derace Moser, all-American running back from Texas A&M, and Bill Lyda, Oklahoma 44-yard sprinter, were also killed in stateside plane crashes during training.

Philadelphia Phillies rookie pitcher Barney Mussill was nearly blinded when a defective mustard-gas canister he was holding leaked toxic fumes. He had appeared in only sixteen games in 1944 before being called into service. Mussill would never make it back to the big leagues after the war.

St. Louis Cardinals second baseman Creepy Crespi was undergoing armor training at Fort Riley when the tank he was in overturned. He broke an injured leg that was already keeping him from playing ball for the post team. His injuries were so severe that

BELOW: *A Navy recruit in New York carries his gear at an East Coast training base.* Navy Recruiting Bureau photo

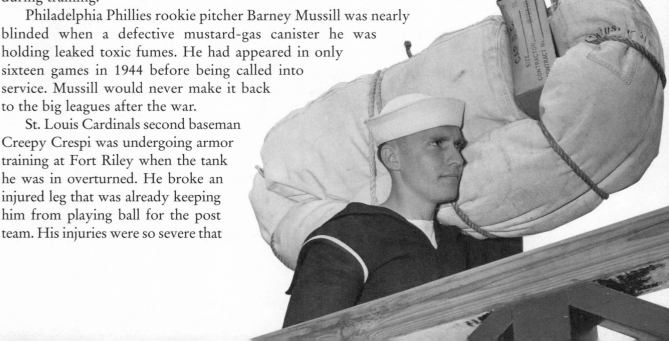

Crespi was discharged. He was left with a limp that prevented him from playing baseball again.

Pro boxer Walter Jack Palahnuik survived a fiery crash in a B-24 bomber while stationed in Arizona. Reconstructive surgery repaired most of his injuries, and soon after leaving the Air Force Palahnuik turned to acting. He would become a well-respected character actor known better as Jack Palance.

Super Teams in the Armed Services

Military training courses could take months, and as more and more professional and college athletes arrived, sports teams formed to play against others in the area.

From 1942 through the end of the war, some of the best teams, especially in baseball and football, were military teams loaded with both collegiate and professional players. They were even better than some of the collegiate teams known as traditional powerhouses before World War II.

The Army Air Forces Flying School in Waco, Texas, was stocked with baseball talent in 1942. Besides minor league players such as outfielder Walter Evers and pitcher Mickey Mandjack, the Waco team boasted catcher George "Birdie" Tebbetts of the Detroit Tigers, Washington Senators outfielder Bruce Campbell, Buster Mills of the Indians, and Senators pitcher Sid Hudson. They also had the Popovich brothers, Nick and Mike, who learned their pitching and catching skills throwing to each other as boys.

Tebbetts had been with Detroit since 1936 and played in the 1940 World Series. He was called up in 1942, then came back for another seven years in 1946. Campbell had played with Tebbetts on the 1940 Tigers team. But after being drafted in 1942 and serving in World War II, he would never again play major league baseball. Buster Mills left the Indians in 1942 for the military and tried to come back in 1946, but called it quits after just nine games. The other ballplayers never got their shot at the big leagues.

Another great military team was stationed at Randolph Field in San Antonio. White Sox outfielder Bibb Falk had a warrior mentality about training and assembled a well-drilled team. "He ran our Army team just like he would a pro team,"

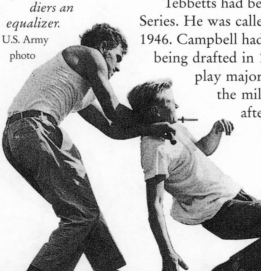

recalled major league pitcher Dave Ferriss. "He wouldn't stand for any fool-ishness: we were there to play ball and to win."

Armed Services Differ on Athletic Participation

While the Army—largest of the military services—was well stocked with ath-letes, it would not allow them to compete in any organized sports that might interfere with their military training. Once soldiers had been reassigned to regular Army units, they could play for unit and post teams.

The Navy, on the other hand, encouraged these transplanted athletes to compete during training courses, creating overnight powerhouses, especially in college football. The Great Lakes Naval Training Station in Illinois seemed to be hording the best athletes, including Duke University's Steve Lach and future Hall of Fame halfback Marion Motley, who, at 235 pounds, was considered an unstoppable block of granite. (After World War II Motley would become an all-pro full-back with the Cleveland Browns and Pittsburgh Steelers, and in 1950 he would lead the league in rushing with 810 yards.)

ABOVE: *An Army lieutenant at Camp Lee practices a bay-onet lunge at an enemy "soldier."* U.S. Army photo

If opponents keyed on neutralizing Motley, they then had to deal with another fairly decent running back: Minnesota's Bruce Smith, named Armed Forces Player of the Year in 1942, who already had an impressive pedigree before joining the Navy. In 1940 and 1941 he was with Minnesota's undefeated national champi-onship team, and he won the Heisman Trophy in '41. (After WWII, Smith would play briefly for the Packers and Rams before leaving the game due to injuries.)

Mickey Cochrane, Athletics catcher and American League Most Valuable Player in 1928, backstopped for the World Champion Detroit Tigers, earning a second MVP award in '34. But his career was cut short when he was hit in the head by a brush-back pitch in 1937 while playing for the Tigers; the ball fractured his skull and knocked him unconscious. He parlayed his baseball savvy into a successful career as coach and manager for several teams. During the war years he was in charge of the Navy's Great Lakes physical training program; In 1947 he was inducted in the Baseball Hall of Fame.

Another future Hall of Famer, Charley "Mechanical Man" Gehringer, was a slick fielding second baseman who played in six All-Star Games. He was with the Tigers for back-to-back World Series, losing to the Cardinals in 1934 but taking the crown the following year against the Cubs. In 1942 the Navy sent him out to the West Coast, where he worked with their physical fitness program through the end of the war.

Joe "the Jet" Perry, a two-hundred-pound fullback, was crashing the line for the Naval Training Station at Alameda, California, when he was discovered by the San Francisco 49ers. (In 1949 he would lead the All-America Football Conference in rushing yards. After the AAFC was dissolved and the 49ers joined the NFL, Perry again led the league in rushing, with 1,018 yards in 1953 and 1,049 yards the following year. In 1969, the Jet was inducted into the Pro Football Hall of Fame.)

After seeing combat in the South Pacific, Coast Guardsman and former high school football star Emlen Tunnell would return to San Francisco in August of 1944 and in his spare time play football for the base team. He recalled, "Our team was called the Coast Guard Pilots, and we weren't afraid of anybody for two reasons, one logical and one illogical. The illogical reason was that we didn't know any better. The logical reason was that 75 percent of our players had seen a year or more of combat duty, and we were comforted by the truth that no matter how tough the opposition might be, they wouldn't fire aerial torpedoes into our huddle."

At the Bainbridge Naval Training Station, high school running back Charlie "Choo-Choo" Justice was a mere teenager playing among former collegiate and pro gridiron stars. But Choo-Choo pulled his weight and led the Bainbridge squad to an undefeated season in 1943. (In 1946 he would play for the Tar Heels of North Carolina and shatter NCAA records in combined yardage for rushing and receiving.)

Colleges Welcome Military Recruits

Bob Neyland commanded his Tennessee Volunteers with military-like regimentation, something he learned as both a West Point graduate and an Army major in World War I. He led the Vols to championship seasons in 1938, '39, and '40, largely by destroying their opponents.

He would return to service in 1941, rise rapidly through the ranks to one-star general, then return to Knoxville for another championship in 1951. He would coach in 216 games, and his teams were so dominant that they held their opponents scoreless in 106 of those games.

But college athletics would change dramatically after December 7, 1941, and through 1945 while Bob Neyland was doing his duty in the China-Burma-India Campaign.

During the war years, some of the best football schools had many pro and

BELOW: *High school football player Emlen Tunnell joined the Coast Guard and was sent to the South Pacific. After the war, like so many other hardened veterans, playing college and professional football was a breeze, certainly after dodging bullets, artillery shells, and torpedoes. Tunnell would rack up Hall of Fame stats during a stellar NFL career.*
AP Wide World photo

college athletes filling out their rosters while studying military courses. Unlike military training sites, these colleges and universities provided classroom space to recruits learning specialized skills, such as languages or pilot preflight training. More than 125 colleges and universities opened their campuses to the armed forces. With so many athletes suddenly on campus for military studies, these schools had virtual all-star teams in a variety of sports.

One such athlete was Northwestern triple-threat quarterback Otto Graham, who graduated in 1943, joined the Navy, and was sent to the University of North Carolina at Chapel Hill as a naval aviation cadet. There he played both fullback and quarterback on a team loaded with college all-Americans and pro athletes, all going through preflight training.

(After World War II, Graham led the Cleveland Browns to four All-America Conference championships. Then in 1949, when the Browns joined the National Football League and were considered just a second-rate bunch of bums by the other established teams, they upset the New York Giants and Los Angeles Rams to take the NFL crown. The Browns would play in the National Football Conference championship game every year from 1949 through 1954, winning the crown again in '53 and '54. And Otto Graham, who was trained to fly Navy planes but never went overseas to fight, was the Browns quarterback through all those glory years. In 1953 and 1955 he led the league in passing, with 2,722 yards and 1,721, respectively. Even today Graham is considered by many to be the greatest quarterback ever to play football.)

The V-5 aviation program for Navy and Marine Corps bomber and fighter pilots at the University of North Carolina and other campuses was developed by former Navy all-American halfback Thomas Hamilton, who would rise through the ranks to eventually skipper the aircraft carrier *Enterprise*.

Other athletes who went through Navy preflight training included John Wooden, a pro basketball player for the Indianapolis Kautskys, who would later coach UCLA to a string of collegiate championships; Chicago Cardinals pro football quarterback Paul Christman; Boston Red Sox outfielder Ted Williams, who belted a .406 batting average during the 1941 season; and a little-known high school baseball and soccer player from Andover Prep School, George Walker Bush, who would become the Navy's youngest pilot. Bush had enlisted in the Navy on his eighteenth birthday, just a few days after the crucial battle of Midway, when Navy pilots ushered in a new era of sea warfare: carrier-launched aircraft.

ABOVE: *Fresno State's pole vaulting champion Cornelius Warmerdam (right) won the AAU crown and, by 1942, had set a world record height that would stand for more than a decade. Considered one of America's greatest athletes who never had an opportunity to compete for an Olympic medal, the Flying Dutchman would join the Navy and serve as a fitness instructor at the Navy preflight training school at Del Monte, California.*
U.S. Navy photo

The accelerated V-5 program to rush skilled pilots to both Europe and the Pacific stressed physical activities. Besides hand-to-hand combat, all cadets competed in nine specific sports to develop agility and stamina: basketball, boxing, football, gymnastics, soccer, swimming, track, and tumbling.

Fresno State College's Cornelius "Dutch" Warmerdam set several pole vaulting records and was priming for the Olympics when the 1940 Games were cancelled. During World War II he served as a physical fitness instructor for the Navy's preflight training program at Del Monte, California. (After the war he continued as a track and field coach and felt he was too old to compete in the Olympics, which resumed in 1948. Many feel the Flying Dutchman was the greatest track athlete never to have had a chance to go for the gold.)

A look back at football's 1943 college all-Americans shows just how many great athletes were in Navy training courses at colleges throughout the country: end Joe Parker at Texas, tackle James White at Notre Dame, guards John Steber at Georgia Tech and George Brown at the Naval Academy, and backers Robert Odell from Penn, Bill Daley at Michigan, and Otto Graham of Northwestern.

On that same all-American squad was center Casimir Myslinski of West Point, along with Patrick Preston of Duke, and Ralph Heywood of Southern Cal, both Marine Corps trainees. The only nonmilitary all-American on that 1943 team was Creighton Miller of Notre Dame.

ABOVE:
Northwestern super-star Otto Graham was a dominant force on the field. But in 1943 he joined the Navy and took his preflight training at the University of North Carolina, where he played both signal caller and fullback.
National Archives photo

Playing for a Former Rival

But just as quickly as these schools welcomed military trainee/athletes, they could just as quickly lose them. Notre Dame lost its starting quarterback, Angelo Bertelli, midway through that 1943 season. Still, his numbers were good enough to earn him the Heisman Trophy that year. (The old Boston Yanks would select Bertelli as their number-one draft choice the next year.) The runner-up in the 1943 Heisman race was Pennsylvania's Robert Odell.

Elroy "Crazy Legs" Hirsch had been an all-American halfback at Wisconsin in 1942. He joined the Marines and transferred to the University of Michigan for Marine Corps V-12 training. While at Big Ten rival Michigan, he was again an all-American. Hirsch became a four-sport letterman for the Wolverines, including playing for championship teams in both basketball and baseball.

But Michigan also lost all-American Bill Daley, along with six other football players, after just two months of the '43 season. While the Navy was more than willing to allow its trainees to participate in athletics, it rarely deferred their transfers until the end of football season once that training was completed.

Schools Shut Down Sports Programs

Many colleges had lost so many players that they couldn't field a competitive team, especially as the war dragged on.

In 1944 Ike Armstrong, University of Utah's football coach, held tryouts and was so disgusted with the group of seventeen-year-olds who turned out that he shouted: "All boys who shaved this morning step forward." With this simple formula he selected his starting team.

Many schools had to abandon athletics altogether for the duration of the war, simply because Army cadets were using all of the athletic facilities for military training. By 1943 the NCAA called off wrestling, fencing, cross-country running, and gymnastics, and more than three hundred schools cancelled their football programs, but not because there weren't enough athletes for the teams. Many schools relinquished their gymnasiums, swimming pools, and outdoor stadiums to the Army for physical fitness requirements. This left the school's teams with no place to train or practice.

Also, with constant training, from 6:00 A.M. to 10:30 P.M., six and a half days every week, Army trainees had neither the time nor the energy—nor permission from the Secretary of the Army—to play intercollegiate sports.

They were too busy preparing for combat.

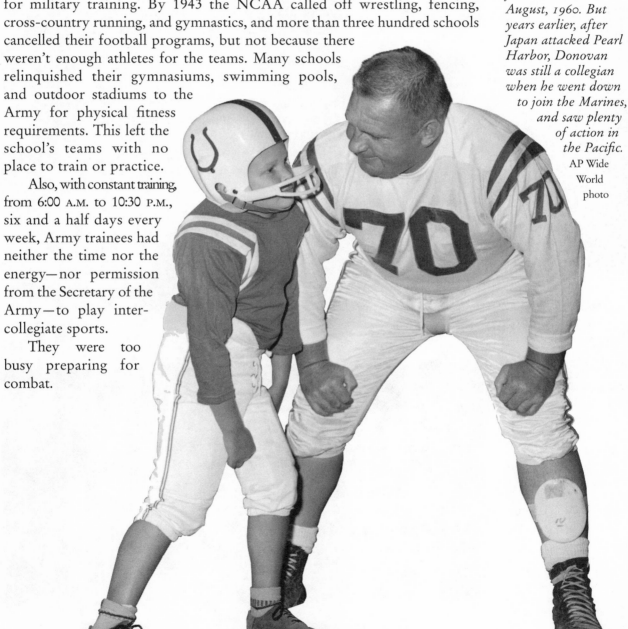

BELOW: *Baltimore Colts lineman Art Donovan took time to show seven-year-old Stevie MacGregor, a young fan, football fundamentals in August, 1960. But years earlier, after Japan attacked Pearl Harbor, Donovan was still a collegian when he went down to join the Marines, and saw plenty of action in the Pacific.* AP Wide World photo

Basketball Devastated During the War Years

"Pro basketball's reputation had been less than stellar in the 1930s and early '40s. . . . Games often became bloodbaths, especially under the basket. The frontcourt was no place for the squeamish, and the front row, where fans sat who were just as rough and raucous was no place for women and children. Basketball was a very hard game."

—*George Mikan*

"Basketball is like war in that offensive weapons are developed first, and it always takes awhile for the defense to catch up."

—*Red Auerbach*

BASKETBALL IN THE LATE 1930s WAS A SLOW-MOVING RELIC that included a center jump ball after every basket—after *every* basket! Slam dunks were unheard of. Even behind-the-back passes and through-the-legs dribbling were considered showing up the other team. Jump shots were called set shots because, quite simply, nobody jumped. And the most common "fast break" was when both teams dashed to the locker room at halftime.

BELOW: *During basic training and unit maneuvers at Camp Rucker in Alabama, the 81st Infantry Division basketball team played against military, semipro, and collegiate teams in the area.* 81st Infantry Division photo

LEFT: *In Mississippi, the Greenwood Army Air Field championship basketball team was nothing but Smiths—Bill, Gordon, Otis, Bob and Jim—and none of them were related. Their coach, Sergeant Bill Metz, was odd man out.*
Army Air Forces photo

Collegiate basketball was far more popular than pro ball, though no team or league had a truly national following. In fact, few college teams even played against others outside their region of the country. And pro leagues were also regional in scope. Five teams that did have a following, primarily in the East, were the Philadelphia Sphas, and the all-black New York Rens, the Black Washingtonians, the barn-storming Harlem Globetrotters, and Renaissance Big Five, which toured the country from 1932 to 1940 and were arguably the best hoops team around, black or white.

Several of the Black Washingtonians worked for Grumman Aircraft. While they would initially be exempt from the draft during World War II, they could only play for the team on weekends because of shift work at the factory.

College Popularity Leads to National Tourneys

College basketball got a big boost when, in 1938, New York's Madison Square Garden invited the top teams from around the country to play in the National Invitational Tournament. For many teams, this was the first opportunity to play against others outside their own league. Temple University easily beat Colorado 60–36 in that first NIT.

One player who dominated the collegiate scene in the late thirties was Stanford's three-time all-American and two-time collegiate player of the year, Angelo "Hank" Luisetti, who was destined to kick-start the stodgy pro leagues with his one-hand push shot and flamboyant style, making a mockery of the standard two-hand set shot. Luisetti would lead Stanford to three Pacific Coast Conference titles and selection as collegiate team of the year in 1936–37.

But in 1944, while in the Navy, Luisetti contracted spinal meningitis, and he never regained his health. Doctors cautioned that he should never again exert himself on the basketball court. Luisetti was one of the greatest players never to play pro basketball.

In 1939, after seeing the potential of tournament play, the NCAA created its own post-season tournament, pitting the top four teams from both the east and west divisions. The Oregon Ducks of the Pacific Coast Conference beat the Big Ten's Ohio State Buckeyes 46–33 in the NCAA's own championship tournament.

RIGHT: *Despite the brisk weather, aviation engineers based on Iceland in 1942 enjoyed a basketball game.* U.S. Army Signal Corps photo

With the military gearing up for the conflicts in Europe, Colgate center Bob Goslin was drafted in early 1941 and assigned to the cavalry before transferring to the Army Air Corps.

The 1942 NCAA tourney was held just weeks after the Japanese attack on Pearl Harbor. The nation was still scrambling to mobilize for war, and young men everywhere, including college basketball players, knew it was just a matter of time before they received their draft notices.

Stanford, which had won the Western bracket in '42, took the championship trophy, beating Dartmouth's Big Green Indians, 53–38. By the following season, both teams would lose key players to the military.

In 1943 the NCAA champion Wyoming Cowboys would lose the services of Player of the Year Kenny Sailors, who joined the Marines. Three other Cowboys who left for military service immediately after the tournament were Jim Roney, Floyd Volker, and Jim Weir. But Wyoming was not unique in seeing its roster depleted by the war. With the military massing for the invasion of Fortress Europe in 1944, every major collegiate team was affected.

Loyola University all-American Marv Colen was assigned to an ordnance unit and served in France.

The University of Missouri had the Potosi Twins in 1944: Cliff and Beau Minx, who played round ball just for the fun of it. Together they had a unique strategy, which Beau revealed: "My brother, being a forward, would get more fouls on him. So when he got four fouls—at halftime or sometime—we'd change jerseys," thus allowing both of them to remain on the court longer together. In 1945 the Navy would finally separate the twins, with Cliff remaining stateside while Beau shipped off to Hawaii.

Another Midwestern powerhouse would be decimated by the manpower demands of World War II. The entire Oklahoma A&M team was called up after the 1943 season, though Bob Kurland, at seven feet, was deemed too tall. (The Army's maximum accepted height was six feet, six inches.) Kurland returned to A&M and became one of the dominant big men in the game.

Influx of Recruits Play College Ball

Some college basketball programs were helped immensely by the war. With on-campus military training programs, such as the Navy's aviation courses, those schools saw an influx of student-athletes, who filled the rosters of departing basketball players.

One such school was Dartmouth, which loaded its squad with athletes from other teams. Among those players were Bob Gale from Cornell, Larry Leggatt of New York University, and Dick McGuire of St. John's. Together they marched right into the 1944 NCAA championship game but lost in overtime to Utah on a last-second shot, 42–40. Soon afterward the three Dartmouth players completed their military training and joined the Navy.

For the second year in a row, Oklahoma A&M saw its entire squad called into the military, except of course for Bob Kurland, who towered over opponents. With the help of Floyd Burdette, who would soon join the Army Air Corps, and Doyle Parrack, who was released from military service to help on the family farm, Oklahoma A&M won the NCAAs in 1945, beating New York University, 49–45.

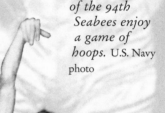

BELOW: *After the Japanese were routed from the Marianas, Navy Seabees—construction battalions—were called in to fortify dock facilities and rebuild damaged airstrips.*

During their free time, members of the 94th Seabees enjoy a game of hoops. U.S. Navy photo

A&M would win the NCAA again in 1946. With the war over, an influx of returning lettermen from the 1943 and 1944 teams created a logjam for positions on the squad. One player of note was forward Sam Aubrey, who left the 1943 squad, was severely wounded in combat, and was told he might never walk again. Aubrey made that team in 1946 and enjoyed beating North Carolina, 43–40, for Oklahoma A&M's second straight NCAA title.

Harry Boykoff, at six feet, nine inches was the man in the middle at St. John's, earning all-American honors in 1943. Months later, even though he was three inches over the Army's height restriction, Boykoff demanded and received an exception to policy, allowing him to serve. "I went to West Point as a GI Field Artillery instructor." Boykoff hadn't played basketball in more than two years, but when he returned to St. John's he would once again make the all-American team in 1945–46.

Andy Phillip had been a prominent baseball prospect with the St. Louis Cardinals but instead became the sparkplug as one of the Whiz Kids at the University of Illinois in the early 1940s. In another time Illinois could have dominated college basketball for several years, but World War II tore the team apart. Phillip joined the Marine Corps in 1943 and served in the Pacific Campaign. He would return to Illinois and earn selection to the all-American team, then go on to play eleven years in the NBA, playing on five all-star teams. The other four starters from the Illini Whiz Kids— Jack Smiley, Art Mathisen, Ken Menke, and Gene Vance—all joined the Army, dismantling what a majority of college coaches felt was the best collegiate team of all time.

By 1944 eighteen-year-old freshmen were allowed to suit up, joining upperclassmen who couldn't serve in the military

BELOW: *Stanford All-American and collegiate player of the year Hank Luisetti was destined to be a superstar long before the term was invented. He joined the Navy and in 1944 contracted spinal meningitis and was advised that the physical strain of basketball might be too risky.* Photo courtesy of Stanford University

(having failed the induction physicals) and military recruits who were on campus to complete their training.

Jumping Joe Fulks, basketball player at Murray State in Kentucky, also served in the Pacific during World War II. Once the Japanese had surrendered, Fulks would play with Andy Phillip on an Army team with other pro and college stars. Jumping Joe would return to the States and sign with the Philadelphia Warriors of the fledgling Basketball Association of America League. He would lead them to the championship in 1947, while scoring a league-high 1,389 points.

LEFT: *Seton Hall's All-American Bob Davies—dubbed the Harrisburg Houdini—served on a sub chaser during the war. He would come back and win all-star honors four years running with the Rochester Royals.* Photo courtesy of Seton Hall University

The Little-Known Professionals

After the East Coast's American Basketball League struggled to survive in the early 1930s, the National Basketball League formed in 1937, consisting of thirteen teams based in the Midwest. Corporate sponsorship by Goodyear and Firestone created two rival teams in Akron, Ohio, while General Electric established a team in Fort Wayne, Indiana. Ten more independent teams, such as the Indianapolis Kautskys and Sheboygan Redskins, filled out the NBL.

John Wooden, who played for the Kautskys, served in the Navy during the war. (After the war he had several coaching stints and led UCLA to a string of NCAA titles.)

To attract collegiate stars used to playing a faster game, the NBL abolished the time-clogging center jump after each basket. Among the many collegians who signed with the NBL were Bob Davies and Otto Graham, both of whom, like Wooden, would be called into the military after the attack on Pearl Harbor.

Struggling to Survive

Based in small cities in the north-central region of the country, the NBL struggled to keep its franchises. In fact, the league nearly folded during the war, when so many players were drafted by the military.

The 1942 NBL season began just two weeks after Pearl Harbor, and several of its players were called up, including Oshkosh all-stars forwards Bob Carpenter and Herm Witasek, Fort Wayne's Bob Calihan, Lee Huber of the Akron Goodyear Wingfoots, Bob Dietz and Ernie Andres of the Indianapolis Kautskys, Jack Ozburn of the Toledo Jim White Chevrolets, and Chicago Bruins Stan Szukala and Bill Japac.

In 1943 the war again took a heavy toll on the NBL. Goodyear dropped its Akron team. Indianapolis and the Chicago Bruins called it quits, but the Windy City still fielded a team, after the local Studebaker plant stepped forward as a sponsor.

The Stubebaker plant had been converted to build military vehicles, making all of its workers exempt from the armed forces. And those workers included the Chicago Studebakers players, several of whom were "stolen" from other teams. Sonny Boswell, Bernie Price, and Duke Cumberland came from the Harlem Globetrotters (which originated in Chicago), Dick Evans and Mike Novak were picked up from the defunct Bruins squad, and Paul Sokody came over from the Sheboygan Redskins. The addition of the three Globetrotters players meant Chicago would field the first integrated team in league play.

Reece "the Goose" Tatum of the Globetrotters didn't join his teammates at the Chicago Studebaker factory and was drafted into the Army Air Corps. After basic training, Tatum was sent to Lincoln Air Base in Nebraska, where he played basketball and entertained the crowds with his antics and ball-handling skills. With a wingspan of eighty-four inches, Tatum perfected his trademark hook shot while in the military.

With room for only thirteen players (after losing four to the military) the Studebakers could not save the other teams in the NBL, and so by the beginning of the '43–'44 season, only four teams remained. Two more were added the following year, while the Cleveland franchise changed names and shuffled its lineup, picking up players from the teams that had folded.

BELOW: *St. John's All-American Harry Boykoff was considered too tall for the military, but after he lobbied for an exception, he was sent to West Point to be an artillery instructor.* Photo courtesy of St. John's University

The 1945–46 season was the first after the war, welcoming back both former NBL and prewar collegiate stars. This influx of talent prodded several franchises to join the league, which ballooned to twelve teams for the '46–'47 season. But in 1946 the NBL was no longer the only major basketball league in the country.

LEFT: *The Fighting Illini's Whiz Kids of the early forties were considered by many coaches and writers as one of the greatest collegiate teams ever assembled. But WWII took its toll and dismantled this hard court juggernaut. Coach Mills (left) had a right to be proud of his squad—which included Art Mathisen, Jack Smiley, Gene Vance, Ken Menke, and Andy Phillip—but by 1944 he filled out his roster with freshmen and others who couldn't serve in the military, mostly due to physical limitations. Andy Phillip, who also played minor league baseball with the Cardinals, led the Whiz Kids until he joined the Marines, serving in the South Pacific.* Photo courtesy of the University of Illinois

Fledgling League Forms

After World War II, owners of large venues in major East Coast cities saw a resurgent interest in sports and sought to use their arenas for more than just pro hockey and college basketball games.

The popularity of college basketball doubleheaders at Madison Square Garden led to similar efforts in other large arenas. But there was more money to be made by creating a new pro league rather than just raking in the revenue from college games.

During the summer of 1946, eleven of these arena owners got together and formed the Basketball Association of America, with franchises concentrated in the northeast and central states. These new teams—including New York, Philadelphia, Boston, Cleveland, Detroit, and Chicago—had a much larger fan base than the smaller cities of the NBL, but they could not attract the same caliber of player.

For two seasons the NBL and BAA struggled. Then in 1948 the four strongest teams in the NBL—Minneapolis, Fort Wayne, Rochester, and Indianapolis—jumped ship, linking up with the BAA. The merger was beneficial to all teams involved, allowing the big-name players of the NBL to play in the larger arenas of the BAA.

One of those big-name players was Seton Hall all-American Bob Davies, the Harrisburg Houdini, who had served in the Navy on a sub chaser during the war. He would sign with the Rochester Royals and be selected as an all-star four years running.

BELOW: *John Wooden was a prominent Big Ten basketball player at Purdue, then played pro ball with the Indianapolis Kautskys before joining the Navy. After the war he would lean toward coaching, eventually developing UCLA into the greatest dynasty in college basketball.* Photo courtesy of Purdue University

Another Navy veteran and teammate of Davies, if only briefly, was Northwestern all-American basketball player Otto Graham, who went on to play quarterback for the Cleveland Browns in the new All-America Football Conference. He would lead the Browns to four league titles, then, after the Browns joined the National Football League in 1950, would guide them to that crown also.

The NBL quickly added four new teams and maintained its status as the better league, though the BAA had moved up a notch when it added the four former NBL defector teams.

To cap off its drawing power in 1949, the NBL created a new team, the Indianapolis Olympians, made up of the NCAA Champion Kentucky Wildcats graduating seniors and members of the 1948 U.S. Olympic basketball team. Soon afterward, the BAA and NBL negotiated a merger, creating the National Basketball Association, with seventeen teams divided into three divisions.

Integrating Basketball

Like Negro Leagues baseball players, black basketball players were not permitted to play in the big leagues. There were several dominating black teams, such as the Rens and the Globetrotters, who took on all comers and more than held their own. And there were a few integrated teams, such as the Chicago Studebakers during the 1943–44 season, and the Dayton Metropolitans in 1946–47.

But it would take until the 1950–51 season before NBA teams drafted black players. And one of the first black players to join the NBA was Nat Sweetwater Clifton, selected by the New York Knicks.

In 1943 Clifton had played for Xavier University in New Orleans and was chosen MVP of the Southern Conference. He then served in the Army from 1944 to 1947, including a tour in Europe.

Clifton felt his Army experience gave him an edge over other black basketball players: "I had been in the Army and I was a disciplined, quiet kind of guy. I was used to following orders. I suppose it was why I was chosen to play in the NBA because there certainly were blacks better than me." (Clifton would play for seven years with the Knicks, earning all-star honors in 1957.)

An Olympic Hero Returns

Six years after the Nazis surrendered, Goose Tatum and the Harlem Globetrotters returned to the Olympic Stadium in Berlin, on August 22, 1951, to play a game outdoors. More than 75,000 German spectators were packed in to see this American contingent of black athletes.

Fifteen years earlier, America's Olympic team, led by what the Nazis had called the Black Auxiliaries, had overwhelmed the host country's Aryan super athletes, won numerous medals, and became instant celebrities to the German masses. Adolf Hitler had witnessed many of the events and proudly cheered his own athletes when they won, but he was absent from the stadium when it came time to congratulate any of the black American athletes.

During halftime at the Globetrotters game in Berlin in 1951, an American helicopter circled the stadium, then landed on the field. Stepping out from that helicopter was Olympic hero Jesse Owens, wearing the four gold medals he had won in that same stadium fifteen years earlier. Once again the German masses cheered as Owens raised his arms in victory. Then, as he had done at the 1936 Olympics, Jesse Owens circled the track to a chorus of cheers.

7. Confused Beyond Imagination: The China-Burma-India Campaign

the NIPPONESE NEMESIS

"THERE ARE NINE YANK AIRMEN WHO WILL GIVE YOU ODDS THAT THEY CAN MAKE ANY NINE-LIVED CAT TURN GREEN WITH ENVY. THEY'RE MEMBERS OF A COMBAT CREW THAT PLAYED TAG WITH BORROWED TIME SO OFTEN ON A BOMBING MISSION THAT THE LAW OF AVERAGES IS IN GRAVE DANGER OF BEING REPEALED."

—*Sergeant Ed Cunningham, January 20, 1943, in India, for* Yank *magazine*

OPPOSITE: *Fighter planes of the Flying Tigers provided escort protection for transport planes delivering supplies and ammunition to combat units in China. Michigan running back and Heisman Trophy winner Tom Harmon was one of those fighter pilots.* National Archives photo

ON A GEOGRAPHICAL MAP, THE ISLANDS OF JAPAN resemble a dragon looking out to the Pacific. Surrounded by water, Japan in the early 1930s longed to be the ruling power in Asia. The dragon, with its massive armed forces, turned around toward the mainland and invaded Manchuria in 1931. Then it set out to conquer all of China before heading south toward Indonesia, Australia, and New Zealand.

To break the dragon's back on the Asian mainland, American and British units supported the rebel Chinese Nationalist forces. But without food and medicine, fuel and ammunition, the Chinese had little chance against the powerful Japanese.

In 1937 Claire Chennault—an ace aviator who in his younger days had formed a team of barnstorming stunt flyers called Three Men on a Flying Trapeze that crisscrossed America—was serving as a consultant to the ragtag Chinese Air Force. He scrounged for anything that would fly and began training Chinese pilots to counterpunch the far superior Japanese aviators. His strategy was simple: Avoid individual dogfights but hit hard, hit with precision, and hit as a team. Ever the commander, Chennault was also the pitcher for his hard-hitting softball team.

Chennault used his connections and influence within the aviation community to have one hundred Curtiss P-40 aircraft diverted to China, then prodded seventy-five U.S. Army and Navy pilots to leave the military and sign on with him, forming the American Volunteer Group, dubbed the Flying Tigers. They were paid six hundred dollars a month plus five hundred dollars for every Japanese plane they shot down.

ABOVE: *John "Flying Dutchman" Kitzmiller was a triple threat ball carrier for the University of Oregon. During the war he was an Army captain with the 10th Air Force in India.* Photo courtesy of the University of Oregon

Flying the Hump

From distant air bases in Burma and India, the Allied aircrews flew relief supplies to the Chinese. But these flights over the Himalaya, nicknamed the Hump, were extremely dangerous. More than four hundred supply planes crashed while flying the perilous Hump, either shot down by Japanese planes or forced down by bad weather. During the CBI Campaign, Mother Nature truly was one hell of a mother!

George Varoff, world champion pole vaulter, was on one of those planes that was shot down. He survived the crash, then avoided enemy patrols with the help of Chinese partisans and made it back to his base.

Boze Berger was a multitalented athlete at the University of Maryland, where he was an all-American basketball guard, third baseman, and halfback. He played major league baseball from 1932 to 1941. When his Army Reserve unit was activated after Pearl Harbor, Berger gave up sports and served in the China-Burma-India area of operations.

John Kitzmiller, Oregon's Flying Dutchman and triple threat on the gridiron, was a captain with the Tenth Air Force in China. One of his fellow officers was Lieutenant J. Hall Surface, Jr., a nationally ranked tennis player who had led the Texas Longhorns to the college crown and was a member of the Davis Cup team in 1936 and '37.

ABOVE: *C-47 cargo planes of the Air Transport Command flew the perilous Hump—the Himalaya—from bases in India and Burma to Allied units in China, delivering up to 45,000 tons of supplies every month during the height of the campaign. One of those transport pilots was the Senator's all-star third baseman Buddy Lewis.*
U.S. Air Force photo

Buddy Lewis "Waves" Goodbye

Another pilot who braved the Hump was Washington Senators third baseman John K. "Buddy" Lewis, a former American League all-star. He broke in with the Senators in 1935 and anchored the hot corner for six years, through the 1941 season.

After joining the Army Air Corps and before leaving for the Pacific Campaign, Lewis had returned to watch his teammates warm up for one last baseball game, even joining them for batting and fielding practice. But then Lewis put his Army uniform back on and waved goodbye to his teammates, saying he'd stop back around 4:30 that afternoon.

Suddenly during the fourth inning, and precisely at 4:30, a huge Army Air Corps transport plane dove down across the ball field and climbed back over the stadium, scaring most of the spectators, who thought some crazed pilot

was going to crash into the field. But it was just Buddy Lewis saying good-bye to the fans and the friends and the game he loved . . . at least until after the war.

Later, while stationed in India, Lewis flew a transport plane eight to twelve hours every night over the Himalaya, delivering reinforcements and supplies to the Chinese partisans.

Lewis would return to the Senators—after more than three hundred flying missions and two thousand hours in the air—to play in sixty-nine games in 1945. His first time at bat after returning from the Pacific, Lewis faced White Sox pitcher Earl Caldwell, who was having a problem finding the strike zone. It didn't help that umpire Bill McGowan wasn't cutting him any slack. After throwing what he felt were two strikes, Caldwell stormed off the pitcher's mound and confronted McGowan, who responded: "This is Buddy's first time at bat after being in the war, and there ain't no way you're going to throw a strike."

Caldwell stomped back to the pitching rubber, and, not willing to serve up a marshmallow that Lewis could whack over the fences, he simply threw two more balls and gave him a free pass. Lewis quickly got back into playing condition and played baseball, mostly as an outfielder, through the 1949 season.

LEFT: *For units not on the front lines— such as the 1st Transport Squadron and 858th Engineers when they were stationed at Assam, India—there was down time for recreation including a baseball game between the two.*
U.S. Army photo

BELOW: *A 40-mm anti-aircraft gun crew in India watches for enemy planes in April 1944.*
U.S. Army photo

Old 98 Bails Out

Other Allied planes bombed and strafed Japanese camps in China and northern Burma. Fighter planes also shot down 286 Japanese aircraft over the China-Burma-India region.

Heisman Trophy winner and Michigan all-American football player Tom Harmon was one of those fighter pilots, serving with the 449th Fighter Squadron, Fifty-first Fighter Group. The nickname for Harmon's plane was simply "98," his jersey number as a Michigan Wolverine from 1938 to 1940. A familiar sight on Big Ten gridirons was Harmon streaking downfield with his jersey shredded and flapping behind him, torn by opposing players trying to tackle the elusive Old 98.

Besides the Heisman, Harmon had also won the Maxwell Trophy, Washington Touchdown Trophy, and Big Ten MVP award in 1940 before joining the Army Air Corps and shipping out for the CBI Campaign.

During one mission over China, Harmon shot down two enemy planes, but his own P-38 Lightning was also hit, and he crashed into hostile territory. After he failed to return to his base that day or the next, Harmon was initially declared missing in action. Fortunately he survived the crash, and after thirty-two days in hostile territory, with the help of Chinese guerilla forces he made his way through the jungles back to friendly territory.

Hammering Hank Faces Danger

While in the China-Burma-India Campaign, Detroit Tigers slugger Hank Greenberg—the 1935 American League most valuable player—was in charge of a squadron from the Twentieth Bomber Command.

Simply traversing the Himalaya was an adventure, as Greenberg remembered: "Flying the Hump is a pretty nerve-racking experience. I went over it five times and you're always worried about the weather. It's rare that you have a clear day. If you fly over the weather, you're sweating it out in fear you won't be able to find your landing field when you come down through it. If you fly through the weather, you're constantly afraid you'll hit one of those mountain peaks.

ABOVE: *Michigan's Old 98 was running back Tom Harmon, who won the Heisman Trophy in 1940, then joined the Army Air Corps. While serving in the China, Burma, India theater, Harmon was a fighter pilot and his plane was dubbed simply "98."* Photo courtesy of the University of Michigan

RIGHT: *Tigers slugger Hammering Hank Greenberg served with the 20th Bomber Command in the CBI. It was a long way from Detroit, where he terrorized American League pitchers and was the MVP in 1935.* AP Wide World photo

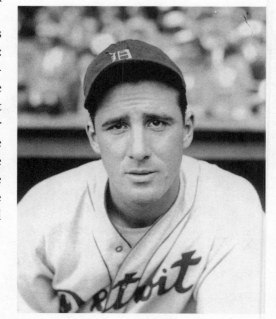

"Always in the back of your mind is the fact that if anything goes wrong the plane can't be landed. It's an awe-inspiring yet terrifying view. That rugged scenery was desolate but breath-taking."

Greenberg was almost killed in the CBI Campaign when a B-29 bomber crashed as it was taking off from an air base he was at. The American League home run hitter and others rushed to the plane to rescue the crew as the bombs inside exploded, knocking Greenberg to the ground.

"As we were running there was a blast when the gas tanks blew up and we were only thirty yards away when a bomb went off," Greenberg recalled. "It knocked us right into a drainage ditch alongside the rice paddies while pieces of metal floated down out of the air. I was stunned and couldn't talk or hear for a couple of days, but was otherwise undamaged."

Luckily the bomber crew also survived the mishap unharmed.

Ground Fighting in the CBI

The Japanese had planned on conquering China quickly, without much of a fight. But as the war dragged on, the soldiers of the Rising Sun became weary. The mighty dragon had to rest and lick his wounds, but the Allies wanted to keep him on the run.

American and other Allied ground troops rushed in and fought side by side with the Chinese, hoping to drive out the Japanese. One of the American commanders in the China-Burma-India Campaign was two-star general Dan Sultan, who had played collegiate football at West Point. (One of his team-mates at the Point was Dwight D. Eisenhower, who had his hands full fighting the Germans in the European Theater.)

Green Bay Packers halfback Johnny "Blood" McNally, who was voted to the all-pro squad of the 1930s, later served in China as a cryptographer,

BELOW:
Merrill's Marauders distinguished themselves in the CBI campaign.
National Archives photo

analyzing coded radio and teletype transmissions from the enemy, trying to figure out what their next move was going to be. A lot of it was guesswork, but American forces in both Pacific and European battles depended on code-breakers like Johnny Blood to figure out what the enemy was doing so they could be ready for it.

One of the major problems of the CBI Campaign was getting supplies to those combat units probing deep into inhospitable territory. Parachute drops were partly successful, though often enemy soldiers intercepted supply drops before Americans could get to them. Tragically, a common ploy was for Japanese troops to converge on the descending parachutes, then wait and ambush the American and Chinese soldiers desperate for the resupply.

Army Brigadier General Robert Neyland, stationed in Calcutta, was one of the senior officers responsible for getting vital supplies to the partisans and Allied units that needed them. As a West Point grad and World War I veteran, Neyland was notorious for regimentation, which he had honed on the gridiron at Knoxville as head coach of the Tennessee Volunteers. He would lead the Vols to league and national championships prior to World War II, join the fight in the CBI, and then return to Knoxville and spearhead another drive to a third national championship in 1951. Bob Neyland, the coach or the general, would accept nothing less than total victory.

To establish a ground route across Burma and into China, Army engineers cut a trace through impassable terrain, but half the time monsoon rains brought the work to a muddy halt.

One of those engineer officers working on the Ledo Road was

RIGHT ABOVE:

Johnny "Blood" McNally made the NFL's 1930s All-Pro team while slicing through opposing defenses for the Green Bay Packers. During WWII he was assigned as a code buster in China. AP Wide World photo

RIGHT BELOW:

American pilots volunteered to support Chinese partisans in the early 1940s against Japanese invaders. After the attack on Pearl Harbor, these Flying Tigers became part of the Army Air Forces. Office of War Information photo

Lieutenant Colonel William Green, who more than a decade earlier had served as a human bulldozer on the University of Illinois football team, clearing a path as blocking back for the great ball carrier Red Grange.

Many American and Allied servicemen would lose their lives in the prolonged CBI Campaign, but the decimated Japanese forces eventually withdrew, giving up their goal of conquering China.

Future Baseball Execs Pull Duty

Gene Autry, the singing cowboy, joined the Army Air Corps and flew cargo planes to India. (After the war he would invest in an American League expansion team for Southern California, which would be called the Angels.)

David Grote interrupted his studies at Xavier University to join the Navy, seeing action in the China-Burma-India Campaign, followed by several European conflicts, including Italy and France. (He was with the front office of the Cincinnati Reds by 1948 and then moved up to become National League president in 1951.)

Leisure Time in the CBI

With the Japanese relinquishing control of the China-Burma-India Campaign, there would be time for relaxation, which for many GIs took the form of athletic competition.

PFC Johnny Boulos, who had played soccer in the States with the Brooklyn Hispanos, literally had his pants torn off while playing soccer in India—not as dangerous as being shot down, but embarrassing just the same.

Freckles Brown, a rodeo cowboy who rode saddle broncs, barebacks, and bulls in civilian life back in the States, was a paratrooper in China. He would organize a rodeo for the GIs once the fighting ceased, participating in several events and winning the all-around title, with a composite score higher than any other participant's. (After World War II the "Un-sinkable Freckles Brown" would appear in eight national finals rodeos and win the World Champion Bull Rider crown in 1962.)

Earle Meadows, the 1936 Olympic gold medalist in the pole vault, with a jump of 14 feet 3 inches, was also assigned to the China-Burma-India Campaign. During a track meet pitting GIs against their Chinese allies, Meadows easily cleared 14 feet, a Chinese record for the pole vault at the time.

BELOW:
Muleskinners of the 612th Field Artillery Battalion haul 75-mm pack howitzers across a stream in Myitkyina in Burma in 1944.
U.S. Army photo

Tennis Pros and Amateurs Join the Fight

"TENNIS PLAYERS JUST DIDN'T RATE WITH THE VIRILE BREED OF HE-MEN REPRESENTED BY BABE RUTH, JACK DEMPSEY, RED GRANGE, JOHNNY WEISSMULLER, TOMMY HITCHCOCK, WALTER HAGEN AND BOBBY JONES. . . . IT'S ENOUGH TO SHOW THAT TENNIS HAS GONE OFF TO WAR AS HAVE ALL OTHER SPORTS AND THAT, DESPITE THEIR LOVE—FORTY AND LIP SERVICE TO THE SOCIAL AMENITIES, THE BOYS IN THE ICE CREAM PANTS AREN'T ANY COMFORT TO TOJO OR ADOLF."

—*Allison Danzig*

"LIKE LEAVES, THE TENNIS PLAYERS WERE QUICKLY CARRIED ALONG BY THE WINDS OF WAR."

—*Gianni Clerici*

BY THE LATE-1930s HITLER HAD UPSET THE PRECARIOUS balance of powers in Europe, and international sports virtually came to a standstill. After the 1936 Summer Olympic Games in Berlin, the spectacle was suspended for nearly a decade.

Sportsmanship and fair play could hardly be more out of place while German tanks were rumbling across Poland and Japanese troops were slaughtering thousands of innocent Chinese civilians.

During the war years, the hallowed grounds of Wimbledon—the All-England Tennis Club— were used as a civil defense center. With German bombs raining down on London and south Britain, there was no time for the frivolity of grass court tennis. Another crown jewel of tennis establishments, the red clay courts at Roland-Garros in Paris, was turned into a concentration camp during the Nazi occupation of France.

The 1939 U.S. Davis Cup team—Joe Hunt, Frank Parker, Bobby Riggs, and Jack Kramer— lost to Australia, three games to two. It would be the last truly international competition American tennis players would play in until

BELOW: *Don Budge won the Grand Slam in 1938, a year after going head-to-head with German champion Baron Gottfried von Cramm in Davis Cup play. Despite receiving a motivational phone call from Adolf Hitler just before their match, von Cramm couldn't hold off the young American.*

Just a few years later Budge was serving with the Army Air Forces while von Cramm was fighting on the Russian front. Library of Congress photo

after World War II. Within a few years all four members of that 1939 team would be in the armed forces. Riggs joined the Navy and served as an athletic instructor at Hawaii and Guam, often playing tennis matches for the troops throughout the Pacific during lulls in the fighting.

Virtually all of America's top men's players joined the military during the war years. Art Larsen dabbled in tennis prior to joining the Army but never played it seriously. He wound up in France with the Seventeenth Cavalry Squadron as a machine-gunner. "Suddenly, out of nowhere, a fleet of bombers began strafing and bombing us," Larsen recalled. "Our own Air Force had mistaken us for Nazis. Half the troop was killed. I came through unscratched, but then and there I developed the complex I'm still trying to shake."

Larsen would also see action in Belgium and Luxembourg before returning to California, where he would receive psychological treatment for his fear of getting killed in combat. Veterans Administration doctors recommended tennis, which Art picked up with feverish passion, turning his fear into boundless energy . . . and the national singles championship.

Davis Cupper Joe Hunt was a gifted athlete who played varsity football for the Naval Academy before heading to the Pacific aboard a destroyer, followed by a stint in the Atlantic. Along the way he captured the national singles championship in 1943, beating Coast Guardsman and Davis Cup teammate Jack Kramer.

But Hunt yearned to be a flyer, and he transferred to naval aviation. While learning to fly a Grumman Hellcat at Daytona Beach, Navy Lieutenant Joe Hunt lost control of his plane during gunnery practice and crashed at sea. The U.S. Navy lost a fine young pilot. U.S. tennis lost a great champion.

Bryan "Bitsy" Grant was called the Mighty Atom. His near-perpetual crown was the Southern Championship, which he won eleven times in twenty-five years. Among his other wins were the National Clay Court titles in '30, '34, and '35. During World War II he would be assigned to the Fifth Air Force.

Another all-around athlete was Gardnar Mulloy, who played end and halfback for the University of Miami and was on the school's boxing team. But it was on the tennis courts that Gar really made his mark, serving on five Davis Cup teams and pairing up with Billy Talbert to dominate every doubles tourney they entered. As a lieutenant commander in the Navy, Mulloy commanded a landing ship, LST 32—dubbed Mulloy's Joy Ship—which saw action off the coast of Italy and supported the amphibious landings at Sicily, Salerno, Anzio, the Isle of Melba, and southern France. To stay in shape Mulloy even plotted out a tennis court on the deck of a warship and banged tennis balls off the bulkhead, determined to get back into competition as soon as he could.

Though he was forty-three years old and thus exempt from military service, J. Gilbert Hall enlisted in the Army in 1941 and served in Europe with the Eighth Armored Division, commanding a tank crew in the closing months of the war.

The Eighth Armored Division would see action in France, Holland, and Germany, winding up their European Campaign in the Harz Mountains when Germany surrendered. After World War II Hall picked up his racket again and captured the veterans' singles title several years running.

At eighteen, teen phenom Jack Kramer was selected to America's Davis Cup squad, where he teamed up with Joe Hunt. Later he played doubles with Ted Schroeder to capture the national crown, just one of an astonishing string of titles for the pair. Tennis was not Kramer's first ambition, though, when he was growing up. Team sports such as baseball, football, and basketball occupied most of his time, and young Jack looked forward to being a big-league baseball player.

But after being battered in a football game, Jack was encouraged to try something a little less violent—such as tennis, which he had felt was a "sissy game" until he finally tried it and liked it. He won the national interscholastic title when he was seventeen.

In 1943 Kramer joined the Coast Guard but took time off to play in the nationals at Forest Hills, where he lost in the finals to his Davis Cup teammate Joe Hunt. After boot camp Kramer ended up in the Pacific on a landing ship and participated in five island invasions. He would not return to tennis full-time until he left the service in 1946. Within a year he was back at the U.S. Nationals and beat another ex-serviceman, Tom Brown, in the finals. The two met again

BELOW: Two sports superstars—baseball's Babe Ruth and tennis champ Bill Tilden—worked tirelessly during the war years putting on sports exhibitions to raise money for numerous charities. Photo courtesy of the Citizens Savings Hall of Fame

the next year, in the finals at Wimbledon, and Kramer took the title in three sets.

Tom Brown, Jr., was known as the Flailer for his jerky style on the court. After playing collegiate tennis in 1943 with the University of California he joined the Army as a "ground-pounder"—infantry, all the way, for three years.

Another doubles duo separated by the war was Wilmer Allison and Johnny Van Ryn. Allison, national champ in 1935 and known radio enthusiast, joined the Army Air Forces and was given the task of establishing radio relay stations overseas. Ryn chose the Navy for his duty assignment.

J. Edward "Budge" Patty won the national juniors title in '41 and '42 but spent most of his time on the French Riviera. In the service he came back to the states for training and then returned to fight on the European continent he knew so well.

Among the many other nationally ranked amateur and professional tennis players serving in the armed forces were Ramsay Potts, who served as a pilot in the Middle East; collegian Kendall Cramm, who died when his ship was torpedoed in the Pacific; and national amateur champion John Doeg, who was on a convoy run to Murmansk when his ship was torpedoed by a Nazi submarine.

Army Air Forces Sergeant Frank Parker, while stationed at Muroc Field in California, won the U.S. tennis crown in 1944; national champion Ted Schroeder served in the Navy; American Davis Cup team player Lester Stoefen joined the Army; another Davis Cupper, J. Hal Surface, put in two and a half years in the China-Burma-India theater; Tulane college champion Ernie Sutter had his right arm was severely wounded when he was part of the Allied invasion of North Africa.

David Freeman was the junior national tennis champion in singles and doubles in 1937 and U.S. singles badminton champion from 1939 to 1942 and 1947 to 1948. The Pasadena Flash would spend two years in the Army, with the Medical Corps in Panama's Canal Zone.

Other tennis players fighting in World War II were Seattle amateur Bob Vaupell, another pilot decorated for his actions at Guadalcanal; Frank Kovacs, the Clown Prince of Tennis and an Army junior officer in the South Pacific; mixed doubles player Clovey La Croix, who was wounded by shrapnel when the Navy cruiser he was on came under attack while patrolling the South Pacific; Rice champion Frank Guernsey, who served as a pilot in the Aleutians Campaign; and Greg Mangin, who served as a gunner on a Flying Fortess bomber. Dick Savit joined the Navy at the end of WWII and was discharged in 1946. (After the war Savit would rise through the national rankings, winning Wimbledon in 1951.) Pancho Gonzales served briefly in the Navy and then three years after the war captured the U.S. men's singles crown at Forest Hills. He would win again in 1949.

In the mid-1930s, Fred Perry was virtually unstoppable, winning Wimbledon three years straight from 1934 to 1936, the U.S. crown in 1933 and 1934 and again in 1936, plus the Australian Open in 1934, and the French title the next year. During the war he served as a physical training instructor at the Army air base at Santa Ana, California.

When he was young, diabetes prevented Billy Talbert from doing anything strenuous, but doctors would allow him to keep in shape by playing tennis. Talbert not only got his exercise on the courts, he excelled at tennis and was chosen for the junior Davis Cup squad in 1938.

Though his diabetes barred him from enlisting, Talbert worked for the Navy during the war years and continued to play tennis. But he really made his mark as a doubles player, teaming up with Gardnar Mulloy to win the doubles title at Forest Hills in 1942. Their opponents in the title match were two other servicemen, Bob Falkenburg and Jack Tuero.

Together Talbert and Mulloy were invincible, winning eighty-four of the ninety doubles tournaments they played in. Only the disruption of the war years kept this dominant duo from capturing every major tournament.

And then there was a related sport that has never received much recognition in the United States: ping-pong, or table tennis. Prior to World War II, five-time national champ and world doubles champ Sol Schiff had toured Europe, where the sport was very popular.

After joining the military, Private Schiff attempted to hook his barracks buddies at Camp Shelby, Mississippi, into playing ping-pong. And he boldly predicted in 1944 that future champions of the sport would come from the military ranks and would lead the sports surge in popularity.

Supporting the War Effort

When war broke out in Europe in September 1939, German U-boats were prowling the Atlantic, endangering any ships, including luxury liners, caught on the high seas. British tennis player Mary Hardwick was in the United States at the time, and her family urged her not to return home and risk an Atlantic crossing.

As a way to support herself and raise money for the war effort, Hardwick toured the country, holding tennis exhibitions at basic training camps, air bases, and Navy ports. Often after exhibition matches, Hardwick would invite servicemen or -women to try their luck against her. Hardwick raised thousands of dollars for British War Relief, the American and Canadian Red Cross, and the USO.

British Davis Cup player Charles Hare, who had moved to the United States in 1937 and had applied to become a U.S. citizen, traveled with Mary Hardwick as she crisscrossed the country. Eventually they were married. Soon Hare joined the United States Army.

Another tennis player who spent considerable time during the war years playing in exhibition matches to raise millions of dollars was seven-time U.S. National and triple-crown Wimbledon champion Bill Tilden.

During 1944 and '45, in his fifties, Tilden tirelessly traveled around the country, playing in more than two hundred fund-raisers plus exhibitions at military compounds.

Defeating Hitler's Champion

The undisputed king of tennis from 1937 until he joined the Army Air Forces in 1941 was Don Budge, who snared the elusive Grand Slam—the Australian, French, and U.S. championships, and Wimbledon—in 1938. But while only a few tennis champions have won the big four in the same calendar year, Budge considered a Davis Cup match his greatest ever: "I was pitted against Germany's Baron Gottfried von Cramm . . . in 1937," Budge recalled.

The winner of this pairing would still have to meet the defender, England, in the Challenge Round, but in just about everyone's view the 1937 Davis Cup would certainly go to the survivor of the U.S.-Germany meeting. This possibility was not lost on a man called Adolf Hitler, whose Nazi pride was still chafing over the Olympic triumphs in Berlin a year earlier of a non-Aryan named Jesse Ownes and the Black Auxiliaries. Before the match had even begun, Hitler's interest in it was apparent.

While still in the locker room, "Gottfried and I were hustled along so that we hardly had time to

BELOW: It was a potent Davis Cup team for the U.S.—Gardnar Mulloy, Bill Talbert, Frankie Parker, and Ted Schroeder—but with the demands of the military they were all called on to do their part. Parker served with the Army Air Forces in California; Schroeder was in the Navy; Talbert had diabetes and couldn't join the service but he helped out the Navy whenever they needed him. Mulloy excelled at football and boxing with the University of Miami, then teamed up with Talbert to play doubles tennis. During his stint with the Navy, he commanded "Mulloy's Joy Ship," a landing transport that saw plenty of action during landings in Italy and southern France. AP Wide World photo

acknowledge each other," Budge said. The club phone rang, and an attendant picked it up. Al Laney recalled the conversation in his article, "Budge-Von Cramm Davis Cup Match."

"'Mr. von Cramm,' he said. 'Long distance for you sir.'

"'Yes, hello. This is Gotfried Cramm.' He spoke English impeccably. Gottfried finished speaking to the operator and suddenly switched to German. 'Ja, mein Fuhrer,' was the first thing he said.

"He said, in fact, little else but 'Ja, mein Fuhrer,' for the rest of the conversation. He spoke with respect but showed no emotion. Finally, after a couple of minutes or so, Cramm hung up.

"'Excuse me, gentlemen,' Gottfried said matter-of-factly. 'It was Hitler. I don't know why he called me,' That was all he offered and there was time for no more.

"I think one reason why Gottfried irritated the Nazis so particularly in refusing to go along with them was that he looked and acted exactly as the Nazi propaganda said all Germans should. He was six feet tall, with blond hair, of course, and cold blue eyes, and a face that was handsome to a fault. And more, Gottfried emitted a personal magnetism that made him dominate any scene he was a part of."

Budge would go on to win the hard-fought match against an opponent he had the highest respect for on the tennis court.

But a few short years later, America would declare war on Nazi Germany, and the match between Budge and von Cramm—just as Jesse Owens's and the Black Auxiliaries' achievements at the 1936 Olympics—would be looked back on as America's earliest victories against Hitler's Aryan "supermen."

Both Budge and von Cramm took up arms, Budge serving in the U.S. Army Air Forces and his German rival fighting the Russians on the Eastern Front, where he would be wounded. Budge would tear a muscle in his right shoulder while running an Army obstacle course. The injury would limit his mobility with a tennis racket, and he would never regain his dominance in the sport he loved.

Welcoming Back a Defeated Combatant

By May 1945 Germany was defeated. Four months later, Japan would call it quits. In the tennis world, one player signified the tragic toll the war in Europe had taken on its combatants.

As part of the Axis powers, Austrian men, including tennis star Hans Redl, fought beside Germany and Italy. Redl would lose his arm in combat, yet when he returned to play at Wimbledon, the crowd did not boo this former enemy. They cheered and in doing so signified that sportsmanship and fair play were once again in style.

8. Nazi Wolf Packs Terrorize the Atlantic

> "SPEED IS UNFORTUNATELY A MOST EXPENSIVE COMMODITY: ALIKE IN BATTLESHIPS, MOTOR CARS, RACE HORSES AND WOMEN, A COMPARATIVELY SMALL INCREASE IN SPEED MAY DOUBLE THE PRICE OF THE ARTICLE."
>
> — *Lord Archibald Wavell, 1931*

OPPOSITE: *An Allied tanker smolders after being hit by torpedoes from a Nazi U-boat. During the Atlantic Campaign more than 2,600 Allied ships were sunk. Toledo University football star Emlen Tunnell joined the Coast Guard and survived two torpedo attacks during Atlantic crossings. Amateur tennis player John Doeg ended up in the drink when his ship was also torpedoed during his first trans-Atlantic journey.* U.S. Naval Institute photo

THE ENGLISH CHANNEL WAS NOT WIDE ENOUGH IN THE LATE 1930s to keep Hitler from picking a fight with the British, who turned to the United States for help. President Roosevelt listened to Winston Churchill's pleas for assistance and agreed to send ships, planes, and supplies to Britain under a Lend Lease Agreement, but FDR avoided a full commitment, refusing to declare war against the Axis until the Japanese made it unavoidable when they attacked Pearl Harbor.

As those transport ships loaded with fuel, food, and supplies and manned by American sailors departed U.S. territorial waters, many were attacked by German submarines, known as U-boats, roaming the Atlantic and waiting to pounce.

Terrorizing the Junction

More than 2,400 seamen perished when 120 U.S. and Allied ships were sunk along America's East Coast, nicknamed Torpedo Junction by the brave men who sailed the Atlantic. Even though their country was not yet officially a participant in World War II, young American men were already fighting and dying to help defend England against the Nazis.

All along the eastern seaboard, cities were under blackout restrictions so those transport ships heading out to sea wouldn't be silhouetted and thus easy targets for the U-boats lurking in the darkness.

On the night of May 12, 1942, the lights at New York baseball stadiums—the Polo Grounds and Ebbets Field—were intentionally left on to find out if they served as a beacon for Nazi subs prowling off shore. Within the week it was decided not to tempt fate. All Giants and Dodgers games would be played during daylight hours, and night games were either canceled or rescheduled. Other stadiums on both the East and West Coasts also curtailed games after dusk as a precaution against enemy assassins and nautical snipers.

ABOVE: *Running back Marshall "Biggie" Goldberg was an All-American with the Pitt Panthers in 1937 and '38. During WWII he saw action in the Navy, in both the Atlantic and Pacific campaigns.* Photo courtesy of University of Pittsburgh

Enemy Probes Come Ashore

Another concern was enemy saboteurs sneaking ashore and unleashing a wave of terror. In fact, on June 13, 1942, a four-man team of Nazi commandos slipped through the coastal beach patrols at Amagansett on Long Island, New

York. Four days later another team sneaked ashore at Ponte Vedra, Florida. Their mission was to blow up aluminum plants in Tennessee, New York, and Illinois; Philadelphia's cryolite plant; plus rail hubs and waterways as far west as St. Louis and Cincinnati.

All eight Nazi spies were eventually caught and tried, without publicity. But their ability to penetrate American defenses after being dropped off by Nazi U-boats sparked an intensive effort to plug the holes in America's coastal defenses and prevent any further probes.

ABOVE: *Convoy duty in the Atlantic was dangerous, as lookouts maintained a constant watch for Nazi submarines, known as U-boats, which worked together in Wolf Packs to pounce on a convoy and sink as many ships as possible before moving off to wait for another convoy.*
National Archives photo

Those Menacing Wolf Packs

Farther out in the Atlantic, the U-boats worked together in what became known as Wolf Packs to attack the vulnerable convoys of ships steaming for northern Europe.

German Luftwaffe fighter planes and bombers based in France and later in Scandinavia also harassed the Allied convoys as they approached the European continent. Hundreds of ships and thousands of men perished in the icy waters of the North Atlantic, many only a few hours from safe harbor.

From September 3, 1939, when Britain and France declared war on Germany, until the end of World War II nearly six years later, more than 2,600 Allied ships were sunk in the Atlantic alone, claiming thousands of lives. Many more sailors and merchantmen were left clinging to life rafts and other debris floating on the choppy seas, hoping to be rescued by friendly ships after theirs succumbed to U-boat torpedoes. But in the frigid regions of the Atlantic, numbness could overcome a seaman within minutes, and many perished in the icy deep.

One of those seamen tossed overboard during an enemy attack was amateur tennis champion and 1930 U.S. Open winner John Doeg, who was on his first Atlantic convoy crossing to Murmansk when his ship was torpedoed.

Enduring Two Torpedo Hits

Emlen Tunnell had broken his neck while playing football at Toledo University and was told he should never attempt to play again, but the next year he was back on the gridiron.

LEFT: *Thousands of Americans were buried at sea or perished when their ships were torpedoed in the Atlantic.* U.S. Coast Guard photo

BELOW: *Iowa running back Nile Kinnick won the Heisman trophy in 1939, and was America's most popular athlete that year, according to the Associated Press. Just days before the Japanese attacked Pearl Harbor, Kinnick was called to active duty with the Navy. He was stationed in the Caribbean, flying a Navy Wildcat fighter plane, searching out Nazi U-boats in the area, when, in early June of 1943 his plane had engine trouble and plunged into the Gulf of Paria. No trace of the plane or Iowa's favorite son has yet been found.* Photo courtesy of the University of Iowa

After being rejected by the Army and Navy, Tunnell joined the Coast Guard. Whenever he got time off, Tunnell would continue to play football, mostly on weekends for the New London, Connecticut, team known as the Fleet City Bluejackets. But eventually he would be assigned to patrol duty and survived two torpedo attacks during Atlantic convoy runs.

(After the war Tunnell would return to the University of Iowa and then became the first black to take the field with the New York Giants. He earned nine Pro Bowl selections and induction to the Pro Football Hall of Fame in 1967. Among Emlen the Gremlin's achievements were 79 interceptions [74 with the Giants and 5 with Green Bay], 1,282 interception return yards, 258 punt returns [8 in a game against the New York Yanks, on December 3, 1950] totaling 2,209 yards, with 5 punts returned for touchdowns.)

The Privateers

Instead of signing up for one of the armed services, some men chose to join the Merchant Marine, which was very much like the Navy armed guard, but they worked for private shipping companies and their pay was much better. Their jobs were just as dangerous because they served on ships crossing both oceans, and German and Japanese submarines, ships, and planes were looking to attack and sink these cargo vessels.

One of pro football's greatest quarterbacks, Sid Luckman of the Chicago Bears, interrupted his Hall of Fame career to sign on with the Merchant Marine and brave those North Atlantic sea journeys, where German U-boats cruised just below the surface.

Luckman had piloted the Bears to the league title in '40, '41, and '43, demolishing the Redskins 73–0 in 1940. In his final championship game before joining the Merchant Marine, Luckman threw five touchdown passes and beat the Redskins 41–21.

(After serving two years of dangerous convoy duty on an oil tanker, Luckman would return to the Bears and again lead them to the league championship in 1946, beating the New York Giants 24–14.)

Texas Longhorns all-conference fullback Bobby Layne and Southern Methodist's Doak Walker had been teammates at Highland Park High School but became rivals in college. Both set aside stellar collegiate careers to join the Merchant Marine and brave the treacherous Atlantic. Both would return to college and rack up All-America honors. (Layne later switched to quarterback and joined the pros in 1948, playing with the Chicago Bears, New York Bulldogs, Detroit Lions, and Pittsburgh Steelers during a fourteen-year all-pro career. Walker scored 128 points his all-pro rookie season in 1950 with Detroit, joining up again with his high school teammate Bobby Layne.)

One of America's greatest athletes, Jim Thorpe, was a merchant mariner on a transport ship carrying delicate cargo: ammunition. The military considered him too old to serve, so he volunteered as a privateer, in one of the most treacherous jobs on the high seas. In his prime Thorpe was an athletic superman, winning gold medals in the decathlon and pentathlon at the 1912 Olympic Games in Stockholm, followed by seven years playing big-league baseball, from 1913 to 1919, and pro football from 1915 to 1929.

Former World Lightweight Boxing Champion Benny Leonard, who retired from boxing undefeated in 1925, was a prominent Jewish boxer who spoke out against anti-Semitism and served with the Merchant Marine for several years before returning to the ring as a referee.

Charlie "King Kong" Keller was a key player on the Yankees' World Series team in 1939, clobbering opposing pitchers for a .438 average. His numbers fell off in the '41 through '43 Fall Classics, but he still compiled a respectable .306 average. In 1944 and 1945 he was prowling the waterways with the Merchant Marine. Injuries after the war limited his baseball appearances, and he finally hung it up after two games in 1952.

Turning the Tables

Those dangerous ocean crossings—sending supplies and personnel to Europe—had to continue despite the dangers of the deep if the Allies had any hope of penetrating Fortress Europe and defeating the Nazis.

ABOVE: *Columbia All-American quarterback Sid Luckman joined the Chicago Bears and led them to the NFL crown in 1940 and '41, then again two years later. He then joined the Merchant Marine and served on an oil tanker traversing the Atlantic.* Photo courtesy of Columbia University

Notre Dame quarterback Johnny Lujack served on a Navy subchaser for eleven months, stalking those menacing U-boats and sending them to their doom. (In 1946 Lujack returned to the Fighting Irish; he posted Heisman numbers the next year.)

Oklahoma lineman Plato Andros prowled the Atlantic sea-lanes on a Coast Guard ship. So did New York Giants first baseman Babe Young. After playing from 1936 to 1942, Babe joined the service and headed to sea for the next three years, returning to the Giants for the 1946 season. (He was traded to Cincinnati the next year and again to the St. Louis Cardinals in 1948, then called it quits.)

Cleveland Indians fireball pitcher Bob Feller served on the USS *Alabama* in charge of a gun crew. Though convoy duty in the North Atlantic kept him busy, Rapid Robert stayed in shape: "I had my rowing machine, my punching bag in the boiler room where it was hotter than hell. And I did my chin-ups and push-ups, and skipping a rope, and running around the ship on my jogging track. Had guys aboard ship lined up waiting to take turns catching for me.

"Even when you're standing around the guns doing nothing, you can do push-ups, deep knee bends, deep breathing exercises, high kicking exercises, stretching exercises. There's all these things you can hang from to keep your muscles in shape."

(Opposing American League batters probably wished he wasn't in such great shape; when Feller returned to the Indians in mid-August of 1945, he picked up without missing a beat, striking out twelve Detroit Tigers batters in his first game back.)

Other athletes serving in the Navy and deployed to the Atlantic included Pitt Panthers all-American running back Marshall "Biggie" Goldberg; Navy running back Jonas Ingram, who had received the Medal of Honor in World War I and would rise through the ranks to be commander of the Atlantic Fleet in 1944; and Duke end Jim Smith, on the destroyer escort USS *Rich*.

With improvements in radar and sonar equipment, the breaking of the Nazis' Enigma codes, and deployment of escorting warships to attack the attackers, the Allies began to chase off the Wolf Packs and sink the no-longer-elusive U-boats. Soon the Nazis abandoned the Atlantic Campaign, and the Allies stepped up the massive resupply efforts, which contributed greatly to the fall of the Nazi regime.

BELOW: *Coast Guardsmen on a destroyer escort celebrate the sinking of a Nazi U-boat in the Atlantic.* U.S. Coast Guard photo

Guarding the Southern Flank

With Nazi U-boats also prowling the waters off South America and threatening the southern coast of the United States, the military maintained a lookout post on Bermuda and kept a garrison in Panama.

Naturally, wherever Americans were stationed, they played sports in their spare time. In Panama they played baseball and attracted the attention of the curious San Blas Indians, who quickly took up America's sport and gave it their own twist.

Assigned to work in Army mess halls, these diminutive locals eventually approached their GI friends to learn the fundamentals of the game. One of those American players was Corporal Mickey Harris, former Boston Red Sox pitcher. The San Blas players quickly caught on. Because of their size they lacked the power to hit home runs, so they relied on speed and daring to score runs. They played baseball in their bare feet, maintained a constant pidgin-English chatter, and added their own dash and flare to the game. On simple grounders, an infielder would scoop up the ball, roll a few times in the dirt, and zip the ball to first base just in time to nail the runner.

Batters added their own dazzle running the bases, all to the amazement of American GIs, who would someday return home and tell their friends about the acrobatic San Blas Indians of Panama.

BELOW: *Outposts such as Fort Victoria on Bermuda and other Atlantic sites (including Newfoundland, Greenland, and Iceland) were built up and manned to support naval operations and monitor enemy activity in the region.* National Archives photo

Golfers Tee Off Against the Axis

"IT IS ALMOST IMPOSSIBLE TO REMEMBER HOW TRAGIC A PLACE THE WORLD IS WHEN ONE IS PLAYING GOLF."

—*Professor Robert Lynd*

AMERICAN GOLFER CRAIG WOOD WON THE U.S. OPEN IN 1941, and despite a bad back that kept him from enlisting in the Marines, he held the title for five consecutive years. Of course, it helped that by 1943 most of the top golfers, both amateur and pro, were in the armed forces. But the simple reason why Wood held his Open title throughout the war was because the tourney was suspended until 1946.

Like all sports in America, golf made sacrifices in support of the war effort. Many of the tournaments that were held from 1942 through 1945 offered their champions war bonds instead of prize money. While bonds had a cash value, they could not be redeemed until after the war.

As in other sports, golf exhibitions were staged throughout the country to raise money for various national support agencies. In late 1942 the U.S. Golf Association announced that 430 golf courses had raised $116,376 for war relief, plus an additional $906,767 in war bonds and stamps.

Spectators were asked to donate to local blood banks, which set up tents nearby, and to bring scrap aluminum and tin foil, grease, and fat.

The defense industry needed rubber to make, among many things, tires and fan belts, fuel hoses, and life rafts. By November 1943 the Professional Golfers' Association was asking local duffers to bring in used and damaged golf balls so the rubber cores could be sent to war plants and reprocessed for use in tanks, jeeps, trucks, and planes.

BELOW: *While stationed in North Africa in 1943, Staff Sergeant Ted Bodle, Jr., visited the pyramids of Egypt. After climbing the Pyramid of Cheops, Bodle teed up a golf ball and hit into the largest sand bunker on Earth!* U.S. Air Force photo

Despite the many exhibitions and fund-raisers, and with most of the top players in uniform, numerous courses, denied the annual income from tournaments, were close to bankruptcy. The Army and Navy, working closely with the Red Cross, considered utilizing golf course clubhouses as convalescent homes or contingency hospitals for wounded servicemen. Situated away from downtown areas, which could be vulnerable to enemy bombs, golf courses offered pleasant surroundings to recuperating GIs. As part of their rehabilitation therapy, amputees wounded in the war were also encouraged to try golfing, not only to give them something to do but to show them that their physical losses did not have to prevent them from playing golf or other sports they had enjoyed before the war.

Other golf courses, such as the Bayshore in Miami, with their expanses of flat land, were used as military training centers. Mock battles involving large numbers of troops could be conducted, sand traps could be turned into dummy minefields, and water traps could be bridged by engineer units.

Among the many nationally ranked golfers who served in the armed forces during World War II were Porky Oliver, considered the first to be drafted, in early 1941; Horton Smith, who drilled at Miami Bayshore (without his golf clubs); Iowa Open champion Denmar Miller, who joined the Army; Lawson Little and Lew Worsham, who joined the Navy; Jimmy Thomson, who signed on with the Coast Guard; and former Publinks champion Frankie Strafaci, who ended up in the South Pacific and gave golf lessons to earn pocket money. Though he was working in a defense plant in Durham, North Carolina, and thus exempt from military service, Charlie Sifford (who would be called the sport's Jackie Robinson in 1961) served with the Twenty-fourth Infantry Division on Okinawa during the Pacific Campaign. Clayton Heafner joined the Army; Missouri's Bob Willits commanded a Navy amphibious boat in the Pacific, earning the Bronze Star for his exploits; and 1938 intercollegiate champion Johnny Burke was killed in North Africa.

Slammin' Sammy Snead joined the Navy and quickly established his shooting skills on the rifle range at the Norfolk Naval Training Station. At the 1942 PGA tournament at

RIGHT: *After joining the Army in 1942, Staff Sergeant Johnny Moran played exhibition golf for Allied troops stationed in Australia and New Zealand. He even played with Fiji bushmen wearing grass skirts.* U.S. Army photo

Atlantic City, Snead would head into the final round tied with another GI, Army Corporal Jim Turnesa. Snead would pull out the win after thirty-six holes of match play.

In 1923 Bobby Jones won the National Open, his first major tournament title. During the next eight years he would dominate the golf world, winning the 1930 Grand Slam—at that time the British Amateur, British Open, U.S. Open, and U.S. Amateur titles. (The modern Grand Slam comprises the PGA Championships, the Masters, and the British and U.S. Opens.)

ABOVE AND BACK-GROUND: *Grand Slam champion Bobby Jones was practically unbeatable from 1923 through '30. During the war years he served with the Eighth Air Force during the bombing campaign of Fortress Europe.* AP Wide World photo

Sportswriter Grantland Rice wrote about Bobby Jones's greatness in 1940, saying: "There is no more chance that golf will give the world another Jones than there is that literature will produce another Shakespeare, sculpture another Phidias, music another Chopin."

Back problems would plague Jones during the 1930s. Then in 1942 he joined the Army Air Corps, serving as a lieutenant colonel with the Eighth Air Force in Europe.

Ben Hogan dominated the pro tour from 1940 to 1942, and then, like Bobby Jones, he joined the Army Air Forces for the remainder of the war. While stationed in Texas he played in and won the Texas Victory Open, earning him a five-hundred-dollar war bond. (After the war Hogan picked up where he had left off, winning the PGA title in 1946 and again two years later. He was also named PGA Player of the Year in '48, '50, '51, and '53—the same years he won the U.S. Open.)

Lloyd Mangrum joined the Army and was wounded fighting at the Battle of the Bulge. He would come back from the European Campaign as the sport's most celebrated hero and enter the 1946 U.S. Open, held in July in Cleveland.

Among the other ex-servicemen who played at the Open were Lawson Little, Ben Hogan, and Vic Ghezzi. Mangrum, Ghezzi, and Byron Nelson (turned down by the military because he suffered from hemophilia) tied in the final round and ended up going head-to-head in two play-off rounds before Mangrum pulled out a one-stroke win.

9. GIs Get First Test in North Africa

"OF ALL THE AMERICAN TROOPS WHO WERE ABOUT TO BUST THEIR TRACES TO GET INTO BATTLE, I SUPPOSE THE RANGERS WERE THE WORST. THAT WAS BECAUSE THEY HAD BEEN TRAINED LIKE RACE HORSES, AND IF THEY COULDN'T RACE EVERYDAY THEY GOT TO PAWING THE GROUND."

—*Ernie Pyle,* Here Is Your War

OPPOSITE: *German anti-aircraft guns at Algiers, North Africa, create a wall of flak as Allied bombers and fighter escorts approach overhead.* U.S. Army Signal Corps photo

HITLER NOT ONLY FORMULATED PLANS TO CONTROL ALL OF the countries within striking distance of Germany, he also set his sights on North Africa to protect the underbelly of Europe.

The British and French had interests on the southern shores of the Mediterranean Sea and had established a military presence there to protect their investments. Hitler and Italian dictator Benito Mussolini viewed these forces as a threat and sent their own troops, including Nazi Germany's best tanks and crewmen—referred to as the Afrika Korps—to drive the Allies out of North Africa.

The French were splintered into opposing factions, some pro-Nazi, some neutral, and others pro-Allies. This bewildering situation in North Africa was dubbed "the goddamned French political mess"—which only confounded the Allies when it came time to establish a toehold in North Africa and try to figure out who was friend or foe.

Comparison of the Opposing Leaders

In November 1942 transport ships from both England and the United States headed for the North African coast with more than 107,000 Allied troops aboard, 75 percent of whom were Americans. (Another 200,000 GIs and Brits would arrive soon after the initial invasion force was ashore.)

Overseeing the invasion of North Africa, dubbed Operation Torch, was Army General Dwight D. Eisenhower. Opposing him was German commander Erwin Rommel, architect of the powerful Afrika Korps. In their youth both had been active in sports: Eisenhower played minor league baseball and was a varsity football player at West Point until sidelined by a leg injury. Rommel enjoyed rowing, tennis, and cycling in the summer; skiing and skating in winter.

ABOVE: *General Dwight D. Eisenhower oversaw the invasion of North Africa, in November of 1942.* National Archives photo

BELOW: *Troop transport ships from England and the United States converged on North Africa in November 1942. To pass the time, many of the GIs listened to broadcasts of college football games piped in over ship intercoms.* U.S. Army photo

Another hard-charging American general was often compared to the imposing Rommel and even had the audacity to challenge the Nazi commander to a one-on-one duel . . . in tanks: "The two armies could watch. I'd shoot at him, he'd shoot at me," explained the flamboyant George S. Patton, Jr. "If I killed him, I'd be the champ. If he killed me . . . well, he won't."

Patton and General Lucian Truscott, two noted horsemen and polo players, led the invasion force. Both commanders were nearly killed during the invasion of North Africa.

To pass the time, the American soldiers, who were crammed onto transport ships steaming the Atlantic south to the Mediterranean and waiting for the signal to storm ashore, listened to a scratchy shortwave transmission of the football game between the Army Black Nights and the Notre Dame Fighting Irish.

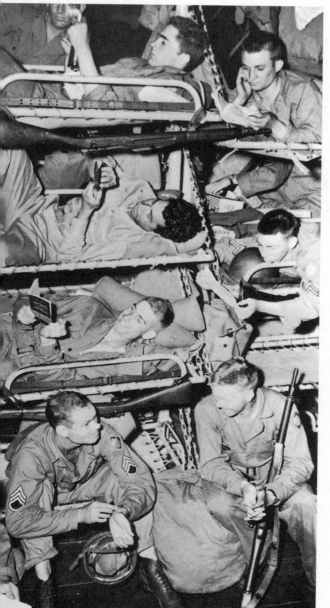

A Make or Break Mission

For the first time, American paratroopers would be sent into combat. Leading the 509th Parachute Infantry Battalion was former West Point swimmer Lieutenant Colonel Edson Raff, who knew his untested airborne troops might have a very short history if their performance in the invasion of North Africa was less than stellar: "Enormous stakes are involved. Not only will we spearhead the invasion, but the future of the paratroops is on the line. If we do well, the airborne will be greatly expanded. If we fail our paratroop units may be disbanded."

Naval Guns Pound the Coast

Prior to troops storming ashore or descending from overhead, naval warships shelled the North African coastal fortifications.

On the warship *Augusta*, flagship for the invasion fleet, the crackle of the ship's loudspeaker announced the opening salvo with the simple chant, "Play Ball!"

One of those naval officers in charge of the gun batteries on his ship was Lieutenant Commander Al Helfer, who had been a four-sport letterman at Pennsylvania's Washington and Jefferson College. He boxed as a heavyweight, played basketball, and ran track, but it was as a bruising fullback who "liked meeting obstacles head on" that Helfer made his mark as a collegian. It was a trait that would carry him well in battle.

After the naval bombardment, thousands of Allied soldiers boarded landing ships and scrambled onto the beaches of North Africa, some under hostile fire from the French, others without any opposition.

Soldiers from a battalion of the First Armored Division—Old Ironsides—joked that the invasion was a cakewalk, that the opposing French forces were merely flicked aside. But their commander, Lieutenant Colonel John Waters, abruptly set his men straight, telling them, "We did very well against the scrub team. [But] next week we hit German troops. When we make a showing against them, you may congratulate yourselves."

Athletes Participate in Torch

West Point cross-country runner George "Bizz" Moore was a forward observer attached to the Ninth Infantry Division—the Varsity Division—during Operation Torch in southern Tunisia when he was wounded in an artillery barrage.

(By July 1948 Moore would be in London competing in the Twelfth Olympiad. His event was the modern pentathlon—a grueling juggernaut that included a 300-meter swim, 5,000-meter steeplechase, pistol shooting, the épée (fencing), and 4,000-meter cross-country run. After five days of competition, Moore would win the silver medal.)

Jack Tripson, who played football with the Detroit Lions, received the Navy Cross—one of the most prestigious of military awards—for his bravery during the invasion. Ernie Sutter, Tulane University's tennis ace, shattered his arm during the assault, and pro halfback Max Partin was also wounded at Tunisia.

Also participating in the Tunisian Campaign was former New York Giants second baseman Andy Cohen, the Tuscaloose Terror, who served with the Twenty-first Engineers and would spend a year in North Africa.

Kansas City Monarchs catcher James "Joe" (or "Pea") Greene was one of the earliest Black Americans to see combat in World War II: "I was in the Ninety-second Division; all colored. But we were all put together with different nationalities as allies. I was in Oran, Algiers . . . in a 57-millimeter antitank company."

LEFT: *Colonel George "Bizz" Moore was a forward observer with the 9th Infantry Division during the North Africa Campaign. After WWII Moore would represent the United States in the Twelfth Olympiad, participating in the modern pentathlon, winning the silver medal.* 9th Infantry Division photo

BELOW: *Among the more than 300,000 soldiers who participated in the North Africa Campaign was Marquette and Cleveland Rams tackle Ed Niemi. After the war he would return home and play for the Chicago Cardinals.* U.S. Army photo

A Paratrooper Who Wasn't

When one American soldier spotted two other soldiers parachuting into Allied territory in North Africa, he became suspicious. Although they were wearing American uniforms, it was odd for just two paratroopers to be descending from above. It should have been hundreds filling the skies.

The suspicious GI pointed his rifle at the two intruders and asked them baseball questions that any American would know the answers to— "Who's the best pitcher for da Bums? What did the Splendid Splinter bat last year?"

When the two bluffed, saying they hadn't heard the latest sports news, the GI knew he had two German spies, trying to drop in behind the lines.

Providing Air Cover

Transport, bomber, and fighter planes were all used in support of the Allied troops, and American athletes played key roles as pilots and crew members.

Second Lieutenant Rocky Byrne, a fighter pilot with the Sixty-fourth Fighter Squadron, played two seasons of minor league baseball before joining the Army Air Corps in 1940. Within days of arriving in Cairo in late October 1942, Byrne was in a dogfight with German fighter planes. On April 26, 1943, after shooting down his fifth and sixth enemy planes, his own P-40 was hit. He was wounded, yet he managed to nurse his plane back to home base.

Walter Scholl, passer for Cornell, flew seventy-two missions and shot down three German planes over North Africa. And tennis star Ramsay Potts was awarded the Air Medal for his actions in the Middle East.

Battling the Afrika Korps

After brief skirmishes with French forces who supported Nazi Germany, the Allies took control of the North African coastal regions of French Morocco and Algeria. Some of the French forces were treated as prisoners of war, while others immediately became Allies in the fight against the Nazis.

Among the French servicemen in North Africa was welterweight boxing champion Marcel Cerdan, who served with the Free French Navy.

With the western African coast secured, the Allies could now establish bases and prepare to fight the fearsome tanks of the Nazi Afrika Korps.

Initially the battle-tested Nazi panzer tankers out-muscled the American tank crews. But by May 1943, with Allied fighter planes there to even the score, it was the Americans and the British who were inflicting the most damage. The Nazis were on the run, retreating east toward Egypt.

But the Nazis still had plenty of punch. "We got shelled every morning at 5:00 at El Alamein [just west of Cairo]. You could set your watch by it," recalled former Olympic gold medalist Ray Barbuti, who won the 400-meter dash and 4x400-meter relay at the 1928 Games in Amsterdam. "I can recall that before I joined the Army I was a rough guy to get out of bed. At El Alamein I found out that I had to get out and into my slit trench by 4:30 if I wanted to stay alive."

LEFT: *B-25 bombers from the Ninth Air Force conducted sorties against enemy fortifications and convoys in the desert of North Africa in 1943.* Army Air Force photo

Missing in Action

During the chaos of battle, it was quite common for GIs to end up as missing in action. They may have been wounded during the chaos of battle and were transported to a field hospital, while their unit continued on without them, only later realizing someone was missing. Other soldiers were captured by the enemy and sent to prisoner of war camps until the end of the war. Still others were shot and buried by the enemy in unmarked graves.

Among the missing in North Africa were Eddie "Buzzer" Berlinski, North Carolina State University football star; Tom Borders, who played football for Alabama in 1938, including a Rose Bowl appearance; and Manhattan College quarter-mile runner Johnny Quigley, who was wounded, came up missing, and later made it back to his infantry unit.

Preparing for the Invasion of Europe

Europe's underbelly was now in Allied control, though not without a heavy cost: the Germans and Italians had lost more than 32,000 men in the North Africa Campaign, while the Americans lost 3,300. More than 238,000 Germans and Italians had been taken prisoner; only 3,102 American GIs had fallen into enemy hands.

BELOW: *Infantrymen weary of trekking everywhere they went quickly learned two basic rules: never pass up any opportunity to relieve yourself or to get off your feet.*

Obviously this soldier took that second rule to heart! U.S. Army photo

One of the German casualties was Luz Long, the 1936 Olympic long jumper who had been bested by American Olympian Jesse Owens. The two had remained long-distance friends, and just days before being killed, sensing his own death, Luz Long wrote a final letter to Owens, the competitor he loved like a brother.

Johnny Burke, the 1938 intercollegiate golf champion, and Foy Draper, a member of the 4x100-meter relay team that won the gold medal at the Berlin Olympics, were also killed during the fighting in North Africa.

. . . of graves and graves and graves. That is our war, and we will carry it with us as we go on from one battleground to another until it is all over, leaving some of us behind on every beach, in every field," wrote Ernie Pyle in *Here Is Your War.*

We are just beginning with the ones who lie back of us here in Tunisia. I don't know whether it was their good fortune or their misfortune to get out of it so early in the game. I guess it doesn't make any difference, once a man has gone. Medals and speeches and victories are nothing to them any more.

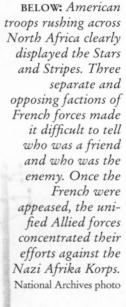

Time for Sports

With the vaunted Afrika Korps now in shambles, Allied air bases and naval ports were rapidly constructed for the tons of supplies and thousands of men that would be arriving soon. Army camps were erected almost overnight, despite the choking desert sands and blast-furnace temperatures.

Among the thousands of military construction workers at North Africa was Navy Sea Bee Deb Copenhaver, former jockey and budding rodeo cowboy. For two years he would manhandle a bulldozer while constructing airstrips on the desert sand. (In December 1945 he returned home and joined the rodeo circuit, taking top honors as World Champion Saddle Bronc Rider in 1955 and '56.)

ABOVE: *Major General George "Blood and Guts" Patton, on board a landing craft, was one of the commanders directing the invasion of North Africa, dubbed Operation Torch.* National Archives photo

Allied bombers took off from those hastily constructed North African airstrips and were soon flying over European cities, blowing up oil refineries and aircraft factories, railroad lines and electrical power plants.

Preparations were being made to strike hard at the Axis powers on the far side of the Mediterranean. Within months an invasion force of Allied troops would cross the Mediterranean and begin the final push toward ending Hitler's domination of Fortress Europe.

But of course, even though the heat and the dust and dirt made it difficult to march in formation or to practice firing their rifles, nothing could stop the Americans in North Africa from a little friendly sports competition when they weren't fighting the Nazis.

But in the rush to ship supplies and equipment overseas, sports gear was not high on the list of combat essentials in 1942. Rather than just sit around and play cards or checkers, the GIs in North Africa looked around for adequate substitutes.

The men used ax handles for baseball bats, much like playing stickball back on the side streets of New York. Army canteens became footballs until dented out of shape. Basketball was mostly a passing game in the 1940s, with very little dribbling, so a balled up uniform tied tight with bootlaces served as an adequate ball. And, just like the old days, an empty box with the bottom

cut out and nailed to a post or a tree became the basket. For some games against nearby British units, the troops used an English soccer ball to play basketball.

Sergeant Manuel Centanio preferred to use that soccer ball to play the sport it was intended for. The former star of the Brooklyn Hispanos and New York Americans soccer squads found enough GIs in Cairo to form four teams that took to the dusty fields of Africa against their Egyptian hosts.

Boxing was always a crowd-pleaser among the French, British, and American troops, with each country putting its best fighters in the ring. The men were separated into amateur and professional brackets.

Some of the more prominent boxers in North Africa included Ezzard Charles and former heavyweight champion Jack Sharkey. Best overall among the Allied boxers in North Africa, though, was not an American but French sailor Marcel Cerdan, welterweight European champion.

During an Allied swim meet in North Africa, one onlooker laughed at the winning time for one of the distance races, boasting that he could have beaten it by several minutes. He hadn't planned to compete in any of the swimming events, at least not until race officials finally dared him to prove his claim by entering the 5,000-meter endurance race. He agreed, and he won the event easily. Only then did he reveal that he was Navy Lieutenant Joe Brock, Big Ten swimming champion from the University of Illinois.

On New Year's Day in 1944—a day when the best collegiate football teams annually played in bowl games back home in the United States—the Arab Bowl was held in Oran, North Africa. Former pro and college players now in the Army and Navy banged heads, without any shoulder pads or helmets, in a game of touch football. Despite the dust swirling up and the heat pushing everyone to exhaustion, the Army all-stars pulled out a win, 10–7, on a last-second field goal.

In an earlier game among the top two teams in the North African Athletic Conference, the Casablanca Rab Chasers squeaked out a one-point victory over the Oran Termites.

Later in '44 the Army and Navy units in North Africa decided to hold a World Series of their own. The baseball field they plotted out on the beach didn't have any fences. Balls hit past the outfielders could roll forever, unless they were hit into right field. Those bouncers ended up in the nearby Mediterranean Sea! To solve the problem, Italian prisoners of war from area camps stood along the beach to stop the runaway baseballs.

And a final note about North Africa: When a local Arab wanted to learn how to play American baseball, one GI volunteered to teach him, but the lessons wouldn't be free. Former major league first baseman Zeke Bonura—who played with the White Sox, Senators, and Giants from 1934 to 1940—gladly taught the Arab sportsman how to catch, throw, and hit a ball, in exchange for free rides on his majestic Arabian stallion.

ABOVE: *Lieutenant Mohammed Derrar of the Spahis French Cavalry with his prized stallion in North Africa, February 1944.* Army Signal Corps photo

Negro Leagues Ballplayers Also Served

"BASEBALL NEEDS NO DEFENDERS OR JUSTIFICATION. IT IS PART OF THE VERY FABRIC OF OUR SOCIETY—JUST AS MUCH AS IF IT WERE WRITTEN INTO OUR CONSTITUTION.

"[THE GAME] HAS BEEN PART OF THE GROWTH OF AMERICA. THIS WAS NEVER MORE APPARENT THAN DURING THE DAYS OF THE WAR WHEN THE ENTIRE NATION FOUND IN BASEBALL A GREAT AND CERTAIN TRANQUILIZER THAT WAS AS VITAL TO OUR SECURITY AS THE SWORD AND SHIELD OF OUR ARMED MIGHT."

—*Senator Kenneth Keating*

BELOW: *On a troop transport bound for Europe, black soldiers were bunked "on the shelf," which meant in the lower decks of the ship.* Army Signal Corps photo

SOON AFTER WORLD WAR I, AND BECAUSE MAJOR LEAGUE Baseball would not allow black ballplayers to participate, a group of businessmen and sports enthusiasts got together in Kansas City to create the Negro National League, in mid-February of 1920. The teams included the Chicago American Giants, Indianapolis ABCs, Detroit Stars, Cuban Stars (of Cincinnati), St. Louis Giants, and Kansas City Monarchs.

One month later the Southern Negro League was created. These teams included the Nashville Elite Giants, Chattanooga Black Lookouts, Jacksonville Red Caps, New Orleans Black Pelicans, Atlanta Black Crackers, and the Birmingham Black Barons.

And three years later, the Eastern Colored League was formed, comprising the Baltimore Black Sox, Brooklyn Royal Giants, Atlantic City Bacharach Giants, New York Lincoln Giants, the Cuban Stars, and Hilldale of Philadelphia.

Though there were plenty of black ballplayers to fill the rosters of every team in the three leagues, finding suitable ball parks where they could play their games was a constant problem. Some teams were allowed to use major league stadiums but, naturally, only when the parent club was not in town. Financing was another problem, and numerous teams went on exhibition tours around the country to pull in more money, playing against white teams, including major league all-star players.

Among the more popular of these Negro League teams that practically lived on the road were the Tennessee Rats, Cincinnati/Indianapolis Clowns, Zulu Cannibals, and Miami Clowns, which combined slapstick comedy with slick fielding and dazzling batting displays. These teams won most of the games they played against white ballplayers, generating talk about the eventual integration of major league baseball.

In some cities that had both major league and Negro League teams, the latter pulled in more fans consistently.

Baseball maverick Bill Veeck even attempted to buy the struggling Philadelphia Phillies, with a plan to deplete the roster and fill it with Negro League ballplayers. The commissioner's office quickly rebuffed Veeck's efforts.

A Turning Point for Negro League Ballplayers

In support of the war, many Negro League teams scheduled games both early and late in the day so that swing-shift factory workers could see their favorite stars play. Free tickets were given to GIs bound for combat overseas and for those coming back.

A common slogan within the black sports community was, "If he's good enough for the Navy, he's good enough for the majors." But initially blacks were accepted into the armed services only to perform menial labor, in such roles as cooks, stevedores, and truck drivers. Many whites felt blacks simply did not have the mental capacity to do difficult tasks, such as fly a plane or fire a tank, and that they could not be relied on in combat. Blacks simply said, "Give us a chance."

With thousands of men needed to fight a war in both Europe and the Pacific, the military finally caved in to pressure to enlist blacks. The Army created all-black armor and infantry units (led by white officers), and the Army Air Corps formed the Tuskegee Airmen, a regiment of fighter pilots, who distinguished themselves in missions over Europe. Other all-black units followed in the engineers and artillery, for example. And without exception, these black units were equal to the task, fighting—and dying—alongside other servicemen and -women.

Major league baseball lost hundreds of players to the war. The Negro Leagues sent many of their finest athletes also, who served in virtually every campaign.

BACKGROUND:
Black enlisted men at their .50-caliber machine gun watch out for enemy aircraft over the bridges of Rheinberg, Germany in 1945. Many of the bridges into the Fatherland were destroyed and had to be rebuilt or amphibious bridges had to be strung together quickly, allowing Allied units to continue the advance. Nazi fighter pilots had instructions to destroy these bridging operations.
U.S. Army photo

Leon Day was considered one of the most dominating pitchers—black or white—in the 1930s and '40s. He was also a good fielder and batter, playing primarily for the Newark Eagles of the Negro Leagues. He joined the Army in time to participate in the landings at Normandy, France, on June 6, 1944. As a member of the 818th Amphibian Battalion, Day steered an Army duck, or amphibious landing craft, from the troop ships to the treacherous shores of Normandy Beach.

(Day returned to the Eagles in 1946, batting a phenomenal .469 and posting a 13–4 record, including a no-hitter, which was a rarity in the hard-hitting Negro Leagues. Day's stats eventually earned him induction into major league baseball's Hall of Fame.)

Another veteran of the Normandy invasion was Willard "Home Run" Brown, center fielder with the Kansas City Monarchs. (In 1947 he would join the St. Louis Browns, appearing in twenty-one games and then returning to the Monarchs.)

Josh Johnson of the Homestead Grays served as an Army officer with the Red Ball Express trucking unit that ran supplies to the frontlines in France and Belgium.

Russell Awkard also played for the Newark Eagles in '40 and '41, as an outfielder. After joining the Army Quartermaster Corps, Awkard was sent to England and then on to France and Belgium.

Frank Duncan was a versatile catcher, primarily for the Kansas City Monarchs. He was drafted, at the age of forty-two, and served six months with the Ninety-second Division.

John "Geronimo" Smith played with three teams before serving with the Army Air Corps from '42 to '45. He would return and play for the Kansas City Monarchs from 1946 to '48 and was recognized as one of the best pitchers in the league.

Monte Irvin, another Newark Eagle, won two league batting titles—the first in 1941 before the start of the war and the second in 1946, after returning from Europe with the Army engineers.

Prior to leaving for the service, Monte Irvin was the popular choice to be the first Negro Leaguer to break the color line and play for a major league team. But his military career interfered with those dreams.

"What happened was I went in the Army and lost my feel for playing and never got a chance to play," Irvin would later recall. "I lost my sharpness when I came out. I wasn't the same player when I came out that I was when I went in." He would eventually join the New York Giants after World War II, and, combined with his Negro Leagues record, post Hall of Fame numbers.

ABOVE: *Negro Leagues ballplayer Monte Irvin won a batting title with the Newark Eagles in 1941, and many fans and players felt he would be the first to break the color line and play in the major leagues. Instead Irvin served with the Army engineers in Europe during WWII and lost some of his playing skills. By the time he was chosen, by the New York Giants, Jackie Robinson was already with the Dodgers.*
U.S. Army photo

John "Buck" O'Neill was a mainstay with the Kansas City Monarchs when they won four consecutive league crowns, from 1939 to 1942. The Monarchs dynasty was dismantled because of the war, when O'Neill and several other key members of the team joined the military. O'Neill served with a Navy construction battalion, ending up in the Philippines once they were retaken in late 1944.

Joe Scott played semipro ball in the Midwest before joining the Army when he was twenty-three. He served with the 350th Field Artillery in France and Belgium. (After World War II his baseball career began with a brief stint as a Detroit Senator, then two years with the Birmingham Black Barons.)

Al Wilmore was a prominent high school pitcher in Philadelphia when he was scouted by the local Negro League Stars. Before joining the team, though, Wilmore served with the 595th Field Artillery in the South Pacific. He would finally take the mound in 1946, earning an all-star berth in 1949.

Charles "Hunkie" Parks was a backup player with the Newark Eagles before the war. He joined the Army and missed out on three full seasons. He returned to the Eagles in 1946 and was on the receiving end of pitcher Leon Day's no-hitter to open that season.

Marlin Carter had stints with a handful of teams during his career, including three tours with the Memphis Red Sox. He joined the Coast Guard and served in the Pacific, ending up in Japan in late 1945. He would return to the Memphis Red Sox and play two more seasons.

James "Red" Moore was dubbed the most perfect first baseman around while playing for a handful of teams prior to the war. He joined the Army in 1941 and served with a combat engineer battalion in France and England, attached to General George "Blood and Guts" Patton's Third Army.

Bob Thurman enlisted in the Army and saw action in the brutal New Guinea Campaign and later on Luzon in the Philippines. While pitching for a unit team there he was discovered and invited to join the Homestead Grays after the war. His best year was 1948, when the Grays won the final Negro National League crown and Thurman batted .341.

Another New Guinea veteran was Sam Hughes, who served with the 196th Support Battalion there. By the time he joined the Army, Hughes had already played pro ball

BELOW: *Black GIs of the 903rd Air Base Security Battalion set up a portable radio during the South Pacific Campaign.*
Army Signal Corps photo

ABOVE: *The 332nd Fighter Group, an all-black P-47 contingent known as the Tuskegee Airmen, arrived in Italy in early 1944. Here they receive a mission briefing at an air base near Ramitelli. As the air war continued and the Tuskegee Airmen proved they were ruthless pilots against their Nazi counterparts, Allied pilots and crewmen requested they be included on every available mission.*
U.S. Air Force photo

for more than thirteen seasons, primarily at second base, and he was selected to more All-Star Games than any other player at that position.

Alfred "Slick" Surratt was also in the Army, at New Guinea and the Philippines. He would return home and play with the Detroit Stars in 1948, followed by four years as a "slick" fielding outfielder for the Monarchs.

Olan "Jelly" Taylor also played for Memphis, dazzling the fans with his nifty fielding at first base. After appearing in three consecutive All-Star Games, Taylor joined the Army—one of the first Negro Leaguers to be drafted. He would rejoin the Red Sox in 1945 and play for two more seasons.

Max "Dr. Cyclops" Manning—given the nickname because he wore thick glasses—was a mainstay on the pitching mound for the Newark Eagles before the war. He served in the Quartermaster Corps and drove trucks with the Red Ball Express, supplying vital supplies, fuel, and ammunition to Third Army units racing across France in 1944. After returning home to resume pitching for Newark, Manning explained, "Being in the service and not playing ball for three years does something to you. It has an effect on you. After getting home again, spring training was almost like therapy. There was a feeling of comfort and it let you kind of get back on track."

James "Pea" Greene was considered the best catcher in the Negro American League while playing with the Kansas City Monarchs from 1939 to '43. He joined the Army's Ninety-second Division and saw action in North Africa and Italy while serving with an anti-tank company. Greene would return to the Monarchs in time for their championship season in 1946.

Charlie Biot, known for his speed in the outfield and on the base paths, served with the 369th Infantry Regiment in the South Pacific and played on the unit's baseball squad. One of his teammates, recruited from a unit located nearby, was Al Wilmore, the teenage pitching phenom from Philly.

Lonnie Summers played semipro ball for three seasons prior to joining the Army in 1942. He climbed into tanks with the 614th Tank Battalion and saw action in Europe. He returned to play in the Mexican League, with two stints catching for the Chicago American Giants, earning him all-star honors in 1949.

Leonard "Fatty" Pig joined the Army in 1940, playing baseball for Army teams wherever he was stationed, including nine months in the Philippines at the end of the war. He would return home from the Pacific and play briefly for the Havana La Palomas in Cuba before joining the Indianapolis Clowns in 1947.

Byron Johnson was an all-star shortstop for the Kansas City Monarchs and Satchel Paige's barnstorming all-stars before joining the Army, serving with the Quartermaster Corps. He wound up at Normandy, France, on D-Day and then rushed into combat during the sweep across northern France.

Andy "Big Six" Watts played semipro ball before joining the Navy. During training at Great Lakes Naval Station in Illinois he played third base for the 1944 championship team, which was loaded with major league stars. The following year Watts was stationed on Guam in the South Pacific. He would return to play for the Cleveland Buckeyes in 1946 and then dropped out of sight for four years before coming back with the Birmingham Black Barons in 1950.

Joe Black was a pitcher with Morgan State in Baltimore when he joined the Army, and "sixteen months after I was drafted before I touched a rifle, I pitched a lot," often holding his own against major league talent. Black would come back and join the Baltimore Elites; he then joined the major league Brooklyn Dodgers several years later.

Larry Doby joined the Navy and was sent to the island of Ulithi in the South Pacific. Also stationed there were major league ballplayers Mickey Vernon of the Senators and Billy Goodman of the Red Sox. The three would often practice together and talked often about Doby getting a shot at the majors when the war was over.

After returning home and playing as an infielder for the Newark Eagles, Doby received an offer to play for the Cleveland Indians—making him the first Negro Leaguer to play in the American League. His major league career would last thirteen years and included six all-star selections and two World Series.

One of the biggest opponents of integrating baseball was Commissioner Kenesaw Mountain Landis. When Landis died in November 1944, his successor was A. B. "Happy" Chandler, former Kentucky governor, who had toured some of the battlefields in the South Pacific. Chandler told a black reporter, "If they [blacks] can fight and die on Okinawa [and] Guadalcanal, in the South Pacific, they can play baseball in America. And when I give my word you can count on it."

In another public statement, Chandler said, "I don't believe in barring Negroes from baseball just because they are Negroes." Still, virtually every major league owner was opposed to integration. The lone dissenter was Brooklyn Dodgers president Branch Rickey, who, on April 9, 1947, announced that Jack Roosevelt Robinson was joining the Dodgers organization. The success or failure of black ballplayers in the major leagues would be determined solely by Robinson, a former Army lieutenant and Kansas City Monarchs rookie shortstop.

10. Pursuit in the Pacific

"In war the power to use two fists is an inestimable asset. To feint with one fist and strike with the other yields an advantage, but a still greater advantage lies in being able to interchange them—to convert the feint into the real blow if the opponent uncovers himself."

—*B. H. Liddell Hart,* Thoughts on War, *1944*

OPPOSITE: *An F6F fighter plane piloted by Ensign Byron Johnson crashes on the deck of the carrier* Enterprise *near Makin Island in November 1943. The carrier's catapult officer, Lieutenant Walter Chewning, risked his own life to rescue the pilot.* U.S. Navy photo

AS JAPAN EXTENDED ITS FORCES FARTHER AWAY FROM ITS home islands, it became vital to conquer and control more territory in the South Pacific. An Imperial Navy unable to resupply and rearm its carriers and warships and repair its damaged ones in safe harbor would be vulnerable to enemy attack.

The Japanese Navy focused on taking the precious oil reserves of the Dutch East Indies, which would extend Japan's range to within striking distance of Australia. The East Indies (now called Indonesia) were lightly defended, with only a small outdated fleet of Allied warships to guard the region.

Mismatch in the Java Sea

This American-British-Dutch-Australian fleet, more commonly known simply as the ABDA, was thrown together to stop Japanese advances in the region. After hearing what enemy warplanes had done to the American fleet at Pearl Harbor, ABDA commanders knew they had little chance of victory, with their World War I-vintage ships and few planes of their own. They hoped only to prolong the fight as long as possible, giving the American ships damaged at Pearl a chance to be repaired and put back to sea.

The waters near Java became the focal point as opposing navies converged in late February 1942.

To a man, the ABDA fleet hoped to inflict some heavy damage on the Japanese, paying them back for the debacle at Pearl Harbor. But from the opening salvo, when Japanese naval guns blasted the ABDA ships from sixteen miles away, it would be a one-sided fight.

The Allied naval guns were not as powerful as Japan's, and American ships had to move in closer while under heavy bombardment. Making

ABOVE: *In the Battle of the Coral Sea, Hellcats from the carriers* Lexington *and* Yorktown *pounced on two enemy flat tops and inflicted heavy damage. Unfortunately, enemy planes hit the Lady Lex and she went down several hours later when an internal gas leak exploded.* U.S. Navy photo

Naval battles in the Pacific involved American and Japanese warships that never fired a shot at each other. Instead, swarms of carrier-launched torpedo planes and dive bombers did the dirty work, with lethal effectiveness. One of those dive bomber pilots was Annapolis boxer John Powers, who scored a direct hit on the enemy flattop Shokaku, *but his plane caught fire from the explosion of his own bomb. For his actions, he was awarded the Medal of Honor, posthumously.*
National Archives photo

this move even more hazardous, the Japanese armada could now unleash its devastating long-range torpedoes.

It became a deadly gauntlet with virtually no escape. With Japanese spotter planes watching and reporting their every movement, it was impossible for the Allied ships to sneak in closer to utilize their own guns or to run and hide to lick their wounds. The relentless Japanese attackers continued to stalk and attack them, decimating the fleet with each encounter.

Of the original ABDA armada of fourteen cruisers and destroyers, ten were hit and sunk. America's largest warship in the area, the cruiser *Houston*, nicknamed the Galloping Ghost of the Java Coast, lost 700 men alone when it was attacked. All told, 1,700 Allied personnel perished at the Battle of the Java Sea, a near-total victory for the Japanese.

Naval Warfare Takes Flight

The Japanese planes that had attacked Pearl Harbor were launched from aircraft carriers hundreds of miles away, ushering in a new era of naval combat.

Previously, "the battleships were supposed to be great heavyweights—much like heavyweight boxers—slow, lumbering perhaps, but with great stamina and ability to absorb punishment and a terrific sock in their 14- and 16-inch guns," wrote Stanley Johnston in *Queen of the Flat-Tops*.

But the coming naval battles in the Pacific would be decided not by the mighty battleships, but by carrier-launched aircraft.

Japanese planes had played a key role in the Battle of the Java Sea, when they were used as observers to keep track of the Allied ships. The ABDA fleet had a few planes available to it, but they remained grounded, for fear of being damaged and unavailable for future fights. It would prove to be a costly tactical error in judgment; there would be no more future battles for the ABDA fleet, now resting on the bottom of the Java Sea.

But learning from the mistakes of their peers, American military leaders quickly saw how successfully the Japanese were using carrier- and island-based planes to serve a variety of roles—long-range striking force, early warning observers, and overhead protectors.

At the same time American code-breakers were intercepting and deciphering Japanese radio and teletype transmissions. By cracking the enemy's codes, the

BELOW: *The Japanese had devastated the U.S. Pacific Fleet at Pearl Harbor, but they failed to sink any American aircraft carriers that were still at sea—a critical mistake they would soon regret. At Coral Sea and Midway, U.S. carrier pilots struck crippling blows and soon the Japanese n aval offensive was in retreat.*
U.S. Navy photo

American military learned that the Japanese planned to converge on New Guinea, northeast of Australia, in May 1942. American warships would be there, hoping to outgun them.

A Crucial Confrontation

The Battle of the Coral Sea—the first-ever engagement of naval forces exclusively using carrier planes—would be determined by inclement weather, combat exaggerations, miscalculations of enemy strength, and just plain dumb luck.

The Japanese believed that, with the U.S. Pacific fleet seemingly wiped out at Pearl and the Allied ABDA armada sent to its doom near Java, there would be no naval opposition to its rampage across the Pacific.

But as damaging as the Pearl Harbor attack had been, none of the precious few American aircraft carriers had been in port during the attack. The Japanese had "awakened a sleeping dragon," with America's biggest weapon—those carriers, with their arsenal of torpedo-bomber and fighter aircraft—still breathing fire and ready for some heavy-duty payback, at Coral Sea.

The two U.S. carriers, named for Revolutionary War battle sites were the *Yorktown* and *Lexington,* with a combined 140 aircraft aboard. The Japanese had a comparable carrier force, including many of the pilots who'd raided Pearl Harbor.

During the initial probes, both sides sent out scout planes to locate the enemy fleets somewhere in the region of the Coral Sea. On May 7 Japanese observer pilots spotted two American ships. In their excitement, the pilots reported an American carrier with one escort.

Immediately seventy enemy planes took off, pounced on the two ships, and sank them. The Japanese pilots boasted of sinking another U.S. flattop, when in fact the "carrier" was an oil tanker, the *Neosho,* accompanied by a destroyer, the *Sims.*

At the same time, ninety-three U.S. planes seemed to come out of nowhere and overwhelmed the Japanese carrier *Shoho,* which went down after being hit by seven torpedoes and thirteen bombs. It was the first enemy carrier to be sunk in the Pacific Campaign.

The next day, while their own planes were stalking the enemy, the *Yorktown* and *Lexington* came under

BELOW: *Crewmen from the Navy submarine USS* Griffin *notch another "kill" on their tote board. American subs played a crucial role in winning the battle of the Pacific.*
National Archives photo

heavy attack. Both American carriers were heavily damaged but remained afloat. Again, Japanese pilots, looking back on the two smoking hulks, reported sinking both. The *Yorktown* limped away for extensive repairs, while the crew of the Lady Lex fought to save the ship. But several hours after the attack, a gas leak caused an explosion, and the proud crew of the *Lexington* was forced to abandon ship. Buzz "Buster" Borries, gridiron superstar for the Naval Academy before the war and who had played varsity baseball, basketball, and football, served on board the *Lexington* at the Coral Sea skirmishes.

To even the score, American planes tracked down two more enemy carriers—the *Zuikaku* and *Shokaku*—and inflicted damage to both. One of those American pilots was former Naval Academy boxer John Powers, who flew a dive-bomber and would plunge perilously close to his target before releasing his bombs. This ensured a direct hit but exposed him to intense anti-aircraft fire. As he dove his Dauntless on the carrier *Shokaku*, Powers knew the enemy ship had to be sunk. Though he scored a direct hit, Powers's plane was hit and engulfed with flames by the explosion of his own bomb.

The *Shokaku* limped back to safe haven and would require many months to repair, eliminating it from future Pacific battles. For his actions, John Powers was posthumously awarded the Medal of Honor.

The Japanese felt confident they had sunk three American carriers at Coral Sea, when in fact only the *Lexington* was sunk. The Americans also lost 66 planes and 543 men, but the Japanese lost 77 aircraft and 1,074 men. The loss of the carriers *Shoho* and *Shokaku*, along with many experienced pilots, would become critical during the next confrontation, the Battle of Midway.

ABOVE: *The Principle of Calculated Risk, plus simple luck, led to an American victory at the Battle of Midway. The aircraft carrier* Enterprise *(foreground), along with her sister ships, the* Hornet *and* Yorktown, *sent out waves of torpedo planes and divebombers, knocking out four enemy flattops.* U.S. Navy photo

The Principle of Calculated Risk

U.S. Navy commanders in the Pacific compared their fight against Japan to David opposing Goliath. In every battle, the enemy would have superior numbers.

Admiral Chester Nimitz, commander of the U.S. Pacific Fleet, knew that if they continued trading pieces—one American carrier sunk, one Japanese carrier sunk, one American battleship damaged, one enemy warship damaged—eventually Japan would win the war simply by attrition. With all the damage they had done at Pearl Harbor, the Japanese already had a decisive edge on battleships. Somehow the United States had to hold out until more warships could be built and deployed to the Pacific.

At the Naval Academy, Nimitz had been a member of the varsity crew team and was an excellent boxer and tennis player. Ironically, while sailing during a Sunday outing, Nimitz got seasick and considered transferring to the Army. The United States almost lost a brilliant naval tactician because of a bout with seasickness!

Nimitz knew the U.S. Navy had to inflict more damage than it suffered if it was to ever get the upper hand in the Pacific Campaign. This gambit was known as the Principle of Calculated Risk. It sounded great in theory, but in reality . . .

The Japanese wanted to create a chain of strongholds, from the Aleutian Islands of Alaska to the Dutch East Indies just north of Australia. In between, they planned to control Midway and Wake Islands and all the island groups in their path, like stepping-stones.

After the battle at Coral Sea, the heavily damaged carrier *Yorktown* headed back to Pearl Harbor for makeshift repairs. She needed another month of overhaul to be back at 100 percent but instead was rushed back to sea to link up with the carriers *Enterprise* and *Hornet* and their armadas of destroyers and cruisers, tankers and submarines for the next confrontation with the enemy, at Midway.

On board one of those escort ships was big-league pitcher Walter Masterson, who played for the Senators from 1939 to 1942. In early May 1942 Masterson was about to take part in one of the pivotal battles of the war in the Pacific. (After his hitch was over he would need a year to regain his pitching skills—"When you get to the position where you don't care whether you live or die, you're kind of strange to be around," he would

BELOW: *The flight deck of the Japanese carrier* Shokaku *is loaded with planes waiting to take off in the Battle of Santa Cruz, mid-October of 1942.*
U.S. Navy photo

lament after the war, suffering from what became known as shell shock. Masterson appeared in only four games in 1945, then twenty-nine the next year. By 1947 he had tamed his inner demons enough to pitch thirty-four consecutive scoreless innings at one stretch.)

Carrier battle tactics relied on both attacking and defending aircraft. The attackers consisted of torpedo planes that approached their target just above the waterline before releasing their "fish" and dive-bombers that came in high then plummeted toward their target, dropping their bombs and pulling up and veering off at the last second. These were usually accompanied by fighter planes needed to take on the enemy defender aircraft. Additional defenders circled over their own armadas, constantly looking out for approaching enemy intruders.

Deadly Consequences

A carrier could launch only one plane at a time, and so a wave of ninety planes might take an hour to get aloft. Landing, refueling, and re-arming below decks was also time consuming. Nowhere were these factors more critical than in the waters surrounding Midway.

On June 4 Japanese planes from four carriers chewed up the American defenders on Midway Island. Other planes loaded with torpedoes were on the carriers' flight decks and ready to launch if any American warships were spotted. But as the first wave of attackers returned from Midway and radioed back that another strike would be necessary to complete the decimation, the order was given to pull the torpedoes off the planes standing by and load them with bombs to finish off the Midway fortifications.

While all this was going on, American bombers and fighters from the *Enterprise, Hornet,* and *Yorktown* took off but lost track of each other.

On board the *Enterprise,* serving as an ordnance crewman, was Stanford University boxer Richard Boone. His job entailed loading bombs and machine gun belts onto the carrier's torpedo bombers and fighter planes. Boone would later return to the United States for additional training to be a radio-gunner on board an Avenger torpedo bomber. (After World War II Boone would turn to acting instead of boxing for his livelihood.)

The *Hornet*'s Torpedo Squadron 8, consisting of fifteen bombers, stumbled onto the four enemy carriers, but because they had been separated from their own fighter escorts the American planes were easily plucked out of the sky by Japanese defender aircraft. Torpedo 6 from the *Enterprise,* and then Torpedo 3 from the *Yorktown* suffered a similar fate. Of forty-one American torpedo bombers, only four survived, and none of their torpedoes found a target.

But in order to knock down the three American torpedo squadrons skimming just above the waves, the Japanese fighter aircraft also had to fly low, leaving their carriers vulnerable to any overhead attack.

On the flight decks of the four Japanese carriers, bombs and torpedoes, fuel tanks and hoses were scattered everywhere as the aircrews scrambled to get their planes back in the air. But suddenly American dive-bombers from the *Enterprise* appeared unopposed and made their descent on the Japanese flat-tops, releasing a full complement of bombs.

The explosions touched off the fuel tanks, bombs, and torpedoes stacked on the carriers' flight decks. In a fiery chain reaction, the munitions and fuel exploded, consuming the planes on three of the Japanese carriers.

The fourth carrier did manage to launch some of its planes before succumbing to the American bombers. Those enemy planes that did escape the inferno pounced on the crippled *Yorktown.*

According to the principle of calculated risk, the Battle of Midway, was a U.S. success. Though the *Yorktown* and the destroyer *Hammann* were sunk, along with 307 men killed and 147 aircraft lost, Japanese losses were far heavier—more than 3,500 lives (including many of the pilots who'd struck Pearl Harbor), 322 planes, three destroyers, two cruisers, and those four prized carriers.

With the Battle of Midway, the tide had finally turned in the war with Japan. Admiral William F. "Bull" Halsey had missed out on Midway because of illness, but soon afterward he was back at the helm of his battle group, issuing the directive "Kill Japs. Kill Japs. Kill More Japs" to every crewman in the South Pacific.

More than thirty-five years earlier, Halsey had played football for the battleship USS *Missouri* against other warship teams. And during football season, Halsey was dispatched to the Naval Academy to serve as assistant backfield coach. The Academy squad had been devastated by the Black Knights of Army by scores of 22–8 in 1902 and 40–5 in 1903. Halsey was the featured back both years, earning the Thompson Trophy as the best athlete in his senior class. The next year the Navy midshipmen eked out a tie. But in 1905, finally, Navy routed Army 10–zip.

Coach Halsey rejoined the *Missouri* after the Academy's victory over West Point in 1905. But in 1942 the U.S. Navy turned its attention to a formidable foe in the Pacific, for there was still plenty of fight left in the Japanese after Midway, and Bull Halsey was gunning for them. Now the Americans would be the aggressor, stopping Japan's plans to throw a net across the Pacific and threaten America's West Coast.

Now, after Midway, the invincible Japanese navy would be the one on the run, licking its wounds and looking for a lull in the fight so it could regroup, reinforce, re-arm, and return to the offensive.

BELOW: *The ill-fated Devastators of Torpedo Squadron Eight flew into a buzz saw during the Battle of Midway, losing 35 of 41 planes.* U.S. Navy photo

11. Slugging It Out in the Solomons

"I WILL HIT 'EM WHERE THEY AIN'T."

—*General Douglas MacArthur*

"ANY BOXER OR FOOTBALL PLAYER CAN TELL YOU . . . BEFORE A GAME OR A FIGHT ONE SITS AND IMAGINES ALL SORTS OF TERRIBLE POSSIBILITIES. EVEN THOUGH DEATH IS UNLIKELY, SERIOUS INJURY IS VERY POSSIBLE. THEN, MIRACULOUSLY, THESE FEELINGS DROP FROM YOU LIKE A SHROUD, AND YOU ARE FREE. YOUR ONLY WORRY FROM THEN ON TO THE END IS SHOWING THE OTHER GUY YOU ARE BETTER THAN HE IS."

—*James Jones*

OPPOSITE: *Navy PT boats carried quite a wallop, seeking out and taking on enemy warships attempting to traverse "the Slot" in the Solomons. Many of these devil boat commanders and crewmen were gifted pro and collegiate athletes, such as Olympic swimmer John Williams, lacrosse All-American Ken Molloy, and pro football players Steven Levanitis of the Eagles and Alex Schibanoff of the Lions.* U.S. Navy photo

THE ENTIRE PACIFIC BECAME A MASSIVE CHESS BOARD AS American and Japanese military leaders moved their navies and other fighting units from one corner to the next, hoping to outmaneuver, and ultimately defeat, their enemy.

The Japanese used the phrase *Hakko-ichiu* ("bring the eight corners of the world under one roof") in describing their attempts to dominate the region. And, just as in chess, both sides used deception to mask their own moves while trying to outguess their opponent.

General Douglas MacArthur knew where enemy troops were positioned throughout most of the Pacific and initially considered slugging it out with them, island by island. But to do that would prolong the fight indefinitely, and so MacArthur instead plotted out leapfrogging—a clear-cut path all the way to Tokyo, bypassing many confrontations and leaving large concentrations of enemy troops waiting for a battle that would never come.

ABOVE: *PT-109 commander John F. Kennedy was quite an athlete in his prep school and college days at Harvard, though back problems would plague him all his life. He also enjoyed competing in regattas back in New England, a distant memory during his perilous tour with the devil boats in the Solomons.* Photo courtesy of the John F. Kennedy Library

But the war in the Pacific was hardly a game of chess to the young men fighting for their country and trying to survive. All they wanted was to get home, alive and in one piece.

Besides fighting the Japanese, the Americans also fought the sweltering heat and monsoon rains of the South Pacific, deadly insects—including swarms of mosquitoes as tenacious and ornery as Japanese dive bombers—and poisonous snakes, hostile natives, impassable jungles that blocked out the sky overhead, and mud that could grab onto a GI's boots and fight him for them, every step of the way, inch by inch.

Assaulting the Solomons

The first major land battle unfolded in the Solomon Islands, a nine-hundred-mile-long chain of isles in the southwest Pacific, located ominously close to Australia, which would be within easy striking range for Japanese planes.

ABOVE: *Army artillery crews on Arundel fired on Japanese units nearby to keep them from moving reinforcements to the New Georgia islands.* Department of Defense photo

The opening salvo would unfold at an unheard-of place that would forever after be known for the struggles and the great loss of life that occurred there: Guadalcanal.

The Japanese already had a small contingent that had cleared enough level ground for an airstrip on Guadalcanal. Soon it would be operational. Then Japanese planes could attack naval convoys trying to reach Australia. But until then they would have to utilize other airstrips farther away.

U.S. Navy and Marine Corps pilots from bases on other islands in the South Pacific were doing their best to keep the pesky enemy bombers and fighters away from the Allied convoys bound for the Land Down Under.

One of those hotshot American dive-bomber pilots credited with enemy kills over Guadalcanal was top Seattle tennis amateur Robert Vaupell, a captain in the Navy who won the Air Medal, Navy Cross, and Purple Heart for his actions.

William "Killer" Kane, tackle for Navy a decade earlier, was at Pearl Harbor when the Japanese attacked and later was a pilot with the flattop *Enterprise*. When his plane was disabled over Guadalcanal, he brought it in for a crash landing.

Marine Private First Class Robert Baum, an aerial radio-gunner, saw plenty of action against Japanese pilots and described what fighting above the clouds was like: "I'm surprised at myself in a way, because I do not get all flustered and excited in the middle of an engagement. This is one game I'm going to beat. When I played baseball I never wanted to sit on the bench, always wanted to play the whole game. And here too, I'm going out every time, and while I'm playing this game, I'm going to play hard, and to win."

Tragically, Baum would later be reported missing in action.

Harold Bauer, a running back at Annapolis in the late 1920s, came to a similar tragic end. As a Marine pilot over Guadalcanal, he was a raging bulldog, often taking on a swarm of enemy fighter planes single-handedly, shooting down nine in less than a month. But his last time aloft, squeezing every ounce of fuel from his empty tanks, Bauer tore into a cluster of Japanese intruders and plunged into the sea. No trace of his plane was found, and Bauer's family accepted his posthumous Medal of Honor.

Lieutenant Bob McLeod, former Dartmouth College halfback, was another fighter jockey, who downed nine enemy Zeroes over Guadalcanal.

Navy Lieutenant Dave Breden, Marquette University's star guard from 1937 to 1939 and a torpedo bomber pilot during the Pacific Campaign, sank two Japanese ships in the waters surrounding the Solomons.

Former Annapolis running back "Jumpin' Joe" Clifton was a daredevil fighter pilot from the carrier *Saratoga* who escorted bombers during raids on the Solomons. Another former Naval Academy running back, Harold Caldwell, was skipper on the *Saratoga*.

Marquette University law student Robert Cannon wanted to be a pro baseball player, but his lineage was more on the legal side of the game. (His father had served as attorney for some of the Chicago players caught up in the notorious "Black Sox" scandal.) Cannon served on the *Saratoga* and then after returning to the states became a court judge and was an unpaid legal advisor to the Major League Baseball Players' Association.

One of the most awesome feats of devil-may-care flying was done by a group of hotshot pilots known as Joe's Flying Circus, headed up by Joe Foss (future American Football League commissioner). During the campaign to clear the skies over Guadalcanal, Foss shot down twenty-six enemy aircraft, and his Circus pilots blasted another forty-six in four months of action.

After bailing out and swimming ashore only to be captured by the Marines, one Japanese pilot who was an avid baseball fan asked which team had won the 1942 World Series. He was stunned to find out the St. Louis Cardinals had beaten the invincible New York Yankees.

The Ground War Begins

Aussie citizens living in the Solomons kept an eye on Japanese movements in the region. These "coast-watchers" promptly reported the buildup on Guadalcanal to

LEFT: *The Japanese were well-entrenched on Bougainville, and it took close-quarters combat to knock them out. A 37th Infantry Division soldier takes aim at an enemy pillbox and heaves a hand grenade, which was about the same size as a baseball. Flame throwers were also used to route the Japanese from reinforced strongholds.* Army Signal Corps photo

LEFT: *Led by Major Greg "Pappy" Boyington, the men of Marine Corps Fighter Squadron VMF-214 were known as "the Black Sheep." In 1943 the unit boasted that they would shoot down one enemy plane for every ball cap sent to them by a World Series player. The St. Louis Cardinals sent twenty caps two months later and the Black Sheep promptly racked up twenty "kills."* U.S. Marine Corps photo

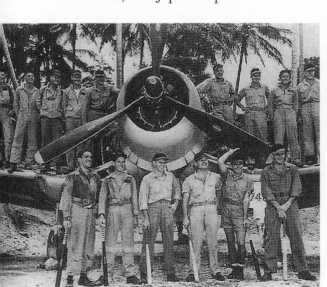

Allied headquarters, which determined that the island had to be seized before the Japanese air bases were operational.

On August 7, 1942, the ten-thousand-strong First Marine Division swarmed ashore. With little resistance they seized the nearly completed Japanese airstrip, which American planes used two weeks later to harass enemy convoys.

At Guadalcanal the Americans learned in hard-fought battles that enemy troops would be well entrenched and would not disgrace their emperor by surrendering. Heavy air and naval bombardment would preface any beach landings at future engagements, but it would still require close-quarters combat to secure every objective. Often the Japanese would fight to the death rather than surrender.

ABOVE: *Troops landing on Rendova Island in the Solomons battled not only enemy forces but also heavy rains, in late June 1943.*
U.S. Navy photo

During several days of intense jungle fighting, the U.S. Marines on Guadalcanal wiped out the Japanese attackers, who had gravely underestimated the Americans' greater numbers and fighting ability. The Guadalcanal Campaign would drag on until February 1943, involving the First and Second Marine divisions and the Army's Americal and Twenty-fifth Infantry divisions.

One of those Twenty-fifth Infantry Tropic Lightning Division soldiers was Captain Charles "Gordo" Davis, a pitcher for the University of Alabama in the 1930s. Gordo—nicknamed that because he was born in Gordo, Alabama—saw several companies of his battalion pinned down by enemy machine gun fire on January 12 and 13, 1943.

"Major Davis led an assault on the Japanese position. . . . When his rifle jammed at its first shot, he drew his pistol and, waving his men on, led the assault over the top of the hill. Electrified by this action, another body of soldiers followed and seized the hill. The capture of this position broke Japanese resistance," states the citation recounting Gordo's actions, which won him the Medal of Honor.

American losses at Guadalcanal were 4,900 killed and 4,183 wounded. One of those injured was Gerald Juzek, a California Angels pitcher in the Coast League, a minor league circuit. He was crippled by enemy machine gun fire and was told he'd never walk again, let alone play ball. (Juzek would rehabilitate his leg and return to the pitching mound on April 1, 1944; he pitched three innings of minor league ball for Los Angeles in the Pacific Coast League.)

Another California minor leaguer, Billey Hebert of the Class AA Oakland Oaks, was killed at Guadalcanal on October 21, 1942.

The Japanese toll at Guadalcanal was staggering: 25,000 dead. They also lost numerous ships and several hundred planes and pilots.

Japan's war machine was no longer viewed as invincible, though the Japanese attempted to continue that false impression for the people back at home, reporting that they were winning every confrontation against the crippled and "inferior" U.S. Navy.

Assaulting Other Solomon Islands

Marine units were dispatched to other islands in the region, where several skirmishes broke out, with the Japanese absorbing most of the punishment.

At Betio, Lieutenant William Hawkins of the Second Marine Division was leading his platoon ashore when enemy machine guns on a well-fortified pier cut into them. Wounded twice, Hawkins knew his troops would not be safe until several remaining machine guns were knocked out.

Hawkins had excelled in baseball and football in high school and at the Texas College of Mines. He used his teamwork skills at Betio to coordinate his men against the Japanese. They knocked out seven guns in all, often with Hawkins standing directly in the line of fire to toss grenades and shoot through the narrow slots of the enemy bunkers. But as night fell on November 21, a Japanese gunner took direct aim at Hawkins, again standing in clear view, and felled him with a machine gun burst.

On nearby Munda, the unforgiving jungles and constant enemy harassment took their toll on the battle-weary American soldiers and Marines. Combat fatigue became another enemy to be conquered.

As a youngster in Green Springs, Ohio, Rodger Young had loved playing baseball, basketball, and football. Though not athletically gifted, he persevered, relying on spunk to compensate for what he lacked on the playing field. Private Rodger Young of the Thirty-seventh Infantry Division—the Buckeyes—would need more of that perseverance and spunk on Munda when a bullet from an enemy machine gun ripped into his shoulder. While his Army buddies provided covering fire, Young crawled as close to the enemy gun emplacement as possible. But he was hit again as he struggled to pull a grenade from his harness and toss it at the enemy position. Rapidly losing blood, he managed to throw two more

BELOW: In a symbolic PR moment, Major Greg "Pappy" Boyington accepts twenty St. Louis Cardinals ball caps and gives Chris "Wild Man" Magee twenty Rising Sun victory stickers. The caps were the Black Sheep Squadron's bounty for shooting down an equal number of enemy war planes. U.S. Marine Corps photo

grenades, knocking out the Japanese machine gunners. But in the aftermath this gutsy athlete from Ohio lay dead on that lonely jungle path on some unknown island in the South Pacific.

At Gavutu Island, a one-man punching bag for Japan was Marine Private Eugene Moore, former pulling guard for the Huron High School football team back in South Dakota. After a swarm of enemy soldiers pounced on his tank and set it afire, Moore decided it was better to be outside and get shot than to stay inside and get burned to a crisp. He opened the hatch and was dragged outside and pummeled with fists, knives, and even a pitchfork, then left for dead. His family was notified of his death, unaware that later a squad of Marines that came to retrieve his body discovered he was still clinging to life.

Time for Some R&R

Once Guadalcanal was secured, the soldiers and Marines were given some R&R—rest and recuperation. They quickly organized competitive sporting matches, pitting the services' best against each other.

In battle for weeks, and totally isolated from any news from home, Lieutenant Hans Gunther, captain of Colgate College's 1939 gridiron squad, lamented during the lull, "I'd give a day's meal to know what teams played in the Rose Bowl."

During the Guadalcanal Golden Gloves Boxing Championship, two middleweights ended up facing each other for the crown but asked for a draw instead. Twin brothers William and Robert Karvelas explained that they had had more than their share of family fisticuffs growing up and would rather save their best punches for the enemy. Tournament judges bowed to their request and presented both with championship medals, cast from the sheet metal of a Japanese Zero.

But even during R&R the men at Guadalcanal knew that soon they would be deploying for the next fight, bringing them closer to the only victory that really mattered—winning the war in the Pacific.

Where the Hell Is Bougainville?

The Japanese abandoned plans to retake Guadalcanal, but they still had plenty of fight left for a knock-down-drag-out battle at Bougainville, another little-known island in the Solomons chain. The Japanese felt so strongly about seizing and controlling Bougainville that Rear Admiral Ijuin Mitsuki cautioned, "If Bougainville falls, Japan will topple."

Japanese troop strength was more than 35,000, with two-thirds of that total deployed along Bougainville's southern coast. Another 6,000 were entrenched to the north, leaving the rest of the island lightly defended.

When the 14,000-strong U.S. Third Marine Division came ashore at Bougainville's Empress Augusta Bay, attacking the center of the island, only 270 enemy troops opposed them. The Japanese, believing the jungle terrain in the central region to be so hostile that the Americans would be foolish to land there, were waiting at both ends of the island.

Once ashore, the Marines attempted to close ground on the larger enemy force by the shortest route, through the heart of an impassable jungle: "the meanest, darkest, and most treacherous battleground in the world," recalled one Marine company commander.

Taking Potshots from Behind

Many Japanese snipers lay in wait for the American patrols, allowing them to pass by, then attacking from the rear. The Solomons battles proved to the Americans that the enemy was a tenacious competitor. Often the Japanese would be lurking in caves and spider holes, and no amount of grenades and mortar fire could eliminate them.

Captain Harry Torgerson, a football hero at New York University, devised a crude apparatus for blasting the enemy from coral caves on nearby Gavutu Island. He attached blocks of dynamite to long boards, then shoved them deep into the caves. If that didn't kill the Japanese, it probably sealed them in.

BELOW: *Bougainville really was one hell of a hell hole! Every night the enemy would probe the lines and take pot shots when they could get close enough, and the next day American soldiers using heavy armor for protection would track down and kill the infiltrators.* National Archives photo

For the first time the Marines also used war dogs to sniff out enemy snipers and tunnel rats. Hundreds of dogs were killed in the Pacific Island campaigns.

Private First Class Al Lindberg, a boxer from Minnesota who had taken the featherweight title at the Guadalcanal Golden Gloves boxing tourney, was killed a short time later in the vicious fighting on Bougainville.

Another athlete at Bougainville was Tulane halfback Bobby Glass, who had played in the inaugural Sugar Bowl in 1935, beating Temple 20–14. At Hellzapoppin' Ridge, an enemy shell exploded close by, killing a fellow marine standing next to him. Shrapnel embedded itself in a tree just above Glass's head. He was unhurt, and very thankful to still be alive.

Solomons Air War Heats Up

By mid-November 1943, forces from the Army's Thirty-seventh Infantry Division and the Twenty-first Marines had secured enough territory for Navy Seabees (construction battalion sailors) to build an airstrip on Bougainville. Soon Allied planes were attacking the Japanese stronghold of Rabaul on New Britain, knocking out 190 enemy planes.

Major Greg "Pappy" Boyington was one of those Marine Corps Corsair fighter pilots tormenting Japanese planes over Rabaul and Guadalcanal. As commander of a group of misfit pilots affectionately known as the Black Sheep, Boyington fast developed a reputation as a tenacious bulldog.

At the University of Washington he had been both a wrestler and swimmer before graduating in 1934. After serving with the Flying Tigers in the China-Burma-India theater, Boyington ended up in the South Pacific, providing fighter escorts to Allied bombers hitting enemy airfields located on Bougainville.

On January 3, 1944, Boyington and his Black Sheep pilots ran into a swarm of enemy fighter planes over Rabaul. After he got his twenty-eight kill, a cluster of Japanese Zeroes pounced on him and tore his plane to shreds. Severely wounded by enemy bullets and shrapnel, Pappy bailed out over water. After several strafing runs, the Zero pilots left him for the sharks. Boyington inflated his life raft and was picked up by a Japanese sub.

For the next six weeks he was interrogated, beaten, and tortured at Rabaul. "The first ten days were the hardest. They wouldn't let anybody help me. They would make me walk on my bad leg, and shove me with a rifle butt to make sure I did. After ten days I was getting pretty ripe . . . I don't know how they stood the smell. Finally they let a doctor wash me."

BELOW: *Major Greg "Pappy" Boyington was a University of Washington wrestler and swimmer in the early '30s. He would head up the notorious Black Sheep Squadron in the Solomons and torment enemy fighter pilots, personally tallying twenty-eight kills. But on January 3, 1944, he was shot down and taken prisoner, sitting out the rest of the war in a POW camp in Japan.* U.S. Marine Corps photo

Boyington remained a POW in Japan until the end of the war. After repatriation he received the Medal of Honor for his Black Sheep exploits.

Another collegiate athlete turned Marine fighter pilot at Bougainville was Bob Barnett, center for Duke when they played in the 1942 Rose Bowl.

Enemy Forces Step Up the Attack

On Christmas Eve, 1943, the central region of Bougainville was secured, though thousands of dug-in Japanese still controlled both ends of the island. But as the Allied air threat heated up from the central airfields, the Japanese pressed the attack to oust the Americans from the island's midsection.

In March, after hacking through dense jungle, 12,000 Japanese came up against 27,000 American soldiers and Marines. The three-week battle was devastating to the enemy: 5,000 dead and 4,000 wounded. American casualties were 263 dead and several hundred wounded.

While additional Japanese troops continued to hold both ends of Bougainville, U.S. military commanders decided instead to bypass them, limiting contact to infrequent skirmishes. Both sides sent out perimeter patrols to ensure that the other wasn't about to unleash a full-scale attack, but the massed Japanese troops would wait indefinitely, itching for a battle that never came.

Well-Deserved Time Off

Just as on Guadalcanal, the Americans on Bougainville were given time to rest before pressing on to other islands in the Pacific. But the GI version of rest was to hold more boxing matches.

The American and Australian troops on Bougainville held a boxing tourney in October 1944 during a typhoon that led to flash flooding. A few days later these same troops would be in battle against the Japanese at the Upper Laruma Valley of Bougainville. By this time the Japanese were merely delaying their inevitable defeat.

Naval Battle Unfolds

Allied ships in the Slot—the waters near Guadalcanal and the other islands of the Solomons—slugged it out with the enemy as both sides attempted to move men and materiel to the frontlines. But with Japanese and Allied submarines

ABOVE: *In 1937 Colorado running back Byron "Whizzer" White led the nation in rushing yards, points scored, and total offense. He would be the number one draft choice the following year for the Pittsburgh Pirates.*

During WWII he was a Navy lieutenant on board a destroyer in the South Pacific, seeking out enemy warships and transports during the Solomons Campaign. He also saw action on PT boats. Photo courtesy of the University of Colorado

and scout planes prowling the area, ships from both sides met their demise in the waters just north and east of Guadalcanal at what became dubbed Iron Bottom Sound.

The Japanese did manage to land a force of 915 troops on Guadalcanal, but another thousand reinforcements on other transports never made it ashore, either sent to a watery grave or turned away by the American picket line of warships.

Throughout the Solomons Campaign, American and Japanese naval forces played a game of cat and mouse in a series of confrontations. All of these naval battles were named for nearby islands and landmarks, including Savo on August 9, 1942 (which had its own series of six battles ending on December 1); Kula Gulf on July 5 and 6, 1943; Kolombangara a week later; Vella Gulf on August 6 and 7; Vella Lavella two months after that; and Empress Augusta Bay on November 2.

Numerous other naval skirmishes occurred throughout the Solomons Campaign, though most of the American forces were focused on stopping the almost-nightly movements of the Tokyo Express trying to navigate The Slot. The Allies did make use of radar to detect Japanese naval movements from a safe distance, firing shells and torpedoes with devastating success and without actually seeing the enemy warships.

Athletes Patrolling the Slot

Navy Lieutenant Commander George Earnshaw was in charge of the anti-aircraft gun crews on the carrier *Yorktown*. He saw combat in the South Pacific, where he was wounded when enemy planes attacked and one managed to score a direct hit on his gun battery.

Before joining the Navy, Earnshaw had been a pitcher and World Series hero for the Philadelphia Athletics in 1930, winning two games against the St. Louis Cardinals. In game two, Earnshaw struck out eight, posting a 6–1 victory. In game five, with the Series tied 2–2, Earnshaw held the Cards scoreless through seven innings, then turned the game over to Lefty Grove for the win. With only one day's rest, Earnshaw came back for game seven and shut down St. Louis once again, 7–1.

The Athletics also appeared in the '29 World Series, beating the Chicago Cubs, and again in '31, losing to the Cardinals. In 1929 Earnshaw led the American League in wins with twenty-four. After nine years in the major leagues and three World Series, Moose Earnshaw called it quits after the 1936 season.

Navy Captain Arleigh Burke led a force of four destroyers—his "Little Beavers"—to harass the enemy in The Slot, sinking three battleships. Former Colorado University all-American halfback Whizzer White was a Navy lieutenant on board one of the Little Beavers, also pulling duty on PT boats.

In 1938 White was the Pittsburgh Pirates' number-one draft choice and led the league in rushing yards, with 567. Two years later he was with the Detroit Lions and again took the rushing crown, with 514 yards. (Whizzer White would return from the Pacific Campaign and later become better known as Supreme Court Justice Byron White.)

Gus Lentz, captain of the Naval Academy's 1925 football team, was a 240-pound block of granite who slugged it out in the trenches every lineman thrives in. But in the waters near the Solomons, his warship, the carrier *Wasp*, was attacked and crippled. Lentz had been hurt earlier in the campaign and was below decks recuperating when the evacuation order was given. Helpless to make it out on his own, he told his shipmates to leave him behind and save themselves.

Hit-and-Run Sailors

Many athletes who joined the Navy were selected to command the potent Devil Boats—those patrol craft built for speed and loaded with firepower, including torpedoes, depth charges, deck cannons, and machine guns. But if they didn't deliver a haymaker with the first punch, these PT (patrol torpedo) boats could not withstand a counter blow, due primarily to their plywood skin.

Since PT boats operated mostly at night, one of their most valuable weapons was radar, which allowed the crews to locate enemy ships and strike first, strike hard, and then run like hell.

Among the Devil Boat skippers and crewmen was an all-star lineup of athletes: Rumsey "Rum" Ewing, captain of the Dartmouth rowing team, commanding PT 191, dubbed *Bambi;* Oregon State's Olympic swimmer John Williams; John Eastham, Texas A&M football star; rowing record holder Joe Burk; Ernest Pannell, Green Bay Packers tackle; Louis Smith and Stuart Lewis, two Golden Bears from the University of California; Syracuse lacrosse all-American Ken Molloy, who skippered PT 326, known as *Carolina Chile;* Detroit Lion Alex Schibanoff; Cedric Janien from Harvard's varsity football squad, in charge of PT 321, nicknamed *Death's Hand;* Steven Levanitis of the Philadelphia Eagles; Princeton swim champion Jim Foran; Franklin and Marshall's Kermit Montz; Wabash's William Hall on PT 329; Notre Dame all-American Bernard Crimmins and his teammate Paul Lillis, star tackle and team captain; and Yale running back Cyrus Taylor, skipper of PT 193, the *Bitchin' Witch.*

Cy Taylor, affectionately known as the Cypress, and his crew were patrolling just offshore near Noemfoor with Montz and his PT 331 crew when they attacked an enemy supply barge. But the two Devil Boats got stuck on a reef, and enemy troops on the island who heard the gunfire closed

ABOVE: *On the grid-iron they would have been the blitzing linebackers cutting through the line and knocking out the quarterback. In the Solomons, PT boat crewmen had a devil-may-care atti-tude as they sought out enemy warships and unleashed a devastating array of firepower. The crew of PT 109, with John F. Kennedy in com-mand (far right), were in the thick of the action, inflicting damage but losing out when it collided with a Japanese destroyer, on August 2, 1943. Two of the 109 crewmen were killed, but the others survived and were later rescued.* Photo courtesy of the John F. Kennedy Library

in for the easy kill. PT 331 managed to back off the reef to safety while Taylor ordered his crew to abandon ship.

To ensure that his boat would not fall into enemy hands, Taylor poured gasoline below decks. But before he could jump clear, PT 193 erupted in flames, and Taylor was severely wounded. He was pulled aboard PT 331 but died that night.

The death of Cy Taylor, like the hundreds of other Devil Boaters who lost their lives fighting in The Slot of the Solomons, only reminded PT skippers and crewmen that they were expendable. That certainly didn't convince them to transfer to safer duty. In fact, many athletes volunteered to serve with this elite group of daredevils.

One of the most famous PT boat skippers in The Slot was John F. Kennedy, son of the former U.S. ambassador to Great Britain. While at Harvard Kennedy played junior varsity football until a recurring back injury flared up. He played freshman golf and rugby and swam the medley relay on a team that went undefeated. He also teamed up with his older brother, Joe, Jr., to lead Harvard to the Intercollegiate Yacht Regatta trophy during his sophomore year.

In 1941 the Brooklyn Dodgers' ownership was struggling to keep the club, and Branch Rickey contacted Ambassador Joseph Kennedy about pur-chasing enough stock to become controlling owner of the team.

"He's got this son, John, who is brilliant in politics but has physical problems," recalled Walter O'Malley, when he asked Rickey about the elder Kennedy's interest in the ball club. "Mr. Kennedy thinks running the Dodgers could be the greatest outlet in the world for John."

But the deal fell through, and Joe Kennedy walked away from the Dodgers, while young Jack Kennedy joined the Navy.

As commander of PT 109, Kennedy was in charge of a thirteen-man crew. On August 2, 1943, PT 109 was patrolling at night in Blackett Strait near the island of Gizo. Along for the ride was one of Kennedy's Ivy League rivals, Princeton lacrosse player Barney Ross (not the professional boxer of the same name).

An enemy destroyer suddenly appeared and rammed the torpedo boat, shearing off the starboard side and killing two of the crewmen. The 109 exploded. Sailors who observed the collision from their patrol boats assumed all of their friends had been killed. With that enemy destroyer prowling around, it was too dangerous to search for any wounded.

Miraculously, all but two of the crewmen survived. But then Kennedy and the others had to swim for nearly five hours to Bird Island, avoiding both enemy patrols and hungry sharks. Over the next five days Kennedy would repeatedly risk his life to save his crew.

Exaggerating Their Claims

Masking their own casualty shortfalls, Japanese pilots boasted that they had sunk thirteen American aircraft carriers, nineteen cruisers, and nine battleships, plus countless auxiliary vessels, and the thousands of men aboard them, at Iron Bottom Sound. This was easily ten times the real U.S. losses.

This exaggerated battle reporting by Japanese pilots and naval commanders became a liability for their own war planners, who had no idea how many American warships—and especially the prized aircraft carriers—remained afloat. Just as at Coral Sea and Midway, the Japanese fell prey to their own pilots' machismo, grossly underestimating the full complement of the U.S. Navy in the Pacific.

By their own calculations, the Japanese believed they had nearly complete control of the high seas. And so they were stunned when swarms of American carrier-based planes pounced with devastating efficiency. Iron Bottom Sound became a graveyard for countless Japanese warships and the troops caught below decks.

A Knockout Punch

The most critical blow to the Japanese occurred on April 18, 1943, when Admiral Isoroku Yamamoto—the military commander who spearheaded the attack on Pearl Harbor and commander of the Japanese Combined Fleet—was killed when his plane was shot down by American P-38 fighter pilots based at Guadalcanal. Yamamoto's death was a dagger in the heart of the Japanese military.

The loss of Guadalcanal and Bougainville plus the naval defeat in the surrounding waters were equally devastating blows to the Japanese. Rear Admiral Ijuin Mitsuki's foreboding vision—"If Bougainville falls, Japan will topple"—would soon prove prophetic.

Though Tokyo proclaimed both encounters as victories, continuing to mislead the Japanese people, in fact the country's military would never recover from these enormous setbacks.

The USS *Juneau*

SHE WAS THE SLEEKEST VESSEL AFLOAT: THE LIGHT CRUISER USS *Juneau.* But in November 1942, along with the numerous other war ships patrolling The Slot, she was a tempting target to Japanese sub commanders.

The night of November 12 had been especially brutal to the thirteen-ship task group that the *Juneau* was maneuvering with, trading punches with enemy warships in the area. It was a costly night for both sides. By morning the American flotilla had only two cruisers and two destroyers still seaworthy, with only the destroyer USS *Fletcher* unharmed.

The *Juneau* limped along, bound for New Caledonia to make repairs. But on the morning of November 13, an enemy torpedo narrowly missed the cruiser USS *Helena* and slammed into the *Juneau*, cutting her in two. Within seconds the ship disappeared, with only 140 of her 900 men still alive and clinging to floating debris and life rafts.

Among the crew were the five Sullivan brothers, who had bucked Navy policy to serve on the *Juneau* together, and two of the four Rogers brothers.

As teenagers in Waterloo, Iowa, George and Frank Sullivan had learned to box, pounding on each other while three younger brothers—Joseph, called Red; Madison, known as Matt; and Albert—tagged along wherever they went. Frank also enjoyed playing baseball, though he had won his share of trophies and medals in the boxing ring.

In 1937 the two oldest Sullivan brothers signed up for a hitch in the Navy and served together on the USS *Hovey*, where Frank was crowned welterweight champion. By mid-1941 they had returned home, though they knew they could be recalled to the Navy if the fighting overseas continued to escalate and the United States was dragged into the war.

After they heard the news about the attack on Pearl Harbor, all five Sullivan brothers enlisted, though Al, who was married and had a child, was exempt. Al insisted on joining up with his brothers and, after protesting to the Navy Department, was allowed to enlist.

In addition, the Navy lifted its policy of splitting up family members so that, in the event of a disaster, no more than one would be lost. The favorable publicity from all five Sullivans serving together would lead to more Navy enlistees.

After training at the Great Lakes Naval Center in Illinois, the Sullivan boys waited in Brooklyn to board the *Juneau*.

Also waiting there were the Rogers boys: Joey, Pat, Lou, and Jimmy. They, too, were boxers, with Joey recording an amazing 130 knockouts and 24 technical decisions, with no losses.

Like the two oldest Sullivan brothers, Joey and Pat Rogers had already served a hitch in the military and had been waiting at home for war to break out. Like the rest of the nation, they were hopping mad after Pearl Harbor and quickly enlisted, in the Navy, along with their two younger brothers.

The Fighting Rogers knew the publicity their service generated might help them in their boxing careers after the war. But first they had to get through the biggest fight of their lives, alive and unharmed.

After demanding that they serve together, the Rogers were assigned to the *Juneau*.

When the Navy Department dispatched a bulletin urging all brothers and close relatives assigned together to seek reassignment to separate ships, Joey and Jimmy Rogers agreed to transfer to a supply ship. Pat and Louie stayed aboard the *Juneau*.

Tragically, all five Sullivan brothers perished when the *Juneau* was cut in two on November 12, 1942. Joey and Jimmy Rogers had transferred off just in time, but they lost their two brothers, Lou and Pat.

The two remaining Fighting Rogers stepped back in the ring after returning home. Joey had lost his edge, though, and called it quits after only a few bouts. Jimmy picked up where his older brother left off, sometimes fighting once a week. But after a ferocious victory that left him dazed, Jimmy and his wife agreed that it was time to hang up the gloves.

BACKGROUND AND ABOVE: *The Four Fighting Rogers brothers—Joe, James, Lou, and Pat—were also assigned to the* Juneau *but, sensing that they could all be lost if the ship went down, Joe and James transferred to another ship. Weeks later they learned that their two brothers had been killed when the* Juneau *was sunk.* Photo courtesy of James Rogers

Boxers Face the Fight of Their Lives

"To lack intelligence is to be in the ring blind-folded."

—*Marine Corps General D. M. Shoup*

"Boxing at all times, except when the Romans pepped it up with their little variation of cast-iron gloves, has been a most inadequate means of combat. It has no more to do with self-defense than a soldier attacking a tank with a pea-shooter. When one considers modern guerrilla training and the many ways of disabling a man, often permanently, that have been developed, the punch seems little less than puerile."

—*Paul Gallico*, The Golden People

"I know that before a bout I am so nervous that it takes every ounce of my will-power for me to sit still.

"That is the hardest time of any combat, whether with guns, fists or shoulder pads. It is then that one needs every ounce of courage one has. It is then that instinct whispers to you and says 'To hell with honor! To hell with what other people will think of you! To hell with the glory of winning, or of losing magnificently, for that matter! You don't want to get into this. You damned fool, what did you ever let yourself in for this for? You'd be a great one to lose an eye just for getting in a ring to make an impression on the women. Get out! Get out! It's almost too late.' You almost do it, too—almost. But somehow, you always stick it out until it is time to climb into the ring."

—*James Jones*

BACKGROUND: *To pass the time while enroute to the China-Burma-India Campaign, troops participate in a boxing tourney on the deck of a transport ship.*
U.S. Army photo

OF ALL THE PROFESSIONAL AND COLLEGIATE SPORTS, BOXING was hit the hardest in World War II. Though baseball and football were also ravaged by the manpower demands of the armed forces, they still fielded teams and still crowned their champions during the war years.

Boxing, with so many title-holders and contenders in the military, put a freeze on virtually all U.S. and world championship bouts until after the war.

At the world level, five of eight titles were put on hold because Americans serving in the military were the champions and couldn't take time off to train or fight.

Abe Green, president of the National Boxing Association, explained the reasoning for the freeze: "A man in service is entitled to complete protection of his championship under all circumstances until he is able to defend it."

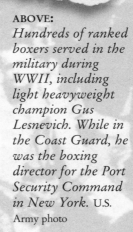

Decimated from Top to Bottom

To explain just how many top boxers were serving in the armed forces during the war, *Yank* magazine reported, on July 29, 1942: "The armed forces are well represented in the quarterly ring ratings of the National Boxing Association. No fewer than four of the eight recognized champions are wearing the uniforms of Uncle Sam. Listed among contenders and outstanding fighters in these ratings are numerous other servicemen.

ABOVE:
Hundreds of ranked boxers served in the military during WWII, including light heavyweight champion Gus Lesnevich. While in the Coast Guard, he was the boxing director for the Port Security Command in New York. U.S. Army photo

"Corporal Joe Louis of the Army naturally tops the heavies as the world's champion. Private Billy Conn, whose broken mitt is all healed, is the leading contender, and Bob Pastor and Lee Savold follow in that order; Melio Bettina and the Navy's Pat Valentine are a step down the ladder as outstanding boxers.

"Gus Lesnevich of the Coast Guard is king of the light heavies, and ranked as contenders are Billy Soose of the Navy, Jimmy Bivins, Booker Beckwith and Charles Ezzard.

"Outstanding are Ken Overlin and Tommy Tucker, both in the Navy, and England's knockout sensation, Tommy Mills.

"Tony Zale, another sailor is firmly entrenched as middleweight champ. Contenders are Georgie Abrams, Tony Martin and Charley Burley. Then come as outstanding, Coley Welch of the Coast Guard, and Fred Apostoli and Steve Belloise of the Navy.

LEFT: *Texas Golden Gloves boxer Don Gerber stepped in the ring against a black bear while stationed at Eagle Pass Army Air Field in Texas.*
Army Air Forces photo

RIGHT: *Heavyweight slugger Maxie Baer served as physical fitness instructor for the 4th Air Service Command at Tinker Field in Oklahoma. His brother, Buddy, at right (who would head for Hollywood after the war), looks on during a choke hold demonstration.* Army Air Force photo

BELOW: *Military policemen at Fort Warren in Wyoming dominated the All-Army boxing championships. The pugilists were, from left to right: heavyweights Ernest McDonald and Robert Nora, light heavyweights James Roberts and Jesse Raybon, welterweight Lawrence Fletcher, and featherweight Rudolph Barrett.* U.S. Army photo

"All branches of the service are up high in the welter division. Sailor Red Cochrane is the champion and contenders are Ray Robinson, California Jackie Wilson of the Army, and Marty Servo of the Coast Guard. Marine Garvey Young is an outstander.

"Sergeant Mike Raffa of the Army, leading contender for the NBA feather title is the only service man to be recognized in the four lower weight brackets."

Both Fred Apostoli and Barney Ross would eventually be selected for *Ring* magazine's Boxer of the Year award. Ross saw heavy action at Guadalcanal, while Apostoli served with a naval gun crew that endured numerous enemy attacks.

Hundreds more boxers—from amateurs, including numerous Golden Gloves winners, to regional pro pugilists and aspiring but still up-and-coming lower-ranked contenders—would enter the armed forces from 1942 to '45.

Boxers' Roles in the Military

Boxers who joined the military fell into three groupings: those who were morale-boosters for the troops overseas, putting on exhibitions, like Joe Louis, who worked tirelessly to entertain the troops; those who served as physical training instructors, at mostly stateside locations, such as Gene Tunney and Jack Dempsey; and those who served in combat, like Barney Ross at Guadalcanal.

The Brown Bomber

Joe Louis had been the heavyweight champ since 1937. In a bout that would come to symbolize the war against Adolf Hitler's racist beliefs, Louis stepped into the ring against German champion Max Schmeling, on June 22, 1938.

Schmelling was a shining example of Aryan superiority, and Nazi propagandists quickly reminded the world that their champion had already proven this point two years earlier when he beat Louis in a nontitle bout.

In the 1937 rematch, Louis was aware that Olympian Jesse Owens had led a contingent of American athletes—black and white—and upset the Germans in their own backyard, at the Berlin Games a year earlier.

Schmelling could redeem some of that lost luster to the Aryan myth by knocking out Louis in the rematch scheduled for Yankee Stadium in June and bringing the heavyweight crown back to the Fatherland. Hitler had even sent him a cable, proclaiming Max Schmelling as "the coming world's champion."

Too bad Louis didn't cooperate. He pummeled Schmeling from the opening bell, knocking him down three times in the first round!

"The Aryan idol, the unconquerable one had been beaten, the bright, shining symbol of race glory has been thumped in the dust. That noise you hear is [Nazi propaganda minister Joseph] Goebbels making for the storm cellar," wrote Jeffrey Sammons in *Beyond the Ring: The Role of Boxing in American Society.*

Barely a month after Pearl Harbor, Joe Louis joined the Army the day after he defended his title, clobbering Buddy Baer and donating his winnings to the Navy Relief Fund, which helped families of those killed in Hawaii. In March he fought again, this time for the Army Relief Fund.

Numerous exhibition matches were held to raise money for the war effort and allowed top boxers, such as Louis, to show their patriotism and keep their names in the headlines. But most of these exhibitions were little more than sparring matches, with a lot of braggadocio but very few knockout punches.

BELOW: *During basic training, men from the newly-formed 81st Infantry Division learn basic boxing techniques.*
81st Wildcat Division Historical Committee photo

RIGHT ABOVE: *Joe Louis—the Brown Bomber—was heavyweight champion when he joined the Army, spending most of his time putting on exhibition bouts to raise money for war relief. He also toured overseas to box for the troops.* Library of Congress photo

Louis, known as the Brown Bomber, would spend his Army tour visiting troops overseas, stateside, and in hospitals. He would also participate in one hundred bouts and exhibitions against other pro fighters, including Golden Gloves featherweight and lightweight champion Sugar Ray Robinson, who served briefly in the Army until a freak fall down a flight of stairs at Fort Hamilton in Brooklyn caused temporary amnesia. Two months later, Robinson received an honorable discharge, just three days before D-Day. (After the war, Robinson won the world welterweight title, in December 1946, and the world middleweight crown in February 1951.)

Pvt. Joe Louis says...

"We're going to do our part ...and we'll win because we're on God's side"

Former Champions Serve

Jack Dempsey, former heavyweight champ from 1919 to 1926, who chewed pine gum to build up his jaw and was known as the Manassa Mauler and Killer of the Ring, served in the Coast Guard, heading up its physical training course, which Dempsey referred to as a "fighting program." He also crisscrossed the country countless times, fighting exhibition matches and raising millions in war bonds. Near the end of the war he would even get a taste of combat, landing at Okinawa, one of the bloodiest battles of the Pacific.

Gene Tunney, who beat Dempsey for the heavyweight crown in 1926, had served in the Marine Corps during World War I, where he fought other Allied boxers in Europe and won the lightweight crown. He retired undefeated in 1928. During World War II he oversaw the Navy's physical training program, and his well-conditioned students were affectionately known as Tunney Fish.

New Zealand heavyweight champion Tom Heeney was in a Navy construction battalion in the Pacific. In July 1928 he had fought Tunney for the heavyweight crown and lost.

Another undefeated heavyweight who joined the service was Eddie Eagan, with the Army Air Corps in the China-Burma-India Campaign. During World War I Eagan was heavyweight champion of Allied forces in Europe, just as Tunney had won the lightweight title. Eagan would also capture the Amateur Athletic Union title and an Olympic gold medal, but he turned down a pro career.

RIGHT BELOW: *Gene Tunney won the heavyweight title in 1926, beating Jack Dempsey. Though he retired from the ring two years later, Tunney would be called on to head up the Navy's fitness regime during the war years.* AP Wide World photo

Brockton's Future Bomber

Rocco Marchegiano played baseball at Brockton High School in Massachusetts before dropping out at fourteen and joining the Army. He was stationed initially at Fort Devens in Massachusetts, where a burly Texan taunted the soldiers in Rocco's unit, challenging anyone to a fistfight.

After his buddies decided that Rocco probably had the best chance against the bully, he agreed to square off. Then he proceeded to pound his opponent's face, knocking the chump out. Years later Rocco would recall, "That fight gave me something. From that time on I felt within myself that nobody could beat me. And I carried that feeling into every one of my fights."

Marchegiano deployed overseas with the Army's 150th Combat Engineers and participated in tearing down the walls of Fortress Europe, when Allied forces stormed the beaches at Normandy, France, in June 1944.

After returning home, Marchegiano picked up boxing just to get into shape and had an unsuccessful tryout with the Red Sox. He soon pushed aside his first love, baseball, after a few successful bouts against other Army boxers. He changed his name to Rocky Marciano and became known as the Brockton Bomber or simply the Rock. (On September 23, 1952, Marciano won the heavyweight crown, and he would defend it six times before retiring with a perfect record of 49–0.)

Boxers Deployed in Every Campaign

Light-heavyweight champion Tommy Loughran served with the Second Marine Division in the Pacific. Former heavyweight contender Bob Paxtor joined up with the Tenth Mountain Division, which engaged in some of the toughest fighting of the war, in Italy.

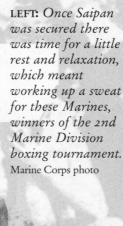

LEFT: *Once Saipan was secured there was time for a little rest and relaxation, which meant working up a sweat for these Marines, winners of the 2nd Marine Division boxing tournament.*
Marine Corps photo

Ezzard Charles drove an Army truck in Italy until his superiors realized they had a boxing sensation in their midst. As a high school senior in 1942, Charles had stepped in the ring and knocked out former light-heavyweight champion Anton Christoforidis in three rounds. He would enter the 1944 Inter-Allied boxing tourney and capture the light-heavyweight crown.

Bantamweight star Midget Smith, who had served in World War I, was also stationed in Italy during World War II. East Coast heavyweight Bob Nestell was wounded during the fighting on Sicily and was evacuated to North Africa to recover from his injuries.

Yank magazine would write in December 1943: "Pedro Montanez, former welterweight contender, who operates a cocktail parlor at San Juan, says there are so many champions and near champions hanging around his place that he's thinking about calling it 'Little Jacobs Beach' [after trainer Mike Jacobs, who handled Joe Louis and Sugar Ray Robinson].

"Some of his customers include Tony Zale, middleweight champion; Willie Pavlovich, light heavy contender, and Sixto Escobar, bantam champion, all of whom are stationed in and around Puerto Rico."

Escobar was working with military policemen on Puerto Rico to improve their fighting skills, while Zale was in the Coast Guard there.

Petey Sarron, former featherweight champ, served as the Army Air Corps boxing coach at Maxwell Field in Alabama. Cleveland heavyweight boxer Eddie Simms was assigned as the boxing instructor at the San Diego Naval Air Station.

Featherweight champion Willie Pep, dubbed the Artful Dodger by sportswriter Red Smith, served in the Army, then transferred to the Navy. During the 1940s, Pep, Joe Louis, and Sugar Ray Robinson were considered the only true ring artists of the decade. In fact, many boxing insiders felt that, pound for pound, Pep was the best of the best.

Jimmy Braddock, former heavyweight champion, was in the Army, while ex-lightweight titlist Lew Jenkins served in the Coast Guard. Lightweight contender Lenny Mancini was wounded in combat during the Battle of the Bulge.

Though not in the armed forces, undefeated lightweight champion Benny Leonard served with the U.S. Maritime Service. He helped train cadets for the Merchant Marine, which saw extensive combat on the high seas, escorting convoys from the United States to Europe.

Numerous Golden Gloves fighters wound up in the armed forces, including Pittsburgh welterweight Bill Garrett, 1938 Illinois heavyweight champion Dick Kist, and New Yorker Johnny Smith.

Once the Europe and Pacific Campaigns were concluded—with the United States and its Allies winning the greatest knockout fight ever—America's pugilists returned to the ring, igniting some of the hottest scrambles for division crowns ever in the history of boxing.

ABOVE: *Two high-profile Marines— boxing champions Barney Ross and Willy Pep— celebrate their discharge together.* U.S. Marine Corps photo

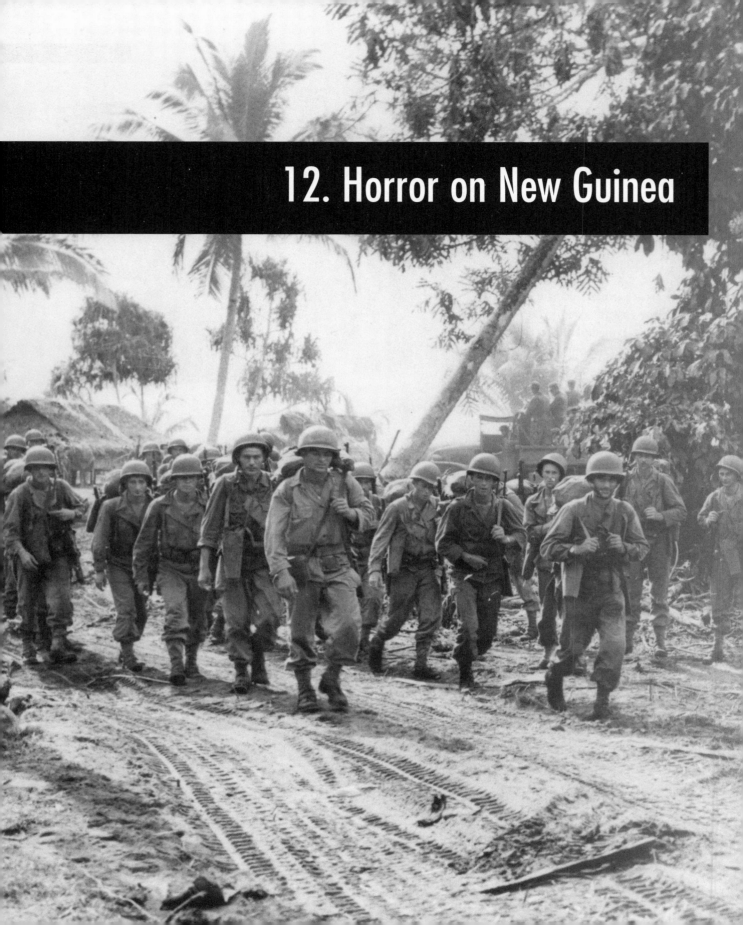

12. Horror on New Guinea

> "I HOPE EVERY JAP THAT MENTIONS MY NAME GETS SHOT, AND TO HELL WITH ALL JAPS ANYWAY."
>
> —*Babe Ruth, after hearing that Japanese soldiers in South Pacific jungles were shouting "To hell with Babe Ruth"*

PERILOUSLY CLOSE TO THE NORTHERN TERRITORIES OF Australia is New Guinea, site of some of the most brutal fighting in the South Pacific.

By late July 1942 the Japanese had sent four thousand troops to capture Buna on the north shore of the island. Their mission was to cross a mountain range and seize vital Port Moresby, which would then allow Japanese warships to cut the Allied supply lines between Australia and the United States, leaving the Land Down Under vulnerable to attack.

The Allies immediately recognized this maneuver and rushed troops from the Thirty-second Infantry Prairie Division and Australian Seventh Division to New Guinea, where they drove the enemy back to the northern side of the island.

But steep, vine-covered cliffs and jungle swamps made any advance on Buna tediously slow, giving the Japanese time to build log bunkers and trenches overlooking every approach. They also constructed mortar-proof gun pits under the massive exposed roots of jungle trees, keeping them hidden until they opened up their guns on unsuspecting American and Australian patrols.

Athletes Dish Out the Punishment

Aerial bombardment by the Fifth Air Force could not dislodge the well-protected Japanese. Only tanks firing point-blank into the enemy bunkers could silence them. But too often tanks could not maneuver in the dense jungle, and ground troops were on their own.

Too many brave young men lost their lives trying to crawl close enough to lob grenades into the enemy positions. But it was the only way to secure the eastern region of New Guinea, and Buna finally fell on January 22, 1943.

Frank "Bulldog" Atkinson, former light-heavyweight wrestler, was involved in close-quarters fighting near Buna and recalled his own version of up close and personal: "We were on patrol and proceeded to pitch camp before we discovered that 25 yards ahead a nine-man Jap patrol lay dug in. At about the same time, it seems, the Japs discovered us. We set

OPPOSITE: *Hopscotching from one island to the next, soldiers of the 127th Infantry advance on Aitape, New Guinea. Ken Gruennert, a catcher in high school back in Wisconsin, and a squad leader with the 127th, used his throwing skills on Christmas Eve of 1942 to knock out enemy gun emplacements with hand grenades. But he was cut down by an enemy sniper.* Photo courtesy of the MacArthur Memorial Museum

ABOVE: *After securing the Admiralties, American troops found an enemy naval gun still intact and turned it against other Japanese strongholds nearby.* Department of Defense photo

out to wipe each other out quiet-like. In the free-for-all hand-to-hand fighting that followed, I broke the arms and legs of at least two Japs, with a flying mare, a back body drop and an Ogasaki dive . . . that's a Judo touch." Atkinson, the human highlight film, saw plenty more action, until he was wounded in 1944 and shipped home.

Ken Gruennert was a squad leader with the 127th Infantry Regiment at Buna. He had been catcher for his high school baseball team back in Helenville, Wisconsin. But on Christmas Eve, 1942, he was crawling through a jungle swamp, edging close to two enemy machine gun nests that had his squad pinned down. Gruennert would rely on the same technique he used as a catcher throwing runners out at second base to heave a few hand grenades at the enemy position. After knocking out the closest one and sustaining a shoulder wound, he crawled toward the second enemy position and blew it to pieces. But before the rest of his unit could move up, he was killed by sniper fire. For his actions, Gruennert was awarded the Congressional Medal of Honor.

Among those Americans fighting on New Guinea were numerous athletes, including Charles Galbreath, all-American tackle at Illinois in 1935; Jimmy Lawrence, NFL running back with the Packers, Cardinals, and Dodgers, who was wounded in action; Negro Leagues infielder Sammy Hughes, who played for the Baltimore Elite Giants before the war and served with the Army's 196th Support Battalion; and Harold Hantelmann, all-American guard for Iowa in 1928, who was injured in the knee by an enemy grenade.

The Bushmasters

One of the most interesting units that fought in the New Guinea Campaign was the 158th Infantry Regiment, the Bushmasters, composed primarily of Mexican-Americans along with Indians from twenty-two tribes in the southwest region of the United States. The Indian men in the regiment, particularly those in

BELOW: *Biak Island, U.S. medium tanks proved their superiority over enemy tanks. Even in treacherous jungle terrain, American armor units provided the infantry with lethal firepower.* U.S. Army Signal Corps photo

LEFT: *To prevent the enemy from delivering fresh troops, supplies and ammunition to front-line units, A-20 planes were employed, using skip bombing tactics to ensure greater accuracy.*
Army Air Forces photo

Company F, were skilled athletes. In high school they played baseball, basketball, and football and ran track. And when the regiment planned any kind of athletic competition between its companies, quite often the Indians from Company F walked away with the bragging rights.

Among the Bushmasters were battalion commander Fred Stofft, a halfback at Glendale High School in California (a teammate of his was Marion Morrison, who would later try his luck with acting and change his name to John Wayne); Ralph Cameron, a Maricopa Indian who enjoyed playing football in Phoenix; heavyweight boxer Jimmy Nocon, who would suffer severe leg wounds at Arare when he tried to rescue a wounded buddy and an enemy machine gun opened up on him; Dixie Walker, a four-letter athlete in high school in Ohio who would receive the Silver Star for his actions at Arare; and Gus Mauzaka, a New Haven athlete who lettered in baseball, basketball, football, and fencing. In New Guinea's dense jungles and in close hand-to-hand fighting, Mauzaka's ability with a saber was invaluable. He was killed when a Japanese soldier stabbed him through the heart with a bayonet.

ABOVE: *In 1938, golfer Frank Moore beat Sammy Snead for the PGA title. Five years later, Moore was stationed on New Guinea, patching up B-24 Liberator bombers coming back from hazardous missions in the South Pacific.*
Army Air Forces photo

Mounting Casualties

Australian and U.S. forces combined would lose 3,095 killed in action, with another 5,451 wounded. But Japan lost a staggering 43,000, including two field armies.

For America's Thirty-second Division, the Red Arrows, New Guinea was its first taste of combat, and the division suffered heavy casualties: 687 killed and 1,918 wounded in action. Another 7,125 soldiers were felled by jungle diseases such as malaria, dysentery, typhus, and dengue fever.

Battle of the Bismarck Sea

The Japanese were still entrenched on New Guinea, to the north at Hollandia. They were licking their wounds but were determined to seize all of the island and control the surrounding waters. They already held Rabaul on the northern end of New Britain (just to the east of New Guinea) and made plans to try to retake Buna. Transport ships were detected leaving Rabaul and heading west into the Bismarck Sea escorted by seven warships on February 28, 1943.

ABOVE: *After each battle there was time for some well-deserved rest before the next confrontation with the Japanese. American units at New Guinea held an all-star baseball game and one of the players was former White Sox and Yankees catcher Ken Silvestri.*
U.S. Army photo

The Fifth Air Force sent its B-25 and B-17 bombers and A-20 torpedo planes along with Australian Beaufighter planes to cut off the enemy convoy, which they quickly destroyed. One of the B-17s was crippled, and the crew was forced to bail out. Japanese Zeroes spotted the parachutes and closed in to strafe the helpless airmen.

Other Allied bomber crews saw this act of cowardice and flashed the news to all forces operating in the area. All of the Japanese transport ships bound for Buna—carrying six thousand reinforcement troops—were hit in the attack, as were those that followed over the next two days. Some of the transports turned about and made it back to Rabaul.

When hundreds of Japanese troops jumped off the other sinking transports, Allied planes and PT boats closed in for a little payback, emptying their machine guns on the enemy troops floundering in the water. Sharks took their share, too, and only a few hundred men were rescued.

It was a devastating blow for Japan: 3,664 men lost at sea, six warships sunk and two more damaged, eight transport ships lost, and twenty planes shot down. The Japanese soon abandoned their efforts to reinforce New Guinea. But there were still many other skirmishes to come in the region, and the Allied forces routed the Japanese from their stronghold on New Britain, before turning their attention to other conquests.

The well-entrenched 90,000 Japanese at Rabaul waited out the war for an attack that never came. General Douglas MacArthur was out to win the war as quickly as possible, not fight it out with every enemy stronghold on every island in the Pacific. The Allies bypassed many Japanese-held islands as they continued their trek toward Japan's home islands.

Allied bombers and fighter planes had knocked out Japanese planes at Rabaul; then Allied planes from nearby Bougainville and other air bases in the region shot down the few enemy planes that remained.

Allied warships also heavily patrolled the surrounding waters, effectively cutting off the Rabaul garrison from its supply lines, simply leaving it to wither away.

Island Hopping

On December 26, 1943, the First Marine Division landed on what they referred to as "green hell" and "the slimy sewer" New Britain, the largest island in the Bismarck Archipelago, where more than 10,000 enemy troops waited.

Torrential downpours turned the rugged terrain and beach swamps into "pea soup." Many Marines were hurt just from falling over slippery tree roots or into deep sinkholes. They had to use all their leg strength just to keep from getting sucked into the muddy bog.

Artillery pieces became stuck and had to be dug out or left behind. Pesky enemy snipers also kept up a constant harassment of the exhausted Marines. During one suicide charge, the Japanese soldiers shouted "To hell with Babe Ruth!" just before they were cut down by small arms fire and grenades. Later, when asked about the incident, the Sultan of Swat himself replied, "I hope every Jap that mentions my name gets shot, and to hell with all Japs anyway."

It would take until February 10, 1944, before the Allies had secured the western sector of New Britain. But the enemy stronghold at Rabaul still remained, though it was enduring continual bombardment from Army Air Corps bombers.

In March 1944, as U.S. and Allied forces continued their northward push, it was critical to remove the Japanese from New Guinea at Hollandia. Seizure of this stronghold would cut off more than 100,000 enemy troops, leaving no avenue for their retreat.

Fifth Air Force bombers worked with carrier planes of Navy Task Force 58 to knock out two hundred enemy planes, while Allied warships unleashed their deck guns on Japanese shore fortifications. This allowed more than 79,000 U.S. troops to hit several locations along New Guinea's midsection in April. Once ashore these forces tightened the noose around 11,000 Japanese garrisoned at Sentani. Many Japanese fled into the nearby Cyclops

LEFT: *Two years after the Japanese had overrun Wake Island, Allied forces were closing in to re-take the remote outpost. In 1944, a B-25 Mitchell bomber drops its payload on enemy positions on Wake, one of many sorties to neutralize the Japanese there.*
National Archives photo

Mountains. Mopping up around Hollandia would be completed by early June. American losses included 159 dead, while the Japanese lost 3,300 killed and another 600 taken prisoner.

Remembering "a Small, Tough Fullback"

Aitape and its two vital airfields, 120 miles east of Hollandia, were secured within a day.

"We were part of a smaller convoy that broke off from the main body for the assault on Aitape," recalled future football Hall of Famer Emlen Tunnell, who served on board the USS *Etamin.* "It was no secret that we were carrying six thousand tons of high explosives. A direct hit would have eliminated all my future worries about [pro football stars] Bobby Layne, Otto Graham, Norman Van Brocklin, Y. A. Tittle, and other tormentors.

"At about 11 P.M. on April 27th, the Japs delivered their second aerial torpedo meant for us. This one was no near miss. It hit on the starboard side, amidships, and blew a hole 27 feet by 27 feet.

"General quarters was sounded, but you don't need any reminder when the Japs are using torpedoes for alarm clocks. Everybody was wide awake about one second after the torpedo hit."

Tunnell and his shipmates were forced to abandon ship. "I looked out toward our ship, listing and smoking only 200 yards away. You always hear ships referred to as 'she,' but I never thought of the *Etamin* as a fighting lady. Our ship reminded me of a small, tough fullback, without much speed, pounding forward every minute of the game."

Small Skirmishes with Strange Names

Other battles in the region would include Maffin Bay, Biak, Noemfoor, Sansapor, Driniumor, and Manus and Los Negros in the Admiralty Islands.

Notre Dame football captain and tackle Paul Lillis was wounded in the invasion of the Admiralties. Joe Kilgrow, former Alabama running back, commanded an anti-aircraft battery credited with shooting down four Zeroes while under fire.

With the devastating losses of the Midway, Solomons, and New Guinea Campaigns, the balance of power had shifted back in favor of the Allies. The Japanese abandoned their offensive plans and reverted to a defensive posture, hoping they could stall the Allied northward advance long enough to regroup and come out fighting strong in later rounds.

Developing "Gameness and Fortitude"

Once they had secured New Guinea, American troops had time for some well-deserved rest and relaxation before the next confrontation with the Japanese.

Gene Tunney, former heavyweight boxing champion and the Navy's director of physical training during World War II, visited New Guinea and talked with General MacArthur about the importance of physical training: "We are better equipped than any other nation in the world to carry on a long war because of sports," Tunney noted.

MacArthur stressed that football and boxing were the best sports for the development of a fighting man, according to *Stars and Stripes*

ABOVE: *American Indians from numerous tribes played a crucial role in the South Pacific, serving in front line combat units. The secretive Navajo Code Talkers sent and received radio transmissions in their own language that the Japanese could never decipher.* Photo courtesy of the MacArthur Memorial Museum

RIGHT BELOW: *Many infantrymen would rather face combat with the Japanese than another day of seasickness on a transport ship! Deploying to the beaches at Bougainville to reinforce the battle-weary Marines, soldiers climb down a cargo net from the President Jackson in November of 1943.* Department of Defense photo

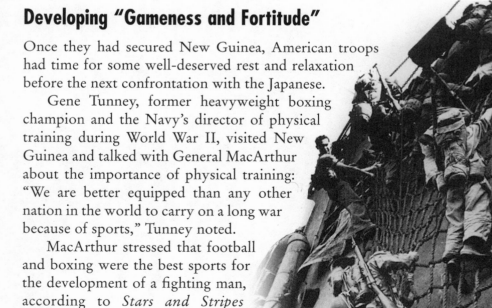

LEFT ABOVE:
"Where the hell is Bougainville?" many Marines wondered as they headed for shore at Empress Augusta Bay in June of 1943. After securing the beachhead and pushing inward, they were able to construct three crucial airstrips that would quickly be used to launch air strikes. U.S. Coast Guard photo

Weekly, October 21, 1944. MacArthur added though that any sport would develop "gameness and fortitude," qualities essential in a fighting man.

With plenty of trees, construction equipment, and time, the GIs on New Guinea built a bowling alley, including pins and balls, claiming that it was the only alley in a combat zone.

By the end of summer in 1944 attention turned to the World Series involving the St. Louis Browns and their cross-town rivals, the Cardinals. GIs on New Guinea heard the play-by-play rebroadcast on shortwave radio. Even Japanese prisoners captured in the New Guinea Campaign tried to listen to the World Series broadcasts.

With so many big-league players serving in the area, New Guinea hosted its own version of the Fall Classic. Participants in the New Guinea Series included Chattanooga minor leaguer Lou Roede, Erv "Four Sack" Dusak of the Cardinals (who would return home and play in the '46 World Series), Phillies pitcher Hugh Mulcahy, Birmingham minor leaguer Carmel Castle, Louis Rosen of the Yankees, Columbus minor leaguer Jack Griffore, White Sox and Yankees catcher Ken "Hawk" Silvestri, Red Sox first baseman Al "Broadway" Flair, and Red Sox minor leaguers Al Kozar and George Byam.

Entertaining the troops from the foul lines was the clown prince of baseball, Al Schacht, who became known more for his pranks and pratfalls than his baseball skills. Schacht's foul-line antics had everyone laughing, something they hadn't done much of during weeks of brutal fighting.

But even tougher battles were still to come.

LEFT BELOW: *Former heavyweight champion and WWI veteran Gene Tunney was in charge of the Navy's athletic training program and visited the South Pacific, where many of his charges, affectionately known as Tunney Fish, were deployed on warships throughout the region.* Library of Congress photo

13. Confrontation in the Frozen Frontier

"By one of those devices that make Uncle Sam's Army oftimes the wonder and despair of foreign strategists, many of the Alaska-based troops hail from the deep South. Alaskans of the Aleutian chain claim 'it rains in Siberia, and the wind just blows it over here.'

"You'll hear the boys from Dixie begin hollering, "Give it back to the Russians.' Not one of them yet has entertained the suggestion of giving it to the Japs."

—*Sergeant Georg Meyers, October 21, 1942, in Alaska, for* Yank *magazine*

OPPOSITE: *An anti-aircraft gun crew stationed at a desolate outpost in the Aleutians watches for enemy planes. In mid-1942 the Japanese had invaded the Aleutians and American units were quickly rushed to the frozen frontier to prevent any further advance toward the West Coast of North America.* National Archives photo

THE ALEUTIAN ISLANDS FORM A ROW OF STEPPING-STONES from Japan to the Arctic regions of North America. These desolate outposts—Unalaska and Agattu, Kiska and Adak, Attu and Amchitka—became the focus of concern in the United States when, on June 3, 1942, Japanese carrier planes bombed Unalaska at Dutch Harbor, killing thirty-five Americans. This could only be a precursor of Japan's intention to invade North America.

U.S. pilots from Patrol Air Wing 4 and the Eleventh Fighter Squadron were sent out to locate the approaching fleet but could not prevent the Japanese from invading the islands. Commanding the Eleventh Air Force's Twenty-eighth Composite Group in Alaska was Colonel William Eareckson, who in 1928 earned first place honors in the Gordon Bennett International Balloon Race. After an air mission that failed to locate any enemy planes, Eareckson submitted the following report to higher headquarters: "Tactical operations for today: No hits, no runs, no errors."

Among the hundreds of other fighter and bomber pilots serving in the Aleutians was Rice University's intercollegiate tennis champion Frank Guernsey. Marv Rickert was an ammunition hauler in the Aleutians. After returning home he would make it to spring training with the Chicago Cubs and battle for the right field position.

ABOVE: *While stationed in Alaska, an American Coast Guardsman teaches softball to the local Eskimos.* National Archives photo

Invasion or Diversion

Fully aware that American aircraft carriers had probably escaped the attack on Pearl Harbor, the Japanese hoped an assault on the Aleutians would lure part of the U.S. fleet to northern waters, making it easier to battle the remaining carrier task forces roaming the Pacific and threatening Japanese troop movements. But American code-breakers figured out that the attack in the Aleutians was simply a diversionary move. The real intent of the Japanese had been taking Midway, which would become a pivotal naval confrontation in May 1942.

Still, because of their proximity to both northern Japan and North America, the Aleutians were a very real threat to Japan and the United States. From air bases in the Arctic, bombers could easily reach either country. In fact, when Jimmy Doolittle's Raiders bombed Tokyo in April 1942, the Japanese first thought the bombers came from air bases in the Aleutians, not from some mysterious American carrier in the Pacific.

The Navy and Coast Guard dispatched warships and patrol boats to the Aleutians to watch for an enemy invasion fleet. Former Oregon State

football player and Philadelphia Athletics catcher John Leovich was assigned to a Coast Guard cutter prowling the Alaskan shoreline. He served on station for three years and lost interest in playing ball after returning home. "My priorities had changed quite a bit [and] when you lost a lot of friends, athletics becomes insignificant."

Freezing Temperatures Take a Toll

For Leovich and the thousands of Americans and Japanese in the northwest, fighting each other in the Aleutians would be only half the battle. Mother Nature proved to be an indiscriminating and formidable foe herself.

Weapons and machinery—including planes and artillery guns—could not withstand the subfreezing temperatures, which turned oil and lubricants into jelly and drained all the energy from batteries. Even more vulnerable to the harsh weather conditions were the soldiers on both sides digging foxholes in the ice-hard tundra, warding off frostbite, or trying to keep a fire going in an Arctic windstorm.

The only combat-ready unit located in the western United States was the Seventh Infantry Hourglass Division in California. They had undergone desert warfare training and were equipped to fight in the North Africa Campaign, not the subfreezing Aleutians. Still, with little cold weather gear, they headed north, invading Attu on May 11, 1943. One of the Army officers at Attu was Lieutenant Cliff Kimsey, who had been an all-American guard at Georgia in 1941.

By the end of the month, and after several brutal battles, the Americans had lost 549 killed in action and had another 1,148 wounded, with more than 2,000 removed from the frontlines because of disease, accidents, and cold weather injuries.

For the Japanese, who fought to the death, 2,350 had been killed. Only 29 disgraced their emperor by surrendering.

The Allies took Kiska next, in mid-August. More than 34,000 Allied troops, mostly American, invaded the island, expecting another bitter fight.

ABOVE: *U.S. submarine S-32 arrives at Dutch Harbor, Alaska, after a successful patrol, sinking three enemy warships and two merchant ships.* U.S. Navy photo

ABOVE: *When the 1942 Alaskan all-star football game was held, numerous collegians played, with other high schoolers filling out the ranks. Among the quarterbacks and running backs in the game were (from left to right) Gordon Hill, who played at Washington State; Bill Jones of Wisconsin Teachers College; Vern Bybee; Steve Pentek from Marquette University; and Charles Wright.*
U.S. Army photo

RIGHT: *More than 800 soldiers showed up for the 1943 GI Olympic Games held on Kodiak, Alaska. In the 120-yard low hurdles, Corporal Bill Combs (far right) took first place.* U.S. Army photo

But all of the occupying Japanese soldiers had already slipped off the island, leaving behind only mines and booby traps. Once the Japanese abandoned the Aleutians Campaign, American bomber pilots stationed there began bombing the Kuriles, north of Japan.

Ballplayers Tour the Frigid North

After the 1943 World Series, several baseball players—including Stan Musial, Dixie Walker, Frankie Frisch, Danny Litwhiler, and Hank Borowy—toured the frozen north and entertained the troops for six weeks.

"Four times a day, seven days a week, they did nothing but answer questions, run off World Series movies and autograph baseballs," reported *Yank* magazine on February 18, 1944. "And still the guys clamored for more."

On one of these occasions, Frank Frisch, known for his acid tongue, had the GIs laughing and cheering at all the right moments. Among the soldiers in their field jackets was a burly Aleut, a mountain of a man, expressionless and stone-still except for his hands, which held a butcher knife he kept flicking with his thumb. Frisch couldn't help but keep a wary eye on this native and finally asked if he understood English and if he cared even a little about baseball.

The Aleut growled back, "Me . . . catcher." Then he pointed his knife menacingly at Frisch. "Me go back to Pittsburgh . . . with you!"

The GIs roared with laughter, but Frisch abruptly ended his spiel and hustled out, hoping the other ballplayers would protect him from bodily harm. Days later they would return home . . . without any stowaway Aleut.

The Triple Nickels

"WE ALL KNEW IT WOULDN'T BE EASY, BUT WE LOOKED FORWARD TO THIS TOUGH JOB WITH EAGERNESS AND SPIRIT. WE KNEW THAT WE WERE PRIVILEGED AND FORTUNATE TO BE AMONG THE FIRST BLACK MEN ON EARTH TO TRAIN FOR PARACHUTE WINGS."

—*Bradley Biggs*

AS BLACKS IN THE MILITARY MOVED INTO MORE COMBAT roles during World War II, they quickly proved they could handle any mission they were given. Shattering the view that they weren't smart enough to think during the chaos of battle, that they might flee rather than fight. One of the most challenging roles belonged to the all-black 555th Parachute Infantry Battalion, nicknamed the Triple Nickels.

Each paratrooper in the 555th was selected for his athleticism, and many were college graduates. Among them was Warren "Cal" Cornelius, East coast light-heavyweight boxer, whose pro record before joining the Army was 96–16; North Carolina A&T College tackle Timothy Armour; Bradley Biggs, who played football with the New York Brown Bombers; Virginia State College football guard Robert Hill; New England lightweight boxer Ted Lowry; "Jabo" Jablonsky, who played football at West Point; Morgan State track and football star Carstell Stewart; and Edward Baker and Jack Warrick, who both played basketball.

During a live-fire training exercise at Camp Mackall in North Carolina, Cal Cornelius would lose

BELOW: *It wasn't Normandy or Holland but when the 555th Parachute Battalion was deployed to the Pacific northwest during WWII, its mission was to fight forest fires created by enemy incendiary bombs carried via the jet stream from Japan's home islands.* Photo courtesy of the U.S. Forest Service

his right hand when a grenade simulator blew up prematurely and he would be mustered out of the Army.

Waiting for Deployment

Other Army airborne units had participated in the invasions of North Africa, Normandy, southern France, and Belgium. Naturally the Triple Nickels assumed they would be following them to Europe sometime in late 1944. But instead, the three thousand paratroopers of the 555th were sent to the northwestern United States, to Pendelton, Oregon, in April 1945 to battle a different enemy.

The Japanese had developed balloon bombs, called the Fu-Go Project, which were sent aloft and carried via the jet stream to North America. Two woodcutters in Montana discovered one of the bombs; a woman and her five children were killed by another near Bly, Oregon.

News reports in early 1945 warned people not to touch these deadly balloons, which measured upward of thirty-five feet in diameter. The Japanese planned to dispatch 15,000 antipersonnel bombs and a staggering 60,000 firebombs to torch America's northwest forests.

The Army Air Corps sent patrol planes out to intercept and shoot down

ABOVE AND BACK-GROUND: *The all-black 555th Parachute Infantry Battalion— the Triple Nickels— trained for combat in World War II and waited for deployment to Europe, but instead they were sent to the northwest United States to defuse Japanese balloon bombs and fight forest fires created by exploded bombs.* Photo courtesy of the U.S. Forest Service

RIGHT: *A smoke-jumper from the 555th Parachute Battalion used his combat training to fight in Operation Firefly . . . to fight fires created by Japanese airborne incendiaries.* Photo courtesy of the U.S. Forest Service

these explosives-laden balloons before they reached the coast. But hundreds had already been launched against the United States, and with the fire season approaching, firefighters were sent to the region, fearing an inferno that could get out of control rapidly if one or more of these balloons detonated in densely forested areas.

The Triple Nickels were rushed through firefighter training and sent to base camps across the northwest, as part of the Fire Fly Project. These "smoke jumpers" would be flown to hazardous sites, where they would parachute in, often over dense forests or rocky mountain tops. Once on the ground, they would put out the fires or dismantle the bombs and secure the area. The 555th became the Army's only airborne firefighters, a precursor of latter-day smoke jumpers.

LEFT: *A smoke jumper from the Triple Nickels jumps into a forested area of the Pacific northwest as part of Operation Firefly.* Photo courtesy of the U.S. Forest Service

BELOW: *While undergoing airborne training at Camp Mackall in North Carolina, the 555th Parachute Infantry formed a football team and played other military and college squads in the area. Some of those players included North Carolina A&T lineman Tim Armour, New York Brown Bombers' Bradley Biggs, West Point's Jabo Jablonski, Carstell Stewart from Morgan State, and Virginia State College guard Robert Hill.* U.S. Army Signal Corps photo

14. Booting the Nazis out of Italy

> "... A RABELAISIAN GAME OF CHESS WHERE THE BOARD HAS A MILLION SQUARES AND THE PIECES CONSIST OF A DOZEN KINGS AND QUEENS, A THOUSAND KNIGHTS, AND SO MANY PAWNS THAT NO ONE CAN EXACTLY COUNT THEM."
>
> —*Sir Ian Hamilton*

ONCE NORTH AFRICA WAS UNDER ALLIED CONTROL, THE next task was to attack Nazi forces deployed along Europe's underbelly. In May 1943 Allied warships and bomber aircraft pounded the islands in the Strait of Sicily. As soon as enemy fortifications there were crippled, Sicily itself came under attack.

Captain Ollie Cordill was one of the hundreds of pilots tasked with traversing the Med. He had flown fourteen bombing missions over Sicily, Cape Bon, and Sardinia when his plane crashed. The former all–Southwest Conference running back from Rice University survived but was seriously injured.

Another football player flying bombing missions in the Mediterranean was Ernie Case, whose plane was blasted on his twelfth mission over Sardinia by a German Messerschmitt fighter pilot. Case bailed out but suffered hip and rib injuries. He and his copilot were captured and taken to a POW camp. Nine months later they managed to escape and sneak back to friendly territory in Italy. (Case would return home in 1946 and after recovering from his injuries played football for the UCLA Bruins as a left-handed quarterback.) Yale Heisman Trophy winner Clint Frank flew bombing missions over North Africa and Italy with the Ninety-eighth Bomb Group.

Sweeping Sicily

The Allies hoped to use Sicily, which was adjacent to Italy's boot, as a stepping-stone to Italy, then drive the Germans back north. Prior to the assault on Sicily General George S. Patton talked with the officers from the Forty-fifth Division, the Thunderbirds, comparing combat to sports: "Battle is the most magnificent competition in which a human being can indulge. It brings out all that is best; it removes all that is base."

OPPOSITE: *At dawn on July 10, 1943, American troops secure the beachhead at Sicily, wading ashore, off-loading ammunition and supplies, preparing for the big push inland.* National Archives photo

ABOVE: *Blood and Guts Patton had a slight fiery streak and he really didn't like to lose, whether it was at the pistol range, the polo field, or the battlegrounds of North Africa, Italy, and northern Europe. Here he scopes out the situation on Sicily.* U.S. Army photo

The Nazis braced for an Allied invasion of either Sardinia or Corsica and were thus caught off guard when, on July 10, 1943, several thousand Airborne paratroopers descended on Sicily. High winds and misdirected transport planes scattered the soldiers along the island's southern coast. Minutes later U.S. troops waded ashore, signaling the start of Operation Husky—the invasion of Sicily. More than 66,000 soldiers and 7,000 vehicles stormed the northern Mediterranean beaches. Opposing them were 30,000 German and 240,000 Italian troops, considered inferior in combat even by their Nazi comrades. Enemy compounds fell quickly, often without any shots fired.

Army troops pushed northward, and on July 22 GIs entered Palermo. General Patton later wrote about the liberation of Palermo: "The street was full of people shouting, 'Down with Mussolini,' and 'Long live America.'"

German units fell back to Messina, but soon 100,000 Italian and German troops were scrambling onto anything afloat to cross the Messina Strait to the mainland. Italian loyalty to Hitler and the Axis was quickly disintegrating and, on September 3, sensing inevitable defeat, the Italians cut all ties to Nazi Germany. Hitler had been concerned about Italian loyalties for some time and even commented to his aides, "The Italians never lose a war; no matter what happens, they somehow end up on the winning side." The Führer made plans with his commander in the region, Field Marshal Albert Kesselring, in case the Italians did surrender or the Allies established a foothold on the peninsula.

Germany established a timetable to incrementally pull back its Nazi forces, allowing rear units the time to shore up fortifications, first along the Volturno River and then the Barbara, Bernhard, and Gustav defense lines. Their final position would be the Apennines Mountains, overlooking the vital Po River Valley with its agricultural and industrial resources.

ABOVE: *A bomber crew from the 97th Bomb Group at Amendola, Italy, pose in front of their B-17. During Operation Strangle, Army Air Force crews flew more than 65,000 sorties while destroying enemy supply lines throughout Italy. Former tennis champ Greg Mangin was a gunner on a Flying Fortress during Strangle, and Michigan running back Bob Chappuis was a radio operator on board a bomber that would be shot down. He was spotted by local partisans who hid him from Nazi patrols for three months and eventually turned him over to a British unit.* Army Air Forces photo

Ashore at Salerno

By mid-September the Allies were ready to continue the pursuit and chose Salerno as the entry point for the invasion of Italy, with the Thirty-sixth Infantry Texas Division making its mark as the first American combat unit ashore. More than 85,000 Allied troops in all were committed to the Salerno Campaign.

But this time the Germans were waiting. They unleashed a torrent of gunfire from bunkers overlooking the beachhead, effectively pinning down the invasion forces scrambling for cover.

Soon the beaches of Salerno were littered with dead and wounded soldiers, wrecked jeeps and trucks, and mountains of supplies blown to pieces by those enemy guns. Private First Class Hans Maier, who played fullback for the New York Americans soccer team, was critically injured at Salerno and had to be evacuated back to the States, where he died several months later. Walter Hess, who played football at West Point with Ike Eisenhower and Omar Bradley, commanded the Thirty-sixth Division's artillery batteries that helped the breakout at Salerno.

Commanding one of the Navy PT boats at Salerno was former heavyweight wrestling champion Jumping Joe Savoldi. The Notre Dame all-American football player was credited with sinking an Italian transport ship during the skirmish to clear the coastal waters.

Allied warships remained offshore, pounding the enemy coastal defenses, while bombers from North Africa and Sicily also softened the German fortifications. Fighting for every inch, Allied units managed to push inland from the Salerno beaches.

On October 1, 1943, Naples was liberated. But among the injured in the battle for that city was amateur featherweight Golden Gloves boxer Carl Palombo, who was hurt by a mortar round.

After winning the Allied championship only months earlier in North Africa, Palombo had hoped to compete in other military bouts, but his injuries were too severe. "I had my heart set on fighting," Palombo stated in 1944, "but in a way I guess I'm lucky to be around. I'm not sure of my chances of doing any more ring work, but the doc says I have a 50-50 chance and that's good enough for me."

Propaganda Broadcasts Sports News

Axis radio in Yugoslavia became popular with American soldiers in Italy because it broadcast major league baseball scores. The GIs ignored the pro-Nazi propaganda messages mixed in with the sports updates.

After the 1943 World Series, when the New York Yankees beat the St. Louis Cardinals four games to one, the Nazis' propaganda minister seized the opportunity to show the world that Germany was not the only country to crack down on religious leaders.

Hitler's spokesman Joseph Goebbels proudly proclaimed: "There are fresh atrocities in the United States. The Yankees [Americans], not content with their pious interference all over the world, are beating up their own cardinals in St. Louis." The German masses assumed he was talking about "Yanks" harassing Catholic Cardinals, not the baseball team.

Continuing the Northward Push

Hill-by-hill and house-to-house fighting continued across Italy as town after town fell into Allied hands.

Begrudgingly the Germans were giving ground, taking up defensive positions along natural barriers, such as rivers that had to be forded or vantage points that looked down on narrow approaches. Two such obstacles—the Rapido River and the Catholic Monastery at Monte Cassino—would be especially costly in American lives.

The Germans established a defensive front, known as the Gustav Line, spanning Italy's midsection and utilizing the imposing Italian Alps with deadly effectiveness. Forward observers posted on virtually every mountaintop watching every avenue of approach could quickly call in artillery fire and aerial bombardment on any Allied advance. Still, Allied trops would have to cross impassable rivers and scale steep mountains if they were going to route the Germans from Italy.

During attacks and counterattacks on Mount Rotundo on November 8, 1943, Maurice "Footsie" Britt—a star end with the University of Arkansas Razorbacks and the Detroit Lions—risked his life to defend his sector from being overrun. Though wounded by mortar fragments, Britt refused to be evacuated. He would later receive the Medal of Honor for his actions on Mount Rotundo.

Seven days after Britt's exploits, Andy Callahan, a former New England boxer who first stepped in the ring in 1926 and fought as a lightweight, welterweight, and middleweight, was killed in Italy.

Soldiers of the Thirty-sixth Infantry Division were given the critical task of securing the Rapido River, east of the Gustav Line. Once a bridge could

be built there, tanks from the U.S. Fifth Army could rumble northward and penetrate the Gustav Line near Cassino. But of the three thousand men who attempted to cross the Rapido on January 20, 1944, barely one hundred made it across, only to be pinned down and cut to shreds by enemy gunners positioned on the overlooking mountainsides.

The two-day assault on the Rapido would result in a staggering 2,128 U.S. casualties: 155 killed, 1,052 wounded, plus hundreds missing or taken prisoner.

Nearby Monte Cassino was famous for its 1,400-year-old Benedictine monastery. Despite the abbey's historical significance, German artillery units utilized the mountaintop location to fire on Allied ground forces approaching in the Liri Valley. Despite appeals from the Vatican, the German gunners refused to move, and Allied leaders—seeing the casualty toll climb every day that Monte Cassino remained untouched—insisted on bombing the entire peak. Too many lives were being lost to be worried about destroying the monastery.

On February 15, 1944, 229 bombers swooped down like rolling thunder and dropped high explosive and incendiary bombs while II Corps artillery lobbed shells, stitching the mountaintop with explosives ever closer to the abbey. Finally, one soldier weary of the enemy bombardments and thankful for the overdue payback, watched the fireworks and shouted out "TOUCH-DOWN!" when several bombs blew apart the abbey at Cassino.

A month later, with Cassino still in German hands, another Allied bombardment was ordered. Finally, in May Allied ground troops penetrated the Gustav Line and on June 6 liberated Rome, the Eternal City.

Assaulting Anzio

While Allied forces were struggling to seize control along the Gustav Line, a second front was opened thirty miles southwest of Rome along the Anzio beachhead on January 22, 1944. With Operation Shingle, the Allies hoped to attack the German Army's Fourteenth Corps from the rear and force them to pull back and regroup.

General John Lucas was concerned about the Anzio landing, saying, "The whole affair has a strong odor of Gallipoli and apparently the same amateur was still on the coach's bench."

But despite General Lucas's doubts, the Anzio landing came off with little fanfare—36,000 men ashore, with just thirteen killed and ninety-seven wounded in strafing attacks. But Allied forces were quickly boxed in before they could get off the beachhead.

The Germans dropped propaganda leaflets, promising that Anzio would be "the biggest cemetery for the Allied forces in World War II." And for four endless months, the Germans tried to fulfill that promise. Enemy artillery pounded the crowded shoreline. One especially devastating weapon was a 280-millimeter cannon mounted on a rail car, which the Germans kept hidden in a tunnel in the Alban Hills.

This gun, dubbed the Anzio Express or Anzio Annie, could fire a 550-pound shell thirty miles and then disappear into its hideaway. GIs at Anzio dug deep into the sand to protect themselves from the incoming explosives. Soon the entire beach was crisscrossed with reinforced trenches, resembling a World War I battlefield. Yet for every round the Germans lobbed at Anzio, Allied artillery and naval guns fired twenty to thirty right back at them.

On May 23 the breakout of Anzio—Operation Buffalo—finally cracked the German perimeter. More than 5,500 GIs were killed at Anzio and another 14,800 were wounded. One of those severely wounded was Footsie Britt, the Detroit Lions end who had been wounded at Mount Rotundo. He was talking on a field phone inside an Italian farmhouse when a German panzer tank fired a

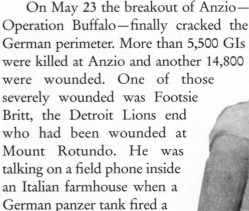

BELOW: *During the Allied Track and Field Championships held in Rome in 1944, four GI participants were Private Zemeri Cox, PFC Dick Ford, Corporal Jack Reynolds (100-meter sprinters), and PFC Willie Steele (high jump and broad jump winner).* U.S. Army photo

ABOVE: *Though the official Olympic Games had been canceled in 1940 and '44, the GI Olympics were held in Rome, in mid-1944, attracting many world-class athletes serving in America's armed forces in Europe. They included former AAU 1,500-meter runner Walter Mehl, Melrose Games 800-meter champion Fred Sickinger, and future Olympian Harrison Dillard.*

U.S. Army photo

single round at the building. The blast tore Britt's right arm off at the elbow and shattered his foot. A promising pro football career was tragically cut short in just that instant, in a farmhouse near Anzio.

Allied Planes Sever German Lifelines

To cripple the German supply routes into Italy, Operation Strangle kicked off on March 11, 1944, with bombers and fighter planes from the Mediterranean Allied Air Forces conducting bombing raids and strafing runs on railroad tracks, mountain convoy routes and tunnels, and coastal shipping ports. During March through May of 1944, 65,000 air sorties were flown, turning these various supply routes to rubble, depriving front-line German units of desperately needed food, fuel, and ammunition.

Bill Mallory, Yale's gridiron captain and all-American in 1923, was a captain with the Army Air Corps in '44 and developed Operation Mallory, a plan to blow up twenty-two of the twenty-four Po River bridges the Germans were using. (A year later, on a flight home, the plane crashed and Mallory was killed.)

Former Davis Cup team member and national indoor tennis champ Gregory Mangin was a Flying Fortress gunner who received the Distinguished Flying Cross for shooting down an enemy fighter plane and keeping others away from his bomber during a mission over Italy. Mangin joked that prior to World War II he played tennis in virtually all the countries he eventually ended up bombing.

Bob Chappuis had been a reserve running back for Michigan in 1942 when he was called into the Army Air Corps. In Italy he served as a radio operator, flying twenty-one missions before his bomber was shot down by anti-aircraft guns. Chappuis avoided capture by hiding out with local partisans for three months, until he made it back to a British unit. (In 1946 Chappuis returned to Michigan and dominated all opponents on the football field. The next year he led the Wolverines to an undefeated season and was second in Heisman voting.)

Olympian Marshall Wayne won gold in high diving and silver in springboards at the Nazi Games in '36. But while he was serving with the Eighth Air Force during a mission to Italy, his plane took a nosedive and Wayne had to bail out, severely injuring his left knee.

Miller Anderson had been a diving champion at Ohio State and was training for the Olympic Games, should they resume after the war. But he was called up and joined the Army Air Corps, becoming a P-47 fighter pilot. On his 112th mission over Verona, his plane was hit by flak. Forced to bail out, Anderson clipped the tail of his plane and broke his thighbone. He was captured by the Germans, who ignored his injuries. Six weeks later American forces liberated the POW camp where Anderson was held, and surgeons determined that his leg would have to be amputated.

Anderson refused. Doctors stabilized his leg with a metal plate and gave him a cane, informing him that he would never walk without a limp. But Anderson refused to give up diving and rehabilitated his leg. (After World War II he returned to Ohio State, where he was a three-time all-American, capturing eleven diving crowns during his collegiate career.)

Army doctor Sammy Lee had competed against Miller Anderson just before both joined the service. He recalled, "The two of us were diving at the nationals in 1942, and we talked about what would happen to us after the war. Miller said, 'Let's make a vow that if we both survive, we'll come back and be Olympic champions.'

"In 1945 I got a letter from Miller saying that he had been shot down over Italy. He had broken his leg, but he reminded me of our pledge to make the next Olympic team. We both did, but he had to do it with a six-inch plate in his leg. Miller came in second in the springboard in London."

Sammy Lee went on to win gold in platform diving at the 1948 Olympics and again in '52. He would take the bronze in springboard diving in '48, standing on the medal stand with his old friend and fellow veteran Miller Anderson.

Pursuit into the Apennines

The 339th Infantry Regiment of the Eighty-fifth Infantry Custer Division pursued the retreating Nazis across the Amaseno River and into the hills west of Priverno in late May 1944. The 339th was commanded by Colonel Brookner Brady, who had been a member of the U.S. Olympic Team in 1932, competing in the modern pentathlon.

Former West Point gridiron player Gus Farwick was in the thick of the mountain fighting. Through the summer of 1944, the Allies continued the attack and the Nazis slowly relinquished ground, though not without cost. Every foot of

BELOW: *During free time the "Anzio Turf Club" conducted horse races, complete with wagering. Sometimes when there weren't enough horses for a race, burros and even a goat or two might sneak up to the starting line.* Imperial War Museum photo

ABOVE: *For three days in July 1944, soldiers of the Fifth Army and Allied air forces flyboys participated in an American-style rodeo . . . though a Roman chariot race was also included. The "chariots" were built from wrecked fighter and bomber planes and any other junk the "gladiator" could piece together* U.S. Army photo

ground was challenged and paid for with blood. Kansas City Monarchs catcher James "Pea" Greene prevented an infantry squad from being ambushed when he spotted a German machine gun crew taking up position on a nearby hilltop near the Arno River, north of Rome.

"I always was a good observer, and I had my binoculars. Two Germans came out with a machine gun. They probably would have wiped out a whole company [of American soldiers] before they realized what was happening. I fired two rounds of high explosives and reached for my binoculars. The first round hit right between the two Germans. Of course both of them went up in the air. By the time they came back down, the other shell hit in there, and they went back in the air."

Greene had saved an infantry squad from certain death and received the combat infantry badge the following month. He would later come close to being ambushed himself by an enemy machine gun. "I was crawling on my stomach and brrrrt, just a line out of a burp gun right in front of my hands, about six inches in front of where my hands were stretched out."

Negotiating the Impassable

As they continued to pull back farther north, the Germans would leave behind dangerous booby traps—25,000 in Livorno alone—which GIs and unsuspecting citizens would later uncover, with tragic results. In the northern Apennines Mountains, the Nazis had taken up position along the fortified Gothic Line, a 150-mile chain of concrete and steel bunkers, tank traps, and minefields forming a deadly gauntlet that Allied ground forces would have to negotiate.

The all-black Ninety-second Buffalo Division (led by white officers), as yet untested in battle, was rushed to the Apennines front. Among its soldiers was Harrison Dillard, who would go on to compete in the 1948 London Olympics, winning gold in the 100-meter sprints and the 4x100-meter relays. Four years later he would take two more gold medals, repeating in the relays plus capturing the 110-meter hurdles title.

Tom Cussans, a Golden Gloves lightweight boxer from Flint, Michigan, was with the Third Battalion, 350th Infantry Regiment along the Gothic Line when his company was outflanked. In close-quarters fighting, Cussans ordered mortar fire directly on their position, startling the Germans but allowing the American soldiers to withdraw to safety.

Enemy artillery camouflaged in the Apennines was fixed on all avenues of approach and unleashed a deadly barrage whenever massed Allied units were spotted.

"Don't Take My Leg"

Athletics minor league pitcher Lou Brissie was one of those soldiers seriously wounded in Italy. In early December 1944, as a weary paratrooper on the front lines with the Eighty-eighth Infantry Division, the Blue Devils, Corporal Brissie was slogging back to the rear with his squad for a long-overdue shower and a hot meal when enemy artillery shells rained down. One exploded just yards away, ripping open his left leg. His leg was shattered between the knee and the ankle, his ankle mangled, both feet broken, and both hands injured. It was seven hours before anyone searched for the squad, and Brissie was the only survivor.

Field doctors determined that to save his life Brissie's leg would have to be amputated, but he pleaded with them, "Send me to somebody who may be able to help me, because I want to play baseball."

Brissie was transported to an Army hospital in Naples (it was Mussolini's former palace at the base of Mount Vesuvius) and Army surgeons there

BELOW: *River crossings in Italy, such as the Po, were especially deadly for American patrols, as Nazi machine gunners, mortar crews, and snipers waited in the surrounding hills and mountains to cut them down.*

Former Negro Leagues catcher James Greene, who played for the Kansas City Monarchs, was great at spotting Nazi snipers with his binoculars and one time saved a large group of his fellow soldiers from certain annihilation when he killed a machine gun crew overwatching the Arno River. U.S. Army photo

ABOVE: *A row of American M-10 tank destroyers shell German strongholds near Bologna, in November 1944.* U.S. Army Signal Corps photo

performed the first of twenty-three operations he would undergo to salvage his leg. Miraculously, Brissie would rehab his leg and return to pitch for the Philadelphia Athletics and Cleveland Indians for seven seasons, inspiring other disabled veterans to live full lives.

Another Eighty-eight Division soldier was Duke quarterback Charlie Haynes, a rifle platoon leader with Easy Company of the 349th Regiment. During the Arno River assault he was gravely wounded when an enemy shell ripped open his chest. Quick evacuation and trauma surgery saved him.

A Winter Lull

Soon foul weather set in and, combined with the lack of ammunition for their artillery, forced the U.S. Fifth Army to delay the attack on the Apennines and wait out the coming winter. But this delay also gave the Germans a chance to deploy reinforcements via the Brenner Pass and resupply their units by coastal supply ships.

Allied PT boats patrolled the coastal waters to intercept those enemy night runners. Among the PT commanders were Stanley Livingston, a Yale swimming champion, and Ralph Pope, who played football and hockey at Harvard.

Hoping to catch the Americans off guard, the Germans launched a counteroffensive on Christmas Day, 1944. This final German attack in Italy was put down two days later. Still the Germans remained entrenched in northern Italy and would hold out through the final days of the war in Europe. Tragically, more than 36,000 Americans were killed and 90,000 wounded fighting in Italy. Major John Hurley, former Washington State College gridiron star was among those killed in action, and wounded was former Philadelphia Athletics pitcher, Lieutenant John Savage, considered the first major leaguer wounded while fighting in Europe.

The '44 Games

Athletics played an important role in the recuperation and relaxation of combat units pulled off the front lines. Throughout Italy there were pickup games of football and baseball wherever there was flat ground a safe distance from enemy gunners hiding in the surrounding hills and mountains.

215

Negro Leagues catcher James "Pea" Greene, who had played with the powerful Kansas City Monarchs when they were dominating the Negro American League, served with an antitank company of the Ninety-second Division at Algiers in North Africa and then in Italy. When the Mediterranean Theater of Operations baseball tournament was held, Greene caught for the winning team. He returned to the Monarchs in time for another Negro American League pennant title in 1946.

Outfielder Ethan Allen had played in the majors for thirteen years with a handful of teams, hanging it up for good in 1938. During the Italian Campaign he served with the Special Services athletic program, coordinating organized sports for the troops during lulls in the fighting.

At the former Mussolini Stadium in Rome, Allied units held their own track and field championships in mid-1944. Among the many athletes participating in the Allied Games was Banks McFadden, who played football at Clemson and later with the Brooklyn Dodgers. He had also participated in track at Clemson and competed in the broad jump, placing third at the Allied Games. The broad jump winner was Fifth Army Private First Class Willie Steele, who held the national junior title. He also won the high jump in Rome. Navy Lieutenant Walter Mehl was the 1,500-meter Amateur Athletic Union (AAU) champion in 1940 while attending the University of Wisconsin. Though chided as an old-timer, Mehl surprised his younger competitors in Rome by again winning the 1,500.

Eight-hundred-meter Melrose Games champion Fred Sickinger, who ran for Manhattan College before joining the Army, easily won the 800-meter race again at the Allied Games.

Many of these winners in Italy would team up to represent the Mediterranean Theater at other armed forces competitions. "We went to Frankfurt to compete against the European Theater in what was called the GI Olympics," recalled future Olympian Harrison Dillard. "I won four gold medals. General Patton was there with his shiny helmet liner and his

BELOW: *Maurice "Footsie" Britt was an elusive end for the Arkansas Razorbacks then joined the Detroit Lions. During heavy fighting in Italy, Britt fought ferociously when his unit was overrun. Despite severe wounds from shell fragments he continued to fight on. For his actions at Mount Rotundo in early November of 1943, Britt received the Medal of Honor. He would later be critically wounded, and would never play football again.* AP Wide World photo

pearl-handled pistols. After I won my fourth medal I heard him say, 'He's the best goddamn athlete I've ever seen.' I felt pretty good about that because Patton himself had been in the Olympics."

Italy Hosts a "Bowl" Game

On New Year's Day, 1945, the Fifth Army gridiron players challenged the Twelfth Air Force athletes in the "first and last" Spaghetti Bowl Game, held at the soccer stadium in Florence.

To prepare for the interservice battle, the Fifth Army players practiced at Montecatini, twenty miles north of Florence. "It had been Mussolini's private physical exercise and massage parlor," noted the team's coach, Louis Bush, who had played at Massachusetts State College in 1934.

While the facilities were top-notch, the only equipment the teams had to practice with were their olive drab long-john underwear shirts for football jerseys and tanker's helmets in place of football shells. Fortunately, the day before the game, a shipment of football uniforms, including pads, shoes, and helmets, arrived from the States.

Coaching the Twelfth Air Force team was George Miller, who had anchored Indiana's offensive line as the center from 1935 to 1937. Among the many pro and collegiate athletes at the game were John Moody, all-American from Morris Brown; quarterback Eugene Stauber, who played for the University of Toledo; Ed Brennan, Syracuse quarterback; Florida halfback Frank Buell; North Carolina State's all-Southern halfback Arthur Faircloth; Dayton University end Joe McShane; University of the South defensive player Arthur Gramman; Texas Tech's Gerald Haston; and Marquette center Ed Niemi, who also played professionally with the Cleveland Rams and Chicago Cardinals. Niemi had already earned the Soldier's Medal for his actions in North Africa.

For the 25,000 soldiers and airmen in attendance, the game also included a cheerleader:

U.S. baton twirling champion Peggy Jean Roan, who was touring with a USO troupe and was "drafted" by the Twelfth Air Force team to rally the vastly outnumbered airmen in the crowd. An Italian burro served as a worthy substitute for the West Point Army mule mascot. Obviously, with the final score 20–0 in favor of the Fifth Army squad, the Italian burro had more of an influence on the outcome of the game than Peggy Jean Roan and her cheerleading abilities.

Afterward a victory banquet was held at the Montecatini spa for both teams. Winning coach Lou Bush noted: "Our game advantage, besides the plays, was a great bunch of athletes who sacrificed their careers to help save America from Hitlerism. All of us—5th and 12th players—fought for principles of peace on earth."

Attending the dinner were boxers Joe Louis and Ezzard Charles, who had been giving boxing exhibitions in Florence; and baseball stars Joe Medwick, Nick Etten, and Leo Durocher, who were visiting the troops overseas during the off-season.

The three also entertained ten thousand GIs at a racetrack near Naples, recapping the 1944 season. Durocher especially had some hilarious tales he never got tired of retelling, and the troops never got tired of hearing, such as the nasty beanball wars he instigated with virtually every team in the league during the 1942 season.

Another big-league player with a keen sense of humor was hurler Lefty "the Gay Castillion" Gomez, who chided the GIs in Italy when he said, "So you guys think you're roughing it? Well, you ought to play 13 years with the Yankees and then get traded to the Boston Braves!" Gomez pitched in five World Series with the Yankees, posting a perfect 6–0 record.

BELOW: *Ships in the harbor at Bari, Italy, burn after a German aerial attack, on December 2, 1943. Two ships loaded with munitions exploded, creating an inferno that consumed the harbor facilities; another sixteen ships were destroyed in the attack.* U.S. Army Signal Corps photo

The Tenth Mountain Division in Italy

> "THEY'LL HAVE TO BUY EVERY YARD OF ITALY WITH BLOOD."

> —*German Field Marshal Albert Kesselring, Commander of German Armies in Italy*

> "THE 10TH NEVER BACKED AWAY FROM A FIGHT AND NEVER LOST AN INCH OF TERRITORY ONCE WE CAPTURED IT."

> —*Lieutenant Bob Dole, injured April 14, 1945*

BELOW: *Roy Mikkelsen won the U.S. ski jumping championship in 1933 and '35 and participated in the Nazi Olympics in Garmisch. He would later join America's Alpine troopers, the 10th Mountain Division.* 10th Mountain Division Association photo

DURING 1939 AND '40, AMERICAN SKIERS AND MOUNTAIN-climbers closely followed the news in Europe and Asia. These outdoorsmen had been overseas and had negotiated the slopes of Finland and Italy and climbed the treacherous Himalaya—all locations where the Germans and Japanese were extending their military might. Naturally, there was concern among mountain buffs that one day the United States would become involved in the war overseas and American troops would have to fight in these higher climes. The Germans alone had fourteen Alpine divisions totaling more than 100,000 troops. The U.S. Army was more concerned about fighting in the jungles of the South Pacific than in the Italian Alps or the mountains of Scandinavia.

Creating the Mountain Troopers

In 1941, as the military geared up for the impending conflict, the call went out for recruits. National Ski Patrol leaders lobbied the Pentagon brass to consider a fighting force comparable to the German, Finnish, and Italian Alpine units. At first the government's only interest was to create a defensive force to guard against an invasion. But one day after the attack on Pearl Harbor, the U.S. Army created the Eighty-seventh Mountain Infantry Regiment and established Fort Lewis, Washington, near Mount Rainier as its home.

Soon outdoorsmen from around the country, often one step ahead of the draft board, signed up for the Eighty-seventh. The National Ski Patrol, formed in the late '30s and consisting of 1,500 volunteers who rescued injured skiers and climbers, was responsible for sifting through the thousands of applicants wanting to join the elite Army Mountain Troopers. While many young men who hated the cold and had never even been on skis or skates were enticed by the glamour of this new fighting force, there were hundreds of others who thrived in the outdoors, including foresters and trappers, backwoodsmen and mule skinners.

Some of winter's most famous athletes were selected, including Norway's world champion ski jumper Torger Tokle, U.S. junior ski jump champ Lyle Munson, U.S. slalom champ Friedl Pfeiffer, Olympic skier Robert Livermore, and Swiss skier and Dartmouth College coach Walter Prager. Dartmouth ski team captain Charles McLane followed his coach into the Army. American ski champion Hannes Schneider encouraged his son Herbert and several future champions to enlist. Many members of college and resort ski teams also joined up.

LEFT: *Bob Dole was quite an athlete at Russell High School in Kansas, lettering in football, track, and basketball. In football he was an end for the Broncos during their 1940 undefeated season, and, as captain of the basketball team, he was selected to the Union Pacific all-star squad. In 1942, at the University of Kansas, he ran the 440- and 880-yard mid-distance races. After joining the Army, Dole was assigned to the 10th Mountain Division, an elite alpine unit loaded with outdoorsmen and athletes. He would later be severely injured during intense fighting in Italy on April 14, 1945, just weeks before the Nazis surrendered.* U.S. Army Signal photo

Establishing the Tenth Mountain Division

By November 1943 the Eighty-seventh had outgrown its accommodations at Fort Lewis and relocated to Camp Hale, nestled in the Colorado Rockies. The unit added the Eighty-sixth Regiment to handle all the newcomers, with both officially under the Tenth Mountain Division.

Former polo champion George Hays had received the Medal of Honor for his World War I exploits and would command the Tenth Division. Roy Mikkelsen, another prominent American skier who joined the Tenth, had won the national ski jumping championship in 1933 and had represented the United States at the 1936 Winter Olympics. Norwegian-born Mikkelsen would proudly serve with the Tenth Division's Ninety-ninth Norwegian American Battalion.

They were trained and ready for deployment, but it would be another year before the unit was called on. Then, after only a few weeks of minor skirmishes, the untested Tenth would be given a mission deemed impossible: protecting Italy's Po River Valley.

The Tenth Mountaineers were facing Germany's Army Group C, which had already experienced five tough years of battle and, to a man, considered the Americans mere novices. But the GIs withstood intense artillery barrages and fierce assaults, refusing to give even an inch. In fact, soldiers of the Tenth

Mountain Division quickly established a reputation for never giving back any territory they'd seized. But routing the enemy was done only after paying a heavy price: 990 died and another 3,000 were wounded during the division's few months of fighting in the Italian Campaign.

A Heavy Price

Among those killed was Tech Sergeant Torger Tokle, the Norwegian ski jumper, who was hit during an artillery shelling near Monte Torraccio. His death only riled up the many American friends he'd made, stirring the already hard-hitting Tenth Mountain troopers to fight even harder to avenge his death.

Former all-American football player Butch Luther from Nebraska was killed while the Tenth was attempting to route enemy forces from Riva Ridge and the surrounding mountains.

Peter Seibert was told he would never ski again after a mortar round ripped his knee apart and burned his face in March 1945. After years of painful rehabilitation, Seibert would strap on the skis again and return to World Cup racing by 1950.

A Kansan Endures

Though the flatlands of Kansas weren't known for their ski slopes, University of Kansas athlete Bob Dole joined the Tenth Mountain Division and would be thrown into the fray almost as soon as he arrived in Italy. April 14, 1945, "was a long day for me, but a short battle," Dole would later recall. "Dotting the sides of Hill 913 [near Bologna] was an intricate system of bunkers and gun emplacements manned by German defenders. Minefields added to their security and our danger."

Dole would remember his fellow soldiers being hit by intensive fire coming from the enemy positions. "From where I crouched, I could see my platoon's radio man go down. I crawled out to retrieve him, but it was too late to do much. After pulling his lifeless form into the foxhole, I felt a sharp sting in my upper right back. Most likely, an exploding shell had ripped into my body, smashing the right shoulder and scattering metal fragments along its path.

BELOW: First Lieutenant E. Polich was in charge of the fledgling Winter Warfare Center on Iceland in early 1943. Initially, military commanders didn't see any need for creating alpine combat units, but by late 1944, the 10th Mountain Division would be needed, to fight the Germans in the Italian Alps.
U.S. Army Signal Corps photo

Whatever it was, it crushed my collarbone, punctured a lung and damaged vertebrae, leaving me paralyzed from the neck down." Bob Dole would eventually regain the feeling in his legs and spend years rehabilitating himself. But he would never be able to use his right arm again.

The Reluctant Enemy

Willie Schaeffler was an avid outdoorsman in Germany in the 1930s. He watched as several of his friends were allowed to relocate to the United States, where they served as ski instructors. But his parents had refused to join the Nazi Party and were thus denied a way out of Germany.

Schaffler was mustered into the German Army and sent to the Russian front, where he sustained injuries in five separate confrontations. Each time he was patched up and sent back into the fight. After the Nazis surrendered, Schaffler became a ski instructor at Garmisch and came to know the American team training for the '48 Olympics. That same year he was allowed admittance to the United States. He got a job at Arapaho Ski Basin in Colorado and ten years later was at Squaw Valley heading up the alpine events for the 1960 Games.

A Lasting Legacy

After the war many of the Tenth Mountain Division veterans would return to the United States and lay the groundwork for many of today's popular ski resorts, including Aspen, Colorado, and the location of their former training site, Camp Hale, now known as Vail, Colorado.

ABOVE AND BACKGROUND: *A caravan of 10th Mountaineers lug backpacks, weapons, and ammunition cross-country during alpine training in Iceland.* U.S. Army Signal Corps photo

Go for Broke

BELOW: *Minoru "Monk" Tateishi was a skilled amateur boxer, but he was better known for his big play abilities as a quarterback in barefoot football. As a Nisei soldier he served in an anti-tank company.* Photo courtesy of the 442nd RCT

"THEY CALL THEMSELVES JUST PLAIN AMERICANS . . . THEY HAVE EARNED THE RIGHT. . . . ANYBODY WHO CALLS THESE DOUGHBOYS 'JAP' IS THE MOST NARROW-MINDED PERSON I KNOW OF. THEY ARE JUST AS AMERICAN AS I AM."

— Major James Gillespie, Commander, One-hundredth Infantry Battalion

"THEY MADE BAYONET CHARGES, FOUGHT OFF COUNT-LESS COUNTERATTACKS, AND HELD THE HIGH GROUND. THEIR FEROCITY IN ACTION AND THEIR DETERMINA-TION TO WIN AGAINST ALL ODDS LED TO THEIR HAVING SUCH HIGH CASUALTIES THAT THEY EARNED THE NAME OF THE PURPLE HEART BATTALION."

—Presidio Army Museum

THE JAPANESE ATTACK ON PEARL HARBOR WAS A SHOCK TO all Americans. There was immediate hatred for those who had perpetrated such a despicable act. When President Franklin D. Roosevelt declared war the next day, thousands of young American men rushed down to recruiting offices throughout the country, eager for some big-time payback.

For the Japanese-Americans in Hawaii and along the West Coast, Pearl Harbor was an assault on them also. Many had been born and raised as Americans. Many didn't even speak Japanese. In fact, they were more American than Japanese, and they were just as ready to fight for their country—for the United States. But they weren't given that chance during the months right after Pearl Harbor. Lieutenant General John DeWitt, the commanding general of western defense in the United States, summed up the feelings of many at the time toward Japanese and Japanese-Americans: "A Jap is a Jap! It makes no difference whether he is an American or not."

Japanese-American families would soon be condemned, forced out of business, rounded up, and moved to detention camps, for fear that a fifth column of spies might assist Japan in an attack on the West Coast. One of the assembly points for detainees was Pasadena's Rose Bowl, site of many memorable football games between Big Ten and West Coast powerhouses. But in April of 1942 it became a parking lot, as Japanese families pulled up in cars and trucks overloaded with possessions, unaware of what

they had done or where they were going: to Manzanar and other detention camps in the Southwest.

The second generation of Japanese-American men, called the Nisei, just wanted a chance to prove their loyalty to the United States and to restore their families' honor. Some of these men had already been serving with National Guard or Reserve units, which were quickly mobilized. The Nisei, however, weren't called to join them on active duty.

Finally, in June 1942, the War Department agreed to induct the Nisei, but in segregated units. Soon afterward more than 1,400 men of the Hawaiian Provisional Battalion—mostly Japanese-Americans from the islands—were loaded onto four transport ships bound for the United States, where they would undergo military training.

Many of the island Nisei were natural-born athletes. After years of working in sugarcane fields, climbing trees to cut pineapple, or hauling in nets on the family fishing boat, their bodies were solid muscle. They excelled not only in swimming and diving but also in boxing and wrestling, judo and karate, baseball and football. Among them were Kenneth Otagaki, a wrestling champion at the University of Hawaii, and Katsumi Kometani, a collegiate swimmer at Michigan State and the University of Southern Cal.

In 1940 Kometani had sponsored a Hawaiian baseball team on a trip to Japan for the Far Eastern Olympics. Throughout its stay, the team was followed everywhere by local policemen, who didn't want any foreigners, especially from U.S. territory, snooping around and seeing Japan's military buildup.

Nisei men in the United States were also sent to basic training. Ironically, they would be serving their country while their own families were confined to detention camps in the deserts of the American Southwest.

LEFT ABOVE: *They were confined to the Manzanar internment camp in California, while their brothers, husbands, and sons served as soldiers with the 442nd Regimental Combat Team in Europe and as translators with the Military Intelligence Service in the Pacific, but the "Chick-a-dee" softball players didn't let their rustic conditions get them too depressed.* Library of Congress photo

LEFT BELOW: *Frank Seto was a pugilist in the Los Angeles area, though his nickname—"Toothless"—may have been an indication of his inability to avoid a punch! He too served with an anti-tank unit in Europe.* Photo courtesy of the 442nd RCT

At Camp McCoy in Wisconsin, the Nisei formed a baseball team and played against other military units on post and local civilian teams in the area. To add a little island flavor Hawaiian singers and ukelele and guitar players dressed in leis and grass skirts entertained the spectators. Though these fun and games did a lot for public relations, the Nisei never forgot that there was a war going on, and they wanted to be a part of it, overseas.

Some of the Nisei who could speak, read, and write Japanese were assigned to the Military Intelligence Service and were sent to the Pacific—to the Aleutians off Alaska and New Georgia, Peleliu, and Iwo Jima—to intercept enemy message traffic. Approximately six thousand Nisei served in the intelligence field during the war, providing valuable information about enemy troop and ship movements.

The majority of the Nisei, though, were formed into the 442nd Regimental Combat Team, which included the One-hundredth Infantry Battalion. The only whites in the unit were the officers. One of these was Jack Johnson, who had played football at the University of Hawaii and was in the National Guard there when it was activated.

After they completed training, the One-hundredth Infantry Battalion was sent to North Africa, then on to Salerno, Italy. The rest of the 442nd would arrive soon after. Very quickly, the Nisei's never-give-up attitude led to the 442nd's motto: "Go for Broke."

From one tough fight to the next, the members of the 442nd displayed their bravery—and their unwavering loyalty to the United States—incurring a staggering 300 percent casualty rate. With a unit strength of 4,500, approximately 18,000 Nisei would serve with the 442nd, each soldier proudly taking the place of those who fell in battle.

Ken Otagaki, the University of Hawaii wrestler, was severely wounded at Cassino in January 1944 when a mortar round exploded near his patrol, killing three and wounding two others. Otagaki lost his right leg and right eye.

Major Jack Johnson was hit by machine gun fire near Cassino, then detonated a mine as he crawled away to find cover. He died at an aid station later that day.

The fighting at Cassino was intense, with both sides lobbing hand grenades at each other. One newspaper reporter figured that, being such good baseball players, the Nisei were probably fairly accurate with throwing hand grenades, which were about the same size as a baseball. The reporter asked one of the Nisei about it and got this answer: "Mister, all you gotta do is trow straight and trow first. Dat's da numbah one theeng, trow first."

One Nisei soldier who could trow straight and trow first was Californian Sadao Munemori, who loved playing baseball before World War II. When a German machine gun pinned down his squad on a hill near Seravazza, Italy, Munemori gathered up some grenades from the other soldiers and crawled within range of the enemy position. He knocked out the machine gun, only to be fired on by another one nearby. Munemori crawled toward that position and eliminated it too with grenades.

He returned to his men, who were sheltered in a bomb crater. But almost immediately, a German grenade bounced in and landed among them. Munemori pounced on the grenade, smothering the explosion. His actions killed him but saved his buddies. On March 7, 1946, Munemori's mother accepted the Medal of Honor awarded to her son.

This medal was the most prestigious of the thousands of medals, including 3,600 Purple Hearts, given to the Nisei of the 442nd Regimental Combat Team—the "go for broke" soldiers who proved beyond a doubt that they truly were Americans.

ABOVE: *Their fathers and older brothers were overseas fighting both the Nazis and the Japanese, but these boys at an internment camp in the western United States, enjoyed a game of baseball to pass the time.*
National Archives photo

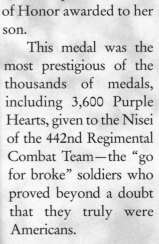

LEFT AND BACKGROUND: *A mortar crew from the "Go for Broke" 442nd Regimental Combat Team prepares to fire on an enemy position near Montennerro, Italy.*
U.S. Army photo

15. Allied Bombers Hit Central Europe

"WAR IS A GAME, BUT UNFORTUNATELY, THE CARDS, COUNTERS, AND FISHES SUFFER BY AN ILL RUN MORE THAN THE GAMESTERS."

—*Horace Walpole, 1788*

"MILITARY TALENT IS GREATLY OVERRATED BY THE WORLD, BECAUSE THE MEANS BY WHICH IT SHOWS ITSELF ARE CONNECTED WITH BRUTE FORCE AND THE MOST TERRIBLE RESULTS; AND MEN'S FACULTIES ARE DAZZLED AND BEATEN DOWN BY A THUNDER AND LIGHTNING SO FORMIDABLE TO THEIR VERY EXISTENCE. IF PLAYING A GAME OF CHESS INVOLVED BLOWING UP OR GUNPOWDER AND THE HAZARD OF LAYING WASTE [TO] A CITY, MEN WOULD HAVE THE SAME GRAND IDEA OF CHESS."

—*James H. L. Hunt*, The Companion, *1828*

OPPOSITE: *The oil refineries of Ploesti, Romania, had to be destroyed to cripple the Nazi war machine. Once American bomber bases were established along the North African coast and later in Italy, missions to Ploesti were flown.* National Archives photo

EARLY IN THE AIR WAR, WHEN NAZI LUFTWAFFE PILOTS flew bombing missions over England they were puzzled by strange ground markings they spotted, always near air base runways. Suspecting that these white chalk lines might be some type of outline for underground defense installations, German pilots frequently dropped a bomb or two for safe measure . . . never realizing all they were bombing were baseball diamonds at American air bases.

Perilous Ploesti

With the Allies taking control of North Africa, bomber and fighter planes were rushed in to fly missions against enemy warships in the Mediterranean and key locations near the Suez Canal. The U.S. Army's Middle East Air Force relied on B-24 bombers, augmented by B-17s from the Tenth Air Force transferred in from India.

The unit launched its first mission against a European target on June 11, 1942, when thirteen bombers hit Ploesti, Romania, and its vital oil refineries, which provided a third of the fuel needed to keep Nazi planes and tanks operational.

This initial strike on Ploesti did little real damage, but it was a huge morale booster, signifying America's willingness to fly alongside the British, who had been conducting missions over Europe for many months. A year later Ploesti still remained a key target, and Operation Tidal Wave was launched on August 1, 1943.

ABOVE: *Joe Kennedy, Jr.—brother of John F. Kennedy who was serving in the South Pacific—was killed on August 12, 1944 when his Liberator bomber blew up en route from England to the European coast.* Photo courtesy of the John F. Kennedy Library

ABOVE: *Whenever a bomber was hit by flak, other airmen watched and counted how many of their buddies bailed out and got their parachutes open. In all, more than 36,000 American pilots and crewmen died when their planes were shot down in the European Campaign. Some of those airmen included Missouri All-American lineman Darold Jenkins, and Colgate gridiron stars Dick East and Jack Scott.* Army Air Forces photo

From five air bases in Libya, 177 bombers of the Ninth Air Force, plus their fighter escorts, took off on a 2,700-mile round trip. With anti-aircraft guns encircling Ploesti, plus German fighter planes swooping down on the approaching formations, the Allied bombers had to fly through a virtual hailstorm of flak and machine-gun fire to reach the oil refineries.

The Allies destroyed two plants, reducing Ploesti's oil output by 40 percent, but fifty-four of the Allied bombers were shot down and 310 airmen were killed, with another 150 taken prisoner. Many other planes were damaged by flak, which injured 54 more crewmen.

"I was a briefing officer in the Libyan Desert, awaiting the return of 28 of our heavy bombers who had that morning to make the tragic low-altitude raid on the Ploesti, Romania oil refineries," recalled Brutus Hamilton, 1936 Olympic decathlon coach for the U.S. team. "Sixteen of those pilots from our small unit gave their lives that day. It's been the saddest day in the history of the 92nd Group. The fact that the raid was considered devastating to the Romanian oil field refineries does not repay us for the loss of our friends. Yet we know that sacrifices must be made in war, that some objectives must be knocked out regardless of cost."

Despite mounting Allied losses, the missions to Ploesti would continue. On the June 10 mission, one of the P-38 Thunderbolt pilots was Stub Hatch, who played polo at Stanford University in 1938. Assigned to the First Fighter Group, Hatch and ninety-five other Thunderbolt pilots that day were pounced on by enemy fighters. Hatch was credited with five kills and two other probables, but twenty-four P-38 pilots didn't make it back from the Ploesti run.

Penetrating Deep Inside Europe

British and American bomber crews stationed in England had been conducting raids on northern European targets for months, long before the establishment of air bases in North Africa. The Brits had been at it since 1939, mostly at night, but when the Yanks arrived they followed the doctrine of high-altitude precision bombing during daylight in order to see the targets from 25,000 feet.

Marshall Wayne, gold medal winner in platform diving and silver medalist in the springboard at Berlin in 1936, joined the Army Air Corps in March 1941 and headed to England, where he flew photo reconnaissance missions and later became a fighter squadron commander.

One of the most famous American athletes assigned to the Army Air Corps in England was pro golfer Bobby Jones, who in 1930 captured the Grand Slam—then the British Amateur, British Open, U.S. Open, and U.S. Amateur. Jones put away his golf clubs and served as a lieutenant colonel with the Eighth Air Force.

Brigadier General Frank Armstrong was the highest-ranking baseball player in the armed forces during World War II. He had played one season with Kinston in the Virginia League before joining the Army Air Corps.

Tom Landry played football at the University of Texas. His older brother, Robert, was killed when the B-17 bomber he was flying over the North Atlantic near Iceland plunged into the icy waters and vanished. Soon after that, Tom enlisted in the Army Air Corps, eventually flying thirty combat missions over Europe with the 493rd Bomb Squadron. His plane

LEFT: *Bobby Jones was an imposing force on the links, capturing golfing's Grand Slam in 1930. During WWII he served with the Army Air Corps' Eighth Air Force.* Photo courtesy of Citizens Savings Hall of Fame

BELOW: *Bombing missions deep inside Europe were extremely dangerous, with German anti-aircraft guns and fighter planes exacting a heavy toll. On this raid, to a Focke Wulf factory at Marienburg, the 8th Air Force lost eighty bombers, involving 800 pilots and airmen.* National Archives photo

crash-landed, but he and his crew survived, and he was discharged in late 1945.

"I went from a scared college freshman . . . to a grizzled war veteran of twenty-one," Landry would later write in his autobiography. "I knew what it meant to look my own fear in the face and go on to do my duty because the lives of my crew and the destiny of my country depended on it."

After returning to the Longhorns, Landry was selected second team all-Southwest Conference fullback and was drafted by the New York Giants and the upstart crosstown rival Yankees of the All-American Football Conference. He signed with the Yankees, who were loaded with other Texas players. But in '49 the AAFC folded and the Giants snatched up Landry. Four years later he took on the dual role as player and defensive coach. He would eventually become head coach of the Dallas Cowboys, leading them to Super Bowl wins in 1972 and 1978.

ABOVE: *After his older brother was killed in a plane crash over the North Atlantic, Texas football player Tom Landry joined the Army Air Corps and flew thirty combat missions over Europe.*

Army Air Corps photo

Ken Kavanaugh played minor league ball with the St. Louis Cardinals in the late 1930s and then played football for Louisiana State, where he won the Knute Rockne Memorial Trophy as the country's best lineman in 1939. From there he played in the trenches for the Chicago Bears on their championship team in 1940–41. During the European Campaign he piloted a B-17 bomber and flew thirty missions over Europe. (Kavanaugh returned to the Bears in time for their championship season in 1946, finally calling it quits in 1950.)

Billy Southworth, a major league prospect who was an outfielder with the Toronto Maple Leafs of the International League and son of the St. Louis Cardinals manager Billy Southworth, survived twenty-five missions over Europe, wearing his lucky Cardinals cap on every flight. On his final mission he thought it might be fun to "bomb" the control tower at his own base in England by dropping a baseball he always kept with him. Ironically, after returning home Southworth was killed when his B-29 Superfortress bomber crashed into Flushing Bay in New York on February 15, 1945.

Another airman assigned to fly fighter escorts for the bomber missions was Lieutenant Monte Weaver, former World Series pitcher and Washington Senator. He was based with the Eighth Air Force in England.

West Point grad William "Spike" Eckert had played first base in high school and intramurals at the Point but had no further aspirations in the game. He would later command the mighty 452nd Bomb Group in Europe and reluctantly became commissioner of baseball in the mid-sixties.

Texas A&M football player Jay Robbins shot down twenty-two Nazi planes while flying a P-38 escorting the bombers deep inside Europe.

Though their bombing missions rarely let up, there was some downtime back at home base, and often the aircrews and the ground support techs got together for some competitive sports. One of those pickup players who was a first baseman in England was Major Clark Gable, better known for his acting skills than his athletic prowess.

The Tragic Statistics of Air War

Despite heavy losses, the air missions had to continue if Germany was to be defeated. Besides hitting military units, the bombers were sent to take out munitions factories, aircraft assembly plants, V-2 rocket sites, and other targets. All of these facilities were heavily protected. No bombing mission was considered an easy one. On virtually every mission, there was at least one plane that didn't return.

Former West Point all-American lineman Robin Olds escorted the big bombers, flying P-38 and P-51 fighters, and had seen far too many of his buddies perish. "There were forty in our squadron [but] air battles took the greatest toll and before I was finished I was the squadron commander . . . I was only 23."

Many airmen managed to bail out only to be captured by the Germans. (Twenty-five thousand U.S. airmen would become POWs.) One of those was Walter "Booty" Payne, star kicker for Clemson College, who was captured with nine other airmen and sent to a POW camp, Stag Luft 1 in Barth, Germany.

Phil Marchildon, Philadelphia Athletics pitcher, was shot down over Denmark. Only he and another crewman from his bomber survived the crash. They then spent a year in a Nazi POW camp. (Marchildon would return to the A's in 1945, appearing in three games. He would play for four more years then call it quits after one game in 1950 with the Boston Red Sox.)

Among those pilots and airmen killed in the air war over Europe were Colgate University football players Jack Scott and Dick East and Ohio State breakaway scatback Don Scott, whose plane crashed over England. Jeff Dickson, "the Tex Rickard of Europe," never made it back from a mission to Germany, and neither did Missouri all-American center Darold Jenkins.

Former Big Ten and AAU breaststroke swimming champion Doc Counsilman was a B-24 bomber pilot who was forced to ditch when his plane was hit by flak over Europe in 1944. (Counsilman would return from the war to lead the Ohio State Buckeyes to an undefeated season, plus the Big Ten and NCAA championships. He was also coach of the U.S. Olympic swim team in 1964 and '76 and led Indiana to six NCAA titles and twenty Big Ten crowns.)

ABOVE: *Army lineman and All-American Robin Olds had a full schedule at West Point, completing his normal studies, practicing and playing with the varsity, and taking flight training for his eventual assignment with the Army Air Corps. Olds would log more than 120 missions over Europe as a fighter pilot.* U.S. Military Academy Archives photo

Tommy Hitchcock, considered the greatest polo player ever—sniper at the long shot, bulldog in a close fight—had been the youngest pilot with the Lafayette Escadrille in World War I. He returned to the cockpit to be one of the oldest pilots in World War II. When asked to compare his polo exploits with his reputation as a fighter pilot, Hitchcock noted, "Polo is exciting but you can't compare it to flying in wartime. That's the best sport in the world. People call duck-shooting a sport. It's not real sport unless the duck can shoot back at you—that's what flying is during war." Tragically, while flying a Mustang fighter plane on a routine training flight with the Ninth Air Force, Ten-Goal Tommy's plane crashed in England, and America lost a true hero and athlete.

Attacking the Fatherland

The Eighth Air Force sent out 376 aircraft on August 17, 1943, to hit two sites deep inside German territory: a ball-bearing plant at Schweinfurt and a Messerschmitt aircraft factory at Regensburg, five hundred miles from the North Sea.

These bombers were accompanied by fighter escorts while crossing the English Channel and partway across the continent. But the "little friends" eventually had to turn back because of limited fuel capacity, leaving the lumbering bombers to fly the rest of the way unaccompanied, relying solely on their own onboard gunners to blast away at enemy fighter planes ducking in and out of the clouds.

Allied bombers would encounter flak and enemy fighter interceptors not only over the two targets but all along the perilous flight. In fact, twenty-one of the B-17 bombers were shot down before they even got to Schweinfurt, and another fifteen were lost on the return trip home. In all, sixty planes were lost in the two raids, with 102 airmen killed and 381 taken prisoner. Though downed over enemy territory, thirty-eight airmen managed to evade capture and made it back to safety, only to fly more missions over Europe.

The Germans increased the protective anti-aircraft gun batteries around Schweinfurt in time for a second major air assault on October 14. Another sixty planes were shot down, with 605 airmen killed or listed as missing in action.

Inclement weather and the harsh winter limited the number of sorties flown by Allied bombers after November 1943. One of those missions, on November 5, involved the 533rd Bomb Squadron, commanded by Colonel Joseph Nazzaro, who had quarterbacked the West Point team in 1933. The mission was to Gelsenkirchen in the Ruhr Valley, which had approximately seven

BELOW: *Ohio State swimmer Doc Counsilman had to set aside his collegiate feats and became a B-24 pilot in Europe. After the war he would return to the Buckeyes and dominate the Big Ten and NCAA, first as a swimmer and later as an aquatics coach.*

Photo courtesy of Ohio State University

LEFT: *On every bombing mission, Allied crew members flew through a gauntlet of enemy fire—flak from anti-aircraft guns below, strafing rounds from fighter planes swooping in from every direction. Hundreds of planes and thousands of brave souls were lost in the air war over Fortress Europe.*

Concrete Charlie Bednarik was a gunner on a B-24 for thirty missions and recalled the flak and anti-aircraft rounds stitching his plane virtually every time out. Office of War Information photo

hundred anti-aircraft guns primed to protect the numerous defense plants in the area. Allied bomber crewmen knew the Ruhr was a killing ground and despised every return mission. Nazzaro's own plane was heavily damaged by flak on this mission and would have to be nursed back to England with an engine smoking.

From November 1943 through January 1944 the Allied bombing effort dropped considerably. But as milder weather was forecast for February, air force leaders prepared to launch a massive campaign of saturation bombing against German aircraft plants and ancillary factories.

The Air War Heats Up

On February 19, 1944, every available Allied bomber—B-17 Flying Fortresses and B-24 Liberators—took off for targets in Germany and Poland. Accompanied by their own fighter escorts to ward off the German interceptors, more than one thousand bombers participated in Operation Argument.

With its own ranks depleted, the German Luftwaffe sent up only a token force to meet the approaching waves of bombers. Thus, only twenty-one of the B-17s and B-24s were shot down. Over the next five days, known as Big Week, Allied bombers kept up a continuous barrage, flying 3,800 sorties.

Walter Truemper was a ball turret gunner on one of those missions to Leipzig during Big Week. In high school in Aurora, Illinois, he was an excellent first baseman and golfer. After high school he attended Northwestern University. On the mission to Leipzig, Truemper unwittingly became a hero.

Two Luftwaffe ME-109 fighters attacked and fired on Truemper's bomber as it neared Leipzig, ripping apart the cockpit and killing the copilot. The pilot was wounded and unconscious, and the plane tipped on its right side.

Truemper and two other crewmen struggled their way to the controls, righted the plane, and tended to the wounded pilot. They nursed the crippled plane back across the English Channel and contacted the control tower for instructions.

After assessing the situation, the squadron commander ordered them to ditch at sea and wait for a rescue boat to pick them up, but the three airmen refused due to their pilot's inability to fend for himself in the water. Twice they attempted to crash land. Then on the third approach the plane plowed nose-first into the ground. For their actions Truemper and one of his fellow crewmen were awarded the Medal of Honor.

Luftwaffe Decimated

The early Allied bombing missions over Europe took a heavy toll: though several key German aircraft plants were severely damaged, 226 bombers had

RIGHT: *During a mission to Ploesti, Romania, a Liberator bomber swoops down to take out another oil refinery.* U.S. Army Air Forces photo

been shot down and 2,600 airmen killed, wounded, or listed as missing in action. The Nazi war machine lost 225 experienced Luftwaffe pilots in the air war, with another 141 injured. As their ranks were depleted, the seasoned Luftwaffe pilots were replaced by inexperienced rookies, untested in battle, who merely wanted to survive the war. They were shoved into the cockpits and ordered aloft but all too often avoided confronting the Allied fighter escorts or the heavily armed bombers.

The loss of the Luftwaffe's best pilots decimated the Nazi fighter squadrons, leaving numerous cities without any air cover to challenge the bombing raids. With the skies over Germany thus neutralized, U.S. and British strategists prepared to step up bombing missions throughout Europe, particularly against the capital of Nazi Germany: Berlin.

Those Hotshot Fighter Pilots

As long as Luftwaffe pilots protected the skies over Berlin, the city was deemed too risky as a target. Anti-aircraft guns surrounding the city certainly shot down their share of planes, but it was the few remaining Luftwaffe fighter pilots who were able and still willing to get up close and personal who were the true menace. Big Week shifted the balance of power, though, and Berlin was promptly moved to the top of the list of targets.

P-51B fighter escort planes were refitted with larger fuel pods, allowing them to accompany the bombers all the way to Berlin and chase off any enemy pilots foolish enough to confront them.

"At the top of the elite world of the Allied air forces stood the fighter pilots," wrote Stephen Ambrose in *D-Day. June 6, 1944: The Climactic Battle of World War II:* "Young, cocky, skilled, veteran warriors—in mass war fought by millions, the fighter pilots were the only glamorous individuals left. Up there all alone in a one-on-one with a Luftwaffe fighter, one man's skill and training and machine against another's, they were the knights in shining armor of World War II. They lived on the edge, completely in the present. It would demean them to call them star athletes, because they were much more than that, but they had some of the traits of the athlete. The most important was the lust to compete. They wanted to . . . engage in dogfights, to help make history."

Jimmy Doolittle, commander of the Eighth Air Force and former world-class racing pilot, was himself a fighter pilot and explained the differences between his breed and those of the bomber command: " . . . the individualistic fighter pilot's 'loner' temperament and inclination [is] to 'take the offensive,' whereas the ideal bomber pilot, with his flight crew behind him, is more apt to be a stoic 'team player' and is better fitted to 'sit there and take it' through flak and fighter attacks as he concentrates on his primary task of getting to and off loading his bombs on the target."

Doolittle planned to fly the first mission to Berlin, just as he had done in Tokyo in 1942, but he was grounded by his superiors, fearing that he might be shot down, taken prisoner, and forced to reveal information about the impending invasion of Fortress Europe, slated for mid-1944.

Proving They Belonged

Sixty-six of the American casualties came from the all-black Tuskegee Airmen, who flew P-47 Thunderbolt, P-51 Mustang, and P-40 Warhawk fighter planes, providing escort and air cover to Allied bombers on more than 1,500 missions over Europe. The Tuskegee Airmen also hit strategic targets such as oil refineries, bridges, and railroad marshaling yards deep behind enemy territory.

"They assembled black men from all over the United States to go into this flying school at Tuskegee Institute," recalled Californian Lowell Steward. "They recruited All-American athletes."

Archie Williams was one of those superb athletes that filled the ranks of the Tuskegee pilots. After winning the 400-meter sprint at the 1936 Berlin Olympics, Williams learned to fly. "I built up my flying time to where I finally got my instructor's rating and my commercial license. That was early in 1941. That's when I found out about this program at Tuskegee Institute." (Williams would become an instructor at Tuskegee for the duration of the war and remained in the Air Force until 1964.)

Initially when they deployed to Europe the pilots from Tuskegee were ignored, often referred to as the Spookwaffe. But once they got the chance to fly on escort missions, they established a reputation that was hard to ignore: "We protected the bombers from enemy attack," explained Steward. "And once our reputation got out as to our fighting ability, we started getting special requests [from white bomber crewmen] for our group to escort their group, the bombers. They all wanted us because we were the only fighter group in the entire air force that did not lose a bomber to enemy action."

Put simply, the Tuskegee pilots would shoot down or chase off any Luftwaffe pilots who dared to approach the bombers they were tasked with protecting. And they performed that task with lethal efficiency.

BELOW: Negro aviation cadets from Tuskegee Institute—known as the Tuskegee Airmen—would later distinguish themselves in the skies over Europe, providing protective escort to Allied bomber planes. Photo Courtesy of the Tuskegee Airmen

The Allies Retaliate

The first Berlin mission, involving five hundred B-17s on March 4, was aborted soon after the planes had taken off due to cloud cover over

LEFT: *While their bombers and crews were off on another mission over mainland Europe, the ground crews left behind in England enjoyed playing football.* Army Air Forces photo

Berlin. But because of communications problems, three bomb squadrons didn't receive the message to turn back. They continued instead to Berlin, where they dropped their payloads despite overcast skies, stunning disbelieving Germans, who felt their capital city was too far from England and too well protected to be hit.

The missions of March 6 and March 8 would be especially devastating to the Germans. The first of these two runs saw 500 Luftwaffe pilots scramble to meet 730 bombers accompanied by 800 fighter escorts. The Germans lost eighty-two pilots that day, followed by another eighty-seven on March 8.

During the first four months of 1944, 1,684 Luftwaffe pilots had been lost, leaving what had three years earlier been a fearsome and dominating air force now in ruins.

An Amazing Comeback

One of the most remarkable stories surrounds Bert Shepard, a young pitcher in the Pacific Coast and Arizona-Texas Leagues, who joined the Army Air Corps and was assigned to the Fifty-fifth Fighter Group in England. On May 21, 1944, Shepard volunteered for a mission to Berlin, flying a P-38 fighter bomber. After dropping down to tree-top level to do a strafing run on a Nazi aerodrome seventy miles from the German capital, Shepard saw other planes in front of him get chewed up in a crossfire of flak. "I'm a mile from the field and they shot my right foot off." He was also hit in the chin and lost consciousness. His plane crashed and exploded. Somehow he survived and was pulled out of the wreckage and taken to a prisoner of war camp, where a German doctor amputated what was left of his leg below the knee.

Another prisoner at the camp made him an artificial stump, and soon Shepard was strengthening his leg, even working on his pitching motion, intent on fulfilling his dream of someday pitching in the major leagues.

In January 1945 Shepard was part of an exchange of wounded prisoners. Seven months later, his dream came true when he was sent in as a relief pitcher for the Washington Senators against the Red Sox. He entered the game with the score 14–1 against the Senators, pitched five innings, and gave up just one run—a respectable outing for any pitcher, let alone one with an artificial leg. It would be Shepard's only big-league appearance, but it was an inspiring moment for thousands of other disabled veterans. He would continue to play in exhibition games around the country, talking to and inspiring hundreds of former servicemen.

Return to Berlin

Allied bombing missions would continue to rock Berlin, but by the end of 1944 the city was in shambles. Lieutenant Colonel Marshall Wayne was a high diver at the 1936 Berlin Games and returned there eight years later with a bird's-eye view, leading B-17 bombers to the once-majestic city where Adolf Hitler was now hiding in an underground bunker.

Another Olympian from the 1936 Nazi Games was Alec Bright, a downhill skier and former Harvard hockey player, who served with the Eighth Air Force in both World War I and World War II.

BELOW: *Bombing runs deep inside Germany, such as Schweinfurt, were a necessity that were not accomplished without great loss of life to Allied bomber crews.* Army Air Corps photo

Concrete Charlie

Pennsylvania teenager Chuck Bednarik, who played football, basketball, and baseball in high school, joined the Army Air Corps and manned a .50-caliber machine gun aboard a B-24 bomber. Bednarik's baptism under fire came with his first mission to Berlin on August 27, 1944. Even after thirty missions, the journey into hell wasn't easy.

He later recalled the intensity of the German ground defenses on those bombing missions, saying, "The antiaircraft fire would be all around us. It was so thick you could walk on it. And you could hear it penetrating. Ping! Ping! Ping! Here you are, this wild, dumb kid, you didn't think you were afraid of anything, and now, every time you take off, you're convinced this is it, you're gonna be ashes."

(Concrete Charlie Bednarik survived those hair-raising missions and returned home, earning a football scholarship to the University of Pennsylvania, where the Bethlehem Bomber was a two-time all-American and recipient of the Maxwell Award in 1948, given to the best college football player in the country. He joined the Philadelphia Eagles in 1949 and was a perennial all-pro.)

The Nazi Rocketeers and the Weary Willies

To swing the balance of power back in their favor, the Nazis were continuing development of their V-1 and V-2 rocket program. These weapons were launched from sites in France, Holland, and Belgium, aimed toward England. Hundreds had already exploded on London and Coventry, killing thousands of innocent British civilians. The Allies drew up a plan to take out these missile sites.

The strategy called for B-17 Liberator bombers called Weary Willies, crammed full of 20,000 pounds of explosives, to take off. The pilot and copilot would bail out while still over England, and the planes would then be flown by radio-control to the target across the English Channel. One of these pilots was Joseph Kennedy, Jr., who had played football at Harvard and was the eldest son of Ambassador Joe Kennedy. On August 12, 1944, he and his copilot climbed into the flying bomb and took off from Fersfield Aerodrome, bound for a V-2 plant near Calais, France.

Twenty minutes out, Kennedy switched on the remote guidance system and two massive explosions disintegrated the plane over Suffolk. No trace of the two pilots was ever found. Project Aphrodite, the Third Air Division's flying bomb, was deemed too dangerous and unreliable and was abruptly abandoned.

ABOVE: *Concrete Charlie, Chuck Bednarik, saw plenty of action aboard a B-24 bomber during the European Campaign. He later played both offense and defense at Penn, earning All-American honors and was chosen the best college player in 1948.* Photo courtesy of the University of Pennsylvania

Dresden Burns

Another important Allied target was Dresden, Germany—a transportation hub where rail lines and roadways converged. These lifelines from Dresden funneled men and materiel to the Eastern Front in the fight against Russia.

On the night of February 13, 1945, British planes dropped incendiary bombs on Dresden, followed with more at dawn and again at midmorning. The following day American B-17s delivered hundreds more bombs.

The entire city was engulfed in flames and 35,000 civilians killed. Naturally the German press deplored the ethics of bombing Dresden, but the British quickly reminded the world what Nazi buzz bombs had already done to innocent British citizens.

Within weeks Germany would surrender, unable to withstand the constant bombing or hold back the Allied ground forces closing in from both the east and west. While it played a decisive role in the European Campaign, the air war had been costly: 36,320 American pilots and crewmen were killed.

ABOVE: *Flying Fortresses of the 8th Air Force strike at the heart of the Fatherland: Berlin, once thought safely out of reach. But Nazi Germany's capitol city sustained some of the heaviest bombing of the European Campaign.* Army Air Corps photo

A Tragic End to the Air War

On April 21, 1945, the B-24 Liberator nicknamed the Black Cat, assigned to the 787th Bomb Squadron, took off for Salzburg, Austria. It was the crew's twenty-third mission.

Among the Black Cat crew were Howard Goodner, who played football at Western Kentucky in 1942 and basketball for the post team during combat-crew training in Colorado; copilot Jack Regan, who played basketball at Queens College and NYU and had been offered a minor league baseball contract by Dodgers manager Leo Durocher; Jack Brennan, who played varsity football at St. Cecilia High School in Englewood, New Jersey; and nose-gunner Harry Gregorian, a welterweight boxer from Detroit, who had pummeled a hapless soldier during a boxing smoker on the transport ships carrying them from the East Coast to England in October of '44.

The war was rapidly winding down and every crewman prayed the Germans would surrender soon. En route to Salzburg, the mission was scratched because of poor visibility over the target area. The squadron turned about and headed for home, passing over the heavily defended city of Regensburg.

Tragically, the Black Cat was hit by anti-aircraft fire. It lost its left wing and plunged in flames. The helpless bomber rolled over in a flat arch. Other aircrews watched desperately for parachutes and prayed, hoping all twelve crewmen had bailed out. But they counted only two chutes. The Black Cat would be the last American plane shot down over Europe in World War II.

LEFT BELOW: *Pilot Richard Farrington and his men were dubbed the Black Cat crew, flying their B-24 Liberator with the 787th Bomber Squadron. Like every crew flying perilous missions over Europe, they needed more than a cat's nine lives to make it through the war alive. But on April 21, 1945, in the final days of the war, the Black Cat took off for another mission — its twenty-third — but over the heavily-defended city of Regensburg, it was hit by flak and crashed. It was the last American bomber lost in the air campaign against Nazi Germany.* Army Air Corps photo

Football Players Go on the Offensive

"MODERN WAR WAS NOT A FOOTBALL GAME. AND MODERN WAR WAS NOT MAN AGAINST MAN—IF IT EVER HAD BEEN. IT WAS MACHINE AGAINST MACHINE. IT WAS INDUSTRY AGAINST INDUSTRY. AND WE HAD THE BEST MACHINE. OUR INDUSTRY WAS BETTER THAN THEIR INDUSTRY. BUT MEN HAD TO DIE OR BE MAIMED TO PROVE IT."

—James Jones

"TWO RIGID, RAMPART-LIKE LINES OF HUMAN FLESH HAVE BEEN CREATED, ONE OF DEFENSE, THE OTHER OF OFFENSE, AND BEHIND THE LATTER IS ESTABLISHED A CATAPULT TO FIRE THROUGH A PORTHOLE OPENED IN THE OFFENSIVE RAMPART A MISSILE COMPOSED OF FOUR OR FIVE HUMAN BODIES GLOBULATED ABOUT A CARRIED FOOTBALL WITH A MAXIMUM OF INITIAL VELOCITY AGAINST THE PRESUMABLY WEAKEST POINT IN THE OPPOSING RAMPART."

—Benjamin Ide Wheeler, 1906

"A PROFESSIONAL FOOTBALL TEAM WARMS UP GRIMLY AND DISPARATELY, LIKE AN ARMY ON MANEUVERS: THE GROUND TROOPS HERE, THE TANKS THERE, THE ARTILLERY AND AIR FORCE OVER THERE."

—Ted Solotaroff

THE BASIC PREMISE OF FOOTBALL IS FOR TWO OPPOSING teams (or armies) to do battle, each taking turns trying to break through the opponent's defensive forces using a variety of weapons (the bruising fullback, the scampering halfback, the fleet-footed end, or the rocket-armed quarterback, to name just the primary "weapons"). At the end of the battle the stronger (or better, or luckier) of the two sides is declared the winner. Afterward, both sides retire for some rest and recuperation and go over the battle plans for their next encounter with another opponent, in another location.

As in any form of physical combat, casualties are expected in football. Often during a long season attrition takes its toll, and a once-powerful team may be decimated by the end of the year. The best teams are the ones that have capable replacements ready to plug those gaps created by injuries. Without reinforcements a team is susceptible to attack in those weakened areas.

"Slugging it out in the trenches," "blitzing the quarterback," and "busting the wedge" are used interchangeably on the battlefield and the gridiron.

Just as in real combat, often it's not the strongest or the better-equipped or even better-trained team that wins the battle. Sometimes the final outcome is based on a last-minute desperation gamble, such as a Hail Mary pass or an end-around sweep.

Football Strategy Like Battle Tactics

Clark Shaughnessy, head football coach at the University of Chicago and a consultant to the Chicago Bears, was fascinated with the battle strategies of an obscure German Army officer named Heinz Guderian, who wrote *Achtung Panzer,* a treatise on tank warfare, in 1937.

Long before his tactics had been proven (and supported by his fellow officers), Guderian felt the tank could be used en masse to produce lightning strikes with devastating efficiency. His blitzkrieg tactics contradicted the tediously slow and laborious use of armor in World War I two decades earlier. Shaughnessy was fanatical with football strategy and applied Guderian's theories to the gridiron, developing the T-formation to a high level of efficiency. The Bears would implement Shaughnessy's radical game plan and go on to decimate the Washington Redskins 73–0 in the 1940 championship game.

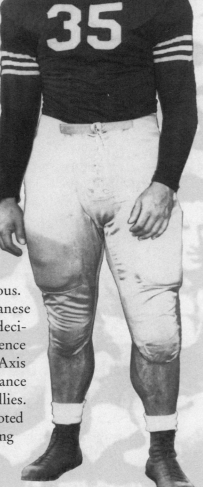

LEFT: *Army fullback Doc Blanchard won the Heisman Trophy in 1945 while playing for the powerhouse West Point.* U.S. Military Academy photo

Guderian's strategies came to fruition as his tanks steamrolled across Europe, from France to Poland and on to North Africa. But the brutal Russian winter stopped his mighty panzer tanks, and after that the Allied forces were able to fight back. The once awesome Nazi war machine would never recover. But Guderian is still considered a battle tactician ahead of his time, just as Shaughnessy is credited as the man behind George "Papa Bear" Halas's Chicago Bears juggernaut.

The comparison between football and war is obvious. During World War II both the Germans and Japanese started with vastly superior war machines but were decimated over the span of several years by Allied persistence and bold, sometimes desperate, tactics. Once the Axis forces no longer had sufficient reinforcements, the balance of power shifted permanently and decisively to the Allies.

In its October 27, 1943, issue, *Stars and Stripes* noted the influence football had on military thinking during

ABOVE: *Hal Van Every, former Minnesota star, would be taken prisoner during the war and remain on the sidelines until being liberated. He would then return to the States and become a Green Bay Packer.*
U.S. Army photo

World War II: "Football strategy is being used all over the world today in tactics designed to outsmart the enemy—so football training should be invaluable in the training of our armed forces. That's the opinion of Lieutenant Commander Mal Stevens, former football coach of Yale and New York University and now mentor of the Naval Training Station team at Sampson, New York.

"'Most of our great admirals and generals—Halsey, Eisenhower and MacArthur, for instance [Bradley and Patton too]—were football players,'" says Mal.

"The individual strategy and thinking as a result of football training and conditioning make for faster and clearer decisions, he believes. Football in many instances, simulates battle conditions. 'The Russians,' he says, 'have been using the old mousetrap play right along—drawing the enemy in and then encircling and side swiping.'"

"Our Navy 'did an end run around Sicily' and the old wedge play 'is the split and divide German method.'

"The air barrage 'helps soften up defenses in battle the same as in football, disorganizing the secondary defense.'

"'All in all,' says Stevens, 'war and football demand highly organized team play in addition to raw physical courage.'"

In combat, that teamwork involved thousands of men from all branches of the armed services, each playing a vital role in both European and Pacific Campaigns, leading to eventual victory.

Fighting it out in the trenches were thousands of collegiate and professional football players alongside men from all professions and backgrounds.

"Hundreds of players who had looked forward to their senior season are now in the field, flying their planes, manning machine guns, or walking the decks of the Navy's fighting craft," said Lou Little, Columbia football coach, in 1942.

"Football is being played harder, faster, perhaps even more fiercely than it has been played before. We have become an offensively minded nation. Defense bonds have become war bonds. The bombers and the ships they buy are weapons of attack, not defense. We must strike, not parry."

Pearl Harbor Disrupts Next Five Years

While war raged in both Europe and the Pacific during the late 1930s, the United States took a wait-and-see stance. One college football coach explained it simply: "Football is the American substitute for war."

But then in early December 1941, all that changed.

News of the Japanese attack on Pearl Harbor reached the United States while the Chicago Bears and Green Bay Packers were slugging it out at Wrigley Field in a divisional playoff game. The Bears won 33–14, but all attention was diverted to more important events occurring halfway around the world.

The following week Chicago nabbed the NFL crown by beating the New York Giants 39–7, but only 13,300 fans attended the game.

The next season many star players were missing, but the league still had enough athletes to continue. But by 1943 several rosters were depleted more than others. To keep teams afloat, players were redistributed. Still, the NFL lost two teams when the Cleveland Rams suspended play and the Philadelphia Eagles and Pittsburgh Steelers merged to form the Phil-Pitt Steagles.

Greasy Neale, hired as the Steelers coach in 1941, was especially disappointed because he had started keeping an innovative "book system," a record of every college football player in the country. "We'd keep track of the players from the start to finish of their college careers," Neale wrote. "Some of the other people around the league made fun of me when they heard about this, but Art Rooney, the owner of the Steelers, said, 'That book will help them be champions in 1944.' I was hoping we'd make it before 1944. Then, of course, the war broke out and in 1942, 20 of my players left for the service. In 1943 we lost more men and the entire league was weakened."

Philly later broke away to try it again on their own, so the Steelers linked up with another war-depleted team, the Chicago Cardinals, to form the Card-Pitt. This team was so pitiful—winless in eleven games—that opposing players referred to it as the "carpet," as in "walk all over them."

The Cleveland Rams took the field again in '44 but would move to Los Angeles two years later. The Boston Yanks were formed in 1944 but merged with the Brooklyn Tigers the next year.

Teams Adapt to Remain Competitive

Many football players fulfilled their military commitment by working in defense-related plants during day shifts, then practicing football after hours and playing games on the weekends as usual. Some players in the Army Reserves, National Guard, or Merchant Marine kept in shape and asked for weekend passes to join their team for games.

Mel Hein had retired from pro ball in 1942 and took over as head coach at Union College at Schenectady, New York. But when Union was forced to drop its football program, Hein stayed on to teach the hundreds of Navy recruits going through V-12 training.

"Just before football season started I had a call from Steve Owens who wanted me to be a Sunday center for the Giants," Hein would later recall. "I had played under him so long I knew the system inside out. And my work at Union kept me in shape. I agreed to the arrangement and during the season of 1943 and 1944 I was the Giants' Sunday Center. Finally in 1945 the boys came home and I packed it in for once and for all."

The league had already instituted a draft of college players, but in 1945 it was changed so that the worst teams would get first crack at the best available collegiate players. But even in 1944, only 12 of the 330 players selected in the draft joined their teams that season. All the others joined the military. Those teams that needed the most help might have a terrific team on paper but still be left with only those players too old or too infirm to join the military.

One of those over-the-hill stars was former Chicago Bears fullback Bronko Nagurski, who had retired from football in 1937 and became a wrestler. In 1943 the Bears asked Bronko for some help, and he obliged, at tackle. In the final game of the season Nagurski was back at fullback and bulled his way to victory one last time before walking away from football.

During his days at New York University, Ken Strong led the country in scoring. He was also good enough in baseball to receive a contract offer from the Detroit Tigers but hurt his wrist in a minor league game. Strong would play for the Giants but retired after the 1940 season. "In 1943, when I was 37 years old, the Giants asked me to come back," Strong remembered. "There was a manpower shortage because of the war and they felt they could use me for kickoffs and place kicks. I didn't really feel old until one day in 1944, when we were playing an exhibition game against the Bears.

"After I kicked off and started downfield, Bulldog Turner, the Bears' great center, came at me. He was just about to hit me when he stopped and said, 'Hell, I can't hit you. You're too damn old!'"

Athletes Deployed Worldwide

By the end of the war, 638 pro football players were in the armed forces, and 21 of them had died. In virtually every campaign pro and college players gave their lives for their country.

Among those killed in the European Campaign were Keith Birlem, an end with the Cardinals and Redskins, who crash-landed in a bomber in 1943; Ed Doyle, killed during the invasion of North Africa in 1942; Georgetown punter Jim Mooney, killed in France; Texas A&M all-American guard Joe Routt, who commanded an infantry company and was fatally wounded; Temple football ace Ed Stecz, killed in Germany; Washington State's John Hurley, killed in Italy; Ohio State running back Don Scott, killed in a bomber crash over England; Clemson's 1939 Cotton Bowl quarterback Aubrey Rion, killed in Europe; Richard Schmon, Princeton team captain, killed in France; Tennessee fullback Bill Nowling, also killed in France;

Johnny Sprague, Southern Methodist's blocking back on the 1935 Rose Bowl team, killed protecting a fellow soldier from a German machine gun.

One tragic example was Army infantry lieutenant Al Blozis, on leave to play tackle for the New York Giants in their 14–7 championship loss to the Green Bay Packers in '44. Less than two months later he was killed in France. It was his first, and only, combat patrol.

Maurice Britt played end for the Detroit Lions during the 1941 season and then, just two days before the attack on Pearl Harbor, joined the Third Infantry Division at Fort Lewis, Washington. Used to crashing into defensive linebackers during his playing days, Britt quickly became known in the Third Herd as a one-man Army for his single-handed actions at Acerno, Italy, in 1943, and again a few months later during an intense firefight when his company of the Thirtieth Infantry Regiment became pinned down. For these two actions Britt received the Silver Star and Distinguished Service Cross, respectively. Wedged between these actions was a battle at Monte Rotundo near Mignano, Italy, in November 1943.

"During the intense fire fight, a bullet pierced his side; his chest, face and hands were covered with grenade wounds," states the award citation from that skirmish.

"Despite his wounds he personally killed 5 and wounded an unknown number of Germans, and wiped out one enemy machine-gun crew. Lieutenant Britt's undaunted courage and prowess in arms were largely responsible for repulsing a German counterattack which, if successful, would have isolated his battalion and destroyed his company."

Britt received the Medal of Honor for this action. Three months later, an enemy artillery shell exploded nearby and Britt lost his right arm . . . and with it his dream of playing pro football again.

The Brutal Pacific

Football players who died fighting in the Pacific included Chuck Braidwood, Cardinals end, fatally injured while serving with the Red Cross in the South Pacific; Alex Santilli, a Fordham tackle who played in the 1942 Sugar Bowl, killed by a Japanese sniper on Saipan; Chicago Bears halfback Young Bussey, died during the Philippines landing in 1944; Eddie Kahn, a guard with Boston and Washington, died from wounds received during the invasion of Leyte in the Philippines in 1945; Detroit Lions fullback Lee Kizzire, shot down over New Guinea in 1943.

BELOW: *Iowa running back and 1939 Heisman trophy winner Nile Kinnick was stationed in the Caribbean as a Navy fighter pilot. But in early June of 1943 his plane went down and Iowa's favorite son was lost at sea.* Photo courtesy of the University of Iowa

Oklahoma all-American end Waddy Young was piloting a B-29 bomber to Japan when it was shot down, killing the entire crew; Georgetown fullback John Barrett was killed on Peleliu; Alabama all-American end Bob Hutson was killed in the South Pacific; Lieutenant Charles Behan, former Detroit Lions player, was killed on Okinawa in May 1945; Marine Sergeant Bob Nanni, former Duke lineman, fell at Iwo Jima.

Another Giants player, end Jack Lummus, was involved in brutal combat on Iwo Jima, leading his Twenty-seventh Marine Regiment platoon through two straight days of fighting. While Lummus was attempting to knock out enemy bunkers, a grenade caught him full force, blowing his legs off. Lummus died the next day.

Iowa's Favorite Son

Another prominent player who tragically died too young was 1939 Heisman Trophy winner Nile Kinnick, University of Iowa running back from 1937 to '39. To put that fantastic year in perspective, Kinnick was also selected Associated Press Athlete of the Year, beating out the Yankee Clipper, Joe DiMaggio, and heavyweight boxing champion Joe Louis.

As part of his Heisman speech, Kinnick stated, "I thank God that I was born to the gridirons of the Midwest and not the battlefields of Europe. I can confidently say that the boys of this country would rather win this trophy than the crois de guerre."

Kinnick was drafted by the Brooklyn Dodgers football team, attended law school, and signed up for the Naval Air Reserve. Then in early December 1941, just days before the Japanese attacked Pearl Harbor, he was called up.

While stationed in the Caribbean, Kinnick flew a Navy F4 Wildcat fighter plane, watching for Nazi U-boats prowling coastal waters. But on June 2, 1943, his engine started leaking oil and then stalled over the Gulf of Paria near Trinidad, and his plane plunged into the sea. Kinnick made it out alive and was sighted bobbing in the water by another pilot, but by the time a rescue boat could be dispatched to the area, he was gone.

Even today, more than sixty years later, Iowans still fondly remember their favorite son and recall his gridiron exploits in the late thirties. For Iowa football fans, the legend of Nile Kinnick will never die.

Singed by the Heat of Battle

Thousands of college and pro football players were wounded during World War II. While many recovered from their wounds and were able to play football again, others suffered crippling injuries, preventing them from participating in the sport they loved. Among those wounded fighting in Europe were Georgia end George Poschner, whose legs had to be amputated after he was wounded in combat at the Battle of the Bulge; Tennessee tackle Abe Shires, wounded in France; Rice's all–Southwest Conference halfback Ollie Cordill, injured in a plane crash while flying missions over Italy; and Harvard guard James Gaffney, who lost his right leg during fighting near the Moselle River in France.

In the Pacific, some of those football players injured included tackle Bernie Gallagher of Pennsylvania, who was wounded on Okinawa but would return to play college ball; Illinois and Purdue all-American guard Alex Agase, injured in both the shoulder and leg while serving with the Fifth Marines in the South Pacific, who would recuperate and return to Illinois; running back Jimmy Lawrence, who played with the Chicago Cardinals, Green Bay Packers, and Brooklyn Dodgers and was wounded in combat on New Guinea; and Philadelphia Eagles guard Jack Sanders, who lost his lower left arm while fighting on Iwo Jima but returned to play for the Eagles in 1945.

Also injured on Iwo Jima were Pennsylvania fullback Bert Stiff; Holy Cross and Brooklyn Dodgers lineman Si Titus; Iowa all-American guard Harold Hantelmann, injured by an enemy hand grenade at Buna on New Guinea; and Notre Dame tackle Paul Lillis, hurt in the Admiralties Campaign.

Present and Future Stars Served on the High Seas

Among the many other prominent players who served in the Navy, Coast Guard, and Merchant Marine during World War II was Byron "Whizzer" White, Colorado's all-American halfback, who led the National Football League in rushing for the Detroit Lions in 1940. He served with a naval destroyer squadron nicknamed the Little Beavers and saw plenty of action in the waters off Guadalcanal. (After returning home, White would later become a Supreme Court Justice). Annapolis halfback Buzz Borries was on board the carrier *Gambier Bay* when it was sunk in the Battle of Leyte Gulf near the Philippines. After forty-two hours in a life raft, with the battle still raging, Borries was finally rescued.

Chicago Bears quarterback Sid Luckman served in the Merchant Marine, pulling convoy duty in the North Atlantic. Named as one of the greatest quarterbacks in NFL history, Luckman led the Bears to the NFL championship game in 1940, playing against the highly favored Washington Redskins and stunning them

BELOW AND BACKGROUND: *The mighty Sooners of Oklahoma didn't lose a conference game in 1943 or '44 despite many of its players leaving for the military. Still, head coach Dewey Lester understood: "Football is the ideal sport for training youngsters to the mood of war. There's simply no acceptable substitute for the rugged give-and-take of free-wheeling body contact."* Photo courtesy of the University of Oklahoma

with a 73–0 shellacking; University of Texas quarterback Bobby Layne served with Luckman in the Maritime Service. (In 1945 Layne returned to Texas and became an all-American, then joined the Bears. Lane led the Detroit Lions to the league championship in 1952, '53, and '57, breaking league records with 196 touchdown passes and 26,768 yards passing).

"Jumbo" Joe Stydahar was the Bears' first draft choice in 1936 when the National Football League owners came up with a selection process for college players. Jumbo Joe went on to become one of the famous Monsters of the Midway. During the Pacific Campaign he was in charge of a gun crew on the carrier USS *Monterey,* which saw action in the Gilberts, Carolines, and Marianas, the Philippine Sea, Leyte Gulf, and Okinawa. (Stydahar returned to the Bears and played two more seasons, capping a Hall of Fame career that included five western division titles and three league crowns).

Another "greatest" quarterback was Northwestern's Otto Graham, who served in the Navy. (Afterward he joined the Cleveland Browns of the All-America Conference and led them to four straight league titles).

One of Graham's Cleveland teammates after the war was University of Nevada all-American fullback Marion Motley. Motley joined the Navy in 1944 and underwent training at Great Lakes Naval Training Station, where he played football under coach Paul Brown. Motley and Graham would join forces again in the pro ranks, playing for the Cleveland Browns. Motley and Browns teammate Bill Willis were the first two black players to join the All-America Conference, breaking down the invisible barriers preventing blacks from playing pro football.

Toledo athlete Emlen Tunnell broke his neck and was told he could never play football again. He joined the Coast Guard, only to have his ship torpedoed twice during convoy operations in the Atlantic. (Tunnell would return to the University of Iowa, then join the New York Giants in 1948. His pro career was marked by nine Pro-Bowl appearances, an NFL title in 1956, and entry into the Hall of Fame in 1967.

Len Ford served in the Navy and then returned to play for the Michigan Wolverines, earning all-American honors followed by five all-pro selections with the Los Angeles Dons and Cleveland Browns.

Norm "Stub" Van Brocklin attracted baseball scouts while pitching at Acalanes High School in California, but he was only interested in playing football. He joined the Navy after his junior year, got his high school diploma while in the service, and served for three years before returning home to play quarterback at the University of Oregon, where he would become an all-American. (Van Brocklin would take his passing attack to the Los Angeles Rams and led them to the NFL crown in 1951 while setting a single-game passing record.)

Wayne Millner was starting end at Notre Dame and then became known as the money player for the Washington Redskins. But after the '41 season he joined the Navy. "I had charge of a gun crew and I ran it like I'd run a football team," Millner later wrote. "I also worked out and stayed in pretty good shape." (Millner would rejoin the Redskins as player and coach, capping off thirty-three years in the game with his induction into the Pro Football Hall of Fame in 1968).

Joe "the Jet" Perry was playing fullback for a Navy team in California when he was scouted by the San Francisco 49ers. (In 1949 he was the All-America Conference's rushing leader.)

Flying High

Georgia's 1943 Heisman Trophy winner Frank Sinkwich, who tried to enlist but was turned away because of flat feet, was later accepted by the Army Air Corps in 1945. One of Sinkwich's teammates was halfback Charley "Triple Threat" Trippi, who served with the Third Air Force. (Trippi would return to Georgia midway through the 1945 season and led them to an undefeated season the following year. He played eight seasons with the Chicago Cardinals and made it to the Hall of Fame in 1968).

Minnesota all-American halfback George Franck, a marine fighter pilot in the Pacific, survived a dunk in the ocean when his plane was shot down near Wotje Atoll. Northwestern's halfback Bernie Jefferson flew fighter planes in the Mediterranean region and earned the Distinguished Flying Cross for his exploits.

Michigan Heisman Trophy and Maxwell Trophy winner Tom Harmon flew fighter planes, in the China-Burma-India Campaign. After being shot down and reported missing for a month, he returned to friendly territory with the aid of Chinese guerrilla forces. (He returned home and played two years with the Los Angeles Rams.)

Also serving in the CBI was Green Bay Packers and Pittsburgh Steelers halfback Johnny "Blood" McNally, who worked as a cryptographer for the Army Air Force. (While with the Packers, Blood scored thirty-seven touchdowns and played on four championship teams, becoming a charter member of the Football Hall of Fame.)

University of Virginia all-American halfback "Bullet" Bill Dudley played just one season for the Pittsburgh Steelers, earning Rookie of the Year honors in 1942. He then joined the Army Air Corps and missed two seasons as a pilot in the Pacific before returning to the Steelers late in 1945. He was named league MVP the next year, and amassed Hall of Fame stats in nine years.

Chuck Bednarik joined the Army Air Corps right after high school, serving as a waist-gunner on a B-24 bomber.

BELOW: *Northwestern's Otto Graham was a superb athlete in both football and basketball. But his collegiate exploits were interrupted in 1943 when he joined the Navy.* Photo courtesy of Northwestern University

While in Europe he flew thirty bombing missions. He returned to play for the University of Pennsylvania, winning the Maxwell Award as the best college player in 1948. (The next year Concrete Charlie joined the Philadelphia Eagles, and he would be selected all-pro nine times during his Hall of Fame career before retiring in 1962).

Tom Landry was playing freshman football for the Texas Longhorns when he was told that his brother, an Army Air Corps pilot, had been shot down in Europe and was listed as missing in action. Tom gave up his scholarship and enlisted two weeks before Christmas in 1942. He would end up with the 862nd Bomb Squadron in England and fly thirty missions to Germany. He was shot down once. (Landry would return to football and coach the Dallas Cowboys to Super Bowl titles in 1972 and 1978.)

Running back Kenny Washington and his UCLA teammate Woody Strode—known in college as the Goal Dust Twins—were the other two black football players to bust down the race barrier in 1946, signing with the Los Angeles Rams. Strode had served with the Army Air Corps during the war. Coincidentally, at UCLA Washington had roomed with another collegiate star who would go on to a Hall of Fame career, but in baseball: Jackie Robinson.

War in the Trenches: Army versus Navy

While UCLA had the Goal Dust twins, West Point dominated the college ranks with the Touchdown Twins—Doc "Mr. Inside" Blanchard and Glenn "Mr. Outside" Davis—who would each win the Heisman Trophy in successive years and be selected to three all-American teams while leading Army to

BELOW: *Michigan running back Tom Harmon (left) won the Heisman Trophy in 1940, then went off to war, serving as a fighter pilot in the China-Burma-India Campaign.* Photo courtesy of the NCAA

two college titles. Army's domination over college football earned the pow-erhouse West Point squad the nickname as the point-a-minute team, raking up lopsided scores nearly every week.

Army's biggest rival would be, as always, the mighty midshipmen of Navy, another powerhouse loaded with the nation's best, especially during the war. Every year bragging rights within the armed services hinged on the winner of the Army-Navy football game, and cadets and graduates from both service schools packed the stands. But in 1942, in an amazing gesture of sportsmanship, the game was moved from Philadelphia to Thompson Stadium in Annapolis to conserve gas. The move meant only those who lived within ten miles of the site could attend the game; thus it was an all-Navy crowd. (Not even President Roosevelt could attend because he lived outside the ten-mile zone.)

The heavily stacked partisan crowd normally would have tormented the visiting cadets of West Point, but instead those midshipmen on the Army side of the field were told to cheer for "their team" wearing the Black and Gold. They did so, though with little enthusiasm and providing no positive influ-ence on the outcome, as Army lost 14–0.

After the game, West Point coach Earl "Red" Blaik praised the middies on a radio program broadcast later to the troops overseas: "The Army ran into one of the finest charging lines we've ever faced. The Japs and the Nazis had better watch out. Our Navy is tops."

Army player Jim Kelleher echoed that sentiment, adding, "It was like playing against eleven tanks all afternoon. They refused to stop. I sure am glad we're fighting this war along with the Navy."

On the football field, Army and Navy would go at it with all guns blazing, but on the battlefields of Europe and the Pacific, their combined weaponry (including the amphibious forces of the Marine Corps and fighter planes and bombers of the Army Air Corps) were an unbeatable juggernaut.

Pounding It Out on the Ground

Notre Dame quarterback Angelo Bertelli was having a great season in 1943 but had to join the Marines midseason. In fact, Bertelli "was the greatest and the most dangerous football player in America this year," reported *Yank* mag-azine on November 26, 1943. "In the six games he played for Notre Dame's powerful Irish, he became the player of the year and everybody's all-every-thing halfback." In just half a season, his statistics were good enough to earn him the Heisman Trophy. He would later see action on Guam and Iwo Jima.

Lou Groza saw heavy combat in the Pacific Campaign, serving with the Army's Ninety-sixth Infantry Division on Okinawa and the Philippines' Leyte Island. But whenever there was a lull in the action, Lou the Toe would erect a pair of goalposts or even use two palm trees to practice kicking field goals, with a football, volleyball, or basketball. He may have even tried

kicking a coconut once or twice! But practicing in heavy combat boots strengthened his leg, the money-maker that would carry him to a nineteen-year career with the Cleveland Browns.

After one year at Notre Dame, Art Donovan joined the Marine Corps and saw action in the Marianas, Marshalls, and Okinawa. (After Japan surrendered, Fatso Donovan played football at Boston College and then joined the Baltimore Colts for a twelve-year Hall of Fame career).

Charlie Conerly wasn't a known commodity when he served for more than four years in the Marine Corps. He was just a young Marine from Clarksville, Mississippi. But after the war, he would attend Ole Miss and make the all-America squad as a halfback, leading his team to the Southeastern Conference title. (In 1956 he would play a key role as the New York Giants won the NFL Championship.)

University of Minnesota defensive tackle Leo Nomellini served in the Marines and saw plenty of action on Saipan and Okinawa. (Considered one of the greatest defensive players in history, Nomellini made his mark during eight seasons with the San Francisco 49ers.)

Gino Marchetti spent his eighteenth birthday trying to join the Army in 1945. After a brief stint in Germany he would enroll at the University of San Francisco and become all-conference tackle in 1951. (Marchetti would go on to play in ten Pro Bowls and help the Baltimore Colts win the NFL title in 1958 and 1959.)

Verne Gagne had been Minnesota's state wrestling champion in 1943 and won the Western Conference title during his freshman year at the University of Minnesota. During his brief stint with the Marine Corps, Gagne served as a combat defense trainer and played football at El Toro, California. (He would return to Minnesota and resume his wrestling prowess, winning conference titles from 1947 to '49 and NCAA crowns in '48 and '49.)

Prisoners of War

They parachuted deep over enemy territory when their bomber planes were shot down, they were rescued at sea when their warships were torpedoed, or, with the rapid advance of enemy ground forces, they simply got overrun and had to surrender. These were some of the ways American servicemen were taken prisoner by the Germans and the Japanese.

Among the pro and college football players held behind bars during the European and Pacific campaigns were: North Carolina State and Newark Bears star Eddie Berlinski, captured in North Africa; Missouri All-American center Darold Jenkins; University of Minnesota star Hal Van Every; Oregon

State fullback Jim Kisselburgh, Yale tackle Fritz Barzilauskas, and Clemson kicker Booty Payne ended up in POW camps in Germany; UCLA quarterback Ernie Case was shot down over Italy and held prisoner for nine months before he escaped; and Chicago Cardinals halfback Mario "Motts" Tonelli was taken prisoner in the Philippines.

Veterans Return from Overseas

When the war finally ended in 1945, the athletes came flooding back, many returning to college. With such a huge influx of players, NFL owners talked about expansion. But having seen more than forty franchises close up shop since the league's inception in 1920, the owners scuttled that idea.

Instead, the upstart All-America Football Conference was born. It lasted only four seasons but created such teams as the Baltimore Colts, the San Francisco 49ers, and the Cleveland Browns and lured one hundred NFL players and many returning veterans, including Angelo Bertelli and Otto Graham.

The Chicago Rockets signed not only superstar Elroy "Crazy Legs" Hirsch but also many of his teammates from the El Toro Marine Air Base team in California. This touched off a bidding war as both leagues went after talented players from the college ranks, military, and semipro teams.

The AAFC was popular in Cleveland, San Francisco, and Baltimore, but teams had a tough time competing in established NFL cities, such as Chicago, Los Angeles, and New York. Falling by the wayside were the Chicago Rockets, Los Angeles Dons, and Brooklyn Dodgers.

By 1949 the three best AAFC teams—the Browns, 49ers, and Colts—were merged into the National Football League, leaving the other AAFC franchises no choice but to fold. The three "rookie" teams that came over from the "creampuff league" were considered second-rate . . . until the Browns stunned the Philadelphia Eagles in the first game of the '49 season, beating them 35–10. The Browns marched through that season all the way to the league championship game, where they beat the Rams 30–28.

With Otto Graham as the field general and Paul Brown calling the plays from the sidelines, the "creampuff" Browns would be a dominant force in the NFL throughout the 1950s.

The years after World War II were an exciting era for professional football, and hundreds of those gridiron stars and top-ranked collegians had served in the military, both stateside and abroad. They gave America the prime of their youth, but many of their prewar buddies sacrificed their lives or their livelihood due to injury, for their country.

BELOW: *During WWII, Charlie Conerly was just one of countless Marines who served in the South Pacific for the duration. But then he would return and play football for Ole Miss, joining the All-American squad in 1946. Ten years later he led the New York Giants to the NFL crown.* Photo courtesy of the University of Mississippi

16. Penetrating Fortress Europe

"IF I WAS GOING TO STORM A PILLBOX, GOING TO
SHEER UTTER, CERTAIN DEATH, AND THE COLONEL
SAID, 'SHEPHERD, PICK SIX GUYS,' I'D PICK SIX
WHITE SOX FANS, BECAUSE THEY HAVE KNOWN
DEATH EVERY DAY OF THEIR LIVES AND IT HOLDS
NO TERROR FOR THEM."

—*Jean Shepherd*

"THE YOUNG MEN BORN INTO THE FALSE PROSPERITY
OF THE 1920S AND BROUGHT UP IN THE BITTER
REALITIES OF THE DEPRESSION OF THE 1930S . . .
NONE OF THEM WANTED TO BE PART OF ANOTHER
WAR. THEY WANTED TO BE THROWING BASEBALLS,
NOT HAND GRENADES, SHOOTING .22S AT RABBITS,
NOT M-1S AT OTHER YOUNG MEN. BUT WHEN THE
TEST CAME, WHEN FREEDOM HAD TO BE FOUGHT
FOR OR ABANDONED, THEY FOUGHT. THEY WERE
SOLDIERS OF DEMOCRACY. THEY WERE THE MEN OF
D-DAY."

—*Stephen E. Ambrose, D-Day*

OPPOSITE: *On the beaches of Normandy, France, soldiers scrambled out of troop landing ships and waded ashore on June 6, 1944. Facing them were heavily fortified Nazi artillery guns and machine-gun bunkers, killing hundreds of American and other Allied soldiers along the beaches.* U.S. Coast Guard photo

IN AUGUST 1942 ALLIED PLANNERS NEEDED TO ASSESS JUST how formidable German defenses were along the northern French coast before launching an all-out invasion of Hitler's Fortress Europe. A raiding force of Canadian and British commandos, with American Rangers along for the experience, landed at Dieppe and were promptly cut to pieces. Though the Dieppe raid was considered a disaster, the Allies learned many valuable lessons they used in planning the main invasion, slated for mid-1944.

Because of their overwhelming success at Dieppe, the Germans were lulled into a false sense of security, feeling their Atlantic Wall was impregnable.

Preparing to Cross the Channel

The Germans were well aware of a massive invasion force assembling and training in southern England in late 1943 and early 1944, especially near Dover, just eighteen miles across the English Channel from the French town of Calais. Hitler was convinced the Allies would storm ashore at Calais and die on the French shoreline.

But the Dover assemblage, which included inflatable tanks and rusted-out landing craft, was merely intended to deceive curious German

BELOW: *Army commanders George Patton and Omar Bradley talk strategy during the European Campaign. During their days at West Point, both were varsity athletes.* Photo courtesy of the Patton Museum

BELOW: *Thousands of troops were loaded onto transport ships along the southern coast of England, then endured crossing the Channel for the invasion of Fortress Europe, commonly known simply as D-Day. Among the front-line commanders who would soon be in the thick of the fighting at Normandy was Colonel Red Reeder of the 12th Infantry Regiment, a former Army brat respected by his peers and his men alike, who played baseball when he was at West Point and turned down an offer to play in the major leagues, choosing instead to remain an Army officer.* U.S. Navy photo

spies along the English coast, masking the real landing site: the beaches of Normandy, France.

Former Athletes in Command

In charge of Allied forces was General Dwight D. Eisenhower, who played baseball and football during his college years at West Point. Dubbed "one of the most promising backs in Eastern football" by *The New York Times* in November of 1912, Eisenhower suffered a knee injury and later that year gave up football. Prior to attending the Point, Eisenhower had also played professional baseball in the Midwest.

"I was a center fielder," he explained. "I went into baseball deliberately to make money, and with no idea of making it a career." Later, during a summer back home in Kansas, Eisenhower played in the Kansas State League under another name to protect his college eligibility at West Point.

Former Annapolis lineman John Hall was well regarded as a tactician in amphibious missions and played a key role in the planning of the Normandy invasion.

Another Army general involved with the D-Day operations was Omar Bradley, a teammate of Eisenhower's on the West Point baseball squad. Bradley too played semipro ball, during the summer of 1915 when he returned home to Missouri. Bradley also played varsity football and, again like Ike, sustained a knee injury that cut short his gridiron exploits. He would later write about the importance of sports and teamwork in developing the many West Point cadets who made their mark in World War II: "It is almost trite to observe that in organized team sports one learns the important art of group cooperation in goal achievement. No extracurricular endeavor I know of could better prepare a soldier for the battlefield."

At Normandy Bradley, known as the "GI's General," would be directly in charge of the American landing. Prior to boarding transports along England's southern coast, thousands of Army officers were mustered in an aircraft hangar. Bradley used a sports analogy when he addressed his young leaders: "Gentlemen, this is going to be the greatest show on earth. You are honored by having grandstand seats."

"Hell, goddamn! We're not in the grandstand," countered Brigadier General Theodore Roosevelt, Jr., assistant commander of the Fourth Division. "We're down on the gridiron!"

Outspoken George Patton didn't mince words when he explained to a crowd of Brits and Yanks how to avoid this bothersome invasion of the French coast and quickly end all the fighting in Europe: "The sooner our soldiers write home and say how lovely the English ladies are, the sooner American dames will get jealous and force the war to a successful conclusion. And then I'll have a chance to go and kill the Japanese."

The Players at Normandy

A total of forty-seven Allied divisions were committed to the Normandy assault. Twenty-one of those divisions were American. The remaining Allied troops came from Britain, Poland, Canada, France, Belgium, Czechoslovakia, Holland, and Italy (the latter having switched sides soon after the Allied invasion of their homeland).

Opposing the Allied invasion force were fifty-eight German divisions, deployed from the Italian frontier, along the southern coast of France, and up to the Atlantic coast all the way to the Netherlands.

Waiting Impatiently for Battle

Such a massed force required months to assemble, train, and prepare for the Channel crossing. The entire free world was anticipating the invasion, and as days turned into weeks and weeks became months, the soldiers grew impatient.

"Sports was one way to burn off some of the pent-up energy," wrote Stephen E. Ambrose in *D-Day.* "At first footballs were handed out, but most company commanders put a stop to that when the games got too rough and some bones were broken. Softball was better; there were barrels full of gloves

LEFT: *Cadet Omar Bradley played football and baseball at West Point and one of his teammates was Dwight Eisenhower. Twenty-five years later they both spearheaded the invasion of Fortress Europe.* U.S. Military Academy photo

ABOVE: *Red Reeder was quite a football and baseball player in the '20s, in fact, he had a tryout with baseball's New York Giants in 1928 and reluctantly turned down a contract, choosing instead to stay in the Army.*

Sixteen years later he was storming the beaches at Normandy, with the 12th Infantry Regiment and would be seriously wounded six days later. U.S. Army photo, courtesy of West Point Military Academy

and balls and constant games of catch. A number of men recalled that these were the last games of catch they ever played because of wounds received or arms lost during the ensuing campaign."

In October of 1943 GIs became restless when they couldn't tune in to any broadcasts of the World Series between the Cardinals and the Yankees. They had to settle for a fifteen-minute recap on the BBC.

ABOVE: *West Point's 1914 baseball team included Omar Bradley, second from left. During the summer he would return home to Missouri and play semipro ball.* U.S. Military Academy photo

Neptune's Transports

On June 5, 1944, more than five thousand seaworthy vessels, from plywood PT boats to massive battleships, were mustered for Operation Neptune—the movement of troops from Britain to Normandy via the English Channel. All day and through the night a steady stream of troops poured on board the transport ships. Many anticipated their first test in combat but didn't look forward to the rocky trip across the Channel.

"All in all, something of a pre–big game atmosphere developed, in which we, an enormous first team, were exhorted and examined for competence and spirit," recalled Army Captain Charles Cawthon of the Twenty-ninth Infantry Division—the Blue and Grey division.

Minesweepers cleared the approaches of thousands of mines, marking safe passage routes with buoys. Still, twenty-four warships and thirty-five transport and supply ships were sunk in the Channel. Landing craft, many thrown together with plywood, were blown apart by the deadly mines. Shore artillery also opened up on the approaching vessels. More than seven hundred of the small transports were hit. Many of the troops on board drowned in the Channel without ever seeing the coast of France.

Airborne Assault

Prior to dawn on June 6, about 13,000 American paratroopers had dropped onto Normandy to secure key bridges over nearby rivers. Among the paratroopers was Ed Hirsch, a guard with Northwestern's football team; Bernard McKearney, who had joined the New Jersey National Guard's 114th Infantry just so he could play basketball at the Armory and was also a respected boxer in the Camden area; University of New Hampshire halfback

John Hanlon; and Wallace Swanson, a collegiate halfback who received a pro offer from the Philadelphia Eagles but signed up to be a paratrooper instead.

Enemy soldiers fired up at the descending GIs. Swanson later remembered, "I could see very little because almost everything was dark. The sparse light from the moon and stars scattered, showing only vague outlines. What I could clearly see were tracer bullets coming up from gun positions and flak bursts that exposed things with a blast of light."

Private Ken Russell was with Company F, 505th Regiment, ordered to drop on Sainte-Mère-Église and hold the town. As a sophomore back in Tennessee just two years earlier he would have been the starting tailback for his high school's championship team. Instead he had lied about his age to join the Army and would soon be a paratrooper with the 82nd Airborne Division, just in time for a bird's-eye view of the Normandy coast. (He would earn the Bronze Star for his actions in the D-Day invasion and would later be injured in Holland.)

With much of the surrounding marshlands of the French coast flooded, many paratroopers drowned under the weight of their own packs. Nazi gunners picked off many more. Tragically, hundreds of these airborne soldiers would not live through June 6, 1944, better known forever after as D-Day.

BELOW: *The port at Brixham along England's southern coast is teaming with activity as landing ships and transports are loaded with everything needed to sustain a protracted war against the Nazis. No one knew if the inevitable confrontation with the Nazis would last for months, or years.* U.S. Army photo

Naval Guns Pound the Beaches

Just offshore that morning, Allied naval guns opened up on the enemy's coastal defenses, which consisted of thick concrete pillboxes housing machine guns and artillery, thousands of mines buried on the beaches, concertina barbed wire, and other obstacles intended to slow the invasion force just enough to cut them down in a shower of bullets, shells, and explosives.

Colonel Red Reeder of the Fourth Infantry Division, former football and baseball player at West Point, recalled the bombardment unleashed by those Allied ships in his book, *Born at Reveille:* "The thunder from the warships was deafening. The acrid smell of the Navy's powder drifted into our motorboats. Our boat grated on the sand. Its iron gate dropped. I felt as if I were in the kickoff of some terrible football game." Six days after surviving hell's fury of the D-Day invasion, Reeder was severely wounded in combat when an enemy artillery shell exploded close by, shredding his left leg below the knee. The leg would later be amputated.

Sixteen years earlier Reeder had a tryout to play baseball with the New York Giants. His stats were good enough that they offered him five thousand dollars a year, three thousand more than he was making in the Army. But the former Army brat, who needed six years to graduate from West Point, was born to be a soldier, and a damned fine one at that. Reeder reluctantly turned down the Giants offer and eventually got back to West Point in 1947 as coach of the plebe baseball team. He also spearheaded a leadership course to prod future cadets to do their best in every endeavor.

"When the landing [at Normandy] did start, it looked like the Fourth of July," recalled Navy seaman Lawrence Berra, assigned to a Navy rocket boat at Normandy. Just prior to joining the Navy, Berra received a minor league baseball contract to play in the Yankees system. He wouldn't get that chance until after the war, and then Berra, best known simply by his nickname—Yogi— would go on to post Hall of Fame statistics.

BELOW: *Yankees catcher Yogi Berra gets ready for another long season during the spring of 1949. Five years earlier, in June of 1944, Berra was in the thick of the action of a different sort, serving on a Navy rocket boat at the Normandy invasion, better known simply as D-Day.*
AP Wide World photo

Deadly Beaches

Allied landing craft at Utah Beach were blown apart by mines and German artillery shells. Troops bogged down by their heavy

LEFT: *A week after the D-Day invasion, U.S. artillery guns pounded Carentan, France. On June 12 American troops entered the town.*
U.S. Army photo

weapons and waterlogged backpacks were pulled under the waves and drowned.

Lieutenant John Tripson, former Detroit Lions tackle, risked his life in the waters off Normandy by rescuing soldiers struggling to make it to shore after their landing ship was blown apart. Many soldiers were hit by machine gun fire before they could find cover on the beach. Others scrambling ashore were killed when they stepped on mines buried in the sand.

K. C. Roberts, who played linebacker for Nebraska's 1940 Rose Bowl squad, was a naval officer among the thousands of soldiers and Marines who made it ashore at Normandy. And Southern Cal's 1939 all-American, Louis Drnovich, commanded the Fifth Engineer Special Brigade pinned down along the seawall at Omaha Beach, one of the many landing spots along the French coast.

Former Brooklyn Dodger football star Bob Halperin was one of the first Americans to land at D-Day, marking the safe approaches for the thousands who would soon follow. Collegiate wrestler Bill Koll was a combat engineer trying to clear the beaches of the deadly mines buried in the sand. Koll recalled later, "People were falling on either side of you. It was the most frightening experience of my life."

Amid the chaos on the beaches at Normandy, many soldiers kept pushing forward in the face of certain death. Tech Sergeant Frank Kwiatek was a heavy-weapons platoon sergeant at Normandy who quickly became a proficient sniper killer. In his younger days as a welterweight boxer he was known as Hard Tack Murphy. At Normandy Kwiatek was out for a little payback. One of his brothers had been killed at Sicily; then just a few weeks later another brother was killed in Italy. Kwiatek vowed to kill twenty-five Germans to avenge each brother's death.

Though many GIs were killed trying to break out from the blood red shores at Normandy, others eventually succeeded in driving back the Germans, establishing a beachhead that would not be relinquished, despite continuing artillery fire from German 88s and pesky enemy fighter planes strafing the beaches.

To keep the skies over Normandy clear of Luftwaffe fighters, "we were told to shoot anything that moved," recalled Yogi Berra. "I am not sure if he said 'moved' or 'any plane below the clouds,' but we all shot at the first plane below the clouds and we shot down one of our own planes. The pilot was mad as hell, and you could hear him swearing as he floated down in his parachute. I remember him shaking his fist and yelling, 'If you bastards would shoot down as many of them as us the goddamn war would be over.'"

Scaling the Cliffs

Overlooking Normandy's shores were the cliffs of Pointe du Hoc, where the Germans had positioned several big guns that were firing on the invasion fleet at both Omaha and Utah Beaches. Capable of firing 25,000 yards, these guns were blasting the wooden transport ships before they got anywhere close to shore.

Soldiers from the Second Ranger Battalion, led by Lieutenant Colonel James Rudder, were given the difficult task of using grappling hooks and ropes to climb the sheer cliffs and somehow silence those guns. One hundred Rangers were killed in the deadly climb. (At Texas A&M in the early 1930s, Rudder had anchored the offensive line, playing center. He then coached

BELOW: *French teenage girls express their gratitude to the American liberators of Paris, who didn't mind the adulation one bit!*
National Archives photo

high school and college football before his Army Reserve unit was mobilized in 1941.) Rudder's Rangers did manage to knock out the enemy guns at Pointe du Hoc, but they suffered heavy casualties, including Rudder himself, who was wounded twice and lost his leg.

Opening the Floodgates

With room to maneuver, additional troops and supplies continued to pour into France via the Normandy beachhead. Dodgers pitcher Larry French, who closed out his career in 1942 with a 15–4 record, was a Navy supply officer responsible for getting food and fuel, supplies, and ammunition off-loaded.

After going ashore at Normandy, French wrote back to a former Dodgers teammate, "This beach was plenty hot—88-millimeter fire and mines wherever you stepped and the darndest fireworks at night. If you can imagine barbed wire 60 feet through, mined every inch of the way, even hanging on the wire like presents on a Christmas tree: pillboxes 20 feet thick that took a direct hit from 14-inch shells to knock out; sinking ships, dead, injured and living soldiers, sailors, flyers from all the Allies floating in the sea among every type of wreckage, you have a small picture of this beach. It was tough to take and nothing in the world did it, could have completed it, but the guts of our American kids."

Also manning the naval supply route from England to Normandy was Rocco Marchegiano, who played baseball at Brockton High School in Massachusetts and dreamed of playing major league ball. (After returning to the States he took up boxing full time, changed his name to Rocky Marciano, and became a heavyweight champion.)

Negro Leagues all-star pitcher Leon Day piloted one of those vulnerable landing craft at Normandy on D-Day while serving with the Army's 818th Amphibian Battalion.

ABOVE: *As Allied forces rolled across France, towns and villages were liberated from the Nazi stranglehold they endured for years.*

In Montcuit, American soldiers gladly accept a swig of wine from two very appreciative villagers. Imperial War Museum photo

By August Allied units were pouring into France. They included the 1313th General Service Engineers, which built and repaired bridges and roads. Negro Leagues star and future Hall of Famer Monte Irvin was part of the all-black 1313th.

"Defend to the Last" at Cherbourg

With a secure toehold on the European continent, Allied forces set out to seize the vital port at Cherbourg on the Cotentin Peninsula. The combined arsenal of naval guns, air bombardment, and Army tanks and foot soldiers steamrolled the German garrison at Cherbourg, which fell just weeks after Normandy. Hitler had given direct orders to his commander at Cherbourg: "Even if worse comes to worst, it is your duty to defend to the last bunker and leave to the enemy not a harbor but a field of ruins." Prior to surrendering, the Germans mined the harbor, using thirty-five tons of dynamite to destroy the vital piers and jetties at Cherbourg.

Onward to Saint-Lô

The Americans continued the advance toward Saint-Lô but were slowed by man-made mounds of dirt topped by bushes and small trees. These barriers crisscrossing the French countryside were known as hedgerows, and the Germans used them with deadly effectiveness to watch for and ambush approaching American foot soldiers. Former West Point halfback Jimmy Van Fleet was in charge of the Eighth Infantry Regiment pushing inland from the Normandy coast, and he saw many of his soldiers cut down in ambushes from those damnable hedgerows. (Van Fleet would later be promoted to general)

Commanding the Twenty-ninth Division at Saint-Lô was Major General Charles Gerhardt, who had been a quarterback at West Point and capped his collegiate career with a win over Notre Dame. Minor league ballplayer Herman Bauer, who had been league MVP while playing at Grand Forks, North Dakota, was also at Saint-Lô. "He was a helluva catcher I told

RIGHT: *Negro Leaguer Monte Irvin served with the 1313th General Service Engineers in France during the European Campaign. Besides emergency construction to repair bombed roads and bridges, Irvin would also guard German soldiers surrendering en masse.* AP Wide World photo

Yogi Berra one day," wrote his brother Hank Bauer of the New York Yankees, who would also serve during World War II, with the Marines. But tragically, Herman "got killed over in St. Lô. Just stuck his head out of the tank and they just got him."

A month after D-Day, Saint-Lô was secured, and the Normandy Campaign was completed. The Navy had lost 1,102 killed in action, mostly sailors manning the landing craft that were blown apart by mines. The Army casualty count included 16,293 killed in action and another 41,051 wounded.

ABOVE: *The Nazis certainly weren't putting up much resistance, but what really hampered American armor units, such as these tanks from the 31st Battalion, 7th Armored Division near Chartres, France, was the lack of fuel and ammunition, clogged back on the Normandy beachhead.* U.S. Army photo

Assaulting Southern France

While the assault forces that landed at Normandy continued their sweep across northern France and down through the central regions, plans were being made to open a second front along the southern coast, on the French Riviera.

Allied units in Italy, more than 300,000 strong, kicked off Operation Dragoon on August 15, 1944, when ten thousand paratroopers of the First Airborne Task Force descended into the Argens River Valley, some thirteen miles from the coast to secure a major intersection and prevent the Germans from rushing reinforcements to the beaches at Cannes and Hyères.

U.S. and Canadian commandos from the First Special Service Force played a key role in Dragoon by landing on two nearby islands and destroying artillery batteries there overlooking the approaches. This allowed safe passage for the more than three thousand ships and smaller craft involved in the operation. A massive naval armada—including 111 destroyers and 24 cruisers—pounded the beaches of southern France with their deck guns before dawn, while more than four thousand bombers from Italy and Corsica emptied their bomb bays on the coastal defenses. Fighter escort planes also strafed enemy troops, vehicles, and fortifications.

One of those pilots was Bernie Jefferson, who had been a halfback at Northwestern. Jefferson earned the Distinguished Flying Cross for missions over southern France, knocking out enemy anti-aircraft gun batteries prior to the invasion.

At 7:30 the morning of August 15, troop transports moved in accompanied by PT boats and rocket craft (LCT-Rs), which provided cover fire for the men of the Sixth U.S. Corps, commanded by Major General Lucian Truscott, who had also been at North Africa. (Years earlier Truscott had been a prominent American polo player. Another major general and former polo player from West Point who participated in the D-Day invasion was Charles Gerhardt, commanding the Twenty-ninth Division.) The three major units of Sixth Corps participating in the southern France operation were the Third, Thirty-sixth, and Forty-fifth Infantry divisions, with the Forty-fifth serving as the fulcrum in the forty-five-mile-long front.

Just as at Normandy, the Nazis had prepped the beaches with mines, barbed wire, and metal stakes. Allied troops had to clear all these obstacles while dodging heavy machine-gun, artillery, and mortar fire from German defenders holed up in fortified coastal bunkers.

Enemy gunners on the cliffs overlooking Camel Beach, where the Thirty-sixth Division was supposed to come ashore, were blasting the

RIGHT: *French citizens had wept when Nazi soldiers goose-stepped down the Champs-Élysées and brazenly boasted that no enemy would dare to penetrate Fortress Europe, which Hitler predicted would last for a thousand years. But by August 1944, American tanks and soldiers paraded in front of the Arc de Triomphe in Paris.*
Office of War Information photo

landing craft before they could unload their troops. The Texans of the Thirty-sixth Division who did make it ashore had to scale those sheer cliffs and knock out the deadly guns. By the end of that first day, 60,150 Allied troops had landed and established a beachhead, and the German defenders had been killed, captured, or were on the run.

Navy seaman Lawrence "Yogi" Berra and the sailors serving with him on a rocket boat also made the invasion of southern France. Berra later recalled the scene on the beach once the enemy had been routed: "When the beach was secured, when we had taken the beach from the Germans, it was like magic. Hundreds of French people came out of nowhere. They ran out on the banks and shouted and waved. Old people, kids, even some dogs. They carried flowers and bottles of wine." After several years of Nazi domination, the French citizens along the southern coast finally had something to celebrate.

ABOVE: *Troops from the 29th Infantry Division in the Saint-Lô area scamper across a road for cover, in July of '44. Nazi gunners frequently hid behind hedgerows, then opened up, with deadly efficiency, on American patrols. Minor league catcher Herman Bauer was an armor crewmen at Saint-Lô who would make the mistake of taking a peek outside his tank and was killed by one of those damned snipers.* U.S. Army photo

Breakout from Normandy

With Normandy and the Riviera secured, Allied forces were now ready to squeeze the Germans from both the north and south of France.

The breakout from the Normandy area was dubbed Operation Cobra. It started out deadly for members of the Thirtieth Infantry Old Hickory Division, commanded by Leland Hobbs, a teammate of Eisenhower and Bradley at West Point in 1914. On July 24 a massive air strike was planned to decimate the German units opposing the Thirtieth Division, but because of poor visibility over the target area, most of the planes were called back. A few of the bombers didn't receive the message to "abort mission" and inadvertently dropped their loads in the midst of the Thirtieth Division soldiers, killing 25. Sadly, this mistake was repeated the next day when smoke blanketed the enemy locations. Again, Allied bombs rained down on the Thirtieth Division, killing 64 and wounding another 374.

Despite this setback, General George Patton's Third Army, along with other Allied forces, swept across France, to the cheers of local civilians as town after town was liberated. The Germans quickly realized that their own blitzkrieg tactics were being used to perfection by none other than old Blood and Guts Patton.

RIGHT: *A Black soldier with the 12th Armored Division guards war-weary German prisoners in the final months of the war in Europe. Less than one year after Allied forces stormed ashore at Normandy, France, German soldiers laid down their arms and surrendered, hoping to be imprisoned by American units rather than face a Russian firing squad. Negro Leagues star Monte Irvin was one of soldiers who pulled guard duty in France.* Office of War Information photo

Though Hitler had ordered four vital ports along the Brittany coast held "to the last man, to the last cartridge," they were soon under Allied control. The German garrison at Saint-Malo—which vowed to "fight to the last stone"—destroyed most of the quays, locks, and harbor machinery before surrendering. Once these ports were secured, more Allied troops and supplies were rushed over from England to continue the dismantling of Fortress Europe.

Paris fell by the end of August, and every French citizen—and most of the free world—celebrated its liberation. German control of France was rapidly disintegrating along both fronts as Nazi units were encircled and cut off from making an escape.

Nazi Stronghold Crumbles

Those who fought to the end—many on direct orders from Hitler—expended all of their ammunition and destroyed bridges and tunnels to slow down their pursuers but were eventually cornered and wiped out. Thousands of other weary German troops, too weak to fight and with no more ammunition, surrendered en masse. During the fourteen-day Rhone Valley Campaign, more than 32,000 German combatants were taken prisoner.

Negro Leagues ballplayer Monte Irvin, with the 1313th General Service Engineers, which restored damaged bridges and roads and later pulled guard duty on Nazi POWs, remembered the large influx of enemy soldiers too weary to continue the fight. "Hundreds and hundreds of German prisoners were coming through, and we would guard them before they were sent someplace else. The prisoners were just happy to be safe behind our lines because for them the war was over. They were tired, disgusted, disheveled, and were glad to be safe and to have someone feed and house them. They were a sorry sight to behold. Some were very young and some were very old, but they were all completely defeated and glad to be out of the war."

Resupplying the Front

The rapid advance of the Allied ground forces was stretching the supply chain. Hundreds of trucks and their drivers were needed to move food and ammunition, plus precious fuel to the front along narrow roads unable to bear the heavy traffic. Massive road jams of troops and tanks and supply trucks were common on all routes leading from Normandy.

The Germans were on the run, but the Allies could not continue the pursuit because their tanks and trucks were running on gas fumes. Reluctantly, General Eisenhower ordered his units to halt just short of the Belgian and German borders until tanks could be refueled.

A week later convoys of trucks dubbed the Red Ball Express rumbled day and night from Saint-Lô on the Brittany coast to every corner of France. Soon, but not soon enough for Patton, his tanks were rumbling across the French countryside again. As a fiery end when he played football at West Point, Patton had busted a few noses of "enemy" defenders, and now he couldn't wait to inflict a whole lot of pain on "them damn Nazi sons of bitches!"

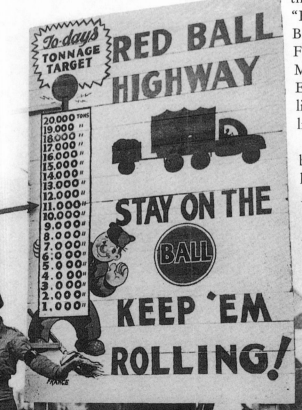

After an eight-year pro career in the Negro Leagues, catcher Josh "Brute" Johnson served with the Red Ball Express as a truck commander. Fellow Negro Leagues pitcher Max Manning also drove a truck for the Express, hustling supplies and gasoline on French roads to the front lines.

Several other Negro Leagues ballplayers manned the vital supply lines in Europe, serving with the Army Quartermaster Corps. They included all-star shortstop Byron Johnson, who played for the Kansas City Monarchs; Jesse "Home Run" Brown, another Monarchs all-star who could hit monster round-trippers whenever he stepped up to the plate (including two in the GI World Series off major league pitcher Ewell "The

LEFT: *As Allied ground forces pushed across France they needed to be resupplied with everything from ammunition to food and fuel. Supply trucks became jammed on the narrow French roadways and could not keep up with those front-line units. Reluctantly, the pursuit of retreating Nazi forces had to be stopped until the logistical problem was solved.*

Within a week, key roads to and from the front were cleared of all traffic and the Red Ball Highway was plotted out so supply trucks and fuel tankers could travel at high speed one way out and another way back to Normandy. Several former Negro Leagues ballplayers were part of the Red Ball Express, as truck drivers, MPs, etc. These included pitcher Max Manning and catcher Josh "Brute" Johnson. Other Black ballplayers were part of the crucial resupply effort with the Quartermaster Corps. U.S. Army photo

Whip" Blackwell, who had a buggy-whip delivery and played for the Cincinnati Reds); and Russell Awkard, who only had a two-year stint in the Negro Leagues, splitting time between the New York Cubans and the Newark Eagles in 1940 and '41.

"Died Like Ants"

Combined, the northern and southern France campaigns were costly for the United States: more than 17,000 GIs were killed and more than 47,000 wounded in the northern campaign; 7,301 died and another 5,361 were hurt in the south.

Author William Styron would later write, "Our generation was not only not intact, it had been in many places cut to pieces. The class just ahead of me in college was virtually wiped out. Beautiful fellows who had won basketball championships and Phi Beta Kappa keys died like ants in the Normandy invasion."

BELOW: *American paratroopers of the 101st Airborne Division proudly hold up a captured Nazi flag after house-to-house fighting in Saint-Marcouf, France.* U.S. Army photo

Among those wounded in action in France were Howie Krist, who pitched relief for the St. Louis Cardinals in the 1943 World Series and was badly injured while hauling ammunition (he returned to the Cards in '46, but his injuries hindered his outings and he was sent down to the minors); hockey star Hector Kilrea, who played for the Detroit Red Wings; University of Tennessee tackle Abe Shires; and James Gaffney, who played guard and served as team captain at Harvard in 1936 and who lost his right leg during battle along the Moselle River.

Captain Matt Urban of the Sixtieth Infantry Regiment, Ninth Infantry Varsity Division, saw that his unit was pinned down in fighting near Renouf, France. He grabbed a bazooka, crawled within range of two panzer tanks firing on his men, and knocked them out. He would be wounded later that same day and have to be evacuated. Urban would catch up with his unit a month later.

At Cornell University Urban had won the 1939 collegiate boxing championship in his weight class. Six years later Urban had earned numerous awards for his battlefield exploits and credited many of the skills he learned as a boxer for helping him survive in combat.

Other athletes weren't as lucky. Some of those many lives cut short during the fighting in France included Richard Schmon, former Princeton football captain; North Carolina tackle Dick Sieck; Washington Senators outfielder Elmer Gedeon, who was killed on April 20, 1944, in an aerial duel over Saint-Pol; University of Tennessee fullback Bill Nowling; Georgetown all-American punter Jim Mooney; St. Louis Browns minor league catcher Art Keller; and West Point center Bill Gillis.

Many of America's finest young men would never know they helped establish a foothold on the European mainland that would lead to the destruction of a Nazi war machine that only months earlier had seemed so invincible.

LEFT: General Dwight D. Eisenhower, supreme commander, gives a pep talk to Screaming Eagles paratroopers just before they board transport planes that will drop them over the French coast, kicking off the assault on the European mainland.
Among those airborne troops was Northwestern lineman Ed Hirsch, Camden area boxer Bernard McKearney, and University of New Hampshire running back John Hanlon.
U.S. Army photo

"THE STRATEGISTS PLANNED THIS CAMPAIGN VERY WELL BUT THEY DID NOT FIGURE ON SO MANY CAVES AND TUNNELS TO PROVIDE THE JAPS WITH A VERITABLE FORTRESS.

"WE TOOK THIS ISLAND THE ONLY WAY IT COULD POSSIBLY HAVE BEEN DONE, BUT A FORTRESS IS A FORTRESS. SEEMED LIKE THIS WAS GOING TO DEVELOP INTO SIEGE WARFARE IN OUR ATTEMPT TO GET ALL THE JAPS OUT OF THEIR CAVES IN THE JAGGED, TREACHEROUS CORAL RIDGES."

—First Lieutenant Richard Kennard,
Eleventh Marines, October 20, 1944

OPPOSITE: *To enemy soldiers, a flag bearer waving the Stars and Stripes was a tempting target, so it was only natural to crouch down until the area was secured. These two soldiers are huddled on the beach at Guam.* National Archives photo

WITH JAPAN BEGRUDGINGLY PULLING BACK ITS TENTACLES, the Allies continued the pursuit, bypassing but isolating some enemy strongholds in the central Pacific—such as Rabaul—while plunging head-first at others. The Japanese were absorbing huge losses on every front, but they still had plenty of fight left, as American soldiers and Marines were soon to find out.

There are numerous island chains scattered northeast of Australia. The Allies planned to invade them in this order: the Gilberts, Marshalls, and Marianas, with the Carolines taken care of along the way. Within these groupings and atolls are separate islands that the Japanese had occupied since the end of World War I (with the exception of Guam) and had turned into virtually impregnable fortresses. These forward-based locations allowed enemy warships and planes to threaten Allied movement anywhere within a triangle from Australia to the Philippines and Hawaii.

Running a Gauntlet

For Allied military strategists, these enemy strongholds had to be eliminated without heavy loss of life. But each presented a variety of obstacles that would have to be overcome: submerged coral reefs would hinder amphibious landing craft from approaching close enough to some beaches, especially in the Gilberts and Marshalls; dense jungles and fetid swamps of the Marianas, Gilberts, and Marshalls awaited those soldiers and Marines who did get ashore.

In the Carolines, honey-combed caves and volcanoes allowed the Japanese to duck inside to safety during aerial and naval bombardments and then pop back out with their own howitzers, mortars, and machine guns to

ABOVE: *Lieutenant George Bush was the youngest pilot in the Navy when he was shot down on September 2, 1944, while on a mission to strike Chichi Jima. He would eventually be rescued.* Photo courtesy of the White House

ABOVE: *Soon after the 2nd and 4th Marines waded ashore at Tinian, in late July 1944, the Japanese launched a desperation suicide charge that was quickly repelled. Former Marquette running back LaVerne Wagner would receive the Bronze Star for his actions at Tinian.* U.S. Marine Corps photo

repel any Allied landing force. Each of these enemy garrisons would fight to the last man. Few enemy soldiers would dishonor their family name or their emperor by surrendering. This was especially true at the invasion of Tarawa in the Gilberts, considered one of the smallest yet bloodiest battles of the entire war.

Blood Red on Tarawa

Before dawn on November 20, 1943, the 16-inch guns of the battleships *Maryland* and *Colorado* pounded Tarawa Atoll, specifically Betio Island, for more than three hours. Carrier planes from Task Force 50 also swooped in, turning the island into a smoldering wasteland. But when Marines from the Fifth Amphibious Corps became bogged down by the razor-sharp coral reef, the Japanese came out of their underground bunkers to unleash a hailstorm of machine-gun fire, killing hundreds of leathernecks in the surf, which soon was streaked blood red.

It would take four days of brutal fighting to secure Tarawa. Only seventeen Japanese were taken prisoner; 4,836 died in the attack or committed suicide. For the Marines, it was a costly piece of worthless real estate: 1,113 killed in action, with another 2,290 wounded.

Lieutenant Colonel Russell Lloyd of the Sixth Regiment, Second Marine Division, lost a close friend at Tarawa and wrote the following for his headstone:

> When the one great scorer
> Comes to write against your name
> He will not write if you won or lost
> But how you played the game
> As Man, Father, Friend, Marine
> Well done.

The Americans learned at Tarawa that the Japanese would be nearly impossible to defeat by bombing and naval shelling alone. It would require ground troops fighting for every inch of ground.

"The Japs were too well dug in," wrote Sergeant John Bushemi while in the Gilbert Islands, for

RIGHT: *The Eniwetok All-Stars, made up of sailors, weren't stocked with major league ballplayers but they still dominated other teams in the Marshall Islands that had better pedigrees.* U.S. Navy photo

Yank magazine on December 24, 1943. "Their blockhouses were of concrete five feet thick, with palm tree trunks 18 inches in diameter superimposed on the concrete. And superimposed on the trees were angle irons made of railroad steel. On top of these were 10 to 12 feet of sand and coral rock. Only a direct hit by a 2,000-pound bomb would cave in or destroy such blockhouses. The Jap pillboxes were built out of sand-filled oil drums, buttressed by heavy coconut logs and then sandbags. Our heavy machine guns and 75s couldn't penetrate these emplacements or knock out the enemy eight-inch shore batteries and machine guns that were awaiting our assault waves."

As brutal as it was, seizure of the Gilberts and elimination of the enemy airstrips there made it easier to launch the next attack, on the Marshall Islands.

LEFT ABOVE: *After heavy fighting in the Gilbert Islands, the 2nd Marine Division returned to Hawaii for a little rest and recreation. While there, they enjoyed a rodeo, Hawaiian-style. Soon they were headed back to the fight in the Central Pacific, for battles on Saipan, Tinian and bloody Okinawa.* U.S. Marine Corps photo

Simultaneous Assault on Makin

At the same time as the Tarawa fighting, soldiers of the Army's Twenty-seventh Infantry New York Division were hitting Makin, also in the Gilberts.

One of the Navy ships supporting the assault on Makin was the carrier *Liscome Bay,* which was hit by an enemy torpedo. Chaplain Robert Carley, former all–Southern California basketball player while at Occidental College, tried to help the wounded to life boats, but in less than thirty minutes the baby flattop sank with 646 men trapped inside. Among those who perished was Dorrie Miller, a heavyweight boxer, who, during the Japanese attack at Pearl Harbor, had rushed to a deck gun on board the *West Virginia* and blasted the enemy planes despite bombs and torpedoes exploding all around him.

Also at Makin was University of Michigan varsity football player and 1935 college all-star Gerald Ford, on board the light carrier *Monterey.* As the flattop's athletic director, Ford kept the crew physically fit and ready for combat. (Ford later received

LEFT BELOW: *Navy lieutenant commander Gerald Ford was fitness director on the light carrier USS Monterey when it deployed to the South Pacific. As a lineman for the University of Michigan football team he was selected for the 1935 All-Star Game and was heavily scouted by several pro teams.* U.S. Navy photo

offers from both the Packers and Lions but chose law school and would eventually enter the political arena . . . something many would consider more perilous than any football game or naval battle.)

Planes from the Monty were launched to intercept Japanese naval and air forces attempting to prevent the invasion of Makin. The *Monterey* also saw action across the Pacific, including the Gilberts, Tinian, Saipan, the Philippines, and Okinawa.

Developing a New Strategy

After the disastrous beach landings at Tarawa, where hundreds of Marines were killed while struggling ashore, military leaders faced harsh criticism. Navy Underwater Demolition Teams or UDTs—commonly known as frogmen—were rushed to the Pacific. Their mission: to sneak ashore before future invasions and blow up any beach obstacles that might hinder the landing forces.

Operation Flintlock kicked off on February 1, 1944, when U.S. Army troops attacked Kwajalein Island in the Marshalls chain while Marine Corps units hit Roi and Namur. Navy frogmen had already scanned the beachheads at both sites to ensure that no barrier reefs would cause problems for the main assault forces. Roi-Namur fell in two days, Kwajalein in four.

Navy ships supported the landings by pounding the enemy fortifications with their deck guns and launching fighter planes and torpedo bombers to keep the skies and seas clear. On board the carrier *Enterprise* cruising the waters around the Marshalls was George Sauer, former Nebraska running back and Green Bay Packer. Minnesota's all-American halfback George Franck was piloting a Marine Corsair fighter plane over the Marshalls when he was shot down and ditched at sea. Enemy coastal guns from Wojte Atoll opened up on Franck, who floated helplessly in his life raft until a gunboat rescued him. A Navy destroyer and fourteen fighter planes also had to be called in to silence the Japanese artillery trying to hit Franck.

Eniwetok was assaulted two weeks later and would take seven days to fall. No survivors were found among the two thousand enemy troops there. At the same time, carrier planes hit Truk in the Carolines, where a massive Japanese air and naval base was located. One of those pilots was Jim Lansing, Fordham University's all-American end in 1941, who scored a direct hit on an enemy warship.

The Three Jewels of the Marianas

Next in the central Pacific island-hopping campaign were the Mariana Islands; the most important of these were Guam, Saipan, and Tinian. Located just

ABOVE: *Nebraska's 1933 All-American running back George Sauer joined the Navy and served on the carrier* Enterprise, *which provided air support in numerous Pacific encounters, including the Marshalls Campaign.*
Photo courtesy of the University of Nebraska

RIGHT: *Minnesota's 1940 triple threat halfback George "Sonny" Franck flew a Marine Corsair fighter in the South Pacific. Near Wojte Atoll he was shot down and enemy gunners used his lift raft for target practice. Miraculously he was soon rescued.*
Photo courtesy of the University of Minnesota

1,500 miles from Japan, air bases in the Marianas would be ideal for the new B-29 Superfortress bombers coming off the assembly lines in the United States. But securing these key strongholds would not be easy.

The Japanese defenders on Saipan, Guam, and Tinian were left without air and naval support when the invasions began. Still they would not be easily routed. Desperate to hang on to these three crucial outposts, they rushed in two carrier attack fleets to counter whatever the Americans were sending to the area.

The Philippines Sea and a Turkey Shoot

The Japanese were under the assumption that the American fleet was in shambles, thrown together with very little punching power left. In fact, on June 13, 1944, the enemy propagandist Tokyo Rose announced that no U.S. warships remained afloat. But instead of the ragtag flotsam the Japanese were expecting, the U.S. Fifth Fleet heading for the Marianas consisted of fifteen aircraft carriers plus more than five hundred supporting warships, submarines, and auxiliaries.

Former Navy lineman Gordon Underwood, submarine commander on the USS *Queenfish,* worked in killer packs to pounce on a Japanese convoy attempting to resupply the entrenched forces in the north Pacific. After the *Queenfish* was stalked by an enemy sub chaser, Underwood guided the sub into the depths of the Philippine Sea and fired a spread of four torpedoes at his pursuers. Three of his "fish" made contact.

Japanese strategists knew the ensuing battle would be costly, but they assumed they would be the ones dishing out the punishment. They hoped to inflict enough damage to delay the Americans' northward sweep toward Japan. Heavy damage was indeed inflicted, but it was mostly one-sided in America's favor.

One of those American carriers prowling the waters of the Philippine Sea was the *Monterey.* Future Hall of Fame football player Joe Stydahar was a junior officer on the light carrier,

BELOW: *During the Great Marianas Turkey Shoot more than 300 enemy planes were shot down in just one day. Without air cover, Japanese forces on Guam, Saipan, and Tinian were pounded by U.S. warships and carrier planes.*
U.S. Navy photo

serving with Michigan lineman Gerald Ford. In the first ever NFL draft, in 1936, the Chicago Bears had selected Stydahar from the University of West Virginia. As one of the Monsters of the Midway, he would play both offense and defense, refusing to wear a helmet until forced to.

On June 19, 1944, both the Americans and Japanese launched their aircraft; it turned into a fiasco for the Japanese. In what was dubbed the Marianas Turkey Shoot, more than three hundred enemy planes were shot down that first day alone. In the next two days, nearly all of the enemy planes were blasted out of the skies, three carriers were sunk, and three others damaged. American losses were one hundred aircraft and two carriers damaged. Among those killed was California football star Kenneth Cotton.

The Japanese fleet was in shambles, but still there, like a thorn in the side, were the Palau Islands, the western part of the Carolines chain, halfway between New Guinea and the Philippines.

On June 15, 1944, the battle for the Marianas began, named Operation Forager, with pre-invasion bombardment of Saipan followed by landings made by the Second and Fourth Marine divisions. The Army's Twenty-seventh Infantry Division followed two days later.

The well-entrenched Japanese held out through early July and then launched a counteroffensive on July 7, which failed. Two days later the remaining Japanese pockets of resistance were eliminated on Saipan. One of the Marines on Saipan was Leo Nomellini, who would anchor the San Francisco 49ers defensive front and play in eleven Pro Bowls. Also seeing action at Saipan was Jim Bivin, former Phillies and Pirates pitcher; college all-American ends Dave Schreiner and Keith Topping; Preacher Dorsett, Cleveland Indians pitcher; and Joe Sabasteanski, center for Fordham's 1942 Sugar Bowl team. One of Sabasteanski's Fordham teammates, tackle Alex Santilli, was killed by an enemy sniper at Saipan.

LEFT: *Marines scale fortifications on Betio (of the Tarawa Atoll). This unknown South Pacific spec on the map would be one of the bloodiest battlegrounds of the Pacific Campaign.*
U.S. Marine Corps photo

While serving with the Second Marine Division on Saipan, Tennessee tackle Dick Huffman was commended for "a display of great courage and initiative in taking charge of his unit at a time when outstanding leadership was needed to rally the forces to continue in the face of terrific fire."

On July 21 soldiers from the Army's Seventy-seventh Infantry—the Hourglass Division—and Marines of the First Marine Brigade and Third Marine Division converged on Guam at Orote Peninsula. The Seventy-seventh was led by Roscoe Woodruff, who had played football at West Point with Dwight D. Eisenhower and Omar Bradley in 1914.

Four days later the Japanese attempted a counterattack to drive the invaders into the Pacific, but their efforts failed. They would continue to resist for two more weeks. Seeing more action on Guam than he ever did while quarterbacking Notre Dame was Heisman Trophy winner Angelo Bertelli.

On July 24 and 25 the Second and Fourth Marines departed Saipan and hit Tinian's north face. The Japanese struck back, launching a desperation suicide charge—many armed only with baseball bats or spears—and again the Marines inflicted more casualties than they incurred. Former Marquette halfback LaVerne Wagner was awarded the Bronze Star "for his outstanding leadership during the battles of Saipan and Tinian."

Of the 58,000 Japanese garrisoned on Saipan, Guam, and Tinian, more than 52,000 were killed or committed suicide.

BELOW: *Saying good-bye to a buddy killed in battle was never easy . . . and would never be forgotten.*
National Archives photo

Bloody Peleliu

Japanese pilots stationed at two Palau islands, Peleliu and Anguar, could harass and cripple the Allied invasion force rushing to the Philippines. Enemy airstrips in the Palaus had to be neutralized, and in June of 1944, Fifth and Thirteenth Air Force bombers maintained a heavy presence over the region. Leading the Mighty Thirteenth was Hubert Harmon, gridiron teammate of Eisenhower and Bradley thirty years earlier. Annapolis running back Harry "Light Horse" Wilson served under Harmon as the Forty-second Medium Bomber Group's commander.

ABOVE: Pushing inland was a nightmare for soldiers and Marines in the South Pacific as they attempted to drive out the enemy, who were often entrenched and not so easily uprooted or killed. Marines at Tinian would soon learn just how stubborn the Japanese could be. U.S. Marine Corps photo

In addition to the bomber missions, the U.S. Third Fleet arrived in early September to launch additional air strikes and met little opposition.

One of the carriers was the USS *San Jacinto*, which launched Avengers and Hellcats. A crewmember on the San Jac was Leo Bird, who played football at Louisiana State University. Art Donovan was also on board the San Jac. Donovan recalled in his book, *Fatso*, "I was the second loader on a 40-millimeter twin mount, and those goddamned Jap dive bombers and torpedo bombers kicked the living shit out of our Navy in '44.

"I remember one night at dusk, these Japanese planes got between two of our ships and while we were shooting at the planes we were actually hitting

RIGHT: Two Marines on the beachhead at Saipan collect their gear in the sand while other landing craft off-load more Marines. Leo Nomellini of the San Francisco 49ers was one of those Marines at Saipan, as was Cleveland Indians pitcher Preacher Dorsett U.S. Marine Corps photo

each other. We almost destroyed one of our own ships. It was really terrible." (Donovan would endure heavy action in other Pacific battles and then return home and carve out a Hall of Fame career with the Baltimore Colts.)

Also on board the *San Jacinto* was the Navy's youngest pilot—a letterman in baseball and basketball and captain of the undefeated soccer team at Andover Prep School—George Herbert Walker Bush. But on September 2, 1944, while on an air strike on Chichi Jima, Bush's plane was shot down. Though wounded when he bailed out, Bush managed to deploy and scramble into his life raft. Two other crewmen couldn't get out of the crippled Avenger in time. The submarine USS *Fishback* was dispatched to the area and rescued Bush before Japanese troops on nearby Chichi Jima could get to him. On board the *Fishback* was Ensign Bill Edwards, a teammate of Leo Bird's at Louisiana State.

Underwater demolition teams were still refining their clandestine tactics but had already saved hundreds of lives by blowing up beach defenses and surveying the approaches for weaknesses. Charles Kirkpatrick, former Naval Academy lineman for the 1930 squad, used the cover of darkness to probe the enemy at Peleliu, photographing enemy fortifications and reporting back to invasion planners.

ABOVE: *A transport ship mockingly called a Water Buffalo churns through the surf as it motors to the beaches of Tinian in July 1944.* U.S. Coast Guard photo

With no enemy air threat, the amphibious forces of Operation Stalemate II invaded Peleliu on September 15 and Anguar two days later. Peleliu was another of the many volcanic islands in the Pacific exploited by the Japanese, who hid in the maze of underground tunnels and caves during heavy bombardment. In addition, they had had time to lay in steel-reinforced bunkers that could withstand heavy pounding from offshore naval guns and aerial bombardment. The entire island became a massive fortress of minefields, concealed pillboxes, and concrete dragon's teeth that would not be easily breached.

LEFT: *The ultimate price of battle.* U.S. Marine Corps photo

After heavy bombardment the first waves of assault troops approached the beaches of Peleliu. Like zombies the Japanese appeared from the smoldering rubble and opened up with heavy mortars and artillery punctuated by the steady staccato of machine-gun fire. Only the continuous effort of individual soldiers and Marines charging directly into the line of fire, inching close enough to throw grenades or sacrificing themselves for their buddies, finally drove the Japanese back. Still, it would take two months of fierce combat to take bloody Peleliu.

One of those courageous Marines was Arthur Jackson, who enjoyed playing football while growing up in Portland, Oregon. During fighting on September 18, Jackson's platoon was pinned down by heavy machine gun fire from a massive bunker on Peleliu. While his buddies covered his approach, Jackson edged close enough to drop a demolition charge through the bunker's gun slits. The explosion rocked the ground and silenced the enemy inside. Jackson then went after ten more enemy pillboxes, knocking them all out that day. Three days later, Jackson was wounded at Bloody Nose Ridge and had to be evacuated. For his actions on Peleliu, Jackson would be awarded the Medal of Honor, presented by President Truman on October 5, 1945.

Duke running back Al Hoover was killed in the thick of combat on Peleliu when he pounced on an enemy grenade to save his fellow Marines.

As in every battle in the Pacific, the Japanese accepted enormous losses—there were only about 300 survivors after Peleliu from an estimated strength of 11,000 to 14,000 when the battle started. U.S. losses were also heavy: 1,252 Marines and 278 soldiers killed in action, with another 5,274 Marines and 1,008 soldiers wounded. One of those killed on Peleliu was John Barrett, former fullback at Georgetown University and star of the 1942 North-South All-Star Game.

Other islands in the Palaus still held 43,000 Japanese troops, but these were cut off from supply or retreat, left to "wither on the vine" as General MacArthur had planned.

Now he could turn his attention to returning to the Philippines—a promise he made to the Filipino people two years earlier. More importantly, with Saipan, Guam, and Tinian secured, air bases were soon operational and ready for the new long-range B-29 Superfortress bombers. An intensive fire-bombing campaign of Japan's home islands was about to be launched in an effort to end the war in the Pacific.

Lounging in Paradise

Once each of the central islands was secure, the soldiers, Marines, sailors, and airmen had time to kick back and enjoy their free time in the tropics. Swimming and fishing, sunbathing and snorkeling in the crystal clear waters of the South Pacific were pleasant alternatives to fierce combat. Catching up on news from home, especially sports, was also important. It was every serviceman's link to home.

Armed Forces Radio established a station on Guam to broadcast programs and recaps of sporting events such as the World Series and college bowl games. One of the announcers on Guam was Buddy Blattner, Cardinals minor league player.

Of course, athletics played a vital role in keeping the troops physically fit and reaffirming the importance of teamwork.

LEFT ABOVE: *Navy construction battalions—the Seabees—were called in whenever a jungle had to be cleared and an airstrip laid down in record time. Or when a baseball diamond was needed, such as in the Marianas for the men of the 94th Seabees.* U.S. Navy photo

LEFT BELOW: *Cardinals outfielder Enos "Country" Slaughter served with the Seabees—a Navy construction battalion—in the South Pacific, clearing jungles to build air strips, docks and compounds . . . and baseball fields where numerous ballplayers couldn't wait to choose up sides and play a game or a few before it was time to get back to the war. In fact, Country Slaughter remembers that at some of the ball games held on Saipan, there were more fans than at a few games he'd played in Philadelphia!* AP Wide World photo

Infielder Andy "Big Six" Watts played for a Navy team on Guam and would later join the Cleveland Buckeyes of the Negro Leagues.

At Eniwetok, volleyball and boxing were the sports of choice. While anyone with a little coordination could play volleyball, it took some experience to step in the boxing ring. One of those fighters with some skill was seaman Buddy O'Dell, world middleweight contender.

Another sailor with an Adonis body and a self-inflated ring record, known simply as Mr. Big, boasted that he could knock out anyone who dared challenge him. His crewmates naturally fell for his dazzling reputation and pooled their money, hoping to make a huge killing when he decked his first opponent. A huge killing was made—when Mr. Big stepped in the ring and immediately hit the canvas, and his crewmates threatened to string him up!

Once Ulithi Island in the Carolines was captured in late September 1944, it was built up to become the center for all naval operations in the region. Hundreds of Navy ships anchored there, if only briefly. Stationed on Ulithi were Negro Leagues superstar Larry Doby and major league players Mickey Vernon of the Washington

Senators and Billy Goodman of the Red Sox. To keep in shape, the three ballplayers practiced together. Doby later recalled, "Of course during that time we would go out with each other and have batting practice, pitching to each other. They mentioned quite often that if blacks got the opportunity [to play in the major leagues] I should have the opportunity to be a baseball player."

(After World War II, Doby would become the first Negro Leagues player to join the American League, playing for thirteen seasons with the Indians and White Sox. In 1952 and '54 he led the league in home runs, and he was selected to the all-star team six times.)

Pittsburgh Pirates catcher Aubrey Epps served with the Fourth Marine Division and captained the baseball team on Saipan. After driving off the enemy in one skirmish, he came across some baseball equipment, including catcher's gear, which of course he claimed as "war booty."

Enos "Country" Slaughter of the St. Louis Cardinals was with a Navy construction battalion, the Seabees, which helped build up the islands in the Marianas, complete with their own ball fields. And with a good assortment of pro and semipro ballplayers to fill out the unit rosters, thousands of servicemen watched the games.

"The bleachers were built out of empty bomb crates and sometimes we had as many as fifteen thousand troops at a game. We were drawing better crowds on Saipan than they were in Philadelphia!" Slaughter laughed.

"You've heard what great baseball fans the Japanese are. Well, when we got to Saipan there were still quite a few of them holed up in the hills. I'll be damned if they didn't sneak out and watch us play ball. We could see them sitting up there, watching the game. When it was over they'd fade back into their caves. But they could have got themselves killed for watching a ball game. Talk about real fans!"

LEFT: *After the area was secured, the 94th Naval Construction Battalion—the Seabees—built a basketball court in the Marianas.* U.S. Navy photo

ABOVE: *After the battles, there was time for sports found only in the South Pacific, like coconut-crab races.* National Archives photo

Bob Feller Does the Right Thing

"I REQUESTED COMBAT DUTY. I PROBABLY COULD HAVE SAT IN HONOLULU DRINKING BEER, BUT THE HELL WITH THAT. I FIGURED IF I WAS IN, I MIGHT AS WELL BE IN ALL THE WAY,"

—Feller told the author Donald Honig for his book, Baseball, When the Grass was Real

ABOVE: : *Cleveland Indians pitcher Bob Feller served as a 40-mm anti-aircraft gun crew captain aboard the warship USS* Alabama. *He would see action in both the Atlantic and Pacific campaigns.* National Archives photo

TWO DAYS AFTER THE JAPANESE ATTACK ON Pearl Harbor, Cleveland Indians fireball pitcher Bob Feller pushed aside a brilliant baseball career, ignored his 3-C deferment, and joined the ranks of thousands of young men enlisting in the armed forces.

"In December 1941 I was on my way to Chicago and about the time I was crossing the Mississippi River the broadcast came over the car radio about Pearl Harbor," Feller recalled later. "I called Gene Tunney . . . he was the head of the armed services athletic program, and he'd been hounding me to get in. So he flew out to Chicago, and I signed up at eight o'clock the next morning at the courthouse."

As a seventeen-year-old from Van Meter, Iowa, Feller joined the Indians in 1936 and quickly earned his nickname Rapid Robert by mowing down opposing batters with a devastating fastball and a wicked curve. He would lead the American League in strikeouts and games won from 1939 to 1941.

By then his father was dying of cancer, and Bob was his family's sole support, which exempted him from military service. Also, because his family owned a farm, Feller could have easily gone home to tend the crops during the war. Still, when America needed men, Feller never hesitated to step to the front of the line.

He could have spent his tour out of harm's way, doing public relations work for the Navy. But Feller volunteered for combat duty instead and was soon right in the middle of it, serving on board the battleship USS

RIGHT BELOW AND BACKGROUND: *Navy gunners stave off Japanese aerial attackers off Saipan.* U.S. Navy photo

Alabama as chief gunnery officer of an anti-aircraft crew.

The *Alabama* escorted Allied convoys across the treacherous North Atlantic while German U-boats prowled in packs—Wolf Packs—waiting to move in and launch a spread of torpedoes at the massed formation of ships before slinking away in the darkness of night.

The *Alabama* would then redeploy to the Third Fleet in the Pacific where it pounded island beaches held by the Japanese and protected American aircraft carriers from enemy planes.

Feller later remembered combat duty in the Pacific: "The Japanese planes would try to get at the carriers. And sometimes they'd come after us. Torpedo bombers. One day our fleet shot down 400-and-some Jap planes; the Marianas Turkey Shoot they called it, just the day after the landing at Saipan.

"Scary? Yes, particularly at night. You're zig-zagging at high speed, and the plane comes in low, to get underneath our shells, sometimes so low they would fly right into a wave or a big swell.

"I'd be up there on the main deck with a bunch of kids, banging away with [twin gun] Bofors. You've got all your other ships out there, and it was nothing unusual to have the ships in the periphery get raked by bullets from our own guns, and a lot of guys get killed."

Feller had stayed in excellent shape while in the Navy, exercising whenever he could, wherever he could on the *Alabama,* and so when he rejoined the Indians near the end of the 1945 season, he promptly took the mound and struck out twelve batters in his first game back.

Though he had lost nearly four full seasons during the war, Feller would go on to win 266 games in eighteen seasons with the Tribe. Based on his consistency and productivity, some experts feel he could easily have won another one hundred games if the war hadn't interrupted his career. But Feller never complained about what could have been. In fact, he was rather proud of his war record.

In 1962 Rapid Robert was elected to the Baseball Hall of Fame.

18. Advancing Across Northern Europe

"It may be observed that, like a jockey, a bold tank general should have his eyes fixed on the winning post, and not, like a cautious transport leader, on the tail of his convoy."

—*J. F. C. Fuller*

"It is at this period that war did indeed become . . . a game of chess. When, following a series of complex maneuvers, one of the two adversaries had lost or won several pawns—towns or fortresses—there came the great battle. Standing on some hilltop from which he could survey the whole field, the entire chessboard, a Marshal skillfully caused his splendid regiments to advance or retreat. Check and Mate, the loser put his pawns away; the regiments marched off to winter quarters, and everybody went about his business pending the next game or campaign."

—*J. Boulenger, 1915*

OPPOSITE: *Army machine-gun crew of the 104th Infantry Battalion covers for a tank of the 4th Armored Division as it crosses a snow-covered field in the Bastogne corridor.* U.S. Army Signal Corps photo

CONTINUING THEIR SWEEP OF NORTHEASTERN FRANCE, THE Allies next turned toward Europe's Low Countries: Belgium, Netherlands, and Luxembourg, often referred to simply as the Benelux. By late August 1944 the U.S. First Army was poised along the Belgian border, but its tanks were thirsty for fuel, and supply trucks were clogged along an impassable route from the beaches at Normandy, France. The First Army could not advance until it could be resupplied.

The once-formidable Nazi war machine was in shambles and retreating back to the Fatherland. An Allied intelligence report assessed what remained of Hitler's military: "The enemy is no longer a cohesive force, but a number of fugitive battle groups, disorganized and even demoralized, short of equipment and arms."

ABOVE: *Infantrymen guarding Germans after the battle of Bastogne, Belgium.* Corbis photo.

Agonizingly, though, the Allied pursuit could not continue, and every hour that they had to wait for the supply and fuel trucks to arrive gave the fleeing Germans a chance to regroup, re-arm, and return to the offensive. Finally, on September 1, elements of the U.S. First Army got the fuel they needed and crossed into Belgium near Mons, where, after three days of heavy fighting, 25,000 German panzer troops surrendered.

Negro Leaguers Play Key Role

Among the GIs who crossed the border from France into Belgium were two Negro Leagues ballplayers—James "Red" Moore and Joe Scott. Moore was considered the "most perfect" first baseman to play the game, with six different teams from 1936 to 1940. He would then serve in the Army from 1941 to 1945, with a combat engineer battalion of the Third Army. Joe Scott was another first baseman, who played semipro ball before joining the Army, also in 1941. He would end up serving with the 350th Field Artillery and saw action in France and Belgium. (His Negro Leagues stint began after he returned home in late 1945, and lasted for five seasons, three of those with the Birmingham Black Barons.)

Holland was the next obstacle en route to Germany and on September 9 the 30th Infantry "Old Hickory" Division liberated its capital of Maastricht. The following day, 5th Armored Division soldiers entered Luxembourg City.

Border Battles

Due north the moment the Allies had awaited for four years finally occurred—they penetrated the German border. The Fifth Armored Division's Eighty-fifth Reconnaissance Squadron, from Luxembourg, crossed over into Rhineland-Palatinate near Stalzenburg at 6:05 P.M. on September 11. First Army elements advanced five miles farther to Trier within twenty-four hours. Units of the Third Infantry Marne Division pushed to within a thousand yards of the West Wall.

All along the extended front, Allied units were at a virtual standstill, waiting for the order to breach the Siegfried Line, the massive manmade barrier Hitler counted on to protect the Third Reich from any invaders. The Allied order to proceed came three days later. But there was also some unfinished business to attend to in central Netherlands.

Paratroopers would be needed for this next mission.

Operation Market Garden

In one of the boldest operations of World War II, more than 16,000 paratroopers of the U.S. Eighty-second and 101st Airborne Divisions and the British First Division filled the skies over Holland on September 17, 1944.

After being dropped from glider planes along a sixty-mile swath behind German lines, the paratroopers of Operation Market Garden rushed to secure vital bridges being held by the Germans, who had orders to destroy them, preventing the Allied troops from making it across the canals and rivers that crisscross Holland.

Individual Valor

One of those paratroopers was Private First Class Joe Mann of the 101st Airborne Division, the Screaming Eagles. In high school at Reardan, Washington, Mann had excelled in football, baseball, and tennis. That September 17 mission into Holland was Mann's first and last combat jump.

The next day, after firing a bazooka to knock out an enemy gun crew, Mann and several other paratroopers were trapped near Best. Twice Mann probed the lines to find an escape route; he was wounded in both arms.

Unable to use either arm to fire a weapon, Mann maintained a vigil all night long, watching for enemy patrols. Grenades were thrown at their position, but his fellow GIs managed to toss them back out, though one grenade did disable their machine gun and blind the gunner. A fifth grenade landed behind the propped-up Mann. Knowing no one could toss it out in time, he laid back on it, smothering the explosion. Mann died minutes later. The following year his father accepted his Medal of Honor.

Another member of the 101st Airborne, one who suffered debilitating injuries, was Dick Foley. Later confined to a wheelchair, he reluctantly had to give up his dream of playing pro baseball but became a scout for the Brooklyn Dodgers.

Seizing Vital Bridges

At the same time as the mass parachute drop, British troops and tanks rushed north to take Arnhem and Nijmegen and those key bridges the Germans planned to destroy. This was the Garden phase of the Allied mission. It took four days of fighting to drive off the Germans. They did manage to destroy and damage some of the road and rail crossings, but their efforts could not stop Allied ground and armored forces from eventually crossing the strategic and symbolic Rhine River.

During a lull in the fighting, two reporters covering the airborne units sought shelter in a damaged building. When they found a radio there, they tried to tune in a broadcast of the first game of the 1944 World Series between St. Louis's crosstown rivals, the Browns and the Cardinals. But in the third inning, just as the Cards started a rally and loaded the bases, German artillery fired a lengthy barrage and the reporters took cover. When the shelling stopped they tried to get back to the game to see how the Cards had done, but somehow the Browns had snuffed out the threat.

ABOVE: *The "Battered Bastards of Bastogne" were surrounded yet refused to give in, hanging on until armor units broke through the enemy lines.* U.S. Army photo

No matter what the Germans threw at them, the Americans also managed to snuff out those rallies, too. Understandably proud of his troops, Lieutenant General Lewis H. Brereton, First Allied Airborne Army commander, said, "The 82nd and 101st divisions accomplished every one of their objectives. In the years to come everyone will remember Arnhem, but no one will remember that two American divisions fought their hearts out in the Dutch canal country and whipped hell out of the Germans."

In the assault to secure those Dutch canals, the U.S. paratroopers had 909 killed and another 3,899 wounded.

Huertgen Forest

While most battles in World War II had a beginning and end, the Huertgen Forest Campaign was little more than a protracted stalemate–though it became a very bloody stalemate for the thousands of American soldiers dragged into it.

The heavily wooded Huertgen and surrounding forests had been well fortified by the Germans prior to the first contact, when the U.S. Ninth Infantry Varsity Division probed the outer woods in September 1944. Matt Urban—a Ninth Division captain who was the collegiate boxing champ while going to

BELOW: *Dense forests blanketed northern Europe, as Allied troops pushed from France into Belgium and Luxembourg. Among the thousands of American soldiers who saw action was future Negro Leaguer Joe Scott with the 350th Field Artillery.*
U.S. Army photo

Cornell—returned from his wounds at Normandy to lead his company into battle near Heer, Belgium. Under a heavy artillery and mortar barrage, Urban attempted to guide his troops in crossing the Meuse River but was severely wounded when shrapnel struck him in the throat. Urban refused to be evacuated until he knew his unit had made it across the Meuse.

The Meatgrinder

Concealed and interlocking bunkers in the surrounding hills allowed the Germans to watch every approach and aim their guns and mortars on every patch of open ground below. But even the dense trees didn't offer Allied units any protection from enemy artillery barrages. In fact, those artillery shells often burst high in the trees, splintering them into deadly wooden spears that impaled hundreds of GIs.

Allied commanders saw that the Huertgen was becoming a meatgrinder, but they couldn't simply bypass it and leave several thousand enemy troops intact. American artillery and P-47 planes blanketed the enemy positions with shells and bombs. On November 2 alone, 7,313 artillery rounds were fired just prior to the Twenty-eighth Division's attack near Schmidt. The soldiers of the Keystone division were decimated.

In mid-November more than 4,500 bombers dropped 10,000 tons of explosives on enemy fortifications. Then the First, Fourth, Eighth, Ninth, and 104th Infantry Divisions hit the line, supported by tanks from the Third and Fifth Armored Divisions.

Through December and January gains on either side were minimal, measured in yards rather than miles.

ABOVE: *American anti-aircraft gunners watch the skies overhead as German and American fighter planes fire at each other. Afraid they might knock down one of the own planes, the AA crews could only observe the dogfight.*
U.S. Army photo

A Dismal Christmas

Minor league pitcher Ralph McLeod was with the Seventy-fifth Division. "Our first action was the breakthrough up in Belgium. I'll always remember the first action . . . the night before Christmas . . . cold . . . snowy."

McLeod would tell a reporter years later, "You got used to the cold. When we had long marches, we started off with an overcoat. Of course to carry an overcoat with an M-1 [rifle] is pretty heavy. The first thing you discarded was the overcoat, no matter how cold it was. All we had was a Red Cross sweater underneath our GI jacket. Come nighttime you cut off a few fir branches and put them on top of the snow, get your roll out, get inside, put your shoes in there so they wouldn't freeze and sleep away. It's an experience I wouldn't want to go through again."

On New Year's Day, 1945, St. Louis Cardinals minor league pitcher Hank Nowak was leading an infantry squad when he was killed in Belgium.

"Surrender" at Schmidt

On February 5, 1945, the Seventy-eighth Lightning Division tried again to take the town of Schmidt, which was still well defended by battle-hardened Nazi soldiers.

Former heavyweight boxing champion Max Schmelling was broadcasting Nazi propaganda radio dispatches to the American troops in Belgium, urging them to surrender rather than be killed in battle.

After four days of house-to-house fighting, Schmidt fell to two regiments of the Seventy-eighth Division. This marked the end of the Huertgen Forest

Campaign, a five-month ordeal that saw nearly 30,000 GIs killed or wounded. The Germans lost a comparable number in dead, wounded, and captured soldiers.

Battle of the Bulge

The once-invincible Third Reich was rapidly collapsing. During the autumn of 1944 Allied leaders were confident the war would be over within weeks. They were mistaken. The Huertgen Campaign was stalled, but in the area around Aachen, the Sixth Panzer Army was forming to defend the region. Allied observation planes spotted and reported this buildup of enemy troops and tanks. But in the region of the Ardennes Forest, the Germans were clandestinely assembling two additional full armies for an all-out assault that Hitler hoped would turn the tide.

To mask their intentions, the Germans ducked into the heavily forested Ardennes, traveling only at night on roads covered with straw. The clattering and clanking of panzer tanks moving into the area was drowned out by German planes continually buzzing low over Allied lines. All communications were done by field phones rather than radio to prevent messages from being intercepted by Allied crytographers. Then, unexpectedly, before dawn on the morning of December 16, 1944—with six inches of snow on the ground and the sun obscured by heavy clouds—two thousand German artillery guns opened up all along the sixty-mile front, from Monschau, Germany, to Echternach, Luxembourg. As soon as the rumble of enemy guns stopped, 200,000 German soldiers attacked the front, being held by 83,000 GIs, many of those untested in battle. Hitler's desperation gambit, Operation Autumn Mist, had begun. By driving a wedge through the Allied lines, pushing west into Luxembourg and Belgium, and seizing the vital port city of Antwerp, Hitler hoped to force a negotiated settlement.

But the German timetable was upset when the American soldiers of the Ninety-ninth Checkerboard Division held off the Sixth Panzer Army to the north near the Meuse River. The Ninety-ninth and Second Divisions would fall back along the Elsenborn Ridge and hold off the enemy assault.

One of the seasoned combat veterans caught in the attack was infantry captain Buzz Baldwin, who had played end and what was called defensive "knifer" for the UCLA Bruins football squad.

ABOVE: *During the Battle of the Bulge, 105-mm howitzers and other field guns and tanks fired almost nonstop to blunt the Germans' final and desperate counteroffensive.*
U.S. Army photo

Clarence Maddern was a minor league outfielder who had joined the infantry and got to tour most of northern Europe—including the Battle of the Bulge—one footstep at a time, sometimes crawling inch by inch. (A year after the war ended, he would get called up to the Chicago Cubs but saw lim- ited action over the next five seasons, playing in only 104 games.)

Another soldier in the middle of the Bulge skirmishes was a young Gino Marchetti, who would later anchor the defensive line for the University of San Francisco. (He would be drafted by the financially troubled New York Yanks, but his rights were relinquished to Dallas in '52. He moved on to the Baltimore Colts, where he would terrorize opposing quarterbacks and become all-pro for the decade.)

When the German attack began, major league baseball players Mel Ott, Bucky Walters, Frankie Frisch, and Dutch Leonard had been in Belgium entertaining First Army troops with their big-league anecdotes. Abruptly, they were whisked away from danger.

Outnumbered at Bastogne

The 106th Division—the Golden Lions—held off the Fifth Panzer Army on the Schnee Eifel for three days, further delaying the enemy timetable. At the crossroads to Saint-Vith and Bastogne, the Twenty-eighth Division fought off the Fifth Panzers and Seventh Army. The Twenty-eighth would fall back to Bastogne, the focal point of the campaign that the Allies called the Battle of the Bulge.

But after receiving intelligence reports that the Allies had thousands of troops waiting to counterattack at Bastogne, the Germans stopped just three miles from the outskirts of the city.

Those intelligence reports proved to be wrong, thankfully for the Americans, who were outnumbered five to one in the region. This failure by the Germans to take Bastogne would doom their plans to continue on to Antwerp. This bulge within the middle of the enemy lines also prevented them from reinforcing their units to either side of Bastogne.

Detecting Enemy Infiltrators

For six crucial days of fighting, most notably by the U.S. Seventh Armored Division—the Lucky Seventh—which sustained heavy losses, the Americans held firm near Bastogne, falling back but preventing any enemy breakthrough. German paratroopers and commandos did manage to infiltrate the lines, dressed in American uniforms and speaking perfect English. To detect these impostors, GIs challenged them with questions only a true American would know.

Senator Kenneth Keating later told how baseball saved many American lives during the Battle of the Bulge: "German troops tried to get behind our lines as spy cover, but baseball proved to be the chink in their well-planned armor. Our forces would halt the jeeps at road blocks and ask such questions as, 'For which team does Bob Feller pitch? What position does Joe DiMaggio play? What's the nickname of the team in Brooklyn?' No screening process ever proved more successful. Baseball was used as a weapon of war to save lives."

Warren Spahn, Cleveland Indians pitcher who was with the Army Engineers and would be wounded by shrapnel in the back of his neck, added: "The Germans had our equipment, our uniforms, even our dog tags. Our password used to be something like, 'Who's the second baseman for the Bums?' They wouldn't know who the 'Bums' were. I used to pity any guy in our outfit who wasn't a baseball fan because he would be in deep trouble!"

To reinforce the decimated U.S. ranks, the 101st and Eighty-second Airborne Divisions were rushed to the front. The 101st arrived at beleaguered Bastogne, along with soldiers from the Tenth Armored Division. Though surrounded by the Germans and ordered to surrender, the Battered Bastards of Bastogne had refused. One of those "bastards" was John Hanlon, football player at the University of New Hampshire, who participated in the parachute drop at Normandy, France, on D-Day.

Farther south, the Fifth Infantry Red Diamond Division and Fourth Armored Division reinforced the battle-weary Army divisions. West Point running back and WWI veteran Bill Hoge led the Fourth Armored as it steamrolled across France and on toward Germany.

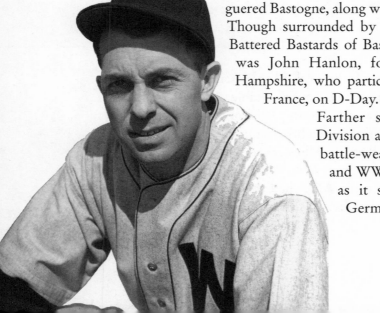

BELOW: *Cecil Travis was an all-star slugging shortstop with the Washington Senators prior to serving with the 76th Infantry Division in northern Europe. As an infantryman he literally walked hundreds of miles and suffered from frostbite during the Battle of the Bulge. He would return to the Senators but his leg injuries would mar his comeback attempt and he never regained his hitting stroke.* AP Wide World photo

The same problem that had plagued American armor units several weeks before—lack of fuel—hit the German panzer units in the Battle of the Bulge. On Christmas Day, 1944, the helpless Second Panzer Division tanks sat idle just four miles from the Meuse River and promptly got pounded by the U.S. Second Armored Division.

Other German units to the north also lacked fuel and became trapped. The German assault was literally running out of gas, and by January 8, Hitler allowed his units to withdraw from the Bulge.

The Greatest, but Very Deadly

Despite Winston Churchill's claim that this was "undoubtedly the greatest American battle of the war," it was not accomplished without enormous losses: 19,246 Americans killed, another 60,050 wounded, and 15,000 taken prisoner.

Among those wounded were former St. Louis Browns and Philadelphia Athletics pitcher Jack Knott, who played for nine seasons before serving with the 104th Infantry Division, and Yankees minor league ballplayer Ralph Houk, who served with the Eighty-ninth Cavalry Recon Squadron and had a brush with the widowmaker when a sniper's bullet punched a hole through his helmet but somehow missed his head. (He would join the Yankees in 1950 and play in two World Series.)

Another minor leaguer who received the Purple Heart during action in northern Europe was Dodgers farmhand Danny Ozark. He never did get to the Bigs as a ball player, but he finally got his shot as a coach and later manager in the early seventies. Texas A&M all-American guard Joseph Routt was an infantry captain who wasn't as lucky.

Knuckleball pitcher Hoyt Wilhelm was playing with the minor league team at Mooresville of the North Carolina State League when he was called up, and he served for three years in the Army. He was wounded in the Battle of the Bulge, but his injuries didn't prevent him from returning to Mooresville and later breaking into the major leagues. (He established himself as one of baseball's premier relief pitchers, relying almost exclusively on a wicked knuckleball pitch.) Another relief pitcher who was a decorated Bulge veteran was Red Sox hurler Earl Johnson.

Golfer Lloyd Mangrum was wounded twice in the Bulge. (After the war he would rejoin the golf tour as the sport's most celebrated war hero and win the 1946 U.S. Open.)

The Reality of Frostbite

Cecil Travis, who served with the Seventy-sixth Infantry Onaway Division, suffered from frostbitten feet, a common ailment for GIs enduring the bitter European winter.

"It was the cold that got to us," Travis would recall later. "You slept where you could, in a barn, anyplace, but there was no heat. We just shivered all night long. At nights you just couldn't get warm. I'll never forget that cold as long as I live."

In 1941 Cecil Travis was the Washington Senators all-star shortstop and was among the league leaders in several categories. Unfortunately, 1941 was the same year that the New York Yankees' Joe DiMaggio hit safely in fifty-six straight games and Ted Williams of the Red Sox topped the majors with a .406 batting average. Both of these feats overshadowed Travis, who had a higher batting average than the Yankee Clipper and led both leagues with 218 hits. It would become "one of the best seasons no one ever heard about."

After the Battle of the Bulge, Travis had trouble keeping up, limping on two badly frozen feet, as his unit pursued a retreating enemy trying to prolong the inevitable. Even after returning to the Senators he would be plagued by his war injuries.

Another soldier whose athletic career was cut short because of the freezing temperatures during the Bulge was George Poschner, who had played left end for Georgia when the Bulldogs beat UCLA in the 1943 Rose Bowl, 9 to zip.

RIGHT: *Minor league pitcher Hoyt Wilhelm joined the Army and saw action in the European Theater. During the Battle of the Bulge he was wounded. After the war he returned to baseball and succeeded as a knuckleballer.* AP Wide World photo by John Lindsay

On January 8, 1945, Poschner was wounded at Kohlhutte, France. Sadly, he was left unattended on the frozen battlefield for two days. Due to his wounds and frostbite, Poschner lost both legs and part of his right hand.

St. Louis Cardinals left-handed pitcher Ernie White, who had played in the 1942 World Series, was trapped by enemy fire and lay sprawled in icy water for a day. The resulting frostbite would later hamper his pitching arm when he returned to the Cardinals.

Operation Northwind

Toward the end of December 1944 the Germans attempted to divert American units from the Ardennes by opening up a second front in north-eastern France, where the U.S. Seventh Army was deployed and braced for an assault along the Lauterbourg Bulge. Fifteen American divisions, encompassing some 250,000 soldiers, manned the region, though many would be pulled out and rushed to bolster the Ardennes offensive.

On New Year's Day, 1945, two German corps attacked, hoping to split the U.S. Fifteenth and Sixth Corps. But the U.S. Forty-fourth and One-hundredth Divisions repelled the attacks, which were the first of many in the Alsace region, all pounding away at the Seventh Army lines.

On January 5, Hitler launched Operation Sonnenwende, or Winter Solstice, to attack the Sixth Corps' right flank and seize Strasbourg, the major city in the disputed Alsace border region. But the Allies, including General Charles de Gaulle's Free French fighters, defended Strasbourg.

Fighting raged in towns all along the front. Finally, on the night of January 24 and 25, the Germans launched a desperation three-pronged attack over the Moder River, which also failed. In all the Germans lost more than 23,000 men killed, wounded, or missing in action, with nearly 6,000 surrendering.

The Allies now prepared for one last hurdle: the final push to Berlin.

George "Blood and Guts" Patton

"To set the cause above renown
    To love the game beyond the prize
To honor, while you strike him down
    The foe that comes with fearless eyes,
To count the life of battle good,
    And dear the land that gave you birth,
And dearer still the brotherhood
    That binds the brave to all the earth."

—Favorite Patton verse

BEFORE HE EARNED THE NICKNAME "BLOOD and Guts" for his daring exploits in the heat of battle, George Patton was a well-known horseman and polo player in international circles. In 1912 he represented the United States in the modern pentathlon, at the Olympic Games in Stockholm, Sweden. The pentathlon comprised five events: shooting a pistol at 25 meters, a 5,000-meter steeplechase, swimming 300 meters, a 4,000-meter cross-country run, and fencing.

The pistol event opened the competition. Though known as an expert marksman, Patton somehow missed two targets completely, though some believe his bullets must have passed through bullet holes he'd already made in the bull's-eye. But because official scorers counted them as misses, Patton stood twenty-first out of forty-two competitors after the first day. He would place in the top ten in the other four events—scoring better than any other competitor—but his poor showing in the pistol event left him in fifth place, with four Swedes placing higher.

During World War II General Patton would make his mark on U.S. military history, starting with the North Africa Campaign, where he and his Nazi counterpart, Erwin Rommel, waged some ferocious tank battles.

Patton would continue his fight against "those Nazi bastards" into France, Belgium, Luxembourg, and on to Germany, then Czechoslovakia and Austria, leading his

RIGHT: *During combat maneuvers in Louisiana in 1941, George "Blood and Guts" Patton drove his men hard, knowing they would soon be going to war.* U.S. Army Signal Corps photo

Third Army troops with an iron will. But Patton cared deeply for his men and drove them hard to keep them alive: "There are no practice games in life. It's eat or be eaten, kill or be killed. I want my bunch to get in there first, to be the 'fustest with the mostest'."

He wanted his soldiers to train and fight as a team, and he often addressed them with sports analogies: "All real Americans love the sting and clash of battle. When you were kids, you all admired the champion marble player; the fastest runner; the big-league ball players; the toughest boxers. Americans love a winner and will not tolerate a loser. Americans despise cowards. Americans play to win . . . all the time. I wouldn't give a hoot in hell for a man who lost and laughed. That's why Americans have never lost, nor ever will lose a war, for the very thought of losing is hateful to an American."

During the closing months of the European Campaign, *Time* magazine wrote, "The Germans had always put more men and guns opposite Patton's outfits. And now Patton was playing his favorite role. He was the swift, slashing halfback of Coach Eisenhower's team. The U.S. public, always more interested in the ballcarrier than in the blockers who open a hole for him, liked Patton's flourishes, his flamboyance, his victories."

Blood and Guts Patton would settle for nothing less than total victory. And once the Nazis were licked, he wanted to spearhead his tanks, turn them eastward, and rumble on toward Moscow and take on Josef Stalin and the whole damn Red Army!

LEFT: *In 1931, the War Department's "Whites" were winners of the Argentine Polo Cup tournament. The team included Major John Eager, Lieutenant Gordon Rogers, Major George Patton, and Major Jacob Devers.* U.S. Army photo

BELOW: *As a junior officer in the Army, George Patton was a well-known horseman and athlete, especially as a sharpshooter. At the Olympic Games in Stockholm, Patton represented the United States in the pentathlon, placing fourth.* U.S. Army photo

Hockey Combatants Become Allies

> "BASEBALL HAPPENS TO BE A GAME OF TENSION . . . FOOTBALL, BASKETBALL AND HOCKEY ARE PLAYED WITH HAND GRENADES AND MACHINE GUNS."
>
> —*John Leonard*

DURING WORLD WAR II, FIGHTING AND SERVING ALONGSIDE American forces were thousands of men and women from Allied countries, such as Canada, Great Britain, Australia, and New Zealand, plus many from the countries occupied by the Axis powers: France, Poland, Russia, and China.

Many foreigners from these countries were living in the United States when war was declared, and thousands of young men returned home to fight for their countries. Others enlisted in America's armed forces, just as many Americans living in England joined the Royal Air Force in the early months of the European Conflict.

While hockey was played in many northern and eastern cities of the United States, most of the players were Canadian. And when Canada's armed forces faced a rapid mobilization in early 1942, these hockey players from north of the border were drafted. In the first year alone, more than seventy players left their teams to join the Canadian armed forces. Another hundred followed the next year, prompting league officials to contemplate canceling hockey for the duration of the war.

As in major league baseball and pro football in the United States, the quality of play suffered as rookies and over-the-hill veterans replaced top-notch Canadian hockey stars.

Stars and Stripes pointed this out in its November 5, 1943, issue: "They're rationing ice hockey for this new season. There'll still be the usual number of games and the usual quota of fights, but as for the actual play—well, with most of the stars off to the wars, the quality of the

stick-work definitely will be on the doubtful side. At the present time, in order to get somebody on the ice to push the puck around, it appears that the magnates will play both ends against the middle by using boys under 18 and old men over 40 who are left behind. With the National League grabbing players who formerly would be in the amateur ranks, the amateur leagues are now so hard put for players that they probably will be going out onto the highways and byways lassoing innocent kids on roller skates."

Several big-league and semipro teams folded because of the lack of players and poor attendance. For example, after the Brooklyn Americans closed up shop, the National Hockey League opened the '42 season with just six teams, in Montreal, Toronto, Boston, Detroit, Chicago, and New York. They played a fifty-game schedule, with the top four teams qualifying for the play-offs. After the New Haven Eagles closed up shop in late 1943, the Eastern Amateur Hockey League only had three teams left.

Those athletes who were playing for American teams before returning to Canada to join the military included Detroit Red Wings forward Sid Abel, who lost two years in the military but returned after the war to post Hall of Fame statistics, and his teammate, goalie Johnny Mowers, who signed on with the Canadian Royal Air Force. Forward Ken Mosdell was playing at Brooklyn when he was inducted in 1942 and served for two years. When he returned from the war, Mosdell joined the Montreal Canadiens and was selected to four all-star squads. Forwards Doug and Max Bentley joined the Chicago Black Hawks in 1939 and '40. Doug missed one season and Max missed two while in the military. Doug was selected to four all-star teams, and Max won the Lady Byng Trophy in 1943, the Art Ross Trophy

BELOW: *Wounded servicemen faced months or even years of rehabilitation after returning home from the European and Pacific campaigns. Disabled veterans in the Philadelphia area were teamed with members of the Falcons minor league hockey team to learn how to skate. Partially blinded veterans Burl DeWitt (left) and Isaac Foster (right) step on the ice for the first time, assisted by Falcons captain Joe Desson.* Veterans Affairs photo

ABOVE: *Bud Wilkinson was the goalie for the Golden Gophers of Minnesota and was also an All-American guard for the football squad in 1935, then took over at quarterback the following year when they won the national championship. During the war years, he served on the carrier* Enterprise, *as hangar deck officer for the Iwo Jima and Okinawa campaigns.*
Photo courtesy of the University of Minnesota

twice, and MVP honors in 1946. (Doug would be elected to the Hockey Hall of Fame two decades later.)

Bobby Carse of the Black Hawks was wounded in France and ended up a prisoner of the Nazis, force-marched to a POW camp in Germany. Kansas City Pla-Mors forward George Gee joined the Canadian Navy and then played for the Chicago Black Hawks in 1945. He had a stint with the Detroit Red Wings before returning to the Black Hawks.

The Bruins' Kraut Line, consisting of forwards Robert Bauer, Milt Schmidt, and Woody Dumart, joined the team in 1936 and left at the same time for the Royal Air Force, with their teammates carrying them off the ice. Bauer won the Lady Byng Trophy in 1940 and 1941, and then again in 1947, while Schmidt was the league's leading scorer in 1939–40, won MVP honors in '51–'52, and was a four-time all-star. The Kraut Line would continue its success for the Ottawa Royal Canadian Air Force team, winning the Allan Cup as the amateur championship team.

Black Hawks goaltender Sammy Lo Presti was forced to abandon his ship after it was hit by a torpedo. He would survive forty-two days in a life raft before being rescued. Cleveland Barons forward Anthony Leswick was a five-foot, six-inch bulldog who "could bring out the worst in a saint," recalled referee Bill Chadwick. After joining the Canadian Navy in 1943, Leswick would return to the New York Rangers in 1945, playing in six All-Star Games during his career; his teammate Bryan Hextall missed just one season and then continued his Hall of Fame stint with the Rangers. Detroit Red Wings defenseman John "Black Jack" Stewart joined the team in 1938 but missed two seasons during the war. (He would play twelve years in the NHL, posting Hall of Fame statistics.)

New York Rangers forward and defenseman Neil Colville served as a navigator with the Royal Canadian Air Force from 1942 to 1945; Brooklyn Americans forward Harry Watson joined the Detroit Red Wings in 1942, then left for the military, returning in 1946.

Dartmouth collegian Jack Riley piloted a PBM seaplane in the Pacific and would play on the U.S. Olympic team in 1948. (He later coached the

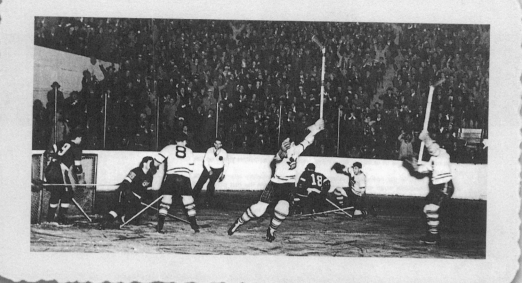

LEFT: *The 1942 Stanley Cup finals, barely four months after Pearl Harbor, pitted Detroit and Toronto, but it wasn't much of a series, with the Red Wings taking the first three games. But after the Maple Leafs denied the sweep, they came back and took the next four games, winning the Cup in Toronto. But soon players from both teams would be heading off to war, fighting for the United States and Canada, alongside Allies from many other countries, including Great Britain and Poland, Australia, and New Zealand.* Photo courtesy of the Ontario Archives

1960 team to Olympic gold at Squaw Valley.)

New York Rangers forward Al Pike played for six seasons, missing two during the war. Boston Bruins forward Roy Conacher posted two twenty-four-goal seasons before joining the military. (He returned in 1946 and became the league's top scorer in 1949.)

Chicago Black Hawks defenseman John Mariucci would serve three years in the Coast Guard and then return to the Hawks. Brooklyn goalie Chuck Rayner played only thirty-six games during the '41–'42 season before serving in the Royal Canadian Navy until 1945. (After the war Rayner was called up by the New York Rangers, was selected to three all-star teams, including MVP honors in 1950, and capped his career with induction into the Hockey Hall of Fame.) Boston Bruins goalie Frankie Brimsek—nicknamed Mr. Zero for posting three consecutive shutouts, twice—missed the '43–'45 season while serving in the U.S. Coast Guard.

North of the border, the war effort also dismantled Canadian teams. The Toronto Maple Leafs lost two key players: center Syl Apps, who became a soldier, and goalie Turk Broda, who joined the Royal Canadian Navy. (Both would return after the war and lead the Leafs to several Stanley Cup trophies before calling it quits, waiting for the Hockey Hall of Fame to add them to its roster.)

Many more pro and collegiate hockey players from the United States and Canada were caught up in the massive manpower sweep of World War II—a conflict that disrupted the lives and careers of millions of young men.

19. Return to the Philippines

> "In my experience, based on many years' obser-vation, officers with high athletic qualifi-cations are not usually successful in the higher ranks."
>
> —*Winston Churchill, February 4, 1941*

WHEN THE JAPANESE ENVISIONED THE "GREATER EAST Asia Co-Prosperity Sphere," their intent was to occupy Manchuria, China, Korea, the Philippines, Formosa, and farther south into the Dutch East Indies and southeast Asia, then utilize every natural resource—including the local populations as a labor force—for their own "prosperity."

Japanese forces attacked the Philippines within hours of Pearl Harbor. Then they overran U.S. defenders in Manila a month later, at Bataan three months after that, and on the fortified island of Corregidor on May 6, 1942. Reluctantly, General Douglas MacArthur left behind the country he loved, but he promised to one day return to the Philippines.

Underestimating the Filipinos

The Japanese mistakenly felt occupation of the Philippines would be peaceful, that they could rely on their Filipino "brothers" to join them in the fight against the white race. But Filipino resistance—supported by U.S. arms and military advisers, many of them escapees from the fighting on the Bataan peninsula and Corregidor in early '42—would be a constant thorn to the Japanese throughout their occupation of the islands. Partisan groups operated and controlled most of the mountain and jungle regions of the country. But their hit-and-run harassment tactics were no match for the Imperial war machine occupying the Philippines, which included approximately 350,000 Japanese troops.

Planning to Return

From 1942 until mid-1944, all available American forces were needed for the Central Pacific Campaign. But once the Allies had secured the Marianas and could rush U.S. planes and warships to these forward locations, they could make plans to finally retake the Philippines.

OPPOSITE: *General Douglas MacArthur (third from left) wades ashore during the initial landings at Leyte in the Philippines in October of 1944, fulfilling his promise to the Filipino people two years earlier that he would return someday.* National Archives photo

BELOW: *U.S. infantrymen advance cautiously through the bombed ruins of Manila's ancient walled city, the Intramuros. Japanese stragglers were holed up in hidden pockets, taking pot shots at American patrols as they passed by.* U.S. Navy photo

Actually, the Navy brass wanted to bypass the Philippines completely and hit Formosa next because it was closer to Japan and could be used for staging the final assault on the home islands. But MacArthur would not break his promise to the Filipino people, and he enlisted the support of President Roosevelt to force the other military strategists to change their minds about sidestepping the islands.

On October 20, 1944, two Allied assault forces involving more than 200,000 men invaded Leyte, one of the central islands of the eastern Philippines. They met very little resistance and by the end of the first day had seized a key air base. General MacArthur waded ashore, proclaiming, "I have returned."

Leading one of those infantry battalions at Leyte was Charles "Monk" Meyer, a West Point running back in the '30s.

MacArthur's Legacy

Dauntless Doug had fulfilled his promise to the Filipino people, and at the same time he got the best of his Navy rivals. He first acquired that nickname from his baseball teammates at West Point, where he played in the first ever game between the Army and Navy cadets, on May 18, 1901. When he first came to bat, the Navy cadets teased him about his father, then governor general of the Philippines, and referred to Doug as a hobo. He went down swinging the first time up, fouled out his next time at bat, but drew a walk his third time at the plate. He then stole second and scored the winning run on an RBI single. The Army cadets won 4–3, and MacArthur thumbed his nose at the midshipmen.

In nearly forty-three years his attitude toward the Navy hadn't changed.

The Battle of Leyte Gulf

The loss of the Marianas in August was a crippling blow to the Japanese. They were faced with the very real possibility that defeat was rapidly approaching. In a desperate gamble, they decided to commit their entire fleet to the next confrontation, hoping to inflict more damage than they received.

Japanese warships continued to roam the northern Pacific, though with extreme caution. In Lingayen

ABOVE: *Three months after U.S. troops returned to the Philippines at Leyte, they were pursuing the Japanese to San Fabian. Wading through streams and rice paddies, hacking trails through dense jungle foliage, the GIs encountered ragtag remnants of the once proud and powerful Imperial Japanese Army.* Department of Defense photo

RIGHT: *Charles "Monk" Meyer was one of West Point's greatest running backs prior to WWII. In the Pacific Campaign he would lead the 127th Infantry Regiment's 2nd Battalion during the invasion of Leyte in the Philippines.* U.S. Military Academy Archives photo

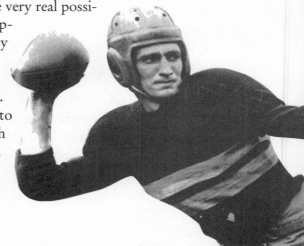

Gulf near the Philippines on August 24, 1944, a Japanese destroyer attacked two U.S. submarines, the *Harder* and the *Hake.* The subs dove as the destroyer approached and fired fifteen depth charges. Though the *Hake* survived the barrage, the *Harder* never surfaced. The skipper on the *Harder* was Texan Sam Dealey, a boxer and runner in high school.

During four patrols in the Pacific, the *Harder* had sunk more than a dozen enemy ships, but on her last mission she could not fire any torpedoes on the enemy warship that tracked her down and tore her apart.

Japan's Last Naval Exploits

Once their intelligence determined that a major invasion force was concentrated in the waters just east of Leyte in the Philippines, the Japanese launched *Plan Sho* (Victory). The Northern Force would attack from the Inland Sea south, while Strike Force A would use the thousands of islands that make up the Philippines to hide their approach from the west, to engage the U.S. fleet in the San Bernardino Strait. At the same time, Strike Force C would approach through the islands from the south. If successful, it would not be detected until it suddenly appeared in the Surigao Strait. All three enemy forces were converging on Leyte Gulf, to cut off the planned invasion.

But the United States controlled the skies over the Philippines, with both carrier-based and land-based planes. Scout planes fanned out in every direction and quickly detected the enemy approach. One of those Army Air Corps crewmen in the Philippines was U.S. amateur golf champion Bud Ward. Sadly, another top amateur golfer, Roy "Bud" Brownell, was killed in the Philippines Campaign.

ABOVE: *The Battle of Leyte Gulf was a disaster for the Japanese, with more than 10,500 killed. American losses— including those from the USS* Kalanin Bay *being buried at sea—were a fraction of that total.* U.S. Navy photo

U.S. carrier planes pounced on Strike Force A on the morning of October 24, sinking the mighty battleship *Musashi* and damaging a heavy cruiser. And American submarines launched a spray of "fish" to sink three cruisers and two destroyers. Strike Force C was intercepted by PT boats and destroyers just as it reached the Surigao Strait that night. Two Japanese

LEFT: *After its planes returned from air strikes on Japanese forces in the Philippines, Task Group 38.3 headed for the Ulithi anchorage, in December 1944.* U.S. Navy photo

battleships and two destroyers were destroyed. The remaining enemy ships scattered.

With virtually no carrier planes of its own, the Northern Force played hide-and-seek, hoping to divert attention from the other two fleets. The enemy did manage to sink the USS *Princeton*, killing 106 men. Three U.S. destroyers were also lost. Kamikazes also took a run at the American warships, plunging from the skies and sinking the carrier *St. Lo*.

Another escort carrier, the *Gambier Bay*, was also lost after absorbing twenty direct hits. One of the last sailors to make it off the Bay was Buzz Borries, the former Navy Academy halfback. He would be left stranded in a life raft for nearly two days while the fighting raged all around him.

All told, American forces lost two destroyers (the *Hoel* and *Johnston*), two escort carriers (the *St. Lo* and *Gambier Bay*), a light carrier (the *Princeton*), and a destroyer escort (the *Samuel B. Roberts*) in the Battle of Leyte Gulf. Former Southern Cal Trojans halfback Howard Callanan was one of those sailors on the destroyer *Hoel* when it went down.

Travis Tidwell was on board during the naval battles of the Philippines. (After the war he would play football at Auburn, earning honors as the Tigers running back.) Ken Cotton, a popular football star in California was killed north of Leyte Gulf, in the Philippine Sea.

Losses They Couldn't Afford

For the Japanese, their desperation gamble was a total failure: four carriers, six heavy cruisers, four light cruisers, three battleships (including the enormous *Musashi*), and nine destroyers were sunk, and more than 10,500 airmen and sailors lost. The remaining warships were rendered helpless, with barely enough fuel to limp back to Japan, where they would be vulnerable to the stepped-up U.S. B-29 bomber raids.

Japanese land forces in the Philippines could no longer depend on naval air protection or gunnery support. Nor would there be any vessels available to resupply or rescue them. The remnants of the Imperial Fleet had abandoned them, leaving them to fight to the death.

Final Push in the Philippines

On December 7, 1944—three years after the attack on Pearl Harbor—U.S. invasion forces swooped in to attack Ormoc on the western coast of Leyte. The Japanese garrison there was well entrenched and offered heavier resistance than it had during earlier assaults on Leyte, in October. Also, ferocious kamikaze pilots attacked U.S. warships overseeing the landing force at Ormoc. These pilots were fanatical, willing to blow themselves to pieces if there was a chance to kill Americans.

One of the hotshot American pilots defending the skies over Ormoc Bay and doing his best to keep the Japanese fighters away from the American warships was Dick Bong, who shot down five enemy planes, bringing his total "kills" to thirty-eight. As a high school athlete in Wisconsin, Bong excelled at baseball, basketball, hockey, and even bowling. But his dream was to be a pilot, and a month after Pearl Harbor he got his wish. In World War II Bong would become the top fighter ace, earning the Medal of Honor.

It would take more than two weeks, but by Christmas Leyte was under Allied control.

Lastly, Luzon

With 250,000 Japanese in place, Luzon was next in the Philippines Campaign. Some 200,000 U.S. troops were tasked with clearing Luzon, landing unopposed to the west at Lingayen Gulf on January 9, 1945. Enemy forces garrisoned on the island had pulled back from the beachhead, unable to withstand the punishing pre-invasion aerial and naval bombardments that had preceded most other amphibious assaults in the Pacific.

Once the Japanese pushed inland, the American forces encountered an elaborate defensive network of pillboxes and connecting tunnels and caves. The entrenched Japanese would not be easily routed. Additional U.S. troops landed south of Manila Bay, on January 31 and soon were engaged in brutal house-to-house fighting in the capital city. At Manila's Rizal Stadium, where so many baseball games

were played before the war, intense fighting was waged, until the capital city was finally liberated on March 3.

At the entrance to Manila Bay was Corregidor—The Rock, site of American humiliation in 1942 when U.S. forces there surrendered. This strategic stronghold was also assaulted and retaken by Allied forces after brutal fighting. Lloyd McCarter was a member of the 503rd Parachute Infantry Regiment, which dropped onto Corregidor. At Gonzaga University, McCarter played varsity football. On Corregidor he braved enemy machine-gun fire to rush an enemy position and knock it out with a hand grenade. Then, despite being wounded, he remained in place to ward off futile banzai charges. Even when he was critically wounded, McCarter continued to shout out the enemy's location so his own mortar crew could fire and wipe them out. For his actions McCarter would later receive the Medal of Honor from President Harry Truman.

Mopping up and Rebuilding

By July the remaining 65,000 Japanese troops were driven into the Luzon hills, where they scavenged for food while trying to elude Filipino guerrillas tracking them down.

Some 190,000 Japanese soldiers had been killed in the Philippines Campaign, while 8,000 Americans were lost. Tragically, as the Japanese pulled back, they destroyed buildings, railways, and bridges, blew up power stations and dams, sank fishing boats, killed farm animals, and severely punished the Filipino people. It would take years to rebuild the country.

One of the Navy construction battalion seamen assigned to help with reconstruction projects was Negro Leagues all-star first baseman John "Buck" O'Neill. After playing on the powerhouse Kansas City Monarchs from 1938 to 1943, O'Neill joined the Navy and missed baseball until he returned for the 1946 season, promptly winning the Negro American League batting title as the Monarchs won the pennant. He would play for the Monarchs until calling it quits in 1955.

Freedom Returns to an Old Ally

It had taken three years for the Allied forces to return to the Philippines, but soon the country became a staging area for several hundred thousand troops slated to attack the home islands. More combat units would be

BELOW: By mid-March of 1945 the Japanese were being pushed back and American troops in northern Luzon were advancing toward Bauang and Baguio. The enemy, though battle-fatigued, still had plenty of fight left in them and relied on the Philippine terrain to slow the Americans down, which only prolonged the inevitable a few more weeks.
Department of Defense photo

arriving from the recently concluded victory in Europe. Kirby Higbe, who led the National League in strikeouts from 1940 to 1943 while pitching for the Dodgers, joined the Army and was sent to Europe with the Eighty-sixth Blackhawk Division. After Germany surrendered, the Eighty-sixth was redeployed to the Pacific for the expected invasion of Japan. (Higbe spent time in the Philippines and then returned to the Dodgers, notching a 17–8 record in 1946.)

Waiting for the impending invasion of Japan was stressful for everyone involved. To take their minds off the anticipated bloodbath, the men played baseball at the bombed-out Rizal Stadium in Manila. Bullet holes and blown-out sections of the outfield wall allowed gate crashers to look on—Manila's own "knot-hole gang"—as semi-pro, major league, and Negro Leagues players from the Army and Navy waged a war of their own for interservice bragging rights.

Joe Garagiola was one of those future big-league ballplayers who would play baseball after the Philippines was secured, backstopping for Kirby Higbe's Manila Dodgers and honing his skills.

But when the games were through, it was back to the daunting task of preparing for the inevitable: the invasion of Japan's home islands that everyone knew would be brutal and deadly.

ABOVE: *A C-47 transport plane drops supplies to the American troops on Corregidor, mid-February of 1945.* U.S. Army photo

LEFT: *The mighty warship USS* Pennsylvania *followed by the* Colorado *leads three other cruisers into Lingayen Gulf, preceding the landing of troops on Luzon, in the Philippines, January 1945.* U.S. Navy photo

20. The Rhineland Campaign

"IN WAR THERE IS NO SECOND PRIZE FOR THE RUNNER-UP."

—*General Omar Bradley*

"A RACING TIPSTER WHO ONLY REACHED HITLER'S LEVEL OF ACCURACY WOULD NOT DO WELL FOR HIS CLIENTS."

—*A. J. P. Taylor*, The Origins of the Second World War

"THE CARDS IN THE GAME OF LIFE ARE THE CHARACTERS OF MEN. . . . BUT WHEN WE PLAY THE GAME OF DEATH, THINGS ARE OUR COUNTERS—GUNS, RIVERS, SHELLS, BREAD, ROADS, FORESTS."

—*Sir Ian Hamilton*, Gallipoli Diary, *1920*

OPPOSITE: *With the German Luftwaffe decimated in the final months of the European Campaign, American anti-aircraft gun crews had little to shoot at. Instead they were reassigned to provide small-caliber artillery support to infantry units pushing into Germany.* U.S. Army Signal Corps photo

ALLIED TROOPS WERE POISED ALL ALONG THE GERMAN border to make the final assault on the Fatherland. Russian troops were gaining ground from the east, while American and other Allied units were tightening the noose from the south and west.

On September 10, 1944, German troops in the border city of Bildchen were startled when U.S. artillery opened up from ten miles away in Belgium. This marked the beginning of the Rhineland Campaign, the assault on Germany's vaunted West Wall. Also known as the Siegfried Line, this chain of defenses included concrete pyramids stacked in rows, which had to be blown apart before Allied tanks could proceed farther. Reinforced bunkers were positioned so that German machine gunners could watch every avenue of approach and cut down anyone daring to enter the killing zone.

The Jewel

Aachen, with 12,000 defenders, was the center of German culture. To underscore the importance of repelling the impending Allied attack, German Minister of the Interior Heinrich Himmler sent this message to the Aachen garrison: "German soldiers! Heroes of Aachen! Our Fuhrer calls upon you to defend to the last bullet, the last gasp of breath, Aachen, this jewel city of German kultur, this shrine where German emperors and kings have been enthroned!"

First Sergeant Bobbie Brown of the Second Armored Hell on Wheels Division led his company on an attack of nearby Crucifix Hill on October 8.

ABOVE: *American servicemen and servicewomen in Paris celebrate the surrender of Nazi Germany on VE-Day—Victory in Europe.* U.S. Army photo

ABOVE: *Soldiers of the 3rd Division's 7th Infantry Regiment scramble up the banks of the Rhine River on March 16, 1945. The retreating Nazi forces had demolished many of the bridges spanning the Rhine so assault boats were called up to get the Americans across, while Army engineers spanned the river with pontoon bridges.* U.S. Army Signal Corps photo

RIGHT: *The bridge at Remagen was the last one spanning the Rhine River and the Allies were determined to seize it before the Germans could blow it up. Among the Army engineers was Boston Braves southpaw Warren Spahn, who was nearly killed when the bridge collapsed, on March 17.* National Archives photo

Hailing from Dublin, Georgia, Brown had notched thirty-nine victories as a boxer. And while playing football for the Army he made the all-star squad in 1927 and received scholarship offers from three universities . . . until they found out he hadn't completed high school.

In fighting at Aachen, Brown's boxing skills would serve him well. After an enemy pillbox pinned down his company, Brown crawled forward to toss a satchel charge inside. But when an enemy soldier suddenly appeared, Brown hopped up and delivered a haymaker, knocking the German backward. Brown then tossed the explosives through the doorway, slammed it shut, and dove for cover, just as the bunker blew apart. He would end up taking out two more bunkers on Crucifix Hill before being wounded during street fighting in Aachen. In August 1945 Brown received the Medal of Honor for his actions at Aachen.

It would take almost three weeks of house-to-house fighting to secure the city, and then the Allies were successful only because the Germans ran out of ammunition.

The Mighty Fortress at Metz

The only bastion on French soil the Germans still held was the fortress city of Metz, with the imposing and seemingly impenetrable fortifications of Fort Driant. With walls nearly seven feet thick, the fort concealed a maze of underground tunnels, which were filled to the rafters with enough food, water, and ammunition to allow the ten thousand German defenders to hold out for months. (Hitler ordered them to hold out "to the last man.") Tangled barbed wire encircled the fort, delaying approaching troops just long enough for Nazi machine gunners and mortar crews manning the ramparts to unleash a deadly barrage.

In early November American troops surrounded Metz, but it wasn't until well into December that the city and its network of forts finally caved in.

Conquest of the Rhine

Hitler had ordered all bridges along the Rhine River blown up before the Allied units could seize them. But many of his troops were too busy fleeing or surrendering to be worried about demolitions.

Once inside German territory, the Allied gains were measured by one vital river crossing—"bouncing the Rhine"—in early March 1945. Though town after town in country after country had fallen, successfully assaulting the Rhine was symbolically equivalent to jockeys coming down the home stretch, with the finish line clearly in sight.

Bill Wood, who led the Thirteenth Armored Division, was another of the many West Point football players under "Blood and Guts" Patton, who believed there was a strong correlation between success on the gridiron and on the battlefield.

Major league outfielder Harry Walker of the St. Louis Cardinals served with a reconnaissance squad operating behind enemy lines, attempting to secure the many bridges that the Germans were desperately trying to blow up. Walker would later recall what it was like, armed with only two machine guns mounted on an exposed Jeep, as hordes of enemy soldiers converged on his position: "Here they come, and I'm trying to stop them, and they wouldn't stop. So that's when I had to start shooting, and I just cut through the whole mess, and they were scattered everywhere, firing back and forth at you, and you're just out there on point like a sitting duck."

Walker had played in the 1943 World Series with the Cards and joined the Army the morning after the Series ended. He would be wounded twice while fighting in Europe and then return to the Cardinals. (In the '46 World Series Walker drove in the Cards' winning run in the final game.)

Murry Dickson, a pitcher with the Cardinals before joining the Army, was an infantryman with the Thirty-fifth Infantry, the Santa Fe Division, crossing the Rhine on March 25 and 26.

Horror at Remagen

Detonation charges on the bridge at Remagen—the last bridge that allowed German units to cross the Rhine— exploded just as GIs of the Ninth Armored Phantom Division started to dash across. The bridge heaved from its supports but miraculously remained standing. The American soldiers quickly scrambled over to cut the detonation wires on the remaining explosives. During the next ten days the Ninth, Seventy-eighth, and Ninety-ninth Infantry Divisions rushed

BELOW: *Reconnaissance squads often worked behind enemy lines, conducting sabotage missions, disrupting enemy maneuvers, and so on. St. Louis Cardinals outfielder Harry Walker pulled recon duty as American ground forces attempted to "bounce the Rhine." His mission was to secure the Rhine River bridges before the Germans could blow them up and stall the Allied advance.* AP Wide World photo

across, despite continued bombing runs by enemy aircraft attempting to destroy the Remagen bridge. Finally, on March 17, without any warning, the bridge collapsed.

One of those Army engineers who narrowly escaped injury on the Remagen bridge was Boston Braves pitcher Warren Spahn, considered one of the best left-handed pitchers ever. "We were trying to complete repairs on the Remagen Bridge so that our trucks could carry weapons to the Front," Spahn recalled. "I checked all the main points and then started to walk toward the bridge. Suddenly, there was a terrible, deafening roar as the bridge collapsed, throwing many of the men and much of the equipment into the deep gorge and water below. We did manage to rescue some of the men but many had been crushed by the falling debris and others drowned."

The tragedy at the Remagen bridge killed twenty-eight and injured another ninety-three American soldiers.

Nazi Remnants Regroup

More than 30,000 enemy troops had been captured in the race to the Rhine, but many other German units were retreating into the mountains to regroup and continue fighting as guerrilla units. U.S. First and Third Armies trapped thousands of Germans in the Eifel Mountains in early March.

Small pockets of enemy resisters and thousands of stragglers were rounded up in mid-March, marking the end of the Rhineland Campaign, which had the highest toll of the war: 50,410 GIs killed in battle with another 165,965 injured.

In the Harz Mountains Hitler had assembled more than 70,000 troops—remnants of the Wehrmacht, many of whom were teenage boys eager to prove themselves but untested in battle—to counterattack to the west. But these

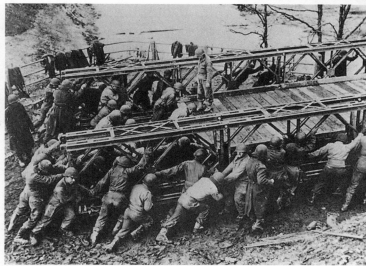

troops were encircled and constricted in April and surrendered before the month was over.

One of those wounded in Germany was all-around athlete Skippy Roberge. Prior to World War II he was a star quarterback, all-American forward in basketball, and infielder for the Boston Braves. (After the war Roberge returned to the Braves, but his wounds had been too severe and he could not remain in the majors. He would play ball a few more years and call it quits in 1951.) Another major leaguer injured in Germany was Emmett Mueller, Philadelphia Phillies infielder. An infantryman killed in Germany was Cleveland Rams end James Hitt.

The Central Campaign

With six full divisions across the Rhine by March 22, the Allies were cutting a path right through Germany's heartland, in what was known as the Central Europe Campaign.

The British were deployed to the north along the Rhine, with the U.S. Thirtieth and Seventy-ninth Divisions complementing them during the attack on Wesel. The largest airborne drop in the European Campaign, Operation Varsity, was made by 21,680 paratroopers of the American Seventeenth Airborne and British Sixth Airborne Divisions. Unfortunately, the Germans were expecting them. In fact, Axis Sally—the enemy radio propagandist with the sexy voice—purred to the paratroopers the night before: "We know you're coming tomorrow and we know where you're coming—at Wesel. Ten crack divisions from the Russia front will be a reception committee."

That "reception committee" blanketed the skies with flak, downing thirty-four troop-carrying planes and gliders of the Ninth Troop Carrier Command, which also lost 41 killed, another 153 injured, and 163 missing in action. The first day alone 159 American paratroopers were killed, and 522 were wounded.

Encircling the Ruhr

With unit cohesion in shambles, ragtag elements of the German Army were rushed to plug holes in the front, which had begun to resemble a massive sieve. En masse, many enemy units were simply surrendering rather than continue to fight. By rushing all available units to the Rhine, Hitler left the

ABOVE: *Army combat engineers ford a stream with a portable bridge, which would allow tanks, jeeps, and trucks to cross deep into the Fatherland. Bouncing the Rhine was the final obstacle to defeating Nazi Germany.*

St. Louis Cardinals pitcher Murry Dickson was with the 35th Infantry Division when his unit crossed the Rhine in late March 1945. National Archives photo

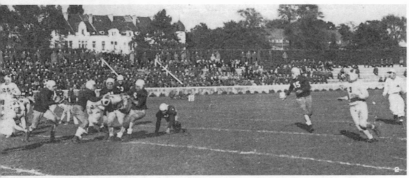

ABOVE: *After the end of hostilities in Europe, the 29th Infantry Division remained in Bremen for occupation duty. During football season the 29th played a team from the 1st Armored Division, blanking the tankers 13–0 at Ike Stadium, named for General Dwight D. "Ike" Eisenhower.* U.S. Army photo

vital Ruhr River industrial region vulnerable. U.S. Ninth Army and First Army units soon enveloped 400,000 enemy troops garrisoned along the Ruhr, and by April 18, they had taken 317,000 of those prisoner.

Serving with the Eighth Armored Division, the Thundering Herd, during its assault on the Ruhr Pocket was tennis player J. Gilbert Hall, who would later return home and win the national veterans' singles title six years running.

Finally, Berlin

On a battle map the Allied offensive looked like hundreds of arrows pointing at one city: Berlin. U.S. forces stopped along the Elbe River though after linking up with Russian troops.

Berlin would be left for the Red Army to conquer.

Mopping Up in Bavaria

Besides Berlin, only two major cities in Germany remained to be taken: Nuremberg and Munich, nestled to the south, in the Bavarian region—Adolf Hitler's homeland. Already battle-weary from continued bombing raids, both Nazi garrisons there were again ordered to "defend to the last bullet."

RIGHT: *American soldiers in Germany finally get the news they were praying for: the surrender of Nazi Germany.* U.S. Army photo

Only brutal house-to-house fighting would decimate the German ranks.

During the fighting in Bavaria, Brooklyn Dodgers pitcher Kirby Higbe kept his arm limbered up by heaving hand grenades at the enemy. Higbe served with the Eighty-sixth Blackhawk Division and barely missed injury when a German artillery shell exploded while he was crossing the Danube River.

U.S. Seventh Army and Third Army units pushed into Austria on May 1, meeting little resistance. And six infantry and two armored divisions entered Czechoslovakia from the west, while the Eastern regions were occupied by Russian forces—a precursor to the Cold War's Iron Curtain.

One of the Czech Army soldiers who saw his country destroyed was long-distance runner Emil Zatopek, who found time during the war to continue his training by running in his Army boots while carrying a heavy backpack. (Zatopek would participate in the 1948 London Olympics, winning the 10,000-meter race and taking a silver medal in the 5,000. After watching him run, one European track coach said "Zatopek runs like a man who has just been stabbed in the heart." At the '52 Olympics he would take gold in both events, plus add a third gold medal in the marathon, an event he had never competed in before.)

ABOVE: *Near Dambach, Germany, an American soldier killed in battle was buried by local villagers, just weeks before the war ended.* National Archives photo

The Führer Dies

Hitler committed suicide in Berlin on April 30. Remembering the desecration of Benito Mussolini's body in Italy, he left orders to have his body burned. On May 8 Germany finally surrendered, marking the end of the war in Europe and the dismantling of the Thousand-Year Reich. American forces in Europe quickly shifted over to occupation duty. With extra time to kill while waiting to rotate back to the States, GIs naturally turned to athletic events, holding them in such venues as the 1936 Olympic Stadium in Berlin and Luitpoldhain Stadium in Nuremberg—the site of many Nazi Party rallies in the 1930s.

21. Two Final Hurdles:
Iwo Jima and Okinawa

"OTHERS ONLY SLIGHTLY OLDER THAN I—LIKE MYSELF YOUNG MARINE CORPS PLATOON LEADERS, PRIMEST CANNON FODDER OF THE PACIFIC WAR—STORMED ASHORE AT TARAWA AND IWO JIMA AND MET UGLY AND HORRIBLE DEATHS ON THE HOT CORAL AND SANDS."

— *William Styron*

OPPOSITE: *After landing on Iwo Jima with little opposition, 4th and 5th Division Marines were pinned down on the beach with scarce protection from enemy machine guns, field artillery, and mortars.* U.S. Marine Corps photo

SULPHUR ISLAND, THE SOUTHERNMOST ISLE OF THE VOLCANO chain, had many names; to the Marines training to assault this next objective, wherever it was in the Pacific, it was known as Island X and Workman Island. Some simply called it the Rock, a name they had used during so many previous no-name island battles.

Once they actually saw it, many soldiers and Marines thought it resembled a floating mummy case, possibly an omen of what was about to occur there. But to military strategists Sulphur Island was known as Iwo Jima, and after the dust had settled it would be considered one of the greatest battlegrounds in Marine Corps history.

A Vital Stepping-Stone

Iwo Jima was situated only six hundred miles from Japan and directly in the flight path of B-29 Superfortresses taking off from bases in the Marianas and headed for missions over Japan. An enemy radar site on Iwo notified the home islands every time American bombers passed overhead, giving Japanese defenders time to rush to their anti-aircraft guns and get their fighter planes in the air to intercept the American intruders.

ABOVE: *Among the thousands of American servicemen participating in the invasion of Okinawa was Coast Guard Commander Jack Dempsey (with rifle), former heavyweight boxing champion.* U.S. Navy photo

The radar site on Iwo Jima had to be destroyed. Then the island had to be assaulted and secured so its airstrip could be used as an emergency landing site for B-29s damaged and unable to make it all the way back to their home base at Saipan, Guam, or Tinian in the Marianas. P-51 Mustangs and P-47 Thunderbolts based on Iwo would then be able to provide fighter escort to the long-range bombers all the way to Japan and back.

But with 21,000 Japanese troops well entrenched on Iwo Jima, it would not be an easy battle. None of the Pacific islands had been easy.

The Enemy Entrenched

As with so many previous encounters in the South Pacific, the Japanese had created an elaborate network of fortified bunkers linked by trenches and tunnels on an island that was little more than five miles long and two miles wide. Deep caves would provide safe shelter for the Japanese during the pre-invasion bombardment that had accompanied other Allied assaults and was fully expected at Iwo Jima. And the brave young men of the Fourth and Fifth Marine Divisions, who were slated for the Iwo Jima Campaign, knew that once the bombardment stopped, thousands of Japanese would appear from nowhere and fight like madmen.

Beginning in November 1944 Army Air Force bombers and Navy warships pounded the enemy fortifications on Iwo Jima for an unprecedented, nonstop seventy-four days. The island trembled, and some of the bunkers were destroyed and cave entrances blocked, but most of the Japanese simply waited out the barrage deep inside that hellish island. By mid-February 1945 the amphibious units were in place, waiting for the signal to launch Operation Detachment.

A Deadly Prelude

Underwater demolition teams attempted to clear the approach to Iwo Jima for the main invasion forces, but enemy guns opened up as they got to the beaches, and the Navy frogmen incurred 170 casualties. On the morning of February 19 U.S. battleships and cruisers, with rocket ships and mortar boats closer to shore, lobbed a full array of explosives at Iwo Jima. Soon the island was obscured by billowing smoke and dust. Once the shelling stopped, air force bombers and carrier-launched Navy planes took their turn.

When the bombing and shelling subsided, the Fourth and Fifth Division Marines began landing on Iwo Jima later that morning, with only scattered fire opposing them. But once the beachhead became clogged with seven battalions of men, plus all their tanks, jeeps, and accoutrements of battle, the Japanese came out of concealment and unleashed their full arsenal, pinning the helpless Marines desperately burrowing into the sand for protection. In the first day alone, 566 Marines were killed and another 1,854 were wounded.

Former Heisman Trophy winner Angelo Bertelli, who played for Notre Dame in 1943 and then joined the Marines, was a platoon leader who narrowly missed injury

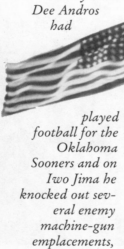

BELOW: *It took four days of brutal fighting before the American flag was raised on Iwo Jima's Mount Suribachi, on February 23, 1945. It would take several more weeks to eliminate the thousands of Japanese soldiers hiding in caves and tunnels on the volcanic island. Often the safest way was to simply blow all the entrances, sealing the enemy inside. Dee Andros had played football for the Oklahoma Sooners and on Iwo Jima he knocked out several enemy machine-gun emplacements, earning a Bronze Star.* U.S. Marine Corps photo

LEFT: *More than 100,000 Japanese soldiers were dug-in and prepared to fight to the death on Okinawa, the final battle before the planned Allied invasion of Japan.* U.S. Marine Corps photo

on the second day ashore, when a mortar round exploded close by. Some of his fellow Marines weren't as lucky.

Scrambling Off the Beach

The Marines realized they would be wiped out if they remained on the beaches, and so, using grenades, flamethrowers, and satchel charges, they pushed inland toward their objective: Mount Suribachi on the southern end of Iwo Jima. Many of the Marines used their bayonets to repel fanatical Japanese, who reacted like cornered animals desperate for escape. It would take four brutal and bloody days of combat to reach the peak of Mount Suribachi for the historic flag raising.

Former Olympic shot putter Harry Bluett Liversedge, who won the bronze medal at the 1920 Games, played football for the Marine Corps's powerhouse team in 1921 and '22, and returned to the Olympics in 1924, was the regimental commander for those valiant Marines who took Suribachi.

The fighting on Iwo Jima would drag on for several weeks as the Marines incinerated hundreds of Japanese soldiers hiding in the volcanic caves or simply blew the entrances, sealing them inside.

Dayton Golden Gloves champion boxer Tony Stein was a one-man wrecking ball. While in Hawaii he had acquired a .30-caliber machine gun from a Navy fighter plane and adapted it so he could brace it against his hip

and obliterate anything he aimed at. Stein called his new weapon a "stinger" and used it to knock out numerous enemy positions. (But on March 1, 1945, while on patrol, Stein was killed by an enemy sniper. A year later his family would sadly receive the Medal of Honor for his actions on Iwo Jima.)

Jay Rebstock had wrecked his knee playing football at Gulf Coast Military Academy in Mississippi. He was classified 4-F, unfit for duty, but after pleading with the doctor at the New Orleans induction center, he was allowed to join the Marines. He was soon assigned to the Twenty-seventh Marine Regiment and thrown into the fight along the east coast of Iwo Jima's Mount Suribachi. Hefting a BAR (Browning automatic rifle)—Rebstock would see many of his fellow Marines cut down by enemy snipers and artillery fire, and only luck separated him from those unfortunate thousands.

Oklahoma Sooners football player Dee Andros was awarded the Bronze Star for knocking out enemy machine-gun nests on Iwo Jima.

Mounting Casualties

Virtually all of the 21,000 Japanese troops on Iwo Jima were killed, while the U.S. Marines lost 6,821 killed in battle. One of those killed was catcher Harry O'Neill, who had played in only one game with the Philadelphia Athletics before joining the Marines.

Angelo Bertelli, the Notre Dame great, took some shrapnel in the shoulder at Iwo Jima. But what stunned him more was hearing that Jack Chevigny, a fellow Fighting Irish running back and former football coach at Notre Dame and Texas, had been killed during the invasion. Marine Sergeant Bob Nanni, an outstanding tackle for Duke's 1942 Rose Bowl team, fell in March.

Rodeo cowboy Fritz Truan, who had won both the bulldogging and all-around champion crowns at the Pendleton Round-Up in 1941, was a proud member of the Cowboys Turtle Association, the early rodeo cowboys organization. During intense combat on Iwo Jima Truan lost his treasured Turtle membership button. After the fight, when he realized it was missing, he risked his life to crawl back to the battlefield, retracing his route to find it. Sadly, Truan was another American athlete killed at Iwo.

Among the wounded were Si Titus, lineman for Holy Cross and later for the Brooklyn Dodgers, and Philadelphia Eagles guard Jack Sanders, who lost part of his left arm. Still hoping to play again, Sanders said, "If Pete Gray can do it," referring to a one-armed pitcher who played major league baseball for the St. Louis Browns during the war years, "then damn, so can I."

A Damn Good Marine

Another pro football player at Iwo Jima was New York Giants end Jack Lummus, who had been an all-American at Baylor University. While leading a rifle platoon near Kitano Point, Lummus destroyed one enemy gun emplacement and wiped out another. Despite being wounded by grenades, he continued to overwhelm position after position.

But then, tragically, an enemy grenade caught him full force, turning his powerful legs into useless stumps. Somehow Lummus managed to stand on what was left of his legs and ordered the rest of his platoon to attack. He was carried back to the Fifth Division field hospital, where he received eighteen pints of blood. The next afternoon, despite excruciating pain, he joked to one of the surgeons, "Doc, it looks like the New York Giants have lost a damn good end." A few hours later Jack Lummus passed away, and the U.S. Marine Corps lost a damn good Marine.

LEFT ABOVE: *Jack Lummus was a bruising All-American end for the Baylor Bears then joined the already potent New York Giants. As a leatherneck at Iwo Jima, he fought ferociously while leading his rifle platoon in destroying several enemy positions. Though wounded, he continued the advance, but after a grenade shredded his legs, Lummus was evacuated from the front lines. Surgeons struggled to save his life, but the next afternoon Lummus gave up the fight.*
AP Wide World photo

LEFT BELOW: *The Japanese couldn't be routed from caves on Okinawa, so the Marines and the Army resorted to flamethrowers. Explosives were also used to blow up cave openings, entombing the enemy. The Marines and the Army suffered 7,300 casualties; the Japanese and Okinawans estimated more than 110,000 lost.* U.S. Navy photo

Last Stand for the Enemy

Okinawa in the Ryukyu Islands is but a "hop, skip, and a jump" from the Japanese mainland. The Japanese no longer had the arsenal to stop an invasion of Okinawa, but they hoped to muster everything they had to prolong the fight as long as possible, to somehow cripple the warships of the U.S. Pacific fleet standing offshore.

Enemy troops on Okinawa were told that any extra time in delaying the Allied invasion might give shipyards in Japan enough time to finish building new aircraft carriers, battleships, and submarines in dry dock and rush them into battle. Those war-weary Japanese troops had no way of knowing that Allied bombers had reduced every shipyard and manufacturing plant in Japan to rubble. Nothing was going to be built in time or in sufficient numbers to delay the inevitable.

Still, the Okinawa defenders—100,000 strong—knew the importance of their seemingly impossible mission, and they were prepared to inflict as much carnage as possible. Their goal, echoed by the Thirty-second Japanese Army, was: "One plane for one warship. One patrol boat for one ship. One man for ten enemy. One man for one tank."

Opposing them were half a million men, including more than 1,500 warships and support vessels and a thousand carrier planes. A British naval task force, with 244 carrier planes of its own, would guard the southern flank of the invasion force.

BELOW: *Soldiers from the 381st Infantry Regiment blast the entrance to one of the hundreds of caves on Okinawa, in June of 1945.* YANK magazine photo

They Fell from the Sky

Kamikazes continued to terrorize Allied warships, and sailors from other vessels in the region watched helplessly as these enemy planes plunged into gun turrets, flight decks, and control towers and exploded in an inferno.

American sailors willing to fight for their country could not fathom an enemy pilot intentionally guiding one of these flying bombs at an Allied warship and committing suicide in honor of their beloved emperor. Still, more than 1,900 kamikaze missions were notched during the Okinawa Campaign, resulting in direct hits on 263 Allied ships. Enemy fighter planes and bombers also attempted to disrupt the landings at Okinawa, but for their efforts hundreds of Japanese pilots were shot down by Allied carrier planes and anti-aircraft gun crews.

Bud Wilkinson, former Big Ten outstanding scholar-athlete and quarterback for the University of Minnesota's 1934, '35, and '36 national championship teams, served as hangar deck officer on the carrier *Enterprise* in support of Iwo Jima and Okinawa. Among the thousands of naval personnel constantly watching overhead for kamikazes at Okinawa was Lieutenant Commander

Larry French, who pitched for the Brooklyn Dodgers in 1942, recording a 15–4 record, before joining the Navy.

The *Enterprise* alone experienced an onslaught of eighty-five enemy planes during a fifteen-minute period. The only way to survive this swarm was through rapid-fire teamwork. In fact, it was well known that the Big E had room for only two types of sailors: the quick and the dead.

Duke end Jim Smith, who played in the '42 Rose Bowl, was on the USS *Bright* when it was damaged by a kamikaze.

One of the most animated football players at Okinawa was Art Donovan, who played briefly at Notre Dame before joining the Marines. Eight months prior to Okinawa, in June 1944, while serving on the carrier USS *San Jacinto* with an anti-aircraft gun crew, Donovan saw how deadly kamikazes could be. "Those goddamn Japs, they were coming down and blowing up our ships left and right," he recalled. "We nearly lost the Navy to those wild bastards. And I figured it was only a matter of time and percentages before the *San Jacinto* took a hit and went down. So I volunteered for the Fleet Marine Force—I raised my fat paw real quick."

Soon afterward, Donovan was on Okinawa as an ammunition handler with a .50-caliber machine gun crew. "I never fired the gun. My job was to make sure the guys who did were never empty. There were Japs all over the place. You'd never really see them, you'd hear their bullets whistling past your ear when you'd get into a fire fight. But it still beat hell out of facing the goddamn kamikazes."

ABOVE: *A familiar scene for American soldiers and Marines hopscotching across the Pacific, from one unknown island to the next. Probably no one participating in this, the invasion of Okinawa, knew this would be their final amphibious landing. They all assumed they would eventually have to invade Japan's home islands later in 1945.* U.S. Navy photo

In all, Allied naval forces suffered 38 ships sunk and 368 damaged at Okinawa, resulting in 9,731 U.S. casualties.

Assaulting Okinawa

A week before the invasion of Okinawa—slated for Easter Sunday, 1945—bombs and shells hammered the island. West Point's 1932 all-American lineman Milt Summerfelt led the bomber group laying waste to Okinawa. Then on March 26 five nearby islands were seized, and, before dawn on April 1, soldiers and Marines rushed ashore.

"We landed Easter Sunday morning. They gave us 72 hours to take that airfield over there, and we took it," recalled ballplayer Hank Bauer. "We walked across it in 15 minutes. Boy, they were waiting for us up in the hills. There wasn't no one around. We set up our defense around that airfield.

"About five o'clock or 5:30 that evening a goddamn Jap airplane tried to land on that airfield. I don't know what he was thinking about with all of them ships out there. He knew them weren't the Jap ships. Well, hell, he never got out of the cockpit."

(Bauer dove into baseball after the war with the same fighting spirit he displayed in the South Pacific. While roaming the outfield with the Yankees, he had a seventeen-game hitting streak in three consecutive World Series, from 1956 to 1958. He also clobbered four home runs in that final tilt, defeating the Braves for the crown.)

Golfer Charlie Sifford was with the Twenty-fourth Infantry Victory Division on Okinawa. (After World War II he would become the first black player to win a Professional Golfers' Association event, taking the Long Beach Open in 1957.)

Another New York ballplayer who saw action at Okinawa was an enormous hunk of granite known as Gil Hodges, considered "the strongest human in baseball." It was even joked that when

BELOW: *Despite its own arsenal of anti-aircraft guns, the battleship USS Missouri could not prevent a Kamikaze (rear upper left) from swooping in dangerously close before exploding.*
U.S. Navy photo

Hodges hit the beach at Okinawa with the Sixteenth Anti-Aircraft Battalion, not only did the Japanese surrender but so did half the Marines!

"Keep Your Head and Ass Down"

The northern sector of Okinawa was secured fairly easily, but most of the Japanese were entrenched to the south and offered stiff resistance along the Shuri line near ancient castle ruins. Some Marines considered the final assault on Okinawa as the most difficult battle of the Pacific Campaign.

"April the 4th we were up in the hills looking for them, and all hell broke loose. For 40-some days it was rough," Hank Bauer remembered. "I got hit the 53rd day I was on there. Got hit with a piece of shrapnel in the left thigh. It went in here on the outside and came out on the other side. Or they took it out on the other side. We went in with 64, and six of us come out. The only thing they ever told us was, 'Keep your head and your ass down.'"

Enemy fighting increased, as the Japanese held firm for nearly two months, including a suicidal counteroffensive on May 3 and 4 that was repulsed by the U.S. First Marine Division.

By May 29 Shuri castle had fallen as the Japanese pulled back to the southern tip of Okinawa. They would continue to hold out until the first week in July. Surprisingly, more than 7,000 battle-weary enemy troops on Okinawa surrendered rather than commit suicide, the more "honorable" choice. The remaining 100,000 Japanese soldiers plus local islanders who were ordered to fight for Japan were killed, many of them entombed in collapsed caves.

Like Nothing Before or Since

Numerous collegiate football players saw action on Okinawa, including Ray Poole, who played end at Mississippi; Pennsylvania tackle Bernie Gallagher, who was wounded but would return to the gridiron after the war; two-time all-American end Alex Agase (chosen while at Illinois in

LEFT: *Dubbed the strongest man in baseball, Brooklyn Dodger Gil Hodges served with the 16th Anti-Aircraft Battalion at Okinawa.* AP Wide World photo

ABOVE: *Wisconsin's All-American end in 1941 and '42 was David Schreiner, who proved capable of dodging opposing tacklers on the gridiron, but wasn't so lucky on the battlefield. He would be killed during heavy fighting on Okinawa.* Photo courtesy of the University of Wisconsin

1942 and again the following year while serving as a Navy cadet at Purdue), who was wounded in the shoulder and leg but would return to play at Illinois; and Rice guard Weldon Humble, in charge of a Marine platoon that endured brutal combat.

Wisconsin all-American end David Schreiner had been considered one of the greatest Big Ten pass catchers prior to World War II. He was killed on Okinawa. Columbia's triple-threat Quarterback Cliff Montgomery would win the Navy's Silver Star for his gallantry in this brutal island campaign.

Ohio State freshman tackle Lou Groza served with a medical unit overwhelmed with casualties at Okinawa. Once the island was secured and the wounded were stabilized, patched up, and evacuated, Groza read a sports brief about a new pro football league in the works, the All-American Football Conference. Within days he'd received a contract offer from Paul Brown, heading up the new franchise in Cleveland. There was only one minor stipulation in the contract: Groza had to come back alive!

With the fall of Iwo Jima, Okinawa, and the Philippines, there remained only one more objective: the invasion of Japan. But with elderly men and disabled war veterans prepared to take up arms, plus millions of Japanese women and children training to defend their homeland, all of them willing to die for their emperor, this final confrontation in the Pacific would also be the most difficult.

Reflections

Years later World War II veteran and University of Texas football coach Darrell Royal would recall these legendary battles of the South Pacific: "A head coach is guided by this main objective: dig, claw, wheedle, coax that fanatical effort out of the players. You want them to play every Saturday as if they were planting the flag on Iwo Jima."

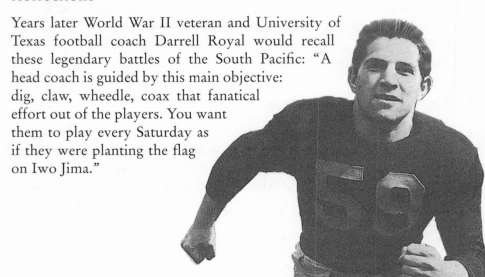

Prisoners of War

> "Shipments of POWs were being put together by the thousands to be sent to Japan. For once the Japanese were being systematic, at least in their own categories of thinking, culling the oldest men, the worst dysenteries, recurrent malarias, badly scarred ulcers, dark-skinned Eurasian Dutch, Australian aborigines, and men of any nationality with red hair or freckles."
>
> — *Gavan Daws*

THE BATTLING BASTARDS OF BATAAN HELD OUT AS LONG AS they could against overwhelming enemy forces that were bombarding their position in early 1942. Though the Japanese were tightening the noose, the American defenders of the Philippines waited for reinforcements that had been promised but never came. Then on April 9 Bataan fell, and the battle-weary defenders were rounded up and force-marched to a prison camp sixty miles to the north. Already weak from four months of combat and little food, the American and Filipino prisoners staggered along the winding road of the Bataan Peninsula.

Martin Gibson was one of the Filipino scouts trapped and captured at Bataan. At the 1936 Berlin Olympics he had placed fourth in the rifle event. (Gibson would survive his internment and represent his country again at the 1948 Olympic Games.) Alvin Poweleit had been a boxer with a devastating knockout punch, but after weeks at Bataan he had wasted away and looked like a skeleton, as did most POWs held by the Japanese.

Those prisoners who fell from exhaustion along the Death March were shot or bayonetted. Those who stopped to help their buddies were beaten back into line. And for those who tried to get a drink from one of the many artesian wells along the route, it would be their last drink. Japanese troops passing by in trucks would club the prisoners with rifle butts. Those who fell in the road were simply run

BELOW: At a prisoner of war camp on Mindanao in the Philippines, Americans remember July 4 and its special significance. It would be more than two years though before they would be free again, liberated when U.S. troops returned to the Philippines. U.S. Army photo

ABOVE: *Major Greg "Pappy" Boyington, leader of the notorious Black Sheep Squadron, was shot down over Rabaul on January 3, 1944 and held prisoner at the Omori Camp in Japan until the end of the war.* National Archives photo

over, repeatedly, until nothing but bloody piles of tattered clothes remained in the dirt.

American and Filipino troops who refused to surrender at Bataan fled into the surrounding hills. Some two thousand swam to the fortified island of Corregidor, which guarded the entrance to Manila Bay. Among the Corregidor defenders was Colonel Paul Bunker, commander of the Fifty-ninth Coast Artillery Regiment.

As a West Point cadet, Bunker was selected as an all-American tackle, then moved into the backfield and made all-American again, as a halfback. But at Corregidor, Bunker could do little to stave off the Japanese artillery shells that rained down incessantly on the tadpole-shaped island.

Finally, after months of intense air and artillery bombardment, the Rock fell on May 6 and those defenders left were rounded up and taken to POW camps in the northern Philippines or other territories held by the Japanese. Among the Americans taken prisoner was Marine Captain Austin Shofner, who had anchored the offensive line for the Tennessee Volunteers. (Shofner would later escape, one of the few who actually succeeded.)

Among those Americans from Bataan and Corregidor who later died in a POW camp was Mason Chronister, the great mile runner from Maryland who set records at the 1940 Penn Relays. And Paul Bunker would die at a POW camp on Formosa, after losing nearly seventy pounds.

Soon after being taken captive, and again at the camps, all prisoners were shaken down. Mario "Motts" Tonelli, former Notre Dame fullback and pro star with the Chicago Tigers, reluctantly gave up his school ring to a Japanese guard who had, ironically, gone to school at the University of Southern Cal—a rival of the Fighting Irish. In fact, in 1939 Tonelli had scored the winning touchdown when Notre Dame beat the USC Trojans 13–6. When no one was looking, the guard slipped the ring back to Tonelli. Motts managed to hide the ring while confined behind barbed wire.

While Japanese guards prized expensive watches and pens taken from the prisoners, they would kill anyone caught with yen, small Japanese flags, or medals that were presumably taken from dead Japanese soldiers.

When Texan Ralph Baggett was captured on Guam, one of his guards confiscated the watch he had won as the shuttle hurdle relay champion at the 1940 Drake Relays.

Former Annapolis running back Richard Antrim was captured when his warship, the USS *Pope,* was sunk in April of 1942. As a POW he frequently spoke out to protest inhuman conditions and treatment, risking immediate death, but the Japanese guards were intimidated by him and made the changes he demanded.

Horrifying Conditions

Prisoners suffering from wounds and disease, and thus unable to do any work, were typically killed. And in the South Pacific, debilitating diseases, from malaria and dysentery to beriberi, dengue fever, and typhus, were rampant.

All other prisoners—including those who were deathly sick but still had a will to live—were assigned to work details, such as the 250-mile long Siam-to-Burma railroad, which utilized more than 61,000 POWs. Of those, 650 were Americans. Approximately one-fifth of all POWs assigned to the railroad project died.

Sports Diversions

Prisoners were allowed rest days at some camps, and those who weren't totally exhausted from the back-breaking labor found other activities to take their minds off their bleak surroundings. In February 1943 the Australians at one of the sub-camps along the railroad staged a "horse race" reminiscent of their country's own Melbourne Cup.

Jockeys wore colorful scarves and selected their "horses," which were simple bamboo brooms with a horse's head painted on them. Prisoners wagered whatever trinkets they still had or sacrificed a bowl of watery rice; then the jockeys galloped around the compound as all the prison spectators, including the guards, cheered them on. At the Tha Muang camp in Thailand, the "horses" were actual prisoners, who lumbered around the camp carrying the scrawniest of jockeys, struggling to hang on.

Tennis player Dick Walker was chosen to help care for the Japanese officers' horses—real horses—at a POW camp on Luzon in the Philippines. Walker toured Japan before the war with fellow tennis great Bill Tilden and had been recognized by one of the Japanese guards who also enjoyed tennis.

If the prisoners were too weak for horse racing, they might bet on frog races or snake races, although usually all of the entrants got eaten soon afterward.

BELOW *At Stalag Luft 1 near Barth, Germany, Allied prisoners enjoy a boxing tournament, with national bragging rights at stake.* Photo courtesy of the Andersonville POW Museum

Little Chance of Escape

Though Allied personnel were trained to do everything possible to escape, the Japanese forced all prisoners to sign a non-escape oath. Those prisoners who were then caught trying to escape were executed in front of other prisoners. Unlike their counterparts in Europe, POWs from Japanese camps could not blend in with the local populace if they did manage to escape. Also, the Japanese offered large bounties to anyone turning in any Allied servicemen on the run.

As Allied forces in the Pacific drove the enemy from one island to the next, the Japanese either executed prisoners of war en masse or evacuated and transferred them to other camps in Japan. One of those POWs was Lou Zamperini, a long-distance runner who finished eighth at the 1936 Olympics in Berlin. After his plane crashed at sea on May 27, 1943, Zamperini was adrift in the Pacific for forty-seven days. He was eventually captured by the Japanese and ended up in a POW camp at Naoetsu, Japan.

Often prisoners being moved from one camp to another in Japanese-held territory were crammed into unmarked transport ships, and many of these were torpedoed or bombed by Allied ships and planes. Thousands of Allied prisoners died as a result.

Maurice Daly and Tom Trapnell, West Point teammates two decades earlier, were on board the *Oryoku Maru* when American bombers pounced on the unmarked transport in the Philippines. Fifteen hundred POWs became helpless pawns, with half of them trapped and killed inside the crippled ship. Daly and Trapness survived, only to be put on another unmarked transport, the *Enoura Maru,* which was also attacked near Formosa. The two long-time Army buddies survived this second attack and were moved to a third ship, the *Brazil Maru,* bound for the home islands. Daly finally gave in to starvation, malnutrition, and the freezing conditions. His buddy Tom Trapnell was by his side when he passed away.

In the Philippines it was known that American prisoners were being held at a camp at Cabanatuan on the island of Luzon. With American forces already ashore at Leyte in the Philippines, it was feared the prisoners at Cabanatuan might be executed.

In late January 1945 a rescue mission was planned involving the U.S. Sixth Ranger Battalion and the Alamo Scouts. Among the contingent sent deep behind enemy lines to rescue the POWs were former Notre Dame quarterback John Murphy; Gibson Niles, who was a cross-country runner at West Point; and Gilbert Cox, football player for Oregon State. The commandos would be traversing rice paddies and open ground and could be easily spotted by passing enemy patrols or scout planes. They would need a lot of luck to avoid being detected and would have to rely on the silence of any Filipinos they might encounter.

In a raid that took barely thirty minutes, the 250 Japanese guards at Cabanatuan were killed and 511 prisoners liberated, though they were still behind enemy lines and had a perilous journey to safety, mostly on foot.

Many of the prisoners had to be carried out on stretchers. Another thirty minutes later, the prisoners and their rescuers had made it across the Pampanga River, where Filipino villagers waited with carts, each pulled by a water buffalo known as a carabao. The emaciated prisoners could ride on the carts for the remainder of the trek, but several insisted on walking—just as they had walked and survived the Bataan Death March.

Overhead, P-61 pilots of the 547th Night Fighter Squadron strafed enemy patrols and convoys searching for the Cabanatuan escapees and their rescuers. The slow-moving caravan would travel through the night and into the next morning until, still five miles behind enemy lines, they met up with an Army convoy of trucks and ambulances protected by infantrymen. The POWs of Cabanatuan were free again, after nearly three years of captivity.

At Santo Tomas University in Manila, male and female prisoners, including civilians living in the Philippines, were housed from 1942 to the end of the war. One of those civilians was Royal Arch Gunnison of the Mutual Broadcasting System. He recalled some of the sports activities that took place behind barbed wire: "Sports were practically our only form of entertainment at Santo Tomas. The Japs let us organize softball leagues and we had 30 teams playing. Sometimes, if they thought we were enjoying ourselves too much, the Japanese guards would come out to a softball game and pick four or five men from each team and cart them off somewhere to dig ditches until the game was over."

Later Gunnison was transferred to a POW camp in Shanghai. "The captain of the guard there was nuts about softball, and wanted to play a game between the guards and the prisoners. We stalled and tried to prevent the game, because we knew so many things could go wrong. But he insisted."

The lopsided game was 27 to zip after just the first inning, and the POWs worried that if they didn't ease up, it might seal their doom. But no matter how often they booted easy grounders, overthrew to first, and wiffed at easy pitches, they still dominated their captors 27–2. "It got so funny that everybody on the side lines, except

BELOW: *Survivors of the Bataan Death March and the siege of Corregidor at the Cabanatuan POW camp in northern Philippines.* National Archives photo

the Japs of course, nearly choked while trying to keep from laughing," Gunnison recalled. "That softball game was practically the only contact in sports we had with the Japanese."

Luckily the guards weren't humiliated enough to retaliate with a little bloodletting.

More humorous antics came out of another game between the Japanese and Americans, only this time the game was held in Hawaii, and the Japanese were the prisoners of war. "The Japs were offering $100 to any of our good players who would join them against us," recalled former Washington Senators pitcher Walter Masterson, in a letter to his old boss, Clark Griffith. Masterson was stationed with the Navy at Pearl Harbor. Another prominent major leaguer playing exhibition games in Hawaii just happened to be the Yankee Clipper, New York Yankees outfielder Joltin' Joe DiMaggio.

"They are very small and extremely light, and the temptation is strong to grab a couple of them by the heels and knock their heads together," Masterson continued, retelling the story of one Japanese hurler who knocked down an American batter with a brush-back pitch. "I took care of that bird next time he came up to bat!" Even in sports, the Japanese and Americans couldn't resist taking shots at each other.

POWs in Fortress Europe

At considerable risk, the Allies knew that the only way to cripple the formidable Nazi war machine was not just to destroy a greater number of tanks and planes, warships, and submarines, but to prevent them from being replaced. And the only way to do that was to bomb defense factories deep in German territory, which were protected by anti-aircraft gun batteries and Luftwaffe fighter pilots.

Thousands of Allied bomber planes were sent aloft from air bases in England to hit hundreds of targets in Europe. As the Allies got a toehold on North Africa, and then Italy, forward air bases were established, allowing bombers to probe even deeper behind the lines. On some of those dangerous missions, as many as a third of the bombers didn't return home.

BELOW *POWs at Stalag Luft 1 near Barth, Germany, punch it out.* U.S. Air Force Academy Library photo

Some planes were blown apart by flak or shredded by German interceptors. Others made it to the English Channel or the Mediterranean and ditched
at sea. And for nearly every bomber that went down, there were crewmen on
other planes counting the number of parachutes that opened before it
exploded or crashed. The luckiest crewmen were those who had time to bail
out and open their chutes. But quite often, waiting for them on the ground
were angry German civilians who didn't appreciate their homeland being
bombed. Over occupied countries, downed airmen were spotted and rescued
by local partisans, protected, and escorted back to friendly lines. Most,
though, were arrested by German patrols and sent to prisoner of war camps.

Of the more than 93,000 American POWs in Europe, three-fourths were
airmen. (The remainder of POWs were captured primarily after fighting in
Tunisia and the Battle of the Bulge.)

Eddie Berlinski, who played football at North Carolina State and later
with the Newark Bears, had been reported missing during the fighting in
North Africa and later turned up at a prisoner of war camp in Germany.
South African tennis player Eric Sturgess was a Spitfire pilot in his country's
air force who was shot down over Italy in October 1944. He spent time at a
POW camp in Germany until the Russians liberated it in May 1945. (Sturgess
returned to tennis and was consistently ranked in the top ten for several years
after World War II.)

Minor league pitcher Bert Shepard was on a mission to Berlin when flak
ripped through the cockpit of his P-39 Thunderbolt. His plane caught fire and
crashed, and he lost consciousness. When he woke up in a German hospital,
Shepard learned that his lower right leg had been amputated. He would then
be sent to a POW camp, where another prisoner made him an artificial leg.

Chicago Black Hawks hockey player Bobby Carse was seriously
wounded in the shoulder and captured by the Germans during the fighting
in France. He was force-marched to a prisoner of war camp in Germany. His
wounded shoulder became infected, but no German doctors were available.
Luckily, one of the other POWs was a Chicago doctor who loved hockey and
had seen Carse play countless times. He was able to save Carse's life.

Missouri all-American center Darold Jenkins had been listed as missing
in action until he turned up on the roster of a POW camp.

The German word for prisoner of war is *kriegsgefageners*, which Allied
POWs shortened to "kriegies." Unlike Japan, which treated Allied POWs
with total disregard, Germany had signed the Geneva Convention in 1929
and in general followed those guidelines in its treatment of its prisoners.

On the other hand, Hitler's Final Solution and Nazi Germany's treatment of Jews, Slavs, and other "undesirables" rivals Japanese atrocities in
both scope and brutality.

Allied prisoners of war in Europe were sent to camps known as stalags. Typically these camps were surrounded by barbed wire and electrified fencing. Sentry towers—mockingly referred to as "goon boxes"—were positioned to observe the entire perimeter of the compound. At night, searchlights scanned the grounds, for prisoners continually probed for any weakness in the gauntlet. "The problem was to do what would make you feel adequate and make the German guards or others frustrated, without pushing it to the point that you might be badly beaten or injured" wrote Dr. Charles Stengler, a psychologist and former POW.

Prisoners were housed in wooden barracks and slept on slat bunk beds, sometimes padded with straw or newspapers. Most barracks had a small stove that was totally inadequate for providing warmth during the bitter winter months.

Norwegian Birger Ruud, who had won a gold medal at the 1936 Winter Olympics at Garmisch, Germany, was sent to a prisoner of war camp along with his two brothers after they refused to cooperate with Nazi occupiers. Teodor Niewiadomski was captured when the Nazi blitzkrieg rolled through his native Poland. While in a POW camp in Nuremberg, Niewiadomski participated in a mock Olympics, winning first place in the frog jump. He recalled that an Olympic flag was made from an inmate's shirt, and medals were fashioned from paper and barbed wire. And when he won his event, an inmate played the Polish anthem on his harmonica. "I looked at everyone—a Frenchman, an Englishman, a Pole—all had tears in their eyes," he would later recall.

A Thriving Economy Behind the Wire

Red Cross food parcels and mail from home were permitted in the European camps. In fact, many prisoners had a thriving black-market business going with camp guards, bartering cigarettes, canned meat and fish, chocolate, and cheese for batteries (to operate hidden radios), film (for pinhole cameras used to make fake identification photos), sports equipment, or for just about anything the prisoners needed, including English-language newspapers and magazines informing the POWs just how the war was progressing. And of course every tidbit of information was passed throughout the camp.

At Stalag Luft III near Zagar, Poland, for example, there were two weekly newspapers—the *Stalag Stump* and *Kriegie Klarion*—which were simple bulletins of news and gossip. Besides box scores and standings of the various sports teams in camp, the *Stump* and *Klarion* included whatever news they could get about major league baseball and pro football.

Regular sports features were included in the newspapers, written by camp columnists, which included Lou Zaris, New Jersey boxer; Minnesota football player Hal Van Every; Pennsylvania center Fay Frink; and Mississippi State's all-American end Bud Elrod.

Prisoners played sports year-round in the camps—soccer, rugby, and cricket for British prisoners, baseball and football for the Americans, hockey in the winter and volleyball in the summer. Boxing and wrestling settled many disputes among prisoners, and golf caused many more arguments.

Prisoners also quickly learned that golf balls hit too close to the perimeter fence were best just left where they were. It was easier to just bribe one of the German guards with some cigarettes or chocolate to smuggle in another golf ball.

There were so many prisoners who wanted to play each of the sports activities that strict schedules had to be posted every day.

The guards conducted surprise inspections at all hours, hoping to detect tunneling efforts or smuggling operations. Those prisoners caught trying to escape were punished severely, often during a massed formation of all the camp's prisoners.

"The Germans used to have a great sport," recalled Charlie Miller, former national commander of American Ex-Prisoners of War. "At night they'd leave their dogs run through our barracks, and everyone would climb the upper bunks. One night, they let 'em go into the Russian barracks, and there was a lot of confusion. When the Germans finally went in, lit the lights, the only thing they retrieved were three halters. The Russians had in fact killed and ate the dogs."

In the final year of the war, as Allied forces cracked Fortress Europe, the Germans relocated Allied prisoners to keep them from being liberated. Often POWs were force-marched to new camp sites. Others were crammed onto freight trains, only to be strafed by Allied planes. As the collapse of Nazi Germany became inevitable, a "standfast" agreement was reached, stating that Allied prisoners would be allowed to remain in camps deserted by German guards, as long as those POWs did not take up arms and become combatants again.

ABOVE: *During the mid-1920s, Maurice Daly played varsity football at West Point, and like many of his teammates, got caught up in WWII.*

After the Japanese attacked Pearl Harbor they headed toward the Philippines and quickly decimated the Army Air Corps and its planes at Clark Field, where Daly was stationed. He would eventually be taken prisoner and endured the Bataan Death March, only to perish three years later on a transport ship bound for Japan in January of '45. U.S. Military Academy Archives photo

USS *Indianapolis* Delivers the Bomb

"ABOARD THE *INDIANAPOLIS*, THESE 'ARTILLERY OFFICERS' BECAME PART OF THE PUZZLE INTRIGUING THE CREW. WHO WERE THEY AND WHAT WAS THEIR CONNECTION TO THE GIANT CRATE AND THE 'BUCKETS'?"

— *Dan Kurzman*

THE HEAVY CRUISER USS *INDIANAPOLIS* HAD BEEN HIT BY A kamikaze and sustained heavy damage while patrolling the waters off Okinawa on March 31, 1945. During repairs in San Francisco, the *Indianapolis* was given one of the most important missions of World War II: transporting the component parts for an atomic bomb to Tinian, a remote Pacific island in the Marianas chain. After the cargo was loaded on board and secured on the hangar deck, guards were posted around the clock. Among the thirty-nine Marine guards detailed to protect the unknown cargo was Private Giles McCoy, who had played shortstop in high school and dreamed of a tryout with the St. Louis Browns.

The *Indianapolis* cast off for the South Pacific, arriving at Tinian on July 26. From there the component parts were off-loaded and moved to a guarded Quonset hut, where they were assembled. The crew of the *Indianapolis* was not told what was being transported, only that it was vital to ending the war.

The Indy departed Tinian bound for Guam. There Captain Charles McVay asked for an escort, but his request was denied because the Indy was considered a fast cruiser that could elude trouble and there had been few sightings of enemy subs or kamikaze planes on its route in recent months. The Indy then headed toward Leyte Island in the Philippines. On the night of July 30 she was spotted at 1,500 yards by an enemy submarine—the I-58—which launched a spread of six torpedoes and ripped apart the ship with two starboard explosions, killing nearly four hundred of her crew. But eight hundred survived the two blasts and jumped overboard, scattering over several miles as the crippled ship drifted and slowly sank. Because the electronics were knocked out, no one from the *Indianapolis* signaled mayday.

It took less than a quarter-hour for the Indy to list ninety degrees and perish. For the hundreds of survivors close by, they could hear their shipmates still trapped inside the smoldering hulk, screaming and pounding on the bulkhead doors.

ABOVE: *Navy lieutenant Charles McKissick had coached football at Texas Christian before joining the crew of the cruiser* Indianapolis.

U.S. Navy photo

Among the crew who made it off the ship were Adolfo Celaya, who played high school basketball in Arizona, and Lieutenant Charles McKissick, who had gone to college at Texas Christian University and coached football. One of the players on his team was Garland Rich, also cast overboard when the *Indianapolis* went down.

U.S. radio operators on Guam picked up enemy message traffic from the Japanese submarine, which claimed to have sunk an American warship. But this claim was dismissed, as were so many other enemy reports, because no U.S. ship in the area had sent a distress signal. For three days, under a sweltering sun, the eight hundred survivors clung to debris and overcrowded lifeboats while swarms of sharks picked off the stragglers. Many, too weak to hang on, simply gave up. Sadly, Garland Rich was one of those who would not survive the ordeal.

Finally, on August 2, a patrol plane spotted the survivors and radioed back their location. By the following day, 316 of the original 1,199 crew of the *Indianapolis* had been rescued. Two of those survivors were Adolfo Celaya (who returned to the basketball courts, earning all-state honors and eventually playing for San Jose State), and Giles McCoy (who played baseball in the St. Louis Browns minor league system but never made it to the big leagues).

On August 6, 1945, the *Indianapolis* survivors heard about the atomic bomb dropped on Hiroshima. News about the Indy's mission and its tragic demise began to trickle out. Many, now knowing the role they had played in bringing a sudden end to the war in the Pacific, didn't know whether to cheer or to cry.

22. Escalating the Bombing Campaign over Japan

"YOU SAW A PLANE BREAK UP. YOU SAW IT CATCH FIRE. YOU SAW TWO CHUTES, ONE OF THEM BURNING. IT COULD HAVE BEEN YOU. IT WAS A SUPERSTITIOUS RITUAL WE WERE PLAYING. THERE WERE A CERTAIN NUMBER OF BLACKBALLS TO BE PASSED OUT. EVERY TIME ANOTHER PLANE WENT DOWN, IT WAS TAKEN OUT OF PLAY."

—*Studs Terkel,* The Good War, *1984*

"A PEOPLE WHO ARE BOMBED TODAY AS THEY WERE BOMBED YESTERDAY, AND WHO KNOW THAT THEY WILL BE BOMBED AGAIN TOMORROW AND SEE NO END OF THEIR MARTYRDOM, ARE BOUND TO CALL FOR PEACE AT LENGTH."

—*Giulio Douhet,* The Command of the Air, *1921*

OPPOSITE: *During the surrender ceremony at Tokyo Bay, American planes put on an awesome show of force, just in case any of the Japanese thought they ever had a chance for a counterpunch in the closing months of the war. The mighty battleship USS* Missouri, *where the surrender document was signed, is in the foreground.* National Archives photo

AFTER AMERICAN BOMBERS FROM THE DOOLITTLE RAID roared off the flight deck of the carrier USS *Hornet* and bombed Tokyo in April 1942, the Japanese quickly established thousands of anti-aircraft gun batteries around every major city and industrial complex. Fighter pilots were recruited and trained to protect the home islands from enemy intruders. The Japanese were confident this defensive gauntlet would be impenetrable. To restore confidence among the masses, the military leadership promised there would be no more American bombers threatening any of Japan's population centers.

After the Doolittle mission and up through November 1943, there were no bomber bases or aircraft carriers anywhere in the Pacific within range of Japan. But once Eleventh Air Force bombers began operating in the Aleutians, B-24s could conduct missions to the Kuriles, just northeast of Japan. And as island after island in the South Pacific fell into Allied hands, bases were set up, closing the distance to Japan.

"When you're on a mission and you saw a Japanese plane go down, you cheered. This was a football game," wrote Studs Terkel in *The Good War*. "When one of your guys went down, you sighed. It was miserable. One of the saddest things I ever saw, when we were flying wing on a plane that got hit, was the barber's chair gunner in the big bubble at the very top.

"He was right there beside us in plain sight, beginning to go down. He just waved his hand goodbye. There was nothing you could do. You couldn't reach out to touch him."

ABOVE: *Newspaper headlines and radio broadcasts announced the dropping of the first atomic bomb on Hiroshima, Japan. Servicemen on Guam are obviously happy about the news.* National Archives photo

Arrival of the Superforts

A major turning point in the efforts to bomb Japan came with the deployment of the new B-29 Superfortress bombers, which could fly farther, faster, and higher than the lumbering workhorses, the B-24s and B-17s. The much larger B-29 could also carry a bigger payload and boasted its own arsenal of machine guns to knock down approaching enemy fighters.

The first B-29s arrived in Calcutta, India, in early 1944 and were deployed to Guam, Saipan, and Tinian a few months later. On November 24, 1944, 110 Superforts of the 21st Bomber Command took off for Tokyo, and even though they dropped a thousand bombs, cloud cover hindered many of the bombardiers. As a result, fewer than fifty bombs exploded even remotely close to their intended target. This problem would continue through December.

In assessing the dismal bomb damage, Air Force strategists determined that, while flying at much higher altitudes kept the B-29s out of range of anti-aircraft guns and fighter interceptors, flying well above the clouds also made visibility over the target a very real problem. Also, even on clear days, bombs tended to stray off course, due to the never-before-encountered jet stream.

The Japanese were just as concerned that their defenses were unable to knock this new threat out of the skies. They ordered their air forces throughout the Pacific to locate the B-29 bases somewhere in the Marianas. Through January 1945 eleven Superfortresses were destroyed on the ground, and another forty-three were damaged.

A Change in Strategy

General Curtis LeMay, commander of 21st Bomber Command (and a well-known sport pilot, who teamed up with others to win the Mackey Trophy in 1937), ordered a radical shift in bombing strategy in hopes of improving

accuracy. LeMay ordered all of the armaments taken out of the B-29s (except the tail gun and its crewman to handle rear defense). This lightening of the load allowed the planes to carry more bombs, specifically napalm and thermite bombs.

Also, instead of flying in massed formations—a tactic that had worked well over Europe—LeMay wanted his bombers to approach the targets in single file. And, no more high-altitude bombing. LeMay wanted his bombers "on the deck" to ensure better accuracy. Pilots and crewmen felt this last measure could be suicidal. At such low altitude they would be easy targets for both anti-aircraft gun batteries and enemy fighter planes.

"Hell, anyone with a peashooter could hit us!" was one sarcastic jab at LeMay's untested strategy.

A trial run of the modified B-29s was conducted on February 24 to Singapore, and the results—destruction of 40 percent of the warehouse district—proved LeMay's theory just might work. On March 9 B-29s from the Seventy-third, 313th, and 314th bomber groups flew past majestic Mount Fuji on the way to the first firebombing mission on Tokyo.

Japanese radar had picked up the approaching bombers, and fighter planes were sent aloft to intercept them. But those Japanese fighter pilots had already seen many other pilots shot down by the B-29 gunners, and so they maintained a safe distance, unaware that most of the guns had been taken out of the B-29s.

Flying in at low altitude, the crews could hear the air raid sirens blaring, and they could feel the heat as the fires from their incendiaries engulfed fifteen square miles of the city. One of those B-29 pilots was Rosy O'Donnell, who had played halfback for West Point when the Black Knights beat Knute Rockne's Notre Dame team 27–0. Another airman was former Oklahoma end Waddy Young, who nicknamed his B-29 Waddy's Wagon. During a mission to Tokyo on January 9, 1945, the Wagon was hit by flak and ditched at sea. There were no survivors.

Pro rodeo cowboy R. Lewis Bowman, who came from a legendary rodeo family, was a navigator

LEFT: *5th Marine Division "Spearhead" boxers tangle during their stay in Sasebo, Japan.* Courtesy of the 5th Marine Division

BELOW: *Waddy Young played end for Oklahoma's football team. When he became a B-29 bomber pilot he nicknamed his plane "Waddy's Wagon." The fun-loving crew re-created their bomber's nose art moniker. But on January 9, 1945, the "Wagon" was hit by flak during a mission to Tokyo and the entire crew perished.* U.S. Army Air Force photo

on B-17s and then became a flight engineer on a Superfort. (He would return home and become a prominent rancher in Arizona.)

Carrier-launched planes also participated in the bombing missions over Japan. Serving aboard the flattop *Enterprise* during the final months of the Pacific Campaign was University of Minnesota football, golf, and hockey star Bud Wilkinson. (In later years he would become head coach at Oklahoma, which became a powerhouse in college football.) Yankees first baseman Buddy Hassett served on the carrier USS *Bennington*, which was positioned just seventy miles off the coast of Japan and sent its planes on missions to Tokyo. (Hassett would never play major league ball again after returning home to New York.)

Unleashing the Firebombs

In rapid succession, the Allies hit Nagoya, then Osaka, and then Kobe in massive firebombing raids. As expected, the attacks had a demoralizing effect on the Japanese people, and the propagandists had a hard time convincing anyone that the Rising Sun was still winning the war. Japan's defense industry was grinding to a halt, as the bombings destroyed factories and feeder suppliers, and absenteeism rose among factory workers looking for safer places to live. Virtually every major city and all industrial centers were targeted in a campaign that lasted through the end of July 1945.

The Final Assault on Japan

Soon after Germany's surrender, several American combat divisions in Europe were given the news in mid-1945 that instead of returning home to the States as they had been hoping, they would instead be redeploying to the Pacific Theater. The final assault on Japan would require 4.5 million men.

The Allies were preparing for their biggest operation of the entire war, the invasion of Japan, which would kick off with Operation Olympic, the landing on the island of Kyushu, slated for November 1. From there thousands of bombers and fighter planes could strike the rest of Japan at will. At the same time a naval blockade would cut off Japan's lifeline of vital resources, while offshore shelling by thousands of warships would decimate hundreds of coastal cities and towns. This would last for four months. Then Operation Coronet—assault on the main island of Honshu, including Japan's largest city, Tokyo—would begin on March 1, 1946.

Among the GIs slated for the invasion of Japan were three baseball superstars: Pee Wee "the Little Colonel" Reese of the Brooklyn Dodgers, Boston Braves left-handed pitcher Warren Spahn, and Boston Red Sox slugger Bobby Doerr.

BELOW: *In mid-1939 Louisville Colonels hotshot shortstop Harold "Pee Wee" Reese would soon be picked up by the Brooklyn Dodgers, where he would roam the middle of the infield for many years. But during WWII, "the Little Colonel" was sent to Hawaii, then, like thousands of other American servicemen, he prepared for Operation Olympic, the dreaded invasion of Kyushu, Japan, in November of 1945. Two atomic bombs, though, convinced the Japanese emperor that his country could not withstand any further devastation. He ordered his military to surrender, and millions of weary Americans cheered the blessed news.*
AP Wide World photo

Twenty-first Bomber Command Chief Curtis LeMay felt his B-29 Superfortresses could simply bombard the Japanese into submission with the devastating effectiveness of firebombs. But after nearly four years of naval confrontations and island-hopping, interservice rivalries demanded that the Army, Navy, and Marines play a major role in the planning for the final assault, appropriately code-named Operation Downfall—the invasion of Japan.

Millions of Defenders

After the brutal and bloody experiences at Guadalcanal, Iwo Jima, and Okinawa, Americans knew an invasion of Japan would literally be a fight to the death, involving millions of Japanese men, women, and children, all trained to give their lives for their beloved emperor.

In April 1945 the Imperial Japanese Army issued "The Decree of the Homeland Decisive Battle," which spelled out what it would take to repel the invaders and ultimately win the war: "We shall throw everything conceivable, material and spiritual, into the battle and annihilate the enemy landing force by fierce and bold offensive attacks. Every soldier should fight to the last moment believing the final victory.

"Our people should fight to the last person to repel the enemy force. It is expected that the enemy might conduct these tactics [attacks by tanks, flamethrowers, and gas] that our civilians—women, old persons, and children—will be forced to march ahead of them to prevent our soldiers from shooting at the enemy. On this occasion, our soldiers should consider that the victory of the Empire is much more important than our own lives and not hesitate to destroy the enemy."

In 1945, as its forces deployed throughout the Pacific suffered defeat after defeat, the entire country of Japan braced itself for the inevitable Allied

ABOVE: *The sixteen-inch guns of the battleship* Missouri *open up on Japanese island fortifications, leaving a devastating "impression" on the enemy.* U.S. Navy photo

LEFT: *American bombers returning from attacks on Japan's home islands.* U.S. Navy photo

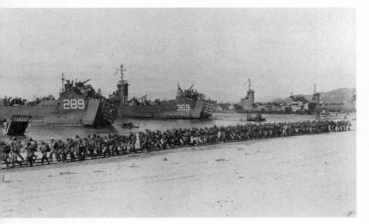

invasion, chanting a popular slogan: "One hundred million die proudly." Women and children were trained with bamboo spears and knives; boys with grenades strapped to their waist were shown how to scramble under an approaching enemy tank and blow it up. The fanaticism of the kamikaze was being taught to the innocents.

Honoring the Emperor

Late in the war the Japanese had introduced a terrifying weapon that devastated hundreds of Allied warships: the kamikaze.

Knowing of the impending invasion, more than five thousand kamikaze pilots were prepared to take to the skies over their homeland and guide their fighter planes—little more than flying bombs—at any approaching ship, sacrificing their lives to kill Americans. At sea, manned torpedoes and suicide boats could do the same, all in honor of the emperor. Japanese military leaders felt that these naval and aerial suicide jockeys could sink enough Allied war-ships to swing the balance of power back in their favor. An invasion of Japan would be nothing short of a massacre, and no American soldier, sailor, airman, or Marine was looking forward to it.

The "Pumpkins"

While other B-29s based at the remote island of Tinian were taking off almost daily on fire-bombing missions, the sleek silver Super-fortresses of the 509th Composite Group stood idle, only occasionally flying off some-where else to practice dropping single ball-shaped bombs jokingly called "pumpkins."

Activity at the far end of Tinian where the 509th was sequestered seemed to heighten after the USS *Indianapolis* arrived and a mysterious crate was off-loaded on July 26. Few people knew that the Indy had just delivered the com-ponent parts for an atomic bomb to be dropped over one of four Japanese cities: Kokura, Hiroshima, Nagasaki, or Niigata.

In command of the 509th was Colonel Paul Tibbets. On August 6 Tibbets flew the B-29 nicknamed the *Enola Gay* and dropped an atomic bomb on the city of Hiroshima, on the southwestern coast of Honshu. Several other B-29 crews were involved in the mission, including scout planes to the primary and alternate sites. One of the scout pilots was Major Claude Eatherly, who flew *Straight Flush* to Hiroshima that morning and reported back that visibility over the target area was good. (Prior to joining the Army Air Corps, Eatherly had played as an end on the North Texas State College football team.)

The atomic explosion, the mushroom cloud, and the overwhelming tidal wave of radioactive dust that enveloped Hiroshima was unlike anything the Japanese had ever seen.

ABOVE: *Battling it out in the football trenches was easy compared to some of the battles they had experienced in the Pacific. When the all-Pacific football tournament was held in 1945, the 11th Airborne Division team won the title.* U.S. Army photo

Power of the Sun

After hearing the news, President Harry Truman broadcast a radio mes-sage to the American people: "The force from which the sun

LEFT: *Leathernecks from the 5th Marine Division enjoy a game of football while on occupation duty in Sasebo, Japan, in late 1945.* Courtesy of the 5th Marine Division

RIGHT: *On the deck of the battleship* Missouri *Admiral Chester Nimitz signs the document marking Japan's official surrender, ending hostilities in World War II's Pacific Campaign.* U.S. Army photo

draws its power has been loosed upon those who brought war to the Far East. . . . If [the leaders of Japan] do not now accept our terms they may expect a rain of ruin from the air, the like of which has never been seen on this earth."

The Japanese cabinet debated whether to continue the fight or accept Truman's demand to surrender. To further persuade the procrastinating Japanese, Truman ordered a second atomic bomb. Major Charles Sweeney piloted the B-29 *Bock's Car* to the primary target, Kokura, which was obscured by drifting smoke from an earlier fire-bombing raid. After twice trying to locate the target, Sweeney headed for the alternate site, Nagasaki, devastating it with an atomic blast just after 11:00 A.M. on August 9.

The Emperor "Swallows Tears"

Despite this second bomb, the Japanese cabinet still could not decide what to do. Finally, Emperor Hirohito urged them to accept the surrender terms, saying, "I cannot bear to see my innocent people suffer any longer. It pains me to think of those who served me so faithfully, the soldiers and sailors who have been killed or wounded in far-off battles, the families who have lost all their worldly goods—and often their lives as well. The time has come when we must bear the unbearable. I swallow my tears and give my sanction to the proposal to accept the Allied proclamation."

After receiving word that the Japanese had surrendered, Admiral William "Bull" Halsey sent a message to his Third Fleet commanders: "Cease firing, but if any enemy planes appear, shoot them down in a friendly fashion!"

By early August most of the American supply ships were already loaded on the West Coast of the United States and waiting for movement orders to steam to North Asia. Combat divisions were already en route to the Pacific when news of the atomic bomb flashed around the world.

On board the escort carrier USS *Matanikau,* serving as fire and damage control officer was U.S. pole vault champion Cornelius Warmerdam, the first to ever clear fifteen feet.

BELOW: *It took nearly four years of brutal fighting, sometimes inch by inch, to defeat the Imperial War Machine of Japan. But finally, FINALLY, on September 2, 1945, the Japanese surrendered, on the USS* Missouri, *anchored in Tokyo Bay.* U.S. Navy photo

Warmerdam had dreams of competing in the Olympic Games, but the Games were cancelled in both 1940 and 1944, when he was in his prime, having won six AAU crowns.

As the *Matanikau* approached the waters near Japan, slated to conduct air strikes on the home islands, Warmerdam recalled, "I saw us as a sitting duck," possibly knowing how inviting a target an American flattop would be to a Japanese kamikaze. Fortunately the atomic bombs prompted the Japanese to give up the fight. (After returning home, Warmerdam also gave up his quest to compete in the Olympics.)

Naturally there was a collective sigh of relief among those service personnel assigned to the invasion of the home islands when Japan's surrender was announced. Loved ones in the States also said prayers of thanks that the conflict was finally over, that the boys would be coming home soon.

The Occupiers

American units began arriving for occupation duty in Japan, to disarm combatants and enforce the terms of the surrender agreement. Among the troops on occupation duty was Negro Leagues all-star infielder Marlin "Pee Wee" Carter, who was serving in the Coast Guard. While his ship was docked in Japan to off-load troops and supplies, Carter witnessed the devastation caused by the atomic bombs and the massive firebombing campaign.

On September 2, aboard the USS *Missouri* anchored in Tokyo Bay, the formal surrender was signed, marking the end of the Pacific Campaign and World War II. Witnessing the signing was Admiral Bull Halsey, who had played football for the *Missouri* just after the turn of the century. Halsey was once again on the Mighty Mo's "winning team" for what would be his greatest victory ever—the defeat of Imperial Japan.

ABOVE: *The offensive squad of the 41st Infantry Division's football team lines up while on occupation duty in the Kure-Hiroshima area of Japan in late 1945.* Courtesy of the 41st Infantry Division

LEFT: *On occupation duty in Japan, military police lieutenant Joe Ochsie, former New York Giants football player, towers over his Japanese counterpart.* U.S. Marine Corps photo

23. Returning Home, Finally

"THERE WERE MEN, SOME OF THEM YOUNG AND SOME FURTHER ALONG IN YEARS, [WHO] SURVIVED THE WAR, AS SO MANY MILLIONS HAD NOT, BUT THEY HAD COME OUT OF IT CHANGED, SOME CRIPPLED IN MIND AND BODY, SOME SIMPLY OLDER AND SLOWER, THEIR REFLEXES DULLED. THEY WEREN'T THE BOYS THEY'D BEEN BEFORE THEY'D CHANGED UNIFORMS, AND THEY NEVER WOULD BE AGAIN."

—*Frederick Turner*, When the Boys Came Back

"FOR ALL SAD WORDS OF TONGUE OR PEN, THE SADDEST ARE THESE: IT MIGHT HAVE BEEN!"

—*John Greenleaf Whittier*

"I'M NO HERO. THE REAL HEROES WERE THE ONES WHO NEVER CAME HOME. THEY HAD A ONE-WAY TRIP TO THE BEACHES AT NORMANDY OR THE ISLANDS IN THE PACIFIC. THE LUCKY ONES WERE STILL ALIVE."

—*Cleveland Indians pitcher Bob Feller*

FOR THE BATTLE-WEARY TROOPS IN EUROPE, AND THEN A few months later for those in the Pacific, coming home was bittersweet. For many months, even years, they had longed for what they had left behind—wives and sweethearts, family and friends. And they wanted it to be just like when they left. But they soon realized it would never be the same. Their war experiences had changed them forever. Many of the people they knew before had also gone off to war, and not everyone made it back.

One prominent sportsman who didn't return home was Paul Bunker, an all-American tackle and halfback at West Point before shipping out to the Philippines. He would be captured when Corregidor fell, survive the infamous Bataan Death March, but succumb to brutal conditions as a prisoner of war in the Pacific. Another of the fallen was Norwegian ski jump champion Torger Tokle, who served with the U.S. Tenth Mountain Division and was killed in Italy.

Sadly, they were just two of the many athletes who gave their lives in World War II.

Eager to Return

For America's athletes, coming home was a mixed bag. The war years had robbed them of precious playing time, whether for just one season or several. It wasn't just a two-year hitch.

OPPOSITE: *As their transport ship arrived at New York harbor, GIs lined the decks to see the beautiful lady with the lamp, the majestic Statue of Liberty.* National Archives photo

BELOW: *In WWII, black servicemen, such as this group boarding a transport ship in the China-Burma-India theater, proved they could fight alongside white soldiers. Soon color barriers, especially in sports, were torn down.* Army Signal Corps photo

Those who joined within days of Pearl Harbor, not to mention those who were already enlisted at the time, would have to serve for the duration of the war, nearly four long years. Some wouldn't return home until 1946 or '47, remaining in Europe or North Asia on occupation duty.

And no one came home immediately after Nazi Germany or Imperial Japan surrendered. Every GI had to earn a number of points before he would receive orders to return. No exceptions were granted for athletes hoping to get home for the next season. Without the required points they had to wait, serving as peacekeepers. When they did finally get back, some were able to rejoin their former teams without missing a beat, including Cleveland Indians fireball pitcher Bob Feller, Detroit Tigers slugger Hank Greenberg, and Chicago Bears quarterback Sid Luckman.

Dealing with Injuries

Others needed time to get back in shape or to recuperate from their war injuries. Washington Senators slugger Cecil Travis never did regain his hitting stroke after suffering from frostbitten feet during the Battle of the Bulge. He would rejoin the Senators and play in fifteen games in 1945, struggle through 1946, batting only .252, and finally retire midway through the '47 season.

Another Battle of the Bulge casualty who wouldn't get a chance to play again was George Poschner. On New Year's Day in 1943, Poschner was playing left end for Georgia against UCLA. The Georgia Bulldogs would beat the Bruins 9 to zip. Two years later, on January 8, 1945, Poschner was severely wounded in combat near Kohlhutte, France, and lay unattended where he had fallen, on a frozen battlefield, for two days. He would lose both legs and part of his right hand. While recuperating at a hospital in Atlanta, he vowed to return to the football field and play again on artificial legs. He never made it back.

Walter Masterson served aboard a ship at Guam and Midway and would need a year to get used to civilian life again and get back into playing shape. He appeared in only four games as a relief pitcher for the Washington Senators near the end of the 1945 season.

LEFT ABOVE: *Cheering servicemen and servicewomen from the China-Burma-India conflict arrive in New York on September 27, 1945 aboard an Army transport ship.* National Archives photo

LEFT BELOW: *Did they ever think they might see the United States again when they first shipped off to Europe? These soldiers, many having experienced things no one else could ever imagine, are obviously glad to be back, having just arrived in New York.* U.S. Army photo

Many veterans—not just athletes—needed time to readjust to the brutal combat they had experienced, to control their war nerves. The term commonly used to describe this ailment was shell shock. "I had only recently returned from the service with three years of athletic rust and a bad case of war nerves," admitted Negro Leagues player Monte Irvin. "I needed to work back into my pre-war playing condition. Neither my arm nor my eyesight was as good as it was before and I wasn't as fast as I had been. I had probably lost a step while I was in the Army, but I couldn't let that stop me." Irvin would regain his baseball skills and break into major league ball on his way to a Hall of Fame career.

One athlete who encouraged other disabled veterans not to give up was minor league pitcher Lou Brissie. Though severely wounded when shell fragments shattered his ankle, broke his left leg and both feet, and injured both of his hands in December 1944, Brissie would return home, endure months of physical therapy, experiment with different pitching styles to relieve the pain in his arm and legs, and eventually pitch for the Philadelphia Athletics.

Cardinals minor league pitcher Johnny Grodzicki arrived home on crutches,

after serving as an Army paratrooper in Europe. On March 30, 1945, during the assault on Berlin, he was severely injured when an enemy shell exploded nearby. Just a few years earlier doctors would have amputated his leg, but surgical techniques developed during the war saved the limb and gave him hope that he might be able to play baseball again. With no feeling in his leg, Grodzicki struggled to keep his balance on the pitching mound at the Cardinals spring training camp in 1946, and he had difficulty fielding bunts and ground balls or covering first base. Still, the team would carry him as a batting practice pitcher, allowing him to remain in baseball.

ABOVE: *Red Cross swimming instructors in West Virginia helped wounded combat veterans rehabilitate and resume normalcy to their lives as much as possible. Former minor league pitcher Lou Brissie was seriously wounded in both legs and hands when an enemy shell exploded nearby in December 1944. He underwent months recuperating and altered his pitching style to lessen the pain and would eventually join the Philadelphia Athletics.* Photo courtesy of the American Red Cross

Another inspiration was Athletics pitcher Phil Marchildon, shot down near Denmark. After a year in a Nazi POW camp, his weight had dropped nearly thirty pounds. Returning home in mid-1945, Marchildon was too weak to play baseball, but he was urged to come back for all the fans who wanted to see him again. Though the Athletics were averaging only 3,000 fans a game that year, nearly 35,000 turned out for Phil Marchildon Night. He would regain his weight and his strength for the 1946 season and played for four more years. Bert Shepard lost his leg when flak from a German anti-aircraft gun ripped through the cockpit of his plane during a mission to Berlin. He ended up in a POW camp, where an Allied doctor, also a prisoner, used scrap wood to make him a prosthetic leg, allowing him to build up his strength. But he never gave up his dream to one day pitch in the major leagues. Despite enormous odds against him, Shepard did fulfill his dream, pitching for the Washington Senators in 1945.

Like Shepard, collegiate diver Miller Anderson was wounded when his plane was hit by flak that ripped into his leg. Doctors threatened to amputate, but Anderson refused because without his leg he would never be able to dive again. It would take months of rehabilitation before Anderson returned to become a three-time all-American diving champion.

Art Larsen had fought in France with the Ninth Army and withstood a terrifying bombardment at Brest. After returning home, he would require months of therapy. Doctors suggested tennis to lick his fear of being killed. Larsen not only licked it, he conquered it on the way to winning the U.S. nationals' singles title.

Clovey La Croix was another tennis player who recovered from battle. After being hit by shrapnel while serving on board a cruiser in the South Pacific, La Croix wanted to thank the doctors who treated him. He decided to help other injured veterans by creating a special tennis racket for amputees.

Because of their injuries, many other disabled athletes could only sit in the stands and watch others play the sports they loved, like Detroit Lions star receiver Footsie Britt. Britt received the Medal of Honor in the Italian Campaign; during a subsequent conflict, an enemy shell exploded nearby, shredding his arm into a bloody stump.

Michigan's Old 98, running back Tom Harmon, who terrorized opposing defenses in 1939 and '40, ripping them for 2,338 yards while scoring thirty-three touchdowns, was a fighter pilot in the China-Burma-India Campaign. Twice his plane was shot down and he parachuted behind enemy lines, making his way into partisan hands and eventually back to friendly forces. But the physical effects—severe burns on his legs when his plane caught fire, the jolt of those parachute landings, and the wear and tear

of evading Japanese forces in mountainous and jungle terrain—took a severe toll. He would return home and struggle through two seasons with the Los Angeles Rams, never quite regaining the explosiveness he had at Michigan.

Returning from War, Going to School

But for many athletes—those who had joined the armed forces right out of high school—the GI Bill of Rights gave them an opportunity to go to college. These battle-hardened veterans had withstood the hardships of war and had grown up fast. By the thousands they were enrolling in colleges and universities throughout the country. And if they couldn't get an athletic scholarship then they'd simply try out for the team and pile-drive any pimple-faced kids who got in their way!

No longer would two-a-day football drills under a sweltering summer sun bother them. Playing in a downpour or pounding it out on an ice-hardened field was nothing compared to what they'd experienced overseas.

"The Army makes you grow up, fast. It's the discipline." emphasized Braves pitcher Warren Spahn. "That had to help me in baseball. I found out that you didn't get pneumonia if you were lying in a trench or on the ice. I fought the fatigue barrier and developed stamina. In other words, I learned that I could do what I made up my mind to do. When you're at maximum effort, which a war demands, you're not cognizant of anything else around you, and that's the same in baseball. You just go out and do it."

Fighting for Their Old Jobs

Many pro athletes just wanted to resume their careers, and the Veterans Act stated that all returning servicemen were entitled to their old jobs at the same pay for a year. But many sports team owners didn't feel the law applied to them. Players were demoted or simply cut without complaint, most unaware they had the right to challenge their treatment. One who dared was minor league ballplayer Al Nimiec, who played for the Seattle Rainiers of the Pacific Coast League. Judge Lloyd Black in federal district court

BELOW: *Bert Shepard was determined to become a major league pitcher, though the war postponed that dream. During the bombing campaign over Europe, he was a fighter pilot, who was shot down when his plane was hit by flak. His leg was blasted to shreds in the attack and he lost consciousness, somehow surviving the crash landing.*

He ended up in a POW camp where a fellow prisoner made a prosthetic stump so he could hobble around without crutches. Shep immediately started rebuilding his leg strength and modified his pitching motion, still intent on getting to the big leagues when the war was over.

In 1945, after returning home, disabled war veteran Bert Shepard finally got in a game with the Washington Senators, inspiring thousands of wounded vets to lick their wounds and get on with their lives. AP Wide World photo

heard Nimiec's grievance and sided with him, stating: "Youth must be served, but not at the expense of men who have worn the uniform." Judge Black also took the opportunity to hammer the restrictions of a ballplayer's standard contract, comparing it to the treatment of slaves. From this and other challenges the short-lived American Baseball Guild formed to act on behalf of the players. It was a forerunner to players' unions in every professional sport.

After withstanding some pretty tough fights with the Germans and the Japanese, American athletes after World War II were ready to make up for lost time. They had survived some of the toughest battles of this century, and yet they were ready to do battle again, on baseball diamonds and football fields, tennis courts and golf courses throughout the country. The athletes who came out of the pivotal era of World War II were about to shatter the record books and create a little sports history of their own.

RIGHT ABOVE: *As a boy, Dwight Eisenhower dreamed of one day becoming a big league ballplayer. At West Point, he was also attracting attention on the gridiron. Circumstances though changed his career plans and, after spearheading Allied forces to victory in Europe, he returned home and was again mustered into service . . . as President of the United States.* U.S. Army photo

RIGHT BELOW: *Wine, women, and song were obviously high on the list of indulgences for these returning servicemen. They're the lucky ones. Thousands more remained overseas on occupation duty, in both Europe and the northern Pacific, waiting to rotate back home.* Department of Defense photo

An Unfulfilled Dream

One athlete who didn't pursue sports after World War II but would leave his mark on world history was General Dwight D. Eisenhower, a talented baseball and football player while at West Point. During the war in Europe he was supreme commander of all forces in the theater. Ike returned home in June 1945 as a conquering hero and soon attended a Giants/Braves ball game in New York. As an avid fan, Eisenhower quickly noticed the drop-off in talent from what he remembered before the war. Finally, in the sixth inning, he asked Giants owner Horace Stoneham, "What the hell has happened to the pitching since I went away to the war?"

After directing the dismantling of Fortress Europe and Hitler's Thousand-Year Reich, Eisenhower turned his attention to politics. Riding a wave of popularity, he became president of the United States in 1953.

Later Ike would share this story about his childhood dream: "When I was a boy growing up in Kansas, a friend of mine and I went fishing, and as we sat there in the warmth of a summer afternoon on a riverbank, we talked about what we wanted to do when we grew up.

"I told him I wanted to be a real major-league baseball player, a genuine professional like Honus Wagner. My friend said that he'd like to be President of the United States.

"Neither of us got our wish."

Bibliography

Allen, Frederick Lewis, *The Big Change: America Transforms Itself, 1900–1950.* Harper & Row, NY 1952
— *Since Yesterday. The Nineteen-Thirties in America.* Harper, NY, 1940
Allen, George with Ben Olan, *Pro Football's 100 Greatest Players,* Bobbs-Merrill Company, Indianapolis, Indiana, 1982
Allen, Kevin, "1980 'Miracle on Ice' wasn't first," *USA Today,* January 15, 2002
Allen, Maury, *Where Have You Gone, Joe DiMaggio?,* E.P. Dutton & Co, NY, 1975
— *You Could Look it Up. The Life of Casey Stengel,* Times Book, NY, 1979
— *Baseball's 100,* A&W Visual Library, NY, 1981
Allen, Thomas B., "The Wings of War," *National Geographic,* March 1994
— and Norman Polmar, *Code-Name Downfall,* Simon & Schuster, NY, 1995
Alvarez, Mark, ed, *The Perfect Game,* Barnes & Noble Books, NY, 1993
Ambrose, Stephen E., *Citizen Soldiers,* Simon & Schuster, NY, 1997
— *D-Day. June 6, 1944: The Climactic Battle of World War II,* Simon & Schuster, NY, 1994
— *The Wild Blue. The Men and Boys Who Flew the B-24s Over Germany,* Simon & Schuster, NY, 2001
— *Eisenhower: Soldier, General of the Army, President-Elect,* Simon & Schuster, NY, 1983
American Heritage and United Press International Editors, *Eisenhower. American Hero,* McGraw-Hill, NY, 1969
Amoruso, Marino, *Gil Hodges. The Quiet Man,* Paul S. Erickson, Middlebury, Vermont, 1991
Anderson, Dave, *Pennant Races. Baseball at its Best,* Doubleday, NY
— "Conerly Was Toughest of the Giants," *NY Times,* 1996
— with Murray Chass, Robert Creamer and Harold Rosenthal, *The Yankees. The Four Fabulous Eras of Baseball's Most Famous Team,* Random House, NY, 1979
Andrews, Peter, "A Place to Be Lousy In," *American Heritage,* December 1991
Antonen, Mel, "The Time of their Lives," *USA TODAY,* December 29, 1999
Asbell, Bernard, *When F.D.R. Died,* Holt. Rinehart and Winston, NY, 1961
Ashe, Arthur R. Jr., *A Hard Road to Glory. The History of the African-American Athlete in Baseball,* Amistad Press
Associated Press Sports Staff, *A Century of Sports,* Plimpton Press, NY, 1971
Astor, Gerald, *June 6, 1944. The Voices of D-Day,* St. Martin's Press, NY
Auerbach, Red, with Joe Fitzgerald, *On & Off the Court,* MacMillan, NY, 1985
Baack, Lawrence J., ed. *The Worlds of Brutus Hamilton,* Book Division of Track and Field News
Bak, Richard, *Casey Stengel,* Taylor Publishing, Dallas, Texas, 1997
Baldwin, Hanson, *Battles Lost and Won. Great Campaigns of World War II,* Harper and Row, 1966
Barber, Red, *The Broadcasters,* The Dial Press, NY, 1970
Barnett, Correlli, *The Battle of El Alamein: Decision in the Desert,* MacMillan, NY, 1964

Baron, Scott, *They Also Served. Military Biographies of Uncommon Americans,* MIE Publishing, Spartanburg, SC, 1998

Bartsch, William, *Doomed at the Start,* Texas A&M University Press. College Station, Texas, 1992

Baumont, Maurice, *The Origins of the Second World War* (translated from French by Simone de Couvreur Ferguson), Yale University Press, 1978

Belden, Jack, *Retreat with Stilwell,* Alfred A. Knopf, NY 1943

Bell, Joseph N., *Bowl Game Thrills,* Julian Messner, Inc, NY

Belote, James H. and William M., *Corregidor, The Saga of a Fortress,* Harper & Row, NY, 1967

Beltrone, Art and Lee, *A Wartime Log,* Howell Press, Charlottesville, Virginia, 1994

Bennett, Geoffrey, *Naval Battles of World War II,* David McKay, 1975

Berkow, Ira, "Larry Doby Crossed Color Barrier Behind Robinson," *St. Louis Post Dispatch,* March 2, 1997
  — *Red: A Biography of Red Smith,* Times Books, NY, 1986
  — and Jim Kaplan, *The Gospel According to Casey,* St. Martin's Press, NY, 1992

Berra, Yogi, with Tom Horton, *YOGI, It Ain't Over,* Harper Paperbacks, NY, 1989

Bevan, Denys, *United States Forces in New Zealand, 1942–1945,* Macpherson Publishing, New Zealand, 1992

Biggs, Bradley, *The Triple Nickles,* Archon Books, 1986

Birdsall, Steve, *Log of the Liberators,* Doubleday, NY, 1973

Bjarkman, Peter C., *The Encyclopedia of Pro Basketball Team Histories,* Carroll & Graf Publishers, NY

Blair, Clay Jr., *MacArthur,* Nelson Doubleday, Garden City, NY
  — *Ridgway's Paratroopers: The American Airborne in World War II,* Doubleday, Garden City, NY, 1985
  — *Silent Victory: The U.S. Submarine War Against Japan,* J.B. Lippincott, 1975
  — and Joan, *The Search for J.F.K.,* Berkley Publishing, NY, 1976

Blum, John Morton, *V Was for Victory: Politics and American Culture During World War II,* Harcourt Brace Jovanovich, 1976

Blumenson, Martin, *The Patton Papers,* Houghton Mifflin Company, Boston
  — "The Struggle for Rome," *American History Illustrated,* June 1983

Bock, Hal, "Revolution: 50 Years Ago, Baseball's Color Barrier Began to Crack," *St. Louis Post-Dispatch,* August 27, 1995

Bollow, John, "Remembering the WASPs," *Saturday Evening Post,* Indianapolis, Indiana, May/June 1995

Bowman, John S. and Joel Zoss, *The American League,* Gallery Books, NY, 1986

Boyle, David, *World War II. A Photographic History,* Metro Books, The Netherlands, 2001

Bradley, Donald, "The Series, 1944: Baseball vs. War," *Kansas City Star,* October 23, 1994

Bradley, Omar N., *A Soldier's Story,* Henry Holt, 1951
  — and Blair, Clay, *A General's Life,* Simon and Schuster, NY, 1983

Bradshaw, Thomas I., and Marsha L. Clark, *Carrier Down,* Eakin Press, Austin, Texas

Brady, Erik, "Pioneer found pain, not fame in pro football," *USA TODAY,* September 20, 1995

Brady, James, "Yogi Berra," *Parade,* July 11, 1999
— "Pee Wee Reese," *Parade,* September 15, 1996

Branch, Elizabeth, "Col. Red Reeder," West Point Assc. of Graduates web site

Brereton, Lewis H., *Brereton Diaries,* William Morrow, 1946

Breuer, William B., *Geronimo! American Paratroopers in World War II*
— *Operation Torch. The Allied Gamble to Invade North Africa,"* St. Martin's Press, NY
— *Devil Boats. The PT War Against Japan,* Presidio Press, Novato, CA
— *The Great Raid on Cabanatuan,* John Wiley & Sons, NY

Broeg, Bob, "Counsilman and Conzelman both made their marks," *St. Louis Post-Dispatch,* June 4, 2000
— "Movie shows how Greenberg worked to become great," *St. Louis Post-Dispatch,* June 11, 2000
— "60 years later, Louis' victory recalled fondly," *St. Louis Post-Dispatch,* June 28, 1998
— *Stan Musial, the Man's Own Story,* Doubleday & Company, Garden City, NY, 1964

Brokaw, Tom, *An Album of Memories,* Random House, NY, 2001

Bruns, Bill, *Sooner,* Josten's Publications, Topeka, Kansas, 1074

Bulkley, Robert J., Jr., *At Close Quarters: PT Boats in the United States Navy,* Government Printing Office, 1962

Burns, James MacGregor, *John Kennedy: A Political Profile,* Harcourt, Brace, NY, 1960
— *Roosevelt: The Lion and the Fox,* Harcourt, Brace, NY, 1956
— *Roosevelt: The Soldier of Freedom,* Harcourt Brace Javanovich, NY, 1970

Burrows, Mike, "Medal tested," Denver Post web site, June 12, 2003

Byrd, Martha H., "Battle of the Philippine Sea," *American History Illustrated,* Harrisburg, PA, July 1977

Campbell, Jim, *Golden Years of Pro Football,* Crescent Books, NY, 1993

Carlson, Lewis, "The Universal Athletic Sport of the World," *American History Illustrated,* Harrisburg, PA, April 1984

Carroll, Bob, *100 Greatest Running Backs,* Crescent Books, NY, 1989

Casewit, Curtis W., *Mountain Troopers!,* Thomas Y. Crowell Company, NY

Cataneo, David, *Baseball Legends and Lore,* Barnes & Noble Books, Nashville, Tennessee, 1997

Center of Military History, United States Army, *The U.S. Army in World War II,* Vol. 1–3, Artabras Publishers, NY, 1190

Chadwick, Bruce, *Boston Red Sox. Memories and Mementoes of New England's Team,* Abbeville Press, NY, 1992

Chang, Thelma, *I Can Never Forget. Men of the 100th/442nd*

Chennault, Claire L., *Way of a Fighter,* G.P. Putnam's Sons, 1949

Childers, Thomas, *Wings of Morning,* Addison-Wesley Publishing, NY, 1995

Chudakov, Grigori, and David E. Scherman, *Allies,* MacMillan Publishing, NY, 1989

Clark, Mark, *Calculated Risk,* Harper and Brothers, 1950

Clary, Jack, *Field of Valor,* Triumph Books, Chicago, Illinois, 2002

Clay, Lucius D., *Decision in Germany,* Doubleday, NY, 1950

Clerici, Gianni, translated by Richard J. Wiezell, *The Ultimate Tennis Book*, Follett Publishing Company, Chicago

Cleveland, Charles B. "Murder on Ice," *Foreign Service magazine*, December 1948

Cloe, John Haile, *The Aleutian Warriors,*

Cobb, Ty with Al Stump, *My Life in Baseball. The True Record,* Doubleday, Garden City, NY, 1961

Coffey, Thomas M., *Decision Over Schweinfurt: The U.S. 8th Air Force Battle for Daylight Bombing,* David McKay, 1977

Cohane, Tim, *Bypaths of Glory*

Cohen, Stan, *The Games of '36,* Pictorial Histories Publishing Company, Missoula, Montana, 1996

Collier, Basil, *The Second World War: A Military History,* William Morrow, 1967
— *The War in the Far East,* William Morrow, NY, 1968
— *The Battle of Britain,* MacMillan, NY, 1962

Comer, John, *Combat Crew. A True Story of Flying and Fighting in World War II,* William Morrow and Company, NY

Commager, Henry Steele, ed., *The American Destiny: Global War,* The Danbury Press, 1976

Compton, Karl T., "If the Atomic Bomb Had Not Been Used" *Atlantic Monthly,* December 1946

Congdon, Don, ed. *The Thirties: A Time to Remember,* Simon and Schuster, NY, 1962

Connor, Anthony J., *Voices from Cooperstown,* Collier Books, NY

Considine, Bob, "Louis Knocks Out Schmeling," *Red Smith's Favorite Sports Stories*

Cooper, Charles, *Tuskegee Heroes*

Cox, James A., "'Tokyo Bombed! Doolittle Do'od It'" *Smithsonian,* June 1992

Craig, William, *The Fall of Japan,* Dial Press, 1967

Cramer, Richard Ben, *Joe DiMaggio. The Hero's Life,* Simon and Schuster, NY, 2000

Curran, Bob, *Pro Football's Rag Days,* Bonanza Books, NY,

Daniels, Jonathan, *The Time Between the Wars: Armistice to Pearl Harbor,* Doubleday, NY, 1966

Danzig, Allison and Schwed, Peter, ed., *The Fireside Book of Tennis,* Simon and Schuster, NY, 1972

Davis, Kevin S., *Soldier of Democracy,* Doubleday, NY,

Davis, Mac, *100 Greatest Sports Feats,* Grosset & Dunlap, NY, 1964

Daws, Gavin, *Prisoners of the Japanese,* William Morrow and Company, NY

Dear, I.C.B., ed., *The Oxford Companion to World War II,* Oxford University Press, NY, 1995

DeArmond, Mike, "Twins at MU: Chapter One," *Kansas City Star,* December 18, 1994

DeChant, John A., *Devilbirds: The Story of Marine Corps Aviation in World War II,* Harper and Brothers, 1947

Deford, Frank, "Almost a HERO," *Sports Illustrated,* December 3, 2001

Deutsch, Jordan A., with David S. Neft, Roland T. Johnson and Richard M. Cohen, *The Sports Encyclopedia: Pro Basketball,* Grosset & Dunlap, NY

Devaney, John, *The Story of Basketball,* Random House, NY, 1976

Dickey, Glenn, *The History of the World Series,* Stein and Day, NY, 1984

Dickson, Paul, *Baseball's Greatest Quotations,* Harper Perennial, NY, 1992

DiMaggio, Dom, with Bill Gilbert, *Real Grass, Real Heroes,* Zebra Books, NY, 1990

Ditrani, Vinny, "When Jackie Robinson Broke Down the Barriers," *Baseball Digest,* Evanston, Illinois, August 1987

Dodd, Mike, "The year Rose Bowl left home," *USA Today,* December 19, 2001

Dole, Bob and Elizabeth, *Unlimited Partners*

Dollinger, Hans, (translated from German by Arnold Pomerans), *The Decline and Fall of Nazi Germany and Imperial Japan* Bonanza Books, 1968

Donovan, Arthur J. Jr., and Drury, Bob, *Fatso, Football When Men Were Really Men,* William Morrow and Company, NY, 1987

Donovan, Robert J., *Eisenhower: The Inside Story,* Harper, NY, 1956

Doolittle, James H., "IMPACT. Daylight Precision Bombing," *American History Illustrated,* Harrisburg, PA, February 1980

Duffy, Joe, "Willie 'Pepped Up' our Friday Nights," *Reminisce,* January/February 1995

Duplacey, James and Eric Zweig, *A Century of Hockey Heroes,* Somerville House, NY, 1999

Dupuy, R. Ernest, *World War II. A Compact History,* Hawthorn, 1969

Durand, Arthur A., *Stalag Luft III. The Secret Story,* Simon & Schuster, NY

Durso, Joseph, *DiMaggio,* Little, Brown and Company, Boston,

Edey, Maitland A., ed. *This Fabulous Century: Six Years of American Life* (volumnes IV, 1930–40 and V, 1940–50), Time-Life Books, NY, 1969
— *TIME Capsule: A History of the Year Condensed from the pages of TIME,* Time-Life Books, NY, 1933 to 1946

Edgren, Robert, "Jack Dempsey's Hardest Fight," *America: An Illustrated Diary of its Most Exciting Years,* American Family Enterprises, 1972

Eighty-ninth Infantry Division Historical Board, *The 89th Infantry Division, 1942–1945,* Infantry Journal Press, Washington

Einstein, Charles, ed. *The Baseball Reader,* McGraw-Hill, NY, 1980
— *The Fireside Book of Baseball,* Simon & Schuster, NY

Eisenbath, Mike, "Mr. Baseball. For Half a Century, Kissell has Taught the Cardinals' Way," *St. Louis Post Dispatch,* March 30, 1997

Eisenhower, Dwight D., *At Ease: Stories I Tell to Friends,* Doubleday, NY, 1967
— *Crusade in Europe,* Doubleday, NY,1948
— *The Papers of Dwight D. Eisenhower. The War Years,* (edited by Alfred D. Chandler, Jr., and Stephen E. Ambrose), Johns Hopkins University Press, 1970

Eisinger, Chester E., ed. *The 1940s: Profile of a Nation in Crisis,* Doubleday Anchor Books, NY 1968

Eskenazi, Gerald, *The Lip,* William Morrow and Company, NY

Esposito, Vincent J., ed. *A Concise History of World War II,* Frederick A. Praeger, 1964

Essame, Hubert, *Patton: A Study in Command,* Charles Scribner's Sons, 1974
— *The Battle for Germany,* Charles Scribner's Sons, NY, 1969

Etkin, Jack, *Innings Ago,* Normandy Square Publications, Kansas City, Missouri, 1987

Ewing, Joseph H., *29 Let's Go!,* Infantry Journal Press, Washington

Falkner, David, *Great Time Coming. The Life of Jackie Robinson from Baseball to Birmingham,* Simon & Schuster, NY

Farago, Ladislas, *Patton: Ordeal and Triumph*, Ivan Obolensky, NY, 1963

Fimrite, Ron, "A Call to Arms," *Sports Illustrated Classic magazine*
— "A Look Back At the Glory Days," *Sports Illustrated Classic*, 1973

Flaherty, Tom, *The U.S. Open, 1895–1965*, E.P. Dutton, NY, 1966

Flanagan, Edward M. Jr., *The Angels. A History of the 11th Airborne Division, 1943–1946*, Infantry Journal Press, Washington

Flower, Desmond, and Reeves, James, eds. *The Taste of Courage. The War, 1939–1945*, Harper and Brothers, 1960

Fowle, Barry W., ed., *Builders and Fighters*

Fox, Stephen, *Big Leagues*, William Morrow and Company, NY, 1994

Francis, Charles E., *The Tuskegee Airmen*

Frayne, Trent, *The Best of Times. Fifty Years of Canadian Sport*, Key Porter Books, Toronto, Canada, 1988

Fried, Ronald K., *Corner Men*, Four Walls Eight Windows, NY

Friedrich, Otto, "Monte Cassino: a story of death and resurrection," *Smithsonian*, April 1987

Fuller, John C., *The Second World War, 1939–1945: A Strategic and Tactical History*, Duell, Sloan and Pearce, 1949

Furlong, William Barry, "How the war in France changed football forever," *Smithsonian magazine*, February 1986

Gallico, Paul, *The Golden People*, Doubleday & Company, Garden City, New York, 1965

Games of the XXIIIrd Olympiad, Los Angeles 1984 Commemorative Book, International Sport Publications, Salt Lake City, UT 1984

Garber, Angus G. III, *Champions! The Greatest Sports Legends of All Time*, Mallard Press, NY, 1990

Garfield, Brian, *The Thousand-Mile: World War II in Alaska and the Aleutians*, Ballantine Books, 1969

George, Nelson, *Elevating the Game*,

Gietscher, Steve, "Go west, young Rams," *Sporting News*, January 23, 1995

Gilbert, Bill, *They Also Served. Baseball and the Home Front, 1941–1945*, Crown Publishers, Inc., NY

Gildea, William, "Donovan Still Casts a Big Shadow," Washington Post, 1986

Givens, Horace, "Hal Schumacher Recalls the Old NY Giants," *Baseball Digest*, January 1984

Glines, Col. Carroll V., *Four Came Home*

Golenbock, Peter, *Fenway*, G.P. Putnam's Sons, NY
— *Wrigleyville*

Goodman, Jack, ed. *While You Were Gone: A Report on Wartime Life in the United States*, Simon and Schuster, NY, 1946

Goralski, Robert, *World War II Almanac: 1931–1945*, G.P. Putnam's Sons, New York, 1981

Gowdy, Curt with Powers, John, *Seasons to Remember*, HarperCollins Publishers

Graham, Frank Jr., *A Farewell to Heroes*, The Viking Press, NY

Gregorich, Barbara, *Women at Play. The Story of Women in Baseball*

Gregory, Robert, *Diz*, Viking

Guderian, Heinz, (translated from German by Constantine FitzGibbon), *Panzer Leader* E.P. Dutton, 1952

Gunther, John, *Roosevelt in Retrospect: A Profile in History,* Harper, NY, 1950

Guthrie, Bill, *Hall of Famers. All-Time Greats of Four Major Sports,* Stadia Sports Publishing, NY, 1973

Gutman, Bill, *They Made it a Whole New Ball Game,* Tempo Books, NY, 1975

— *The Pictorial History of College Basketball,* Gallery Books, NY, 1989

Halberstam, David, ed., *The Best American Sports Writing of the Century,*

— and Glenn Stout, *The Best American Sports Writing, 1991,* Houghton Mifflin Company, Boston, 1991

Hall, Tony, *D-Day.The Invasion in Photographs,* Salamander Books, Stamford, Connecticut, 1994

Halsey, William F., and Bryan III, J. *Admiral Halsey's Story,* McGraw-Hill, 1947

Hamilton, Nigel, *JFK, Reckless Youth,* Random House, NY

Hammel, Eric, *Aces Against Germany,* Pocket Books, NY

Hand, Jack, *Heroes of the NFL,* Random House, NY, 1965

Hansen, C.B., "Unforgettable Omar Bradley," *Reader's Digest,* August 1987

Harris, Sir Arthur, *Bomber Offensive,* MacMillan, 1947

Harris, Mark J., with Franklin D. Mitchell and Steven J. Schechter, "Rosie the Riveter Remembers," *The Homefront: America During World War II,* Putnam, NY

— *Diamond. Baseball Writings of Mark Harris,* Donald I. Fine, NY, 1994

Harwell, Ernie, *Diamond Gems,* Avon Books, NY, 1991

Hastings, Max, *Bomber Command: The Myths and Reality of the Strategic Bombing Offensive, 1939–1945,* Dial Press, 1979

Hechler, Ken, *The Bridge at Remagen,* Ballantine Books, 1957

Heiferman, Ronald, *World War II,* Octopus Books, 1975

Heiman, Lee, Dave Weiner and Bill Gutman, *When the Cheering Stops . . .,* MacMillan, NY, 1990

Hendrickson, Joe, *Tournament of Roses,* Knapp Press, Los Angeles, 1989

Henry, Mark R. *The US Army in World War II,* Osprey Publishing, Oxford, United Kingdom, 2001

Hersey, John, *Hiroshima,* Kno pf, NY, 1946

Herskowitz, Mickey, "A Level Playing Field," *Gameday magazine,* October 15, 1995

Herzog, Brad, "Modeled on a Myth," *Sports Illustrated,* December 29, 1997

Higdon, Hal, *Pro Football, USA,* G.P. Putnam's Sons, NY, 1968

Hirshberg, Al, *Basketball's Greatest Stars,* G.P. Putnam's Sons

Historical Division, U.S. War Department, *American Forces in Action,* U.S. War Department, 1945

History of the Second World War, all issues, BPC Publishing, London

Hockaday, Laura R., "Slick, Strong and Steady," *Kansas City Star,* February 17, 1999

Holland, Gerald, "Is That You Up There, Johnny Blood?" *Fireside Book of Football,* Simon & Schuster, NY, 1964

Hollander, Zander, ed., *The Pro Basketball Encyclopedia,* Corwin Books, Thousand Oaks, CA, 1977

Holm, Jeanne, *Women in the Military*

Holmes, A. Lawrance, ed., *More than a game,* MacMillan, NY, 1967

Holmes, Judith, *Olympiad 1936. Blaze of glory for Hitler's Reich,* Ballantine

Books, NY, 1971

Holtzman, Jerome, "Major League Talent Scouts: Baseball's Unknown Soldiers," *Baseball Digest,* September 1986

Holway, John, *Voices from the Great Black Baseball Leagues,* Da Capo Press, NY
— *Black Diamonds,* Stadium Books\
— *Blackball Stars,* Carroll & Graf Publishers/Richard Gallen, NY

Honan, William H., *Visions of Infamy,* St. Martin's Press, NY, 1991

Honig, Donald, *Baseball America,* MacMillan Publishing Company, NY
— *Baseball. When the Grass Was Real*
— *The NY Yankees l*
— *The October Heroes,* Simon and Schuster, NY, 1979

Hough, Frank O., *The Island War: The United States Marine Corps in the Pacific,* J.B. Lippincott, 1947

Howarth, David, *D-Day, The Sixth of June, 1944,* McGraw-Hill, NY, 1959

Howe, Robert F., "They Turned the Tide," *Smithsonian,* August 2002

Hoyle, Martha Byrd, *A World in Flames: A History of World War II,* Atheneum, 1969

Hoyt, Edwin P., *The Battle of Leyte Gulf,* Pinnacle Books, 1973

Hudson, Alec, *Up Periscope! And Other Stories,* Naval Institute Press, Annapolis, Maryland, 1992

Hyams, Joe, *Flight of the Avenger. George Bush at War,* Harcourt Brace Jovanovich, San Diego, 1991

Ienaga, Saburo, *The Pacific War: World War II and the Japanese, 1931–1945,* (translated from Japanese by Frank Baldwin), Pantheon Books, 1978

Infield, Glenn, *Big Week. The Classic Story of the Crucial Air Battle of WWII,* Brassey's

Irvin, Monte with Riley, James A., *Nice Guys Finish First,* Carroll & Graf Publishers, NY

Jablonski, Edward, *Airwar,* Doubleday, NY, 1971–1972

James, Bill, *The Bill James Historical Baseball Abstract,* Villard Books, New York, 1986

James, D. Clayton, *The Years of MacArthur, 1941–1945,* Houghton Mifflin, 1975

Jones, James, *WWII. A Chronical of Soldiering,* Balantine Books, 1976

Johnson, Dick, and Glenn Stout, *Ted Williams, A Portrait in Words and Pictures,* Walker and Company, NY, 1991

Johnson, Susan F., *When Women Played Hardball*

Johnston, Stanley, *Queen of the Flat-Tops,* Nelson Doubleday, Inc., Garden City, NY

Kahn, David, *The Code-Breakers,* MacMillan, NY, 1967

Kahn, Roger, *The Boys of Summer,*
— *Games We Used to Play*
— *Memories of Summer,* Hyperion, NY

Kariher, Harry C., *Who's Who in Hockey,* Arlington House, New Rochelle, New York

Karst, Gene and Martin J. Jones, Jr., *Who's Who in Professional Baseball,* Arlington House, New Rochelle, NY, 1973

Kashatus, William, "Baseball's Noble Experiment," *American History* magazine, April 1997

Kaufman, Louis, Barbara Fitzgerald and Tom Sewell, *Moe Berg. Athlete, Scholar,*

Spy, Little, Brown, Boston, 1974

Keegan, John, ed. *The Rand McNally Encyclopedia of World War II,* Rand McNally, 1977

— *Six Armies in Normandy: From D-Day to the Liberation of Paris,* Penguin Books, NY, 1983

— *The Second World War,* Viking, NY, 1989

— *Who was Who in World War II,* Thomas Y. Crowell Publishers, NY, 1978

Kelley, Brent P., *They Too Wore Pinstripes,* McFarland and Co., Jefferson, North Carolina, 1998

Kerkhoff, Blair, "Grand Old Player," *Kansas City Star,* August 13, 1996

Kiersh, Edward, *Where Have You Gone, Vince DiMaggio?,* Bantam Books, New York, 1983

Killanin, Lord and John Rodda, *The Olympic Games,* MacMillan, NY, 1976

King, Peter, *Football. A History of the Professional Game,* Bishop Books, 1997

Klinkowitz, Jerry ed., *Writing Baseball,* University of Illinois Press, Chicago, Illinois, 1991

Koenig, Bill, "The War Years," *USA Today Baseball Weekly,* August 16–22, 1995

Kurzman, Dan, *Left to Die. The Tragedy of the USS Juneau,* Pocket Books, New York

— *Fatal Voyage,* Atheneum, NY, 1990

LaForte, Robert S., and Ronald E. Marcello, ed., *Remembering Pearl Harbor,* Scholarly Resources Books, Wilmington, Delaware, 1991

Lalire, Gregory, "With the word at war, the game of baseball contributed to final victory in its own way," *WWII* magazine, September 1993

Lamb, Richard, *The Drift to War, 1922–1939,* St. Martin's Press, NY, 1991

Landry, Tom with Gregg Lewis, *Tom Landry,* HarperCollins, NY, 1990

Lane, Ronald, *Rudder's Rangers,* Ranger Associates, Manassas, Virginia, 1979

Langford, Walter, "Carl Erskine: Was He Best Sore-Armed Pitcher Ever?" *Baseball Digest,* January 1988

— "Larry French: He Saved the Best 'til Last," *Baseball Digest,* June 1984

Laurence, William L., *Dawn Over Zero: The Story of the Atomic Bomb,* Knopf, NY, 1946

LeBlanc, Michael L., ed., *Basketball. Professional Sports Team Histories,* Gale Research, Inc., Detroit, 1994

Leckie, Robert, *The Story of Football,* Random House, NY, 1965

— *Challenge for the Pacific,* Doubleday, NY, 1965

Lee, Marcia, "Clovey La Croix Repays a Debt," *VFW magazine,* March 1951

Leuchtenburg, William E., *New Deal and Global War,* Time-Life Books, New York

Levine, Peter, *Ellis Island to Ebbets Field,* Oxford University Press, NY, 1992

Lewin, Ronald, *Rommel as Military Commander,* Ballantine Books, 1970

— *Ultra Goes to War,* McGraw-Hill, 1978

Lewis, Jerry D., "Yogi Doodle Dandy," *VFW magazine,* May 1980

Liang, Chin-tung, *General Stilwell in China, 1942–1944: The Full Story,* St. John's University Press, 1972

Lieb, Fred, *Baseball As I Have Known It,* Coward, McCann & Geoghegan, New York, 1977

Liddell Hart, B.H., *History of the Second World War,* Putnam, NY, 1970

Lincoln Library of Sports Champions, all volumes, Frontier Free Press, Columbus, Ohio, 1961

Lingeman, Richard B. *Don't You Know there's a War On? The American Home Front, 1941–1945,* G.P. Putnam's Sons, 1970

Linklater, Eric, *The Campaign in Italy,* HMSO, 1951

Lister, Valerie, "Other leagues shared spotlight," *USA Today,* June 7, 1994

Liston, Robert A., *The Great Teams. Why They Win All The Time,* Doubleday, Garden City, NY, 1979

Lord, Lewis, "DiMaggio's America. The Way We Were," *U.S. News & World Report,* March 22, 1999

Lord, Walter, *Day of Infamy,* Henry Holt, 1957

Lorimer, Lawrence, *Baseball Desk Reference,* DK Publishing, NY, 2002

Los Angeles Times, *Book of the 1984 Olympic Games,* Harry N. Abrams, New York, 1984

Lovinger, Jay, ed., *The Gospel According to ESPN. Saints, Saviors & Sinners,* Hyperion, NY, 2002

Luder, Bob, "Longtime KC tennis legend Surface dies," *Kansas City Star,* September 3, 2001

Lundquist, Carl, "One of the Under-Rated Boys of Summer," *Baseball Digest,* May 1989

Maas, Peter, "The Last Great Air Battle," *Esquire,* June 1983

MacArthur, Douglas, *Reminiscences,* McGraw-Hill, 1964

MacDonald, John, *Great Battles of World War II,* MacMillan Publishing, New York, 1986

Macht, Norman L., "Sam Chapman: He Followed the Advice of Ty Cobb," *Baseball Digest,* November 1988

Macy, Sue, *A Whole New Ballgame,* Henry Holt and Company, NY, 1993

Mailer, Norman, "Our War in the Pacific" *Holiday,* November 1960
— *Portrait of a President: John F. Kennedy in Profile,* Little, Brown, Boston 1962

Majdalany, Fred, *The Fall of Fortress Europe,* Doubleday, NY, 1968
— *The Battle of Cassino,* Houghton Mifflin, NY, 1957

Manchester, William, *American Caesar,* Little, Brown and Company, Boston

Marshall, S.L.A., *Night Drop: The American Airborne Invasion of Normandy,* Little, Brown, Boston, 1962
— *Bastogne,* Infantry Journal Press, 1946

Mauldin, Bill, *Back Home,* William Sloane, NY, 1947
— *Up Front,* Holt, NY 1945

Mazzetti, Mark, "The D is For Deception," *U.S. News & World Report,* August 26, 2002

McCallum, Jack, "Fighting Words," *Sports Illustrated,* October 1, 2001

McCallum, John and Charles H. Pearson, *College Football U.S.A. 1869 . . . 1973,* Hall of Fame Publishing, (McGraw-Hill Books), NY, 1971

McCallum, John D., *Southeastern Conference Football,* Charles Scribner's Sons, NY, 1980
— *Big Eight Football,* Charles Scribner's Sons, NY, 1979

McCann, Kevin, *Man From Abilene,* Doubleday & Company, NY, 1952

McCarthy, Dan, "When Army Beat Navy," *VFW magazine,* January 1988
— "Spaghetti Bowl in Italy," *VFW magazine,* January 1986

McCarthy, Joe, *The Remarkable Kennedys,* Dial, NY, 1960

McGuane, Thomas, with Glenn Stout, *The Best American Sports Writing, 1992,* Houghton Mifflin Company, Boston, 1992

McGuff, Joe, *Why Me? Why Not Joe McGuff?*, Herald House, Independence, Missouri, 1992

McGuire, Mark, "One leg a minor setback for Lt. Shepard," *USA Today Baseball Weekly*, April 21–27, 1993

McWhirter, Norris, *Guinness Book of Olympic Records*, Bantam Book, NY, 1983

Mead, Chris, *Champion. Joe Louis,* Charles Scribner's Sons, NY

Mead, William B., "Even the Browns Had a Chance in '44," *The Diamond*, October 1993
— *Baseball Goes to War. Stars Don Khaki, 4-Fs Vie for Pennant*, Farragut Publishing, Washington, D.C., 1985

Medley, Jim, "Marines in Sports: Past, Present and Future," *Marine Corps Gazette*, February 2002

Mellor, William Bancroft, *Patton: Fighting Man*, Putnam, NY, 1946

Messenger, Charles, *The Chronological Atlas of World War Two*, MacMillan Publishing, NY, 1989

Michel, Henri, *The Second World War*, Frederick A. Praeger, 1975

Mihoces, Gary, "Museum sheds light on 'Nazi' Games," *USA Today*, July 15, 1996
— "D-Day helped alter face of athletics," *USA Today*, June 3, 1994

Mikesh, Robert C., *Japan's World War II Balloon Bomb Attacks on North America*, Smithsonian Institution Press, 1973

Miller, Francis Trevelyan, *History of World War II*, Winston, 1945

Miller, Joan, "Nazi Invasion!" *American History Illustrated*, November 1986

Montgomery, Rick, "War and Resurgence," *Kansas City Star*, May 24, 1998

Morison, Samuel Eliot, *History of United States Naval Operations in World War II*, Little, Brown, Boston, 1947–1962
— *The Two-Ocean War: A Short History of the United States Navy in the Second World War*, Little, Brown, Boston, 1963

Moss, Al, *Pac-10 Football*, Crescent Books, Greenwich, Connecticut, 1987

Murphy, Edward F., *Heroes of World War II*, Ballantine, NY, 1991

Murphy, Thomas D., *Ambassadors in Arms*, University of Hawaii Press, Hawaii, 1954

Nack, William, "The Rock," *Sports Illustrated*, August 23, 1993
— "Absolute Zero," *Sports Illustrated*

National Football League Properties, *The First Fifty Years*, Ridge Press/Benjamin Company Books, Encino, California, 1969

Neft, David S., with Roland T. Johnson, Richard M. Cohen, and Jordan A. Deutsch, *The Sports Encyclopedia: Pro Basketball*, Grosset & Dunlap, New York, 1975

Neillands, Robin, *The Conquest of the Reich*, NY University Press, New York

Nemec, David, *Great Baseball Feats, Facts and Firsts*, Signet Books, NY, 1987
— and Saul Wisnia, *100 Years of Baseball*, Publications International, Lincolnwood, Illinois, 2002

Newcomb, Richard F., *Iwo Jima*, Holt, Rinehart and Winston, NY

Newcombe, Jack, ed., *The Fireside Book of Football*, Simon and Schuster, NY, 1964

NFL Official Encyclopedia History of Professional Football, MacMillan Publishing, NY, 1973

Nichols, Charles S. Jr., and Henry I Shaw, Jr., *Okinawa. Victory in the Pacific*, Charles E. Tuttle Publishers, Rutland, Vermont

North, Cheryl Adams, "The Marines Made a Man Out of Me," *Leatherneck* magazine, October 1992

O'Donnell, Kenneth P., *Memories of John Fitzgerald Kennedy,* Little, Brown, Boston 1972

O-Sheel, Patrick and Gene Cook, eds., *Semper Fidelis: The U.S. Marines in the Pacific—1942–1945,* William Sloane Associates, 1947

O'Sullivan, Dan, "1935—Tulane 20, Temple 14," Bowl Championship Series web Site

Owens, Jesse with Neimark, Paul, *Jesse. The Man Who Outran Hitler,* Faucett

Packer, Billy with Roland Lazenby, *Fifty Years of the Final Four,* Taylor Publishing, Dallas, Texas, 1987

Padwe, Sandy, *Basketball's Hall of Fame,* Tempo Books, NY, 1970

Parrish, Thomas and S.L..A. Marshall, *The Simon and Schuster Encyclopedia of World War II,* Simon & Schuster, NY, 1978

Patkin, Max, and Hochman, Stan, *The Clown Prince of Baseball,* WRS Publishing, Waco Texas

Patton, George S., *War as I Knew It,* Houghton Mifflin, 1947

Pepe, Hil, *No-Hitter,* Scholastic Services Books, NY, 1972

Perrett, Geoffrey, *Winged Victory. The Army Air Forces in World War II,* Random House, NY
— *Days of Sadness, Years of Triumph: The American People, 1939–1945,* Coward, McCann and Geoghegan, 1973

Plaschke, Bill, "Race Cards Stacked," *St. Louis Post Dispatch,* March 16, 1997

Pluto, Terry, *Tall Tales,* Simon & Schuster, NY
— "Graham: Still Says He's One of the Guys," *St. Louis Post-Dispatch,* September 24, 1995

Potter, E.B., *Bull Halsey,* Naval Institute Press, Annapolis, Maryland
— *Nimitz,* Naval Institute Press, Annapolis, Maryland, 1976

Potter, Lou, with William Miles and Nina Rosenblum, *Liberators. Fighting on Two Fronts in World War II,* Harcourt Brace Jovanovich, NY

Prange, Gordon W., with Donald M. Goldstein and Katherine V. Dillon, *December 7, 1941. The Day the Japanese Attacked Pearl Harbor,* McGraw-Hill Books, NY, 1988

Price, S.L., "Academy Rewards. Why Army-Navy still matters," *Sports Illustrated,* December 11, 2000
— "The Second World War Kicks Off," *Sports Illustrated,* May 29, 1999

Prioletta, Arthur A., "Nisei soldiers—Second generation Japanese-Americans keep tradition alive," *Okinawa Marine,* October 27, 1989

Pulliam, Kent, "Cleveland helped break barrier in 1946," *Kansas City Star,* September 24, 1995

Puryear, Edgar F. Jr., *Nineteen Stars, A Study in Military Character and Leadership,* Presidio Press, Novato, CA, 1971

Pusey, Merlo J., *Eisenhower, The President,* Macmillan, NY, 1956

Pyle, Ernie, *This is Your War,* Holt, NY, 1943

Raab, Scott, "Zimmer," *Esquire,* July 2001

Rains, Rob, *The St. Louis Cardinals,* St. Martin's Press, NY

Ramsey, Edwin P. and Stephen J. Rivele, *Lieutenant Ramsey's War,* Knightsbridge Publishing, Los Angeles, California

Reader's Digest, Secrets and Spies: Behind the Scenes Stories of World War II, Reader's Digest Association, 1964

Reeder, Russell, *Born at Reveille,* Duell, Sloan & Pearce, NY, 1966

Reichler, Joseph L., *The World Series, 76th Anniversary Edition,* Simon and Schuster, NY, 1979

— *30 Years of Baseball's Great Moments,* Crown Publishers, NY, 1974

Renouvin, Pierre. *World War II and its Origins,* Harper and Brothers, 1969

Ribalow, Harold U., *The Jew in American Sports,* Bloch Publishing Company, 1959

Richman, Howard, "Bad lies of life don't faze him," *Kansas City Star,* June 29, 1997

Riesenberg, Felix, *Sea War: The Story of the U.S. Merchant Marine in World War II,* Rinehart, 1956

Riley, James A., "The Thunder Twins," *The Diamond* magazine, November, 1993

Rizzuto, Phil with Tom Horton, *The October Twelve,* Tom Doherty Associates Book, NY, 1994

Robinson, Jackie, as told to Alfred Duckett, *I Never Had it Made,* Mitchell Hamilburg Agency, 1972

Robinson, Sugar Ray, with Anderson, Dave, *Sugar Ray,* The Viking Press, New York, 1969

Rodgers, Ted, "G.I. Ball," *Sporting News,* June 5, 1995

Rogers, Donald I., *Since You Went Away,* Arlington House, New Rochelle, New York

Rogosin, Donn, *Invisible Men. Life in Baseball's Negro Leagues,* Atheneum, NY, 1903

Root, Gerald S., "Never Far From a Fight," *VFW Foreign Service* magazine, September 1949

Rosenblatt, Roger, "The Atomic Age," *Time,* July 29, 1985

Ross, Bill D., *Iwo Jima. Legacy of Valor,* Vanguard Press, NY

Rushin, Steve, "War and Remembrance," *Sports Illustrated,* July 16, 2001

Rust, Edna and Art Jr., *Illustrated History of the Black Athlete,* Doubleday & Company, Garden City, NY, 1985

Rust, Ken, "The Twelfth Air Force Story," *Historical Aviation Album*

Ryan, Bob, *The Pro Game. The World of Professional Basketball,* McGraw-Hill Book Company, NY, 1975

Ryan, Cornelius, *A Bridge Too Far,* Simon and Schuster, NY, 1974

— *The Last Battle,* Simon and Schuster, NY, 1966

— *The Longest Day,* Simon and Schuster, NY, 1959

Sailer, Steve, "How Jackie Robinson Desegregated America," *National Review,* April 8, 1996

Santos, Kendra, "Turtle Cowboy Ace Still Loves To Win," *National Senior Pro Rodeo Finals,* Las Vegas, NV, November 12–18, 1990

Savage, Jim, *The Encyclopedia of the NCAA Basketball Tournament,* Dell Hardcover, NY, 1990

Schaller, Michael, *The U.S. Crusade in China, 1938–1945,* Columbia University Press, 1979

Schulian, John, "Concrete Charlie," *Sports Illustrated,* September 6, 1993

Schuman, Michael, "The football halls of fame," *Kansas City Star,* January 21, 1996

Schultz, Duane, *The Doolittle Raid,* St. Martin's Press, NY, 1988

Schultz, Paul, *The 85th Infantry Division in World War II,* Infantry Journal Press, Washington

Sears, William R., "Diving the Hard Way," *VFW Foreign Service,* April 1949

2nd World War, West Point Military History Series

Shannon, Mike, *Tales from the Dugout,* Contemporary Books, Chicago, Illinois, 1997

Shapiro, Milton J., *Champions of the Bat,* Julian Messner, NY, 1967

Sherman, Frederick, *Combat Command: The American Aircraft Carriers in the Pacific War,* E.P. Dutton, 1950

Sherrod, Robert, *History of Marine Corps Aviation in World War II,* Combat Forces Press, 1952

Shirer, William L., *The Rise and Fall of the Third Reich: A History of Nazi Germany,* Simon and Schuster, NY, 1960

Shirey, Orville C., *Americans. The Story of the 442nd Combat team,* Infantry Journal Press, Washington, 1946

Shugg, Roger W., and Deweerd, H.A., *World War II: A Concise History,* Infantry Journal Press, 1946

Shukert, Elfrieda Berthiaume, and Barbara Smith Scibetta, *War Brides of World War II,* Presidio, Novato, California, 1988

Sidey, Hugh, *John F. Kennedy, President,* Atheneum, NY, 1963

Siegman, Joseph, *Jewish Sports Legends,* Brassey's, Washington, DC, 2000

Silverman, Al, "The 229th Payday of Mr. Papaleo," *Pageant magazine,* 1960
— *Joe DiMaggio,* Prentice-Hall, Englewood Cliffs, New Jersey, 1969

Simon, Rita James, ed. *As We Saw the Thirties,* University of Illinois, Urbana, 1967

Sirica, John J., "Unforgettable Jack Dempsey," *Reader's Digest,* March 1986

Skehan, Everett M., *Rocky Marciano,* Houghton Mifflin Company, Boston, 1977

Smith, Curt, ed., *What Baseball Means to Me,* Warner Books, NY, 2002
— ed., *The Storytellers,* MacMillan, NY, 1995

Smith, Red, *To Absent Friends from Red Smith,* Atheneum, NY, 1982

Smith, S.E., ed., *The United States Marine Corps in World War II,* Random House, NY, 1969

Smith, Tim Alan, "Gerald Ford, Vice President," *Sports Illustrated,* July 8, 1974

Snelling, Dennis, *A Glimpse of Fame,* McFarland & Company, Jefferson, North Carolina, 1993

Snyder, Louis. *The War: A Concise History,* Julian Messner, 1960

Solomon, Burt, *The Baseball Timeline,* Stonesong Press, NY, 1997

Speer, Albert, *Inside the Third Reich,* Macmillan, NY, 1970

Speidel, Hans, *Invasion 1944,* Henry Regnery, 1950

Sporting News Editors, *Baseball. A Doubleheader Collection of Facts, Feats & Firsts,* Galahad Books, NY, 1993

Squires, Vernon C., "Landing at Tokyo Bay," *American Heritage*

St. John, Bob, *The Man Inside . . . Landry,* Word Books, 1979

Stars and Stripes newspaper

Steele, Michael R., *The Fighting Irish Football Encyclopedia,* Sagamore Publishing, Champaign, Illinois, 1996

Stern, Bill, "GI Gridion Champs," *VFW Foreign Service magazine,* February 1947
— "Pennant Winners," *VFW Foreign Service magazine,* May 1947
— "Baseball's Hardy Perennials," *VFW Bulletin,* June 1945
— "Giants of the Court," *VFW Foreign Service magazine,* January 1946

Stokesbury, James L., "1943. Invasion of Italy," *American History Illustrated,* Harrisburg, PA, December 1977

Stolley, Richard B., ed. *Life: World War II,* Little, Brown, Boston, 2001

Strawson, John, *The Battle for North Africa,* Charles Scribner's Sons, NY, 1979

Sulzberger, C.L., ed. *The American Heritage Picture History of World War II,* Simon and Schuster, NY, 1966
— *World War II,* American Heritage Press, 1970
Sullivan, George, *Pro Football's All-Time Greats,* G.P. Putnam's Sons, NY
— *Great Lives,* Charles Scribner's Sons, NY, 1988
Swift, E.M., "The Olympic Family," *Sports Illustrated,* December 17, 2001
Tajiri, Vincent T., "The Nisei: American Soldier," *VFW magazine,* August 1984
— *The Japanese American soldier in World War II,* 100/442/MIS Museum Foundation, Gardena, California
Tapert, Annette, ed., *Lines of Battle,* Times Books, NY, 1987
Taylor, A.J.P., ed., *History of World War II,* Octopus Books, 1974
Taylor, Phil, "Flying in the Face of the Fuhrer," *Sports Illustrated,* November 29, 1999
terHorst, Jerald F., *Gerald Ford and the Future of the Presidency,* The Third Press, NY, 1974
Terkel, Studs, *The Good War,* Penguin, London, 1986
This Fabulous Century, 1940–50, Time-Life Books
Thomas, David, *Battle of the Java Sea,* Pan Books, 1971
Thomas, Gordon and Max Morgan Witts, *Enola Gay,* Stein and Day, NY, 1977
Thorn, John, ed., *The National Pastime,* Warner Books, NY, 1982
Timanus, Eddie, "Army-Navy: Century of drama," *USA Today,* December 1, 1999
Tingley, Ken, "Jake Early: He Was Known as 'The Chattering Catcher'" *Baseball Digest,* Evanston, IL, November 1985
Toland, John, *But Not in Shame: The Six Months After Pearl Harbor,* Random House, NY, 1961
— *The Last 100 Days,* Doubleday, 1959
— *Battle: The Story of the Bulge,* Random House, NY, 1959
Townsend, Peter, *Duel of Eagles,* Simon and Schuster, NY, 1970
Tregaskis, Richard, *Guadalcanal Diary,* Random House, NY, 1943
Tuchman, Barbara W., *Stilwell and the American Experience in China, 1911–1945,* MacMillan, NY, 1970
Tunnell, Emlen, *Footsteps of a Giant*
Turner, Frederick, *When the Boys Came Back,* Henry Holt and Company, New York, 1996
Tuttle, Dennis, "Still Slingin'" *The Sporting News,* November 7, 1994
U.S. Department of Defense, *The "Magic" Background of Pearl Harbor,* Government Printing Office, 1977
Van der Vat, Dan, *The Pacific Campaign,* Simon & Schuster, NY, 1991
Vancil, Mark, *The NBA at Fifty,* Park Lane Press, NY, 1996
Van Osdol, William R., *Famous Americans in World War II,* Phalanx Publishing, St. Paul, Minnesota
Vass, George, "1939: It was a Vintage Year in Major League History," *Baseball Digest,* February 1989
Veeck, Bill, with Ed Linn, *Veeck as in Wreck,* University of Chicago Press, Chicago, Illinois, 1962
Verrier, Anthony, *Bomber Offensive,* MacMillan, NY, 1968
Vorderman, Don, *The Great Air Races,* Doubleday & Company, 1969
Wallace, Joseph, ed., *The Baseball Anthology, 125 Years,* Harry N. Abrams, New York, 1994

Ward, Gene and Dick Hyman, *Football Wit and Humor,* Grosset & Dunlap, New York, 1970

Ward, Geoffrey C., and Ken Burns, *Baseball. An Illustrated History,* Alfred A. Knopf, NY, 1994

Wendel, Tim, "The Life and Times of Hank Greenberg," *USA Today Baseball Weekly,* October 17–21, 2001

Weyand, Alexander M., *The Saga of American Football,* MacMillan Company, NY, 1961

Wheatley, Ronald, *Operation Sea Lion,* Oxford University Press, 1958

Wheatley, Tom, "Who Was Satch Paige," *Beckett Monthly,* September 1989

Wheeler, Richard, *IWO,* Lippincott & Crowell, NY

Whelan, R., *The Flying Tigers,* Doubleday, NY, 1944

Whittingham, Richard, *The Bears. A 75-Year Celebration,* Taylor Publishing, Dallas, Texas, 1994

Will, George, *Bunts,* Simon and Schuster, NY, 1998

Willenz, June A., *Women Veterans. America's Forgotten Heroines*

Williams, Zinkoff, *Around the World with the Harlem Globetrotters* ,

Willing, Richard, "Chinese fan plays catch across an ocean," *USA Today,* December 12, 1997

Willoughby, Charles A., and John Chamberlain, *MacArthur, 1941–1951,* McGraw-Hill, NY, 1954

Wilson, Kenneth and Brondfield, Jerry, *The Big Ten,* Prentice-Hall, Englewood Cliffs, New Jersey, 1967

Wittner, Lawrence S., ed., *MacArthur. Great Lives Observed,* Prentice-Hall, Englewood Cliffs, NJ, 1971

Wolfert, Ira, *American Guerrilla in the Philippines,* Simon and Schuster, New York, 1945

Wooden, John, *They Call Me Coach,* Word Books, Waco, Texas

Woodward, C. Vann, *The Battle for Leyte Gulf,* MacMillan, NY, 1947

World War II magazine, all issues

World War II, Time-Life Books, Alexandria, Virginia, 1981

Yank magazine, all issues

Yenne, Bill, *Black '41,* John Wiley & Sons, Inc., NY

Young, Desmond, *Rommel, The Desert Fox,* Harper and Brothers, 1950

Zoss, Joel and John S. Bowman, *The Pictorial History of Baseball,* Thunder Bay Press, San Diego, California, 1986

Zumwalt, James, "Our Parents Told Us, 'This is Your Country'," *Parade,* May 26, 1996

Index